On Middle Ground

On Middle Ground

Ground

A History of the Jews of Baltimore

ERIC L. GOLDSTEIN AND DEBORAH R. WEINER

Published in Cooperation with the Jewish Museum of Maryland

Johns Hopkins University Press
BALTIMORE

© 2018 Johns Hopkins University Press
All rights reserved. Published 2018
Printed in the United States of America on acid-free paper
2 4 6 8 9 7 5 3 1

Johns Hopkins University Press
2715 North Charles Street
Baltimore, Maryland 21218-4363
www.press.jhu.edu

Library of Congress Cataloging-in-Publication Data

Names: Goldstein, Eric L., author. | Weiner, Deborah R., author.
Title: On middle ground : a history of the Jews of Baltimore /
Eric L. Goldstein and Deborah R. Weiner.
Description: Baltimore : Johns Hopkins University Press, [2018] |
Includes bibliographical references and index.
Identifiers: LCCN 2017018080 | ISBN 9781421424521 (hardcover : alk. paper) |
ISBN 9781421424538 (electronic) | ISBN 1421424525 (hardcover : alk. paper)
| ISBN 1421424533 (electronic)
Subjects: LCSH: Jews—Maryland—Baltimore—History. |
Baltimore (Md.)—Ethnic relations.
Classification: LCC F189.B19 J53 2018 | DDC 975.2/6004924—dc23
LC record available at https://lccn.loc.gov/2017018080

A catalog record for this book is available from the British Library.

Frontispiece: The bar mitzvah of Louis Stein (detail), 1908. Jewish Museum of Maryland.

*Special discounts are available for bulk purchases of this book. For more information, please
contact Special Sales at 410-516-6936 or specialsales@press.jhu.edu.*

Johns Hopkins University Press uses environmentally friendly book materials, including recycled
text paper that is composed of at least 30 percent post-consumer waste, whenever possible.

To two products of Jewish East Baltimore:

Albert Goldstein (1911–1986) and

Sylvia Feldman Goldstein (1912–2008)

May their memory be for a blessing

Contents

Acknowledgments

During the many years we have each been researching and writing about the history of Baltimore Jews, we have relied on the support and assistance of numerous individuals and institutions. First and foremost, we wish to thank the Jewish Museum of Maryland (JMM), which has served as the home base for this project. Former executive director Avi Y. Decter helped us envision the book and harnessed the resources that made it possible. Deborah Cardin, our liaison with the museum, smoothed the way through the many stages of our work. Joanna Church carried out the massive task of assembling images and obtaining the necessary permissions. Thanks also to current executive director Marvin Pinkert, who joined the JMM after the project was under way.

The following donors provided generous funding to the JMM to underwrite the publication of this book: the Richard and Rosalee C. Davison Foundation, Willard and Lillian Hackerman, the Whiting-Turner Contracting Company, the Leonard and Helen R. Stulman Charitable Foundation, and the Joseph and Harvey Meyerhoff Family Charitable Funds. Additional financial support for the project was provided by the Southern Jewish Historical Society and the Tam Institute for Jewish Studies at Emory University.

We owe a particular debt of gratitude to Gilbert Sandler, the keeper of the memory of Baltimore Jewry. Gil has inspired us with his keen eye for history and his gift for storytelling. We have learned much from his many publications and appreciate the enthusiastic support he has given to our work. The book also owes much to former JMM leaders who pioneered in exploring Baltimore Jewish history and built the collections on which our research is based. We particularly wish to recognize the late Isaac M. Fein, a founder of the Jewish Historical Society of Maryland (the JMM's predecessor) and author of an important institutional history of Baltimore Jews, *The Making of an American Jewish Community* (1971); and Bernard Fishman, the JMM's first professional director, who transformed it into one of the nation's leading Jewish history museums and archives. We also must acknowledge the late

Earl Pruce, compiler of the essential resource *Synagogues, Temples, and Congregations of Maryland, 1830–1990* (1993).

Many current and former JMM staff members influenced this book through their own work and their support as friends, colleagues, and mentors: Elizabeth Kessin Berman, Ilene Dackman-Alon, Karen Falk, Dianne Feldman, Sue Foard, Anita Kassof, Barry Kessler, Barry Lever, Melissa Martens, Virginia North, Erin Titter, Jennifer Vess, Esther Weiner, and Jobi Zink. JMM volunteers offered enthusiastic assistance; special thanks to Ira Askin, Harvey Karch, Vera Kestenberg, and Ed Schechter, and thanks also to Martin Buckman, Sid Rankin, Bernie Raynor, Marvin Spector, and Irv Weintraub.

Devoted archivists and librarians assisted us in our research, including the staffs of the Maryland Department of the Enoch Pratt Free Library, the Maryland Historical Society, the Maryland State Archives, and the Special Collections Department of the Johns Hopkins University Libraries. Special thanks to Susan Malbim at the American Jewish Historical Society, Kevin Proffitt at the Jacob Rader Marcus Center of the American Jewish Archives, Dale Rosengarten at the Jewish Heritage Collection of the College of Charleston, Tom Hollowak in Special Collections at the University of Baltimore's Langsdale Library, and Shirley Aronson at the Maryland State Law Library.

Friends and colleagues provided advice, guidance, and feedback that helped make the book stronger, including Bill Barry, Mark Bauman, Hasia R. Diner, Jessica Elfenbein, Elizabeth Nix, Antero Pietila, Len Rogoff, Jonathan D. Sarna, Lydia Smithers, Frank Towers, Mame Warren, and Hollace Weiner. Special thanks to our friends at the Baltimore City Historical Society for their encouragement; we were each honored to win the society's Joseph L. Arnold Prize for Outstanding Writing on Baltimore History for papers that ultimately became chapters in this book.

Our families provided support and encouragement without which this project could not have been completed. Eric would like to thank his father, Lawrence B. Goldstein, whose Baltimore roots made him an excellent sounding board; his mother and stepmother, Betty Goldstein and Alice Goldstein, who were a much-needed cheering section and gracious hosts during many research trips to the Baltimore area; and his children, Max, Ella, and Jacob Goldstein, whose love and humor made the process of writing less daunting. Deb would like to thank her father and late mother, Ron and Phyllis Weiner, for their lifelong encouragement, and her siblings Lauren, Vicki, and Howard for their sympathetic interest.

Finally, thanks to Bob Brugger, Elizabeth Demers, Juliana McCarthy, and the entire staff of Johns Hopkins University Press for their commitment to this project and their patience as it came to fruition. It has been a rewarding journey.

On Middle Ground

Introduction

Every Marylander knows Old Bay, the popular spice mix that flavors the region's beloved steamed crabs. The seasoning's creator is not so well known. Spice maker Gustav Brunn and his family fled Nazi Germany in 1938 and settled in Baltimore, where Brunn had relatives. He found a job at McCormick's Spice Company but was fired after three days, according to family legend, because the manager discovered he was Jewish. On the advice of local businessman and community leader Myer Strauss, Brunn started his own spice company using a spice mill he had brought from Germany. He rented a small space near the harbor, across from the wholesale fish market.[1]

The first order received by Brunn's Baltimore Spice Company came from Harry Attman's Jewish deli on Lombard Street. The spice business grew, with Brunn's wife, Bianca, keeping the books and operating the mill until the couple could hire another worker. "Baltimore proved to be a good place to get started," their son Ralph recalled. Brunn's broken English posed no barrier: the city had many Yiddish speakers, as well as gentile German meat packers, sausage makers, and bakers, all of whom needed spices. In the early 1940s Gus Brunn developed a blend especially for the seafood purveyors across the street, and he named it in honor of a Chesapeake Bay steamship company, the Old Bay Line. Before long, his spice blend would grace kitchen cabinets in virtually every home in Maryland. The Brunns sold the business in 1986. Four years later, Old Bay was again sold—to McCormick.[2]

The Brunns' story typifies many aspects of the American Jewish experience. They arrived as part of a family migration chain, experienced local antisemitism, received help from the close-knit Jewish community, and succeeded in business as a family. But some aspects of their story are specifically Baltimorean. Because of Baltimore's direct link to the port of Bremen, the city had experienced a massive German migration in the nineteenth century and retained a heavily German character. Also, like many other local manufacturers, the Baltimore Spice Company looked to the South for customers: sausage makers from Virginia to Florida made up a significant part of its customer base. And, of course, the Brunns built their company around the locally important seafood industry. Old Bay took off thanks to the city's love affair with steamed crabs.

Few of the city's Jewish-owned businesses made as strong a mark as the Baltimore Spice Company did with Old Bay. But Gus Brunn's ability to enter the scene and create a classic Baltimore product was echoed in ways large and small by other Jewish participants in the city's commerce and culture. The story of the Baltimore Spice Company offers a prime example of how Baltimore's distinctive characteristics, opportunities, and conditions affected Jewish life—and how Baltimore was in turn changed by its Jewish community.

Baltimore is the only metropolis in the United States that is both a border city and a major port connecting the nation's interior to the world. Perhaps more than any other factor, this position as a bridge between North and South, East and West, has shaped the city's development. Its early prominence as a strategically located harbor and its rise as a manufacturing center followed the pattern of northern seaboard cities, such as Philadelphia, New York, and Boston. As the westernmost port on the East Coast, Baltimore successfully competed with its northern counterparts in forging transportation links and commercial ties with the expanding settlements of the Ohio River valley. Particularly consequential for Baltimore's developing social and political climate, however, were its strong economic ties to the South and the cultural legacy of slavery and racial segregation. As a result of these diverse influences, Baltimoreans have long understood their city to be linked to, yet different from, both North and South, a realization that has sharpened a well-honed sense of place arising from the city's role as the commercial hub of the Chesapeake Bay.

If Baltimore's location at a geographical crossroads has made it a regional hybrid, its demographic history has made it hard to categorize among smaller and larger cities. It ranked among the nation's five most populous urban centers until the post–Civil War era, dropping to the second tier of American cities by the 1870s. Although in many ways it retained its stature as a leading metropolis, its relatively modest size and socially conservative bent imbued it with what journalist Gilbert Sandler described as a decidedly "small town" feel.[3] Thus, in multiple ways, Baltimore has occupied a "middle ground" between regions and cultures, a quality that has often made it a place of contradiction and ambiguity.

Baltimore's Jews have shared in the paradoxes inherent in the city's character as a place both similar to and different from the regions, movements, and trends that collided there. In many respects, the story of Baltimore Jewry—with its dramas of immigration, acculturation, and assimilation—is the story of American Jews in microcosm, but its contours also reflect the city's special locale and culture. Baltimore's status as a commercial gateway to the South; the unique way it experienced the wars of the nineteenth century (as a flash point in the War of 1812 and under federal occupation during the Civil War); the role of its port as a major entryway for German

Founded by Lithuanian-born former peddler Jacob Epstein, the Baltimore Bargain House (pictured here c. 1915) bolstered the city's role as a commercial gateway to the South. The multi-million-dollar-per-year business supplied retail merchants across the region. *Jewish Museum of Maryland.*

migration to the United States; its demographic profile in the early twentieth century as the only American city with sizable populations of both Jews and African Americans—these are but some of the local circumstances that influenced Jewish life.

By revealing how Jews negotiated their place within the particular environment that is Baltimore, this volume explores the interplay of regional and ethnic identity. It also offers a case study in how particular geographical settings, economic conditions, and ethnic and racial landscapes have influenced American Jewish life. Except for New York, few of the nation's major Jewish population centers have received comprehensive narrative treatment in recent decades, even as the field of American Jewish history has blossomed and developed a broader set of scholarly concerns.[4] We help to fill this gap by examining the major issues of American Jewish life within the framework of a wide-ranging narrative history.

We also provide a fresh perspective on the growth and development of Baltimore, a multiethnic city whose various ethnic groups have received too little attention from historians.[5] Beyond simply adding one particular subgroup to the Baltimore narrative, an exploration of Baltimore Jewry sheds light on key aspects of the city's history. The full story of its rise as a trading hub cannot be told without accounting for the Jewish entrepreneurs whose far-flung networks helped the city exploit its advantageous position between North and South. An analysis of why the Jewish community failed to embrace radicalism and secularism to the extent that other Jewish centers did reveals the ongoing impact of Baltimore's socially conservative climate as well as its stature as an ecclesiastical center. Because Jews occupied a particularly fraught place along the city's black-white divide, an analysis of black-Jewish relations greatly enhances an understanding of the larger dynamics of race in a border city. Indeed, the interaction in Baltimore between a Jim Crow political culture characteristic of the South and a European ethnic population characteristic of the North has not received the notice or analysis it deserves.

Baltimore has had its ups and downs through the years. Today it stands in the shadow of Washington, DC, only forty miles away. The metro area no longer has Maryland's largest Jewish population: that honor goes to Montgomery County in the DC suburbs. But Baltimore's history is rich, and Jews have always been an intimate part of it. Without the Jewish community, Baltimore historian Joseph Arnold once wrote, "Baltimore would have been a vastly poorer city in every way." That it received so many Jewish immigrants despite being "widely perceived as a southern city," he argued, was "one of Baltimore's greatest strokes of good fortune."[6] But it was not a matter of luck: Baltimore attracted Jews for sound reasons, and their profound impact stemmed from the opportunities the city provided. In turn, the Baltimore milieu strongly influenced the internal affairs of the Jewish community: even its development as a bastion of American Orthodox Judaism can be traced in part to the city's character. This book aims to illuminate the history of both Baltimore and its Jews, showing how each shaped the other.

Founded in 1729, Baltimore got off to a slow start because the tobacco economy of colonial Maryland worked against the growth of urban centers. In its early years, it remained a small town lacking the business activity that might have attracted Jewish entrepreneurs. Indeed, the city's earliest identifiable Jewish resident was not the prototypical trader, but rather a thief from London who arrived in 1763 as one of the many convict laborers sent to work on local plantations. As the economy began to diversify, however, the Jewish population began to grow. By 1830, enough permanent residents had arrived to form the nucleus of a Jewish community that would steadily expand over the ensuing decades, turning Baltimore into one of the nation's most important Jewish centers. In this volume, we trace the growth and development of Baltimore Jewry from the 1760s to the present.

Baltimore's distinctive setting offered opportunities for advancement that made it a magnet for successive waves of Jewish settlers. The city began to attract enterprising merchants during the American Revolution, when Baltimore thrived as one of the few ports remaining free of a British blockade. After the war, its meteoric rise as a commercial center drew Jewish newcomers whose economic activities helped the upstart town surpass Philadelphia as the second-largest American city. Baltimore's fortunes were buoyed by its status as the East Coast link to the National Road,

Highest Prize 50,000 Dollars.   No. 26434

BY AUTHORITY.

Washington Monument Lottery.

FIRST CLASS.

THIS TICKET will entitle the bearer to such prize as may be drawn to its number, if demanded within twelve months after the drawing is finished, subject to a deduction of fifteen per cent. Prizes payable sixty days after the drawing is completed.

By order of the Managers.

No. 26434   Levi Hollingsworth

Entrepreneur Jacob I. Cohen Jr. arrived in Baltimore shortly after 1800.
His business activities, such as the Washington Monument Lottery, helped to build the city.
Courtesy of the Maryland Historical Society.

the major artery for western trade during the early national period, and after 1823 by the Baltimore and Ohio Railroad (B&O), whose founders aimed to cement the city's standing as one of the nation's most prosperous centers. The city's leading role in the transportation revolution ensured its future as an important trading hub, manufacturing center, and immigrant port of entry. By the 1830s, ships carrying Maryland tobacco to Bremen regularly returned laden with Central European immigrants, including Jews from Bavaria, Prussia, and other places where the promise of Jewish emancipation was falling short.

Starting out as peddlers, petty traders, and craftspeople, these new Jewish arrivals were drawn to Baltimore's economic scene. The B&O offered unparalleled access to growing markets in budding western towns such as Cincinnati and St. Louis, while rail, road, and water routes linked the city to southern trading centers. Building on ties with relatives and coreligionists in these far-off places, Baltimore Jews formed the hub of an ethnic- and kin-based trading network that strengthened the larger economic networks emanating from the city. After the Civil War, Jewish economic activity both benefited from and reinforced the city's position as a gateway between the industrial North and the growing retail market of the postwar South. German Jewish clothing manufacturers and retail emporiums expanded beyond their southern Jewish base to capture the entire southern market, enabling the production of ready-made clothing to emerge as Baltimore's largest industry, a position it held for several decades. In the 1880s, Lithuanian immigrant Jacob Epstein began sending Jewish peddlers southward and soon built his Baltimore Bargain House into one of the nation's largest wholesalers. As both a businessman and a civic leader he became perhaps the city's leading promoter of trade with the South.

The East Baltimore tailor shop of Abraham Kravetz, c. 1908. Baltimore had a large African American population before 1920, unlike other cities with major Jewish communities, making interactions between blacks and Jews much more common. *Jewish Museum of Maryland.*

When the B&O Railroad established a partnership with the North German Lloyd shipping line in 1867, Baltimore's status as a major immigrant port was ensured. Though most immigrants who disembarked in Baltimore moved on to points west, opportunities provided by the city's garment industry and trading networks made Baltimore especially appealing to Jews from the Russian Empire. They constituted the city's largest immigrant group from the 1880s to the 1920s and boosted the Jewish population to 65,000 by 1924.[7] Many got their start as toilers in the clothing industry, where jobs were plentiful. Others found a place in the ethnic economy that formed when Jews crowded into the immigrant neighborhood of East Baltimore. Though tailors, sweatshop operators, and small shop owners often endured years of poverty, their economic foothold was strong enough to provide traction for advancement.

Even after the waves of mass immigration ended and Baltimore's importance as an economic center faded, the city's central location on the eastern seaboard and its low cost of living continued to attract Jewish newcomers, including refugees from Nazi Germany in the 1930s and Holocaust survivors who came after World War II. The late twentieth century saw the arrival of immigrants from Iran, Israel, and the

Rabbi David Einhorn, c. 1865. An advocate of radical reforms to Judaism, Einhorn served Baltimore's Har Sinai Congregation from 1855 until 1861, when he was forced to flee the city because of his vocal opposition to slavery. *Courtesy of the Jacob Rader Marcus Center of the American Jewish Archives, Cincinnati, Ohio.*

former Soviet Union, as well as large numbers of Orthodox Jews from elsewhere in the United States. The well-organized Baltimore Jewish community, responding to world crises from the rise of Nazism to the Iranian revolution, encouraged these migrations and helped the new arrivals to adjust.

In addition to drawing Jews looking for economic opportunity, Baltimore's role as a crossroads made it a gathering place for impressive Jewish thinkers and activists and a seeding ground for a series of Jewish movements and causes. As a result, the city early on attained a position of leadership in the American Jewish world that was disproportionate to the size of its Jewish community. In 1840 Baltimore became home to the first ordained rabbi to settle in America, Abraham Rice, who espoused strict Orthodox standards while offering guidance to Jewish communities nationwide from his post at Baltimore Hebrew Congregation. In 1842, disaffected members of Baltimore Hebrew broke away to form what would later be described as the nation's first successful Reform congregation, Har Sinai, and engaged the firebrand rabbi David Einhorn as their leader. In 1859 the moderate rabbi Benjamin Szold, an ideological father of Judaism's Conservative movement, arrived to lead Oheb Shalom Congregation. The variety of approaches Baltimore Jews took toward religious and cultural adaptation made the city an important focal point in the effort to reshape Judaism in the American setting. Intense ideological debate among the city's rabbis influenced this process, but it was driven above all by the everyday choices and strategies of ordinary congregants who, like most American Jews, pursued a more pragmatic, less ideologically coherent path toward change.

The Eastern European Jews who poured into Baltimore after 1880 created an enclave in the city's eastern section that, while smaller and less cosmopolitan than similar concentrations in New York, Chicago, and Philadelphia, mirrored them in the intensity of its Yiddishkeit.[8] The comparative parochialism of Baltimore at the turn of the twentieth century made it a particularly hospitable place for the nurturing of Orthodoxy, which held a position of authority in local Jewish life that was unmatched in larger Jewish centers. The city emerged as a bastion of traditional Judaism even as Orthodoxy declined nationally in the years before World War II. Ner Israel Rabbinical College, founded in 1933, developed an international reputation and stimulated the growth of other local Orthodox institutions. In the 1970s, Baltimore's position as a nearby and much more affordable alternative to New York City began to draw thousands of Orthodox families. The combination of institutional might and demographic growth gave the Jewish community the highest percentage of Orthodox adherents outside New York and placed Baltimore in the vanguard of the late twentieth century's American Orthodox revival.[9]

Baltimore's role as a leading Jewish community was underscored through its leadership in the American Zionist movement. Local Jews established one of the nation's first Zionist organizations in 1889; eight years later Baltimore was the only American Jewish community to send a delegate to the First Zionist Congress in

Rabbi Jacob Ruderman (*at podium*) and Rabbi Herman Neuberger (*to his left*) at the dedication of a building at Ner Israel Rabbinical College. The two men built Ner Israel into a renowned Orthodox institution. *Jewish Museum of Maryland.*

Basel, Switzerland. Amid the ferment of Baltimore's Zionist scene, Rabbi Szold's daughter Henrietta Szold developed her passionate belief in the importance of Jewish settlement in Palestine years before she founded Hadassah and became one of Israel's most important pre-state leaders. In 1947, Baltimore became directly involved in the struggle for a Jewish state when local Zionists secretly acquired and outfitted an old Chesapeake Bay steamship, which revealed its new name as it approached Palestinian waters: *Exodus 1947*. The ship's dramatic attempt to settle Holocaust survivors in Palestine became, in defeat, a public relations coup and one of the foundational stories of Israel.

On the whole, Jewish communal life during the twentieth century conformed to broad national trends, though in a distinctly Baltimorean way. In the 1920s, "uptown" and "downtown" Jews united to form the Associated Jewish Charities; over the ensuing decades, Jewish leaders went to great lengths to maintain a unified community. The unusually high residential concentration of Baltimore Jews in the post–World War II era undoubtedly helped further this goal. That concentration helped in another way as well: as Jews moved into the American mainstream, Baltimore's intermarriage rate rose, but not nearly as much as elsewhere. Like their counterparts nationally, the city's Reform, Conservative, and Reconstructionist organizations took an increasingly liberal stance in matters of gender, sexual orientation, and inclusivity. The growing divide between these movements and an ever more assertive ultra-Orthodox community polarized the religious scene, with Baltimore's historically strong modern Orthodox movement caught in the middle. Nevertheless, a robust network of institutions and Baltimore's own brand of suburban Yiddishkeit continued to give the community an impressive degree of cohesiveness and strength.

As they put down family roots, gained an economic foothold, and established a vibrant communal life, Baltimore Jews also engaged actively with the non-Jewish world around them. According to the conventional wisdom on American Jewish history, Jews were at a social disadvantage in locales where they had not been among the founding generation. The dynamism of Baltimore society provides a strong counterexample, since the city experienced several new beginnings as it navigated the challenges of wars, blockades, and economic reversals; adapted to successive changes in its ethnic makeup; and recovered from calamities such as the Great Baltimore Fire of 1904.

This dynamism was apparent in 1826, when respected business leaders Solomon Etting and Jacob I. Cohen Jr. successfully lobbied for the right of Maryland's Jews to hold elected office, which the state constitution had denied them. Despite the prejudices of the predominantly rural state legislature, the "Jew Bill" passed because an up-and-coming group of legislators who represented the interests of the city recognized the value of Jewish leadership, capital, and investment to the success and stability of Baltimore, which had been plagued for decades by the uncertainties of a boom-and-bust economy. Just weeks after the bill's passage, Etting and Cohen were elected by their fellow citizens to the Baltimore City Council.

The Jews who arrived from Central Europe after 1820 entered a society with a dominant culture in flux. The huge number of non-Jewish German immigrants challenged the hegemony of the Protestant elite, incidentally making room for Jews who, although socially aloof from non-Jews in their native lands, built important alliances with the German community on these shores. Though Jews focused on building a rich institutional and associational life of their own, their ability to place themselves under a broader "German" umbrella in matters of language, culture, and politics, coupled with their rising economic stature, helped them gain a central role in civic life by the end of the nineteenth century.

Not that antisemitism was absent from the Baltimore scene, as Jews who faced exclusion from neighborhoods, social clubs, and some economic sectors well knew. As elsewhere in America, the fears and prejudices of native-born residents were exacerbated as Jews became a visible segment of the population and began to climb the economic ladder. In Baltimore, however, the response of local elites toward Jewish mobility was profoundly influenced by the city's culture of Jim Crow segregation: residential patterns developed through what journalist Antero Pietila has called a "three-tiered housing market" that strove to rigidly separate African Americans, Jews, and non-Jewish whites.[10] As a result, Jews were hemmed into certain residential districts to a greater extent than in other cities. Nevertheless, as the city's largest new immigrant group of the late nineteenth and early twentieth centuries, Eastern European Jews gained strength in politics, commerce, and the trade union movement. Their rapid advancement offers a potent example of how Baltimore's rich ethnic mix and constantly shifting opportunities provided recurring chances to counter discrimination.

The economic mobility of their immigrant parents gave the generation that came of age in the 1920s the means to demonstrate that they were American—and Baltimorean—in every way. In the years between the world wars, Jews exchanged the crowded immigrant quarters of East Baltimore for working- and middle-class neighborhoods in Northwest Baltimore, such as Forest Park and Pimlico. Although residential discrimination reinforced the concentrated and tightly knit nature of the Jewish community, Jews engaged enthusiastically with the broader city and its culture. They developed allegiances to quintessential Baltimore places, such as City College high school and Druid Hill Park. They played major roles in creating a variety of cultural institutions, from the art museum to The Block, Baltimore's notorious red-light district. With gustatory establishments such as Attman's and Nates and Leons, they fashioned a Baltimore version of the New York deli and even gave the Maryland crab cake their own twist by popularizing the "coddie," which better suited Jewish dietary sensibilities. The interwar years, marked by a fervent participation in local culture along with an almost complete social separation from non-Jews, perhaps saw the purest realization of a distinct Baltimore Jewish identity.

Open around the clock, Nates and Leons deli was an important part of Baltimore's nightlife.
Jewish Museum of Maryland.

Many barriers of social discrimination fell following World War II as the Jewish population grew to more than 100,000. Jews joined the rush to suburbia, yet a complex set of factors—geography, racial dynamics, and the close-knit character of the Jewish community—ensured that they remained residentially segregated as they traded the row houses of northwestern Baltimore City for the more spacious precincts of northwestern Baltimore County. But in other respects they became more entwined than ever in the fabric of metropolitan life. Even as Baltimore declined as a manufacturing center, the growth of suburbia and the redevelopment of downtown offered opportunities to civic leaders, business owners, and real estate developers. Jews not only rooted for the Orioles and the Colts, but were instrumental in bringing these teams to the city. From symphony benefactor Joseph Meyerhoff and art scene leader Amalie Rothschild to Maryland governor Marvin Mandel and trailblazing state senator Rosalie Abrams, they joined the ranks of Baltimore's most influential cultural, philanthropic, and political leaders and also worked on the grassroots level as significant players in the reshaping of a metro area confronted with the challenges of twentieth-century urban life.

Through all of its phases of growth and development, Jewish life in Baltimore was decisively shaped by the presence of a substantial African American community, the largest in any city outside the Deep South before the 1920s.[11] In colonial and early national Baltimore, the presence of slavery undoubtedly helped secure acceptance for Jews as part of the white population, but the large number of free blacks—larger than the number of enslaved blacks after 1810—raised uncomfortable questions for Jews as it did for whites more broadly. In pursuing their fight for full civic equality during the 1820s, for example, Jewish leaders became aware of the need to word the Jew Bill in a way that would steer clear of the explosive issue of civic equality for black freemen. In the 1840s and 1850s, local Jews—like those in other American cities—fought against the nativist threat of the Know-Nothings, who were gaining in political influence nationwide. But in Baltimore, defending the rights of immigrants often meant aligning with the white supremacist platform of the Democrats, who were the major opponents of the Know-Nothings on the local scene.

As sectional tensions racked America and as Baltimore's position as a border city placed it in the forefront of conflict, slavery and secession became key issues on which Jewish civic identity turned. Renegade rabbi David Einhorn was forced to flee the city because of his outspoken opposition to slavery, which he considered anathema to Judaism. Einhorn was atypical, however, even among his own congregants. Although few were active secessionists, most Baltimore Jews shared the racial outlook of white southerners, with whom they had long-standing cultural and economic ties.

The influence of race on Baltimore Jewry was not only a matter of politics and perceptions, it was also a fact of daily life. Baltimore was arguably the first city in the nation where a major population of Jews came in contact with a major population of

With Walter Sondheim Jr. (*front*) presiding, Baltimore's school board was the only one below the Mason-Dixon Line to vote to desegregate immediately after the *Brown v. Board of Education* decision in 1954. Its policy of "free choice" proved ineffective, however. *Courtesy of the Walter Sondheim Jr. Collection, Langsdale Library, University of Baltimore.*

blacks, and the two groups interacted on a significant level. A commercial relationship between African Americans and Jews already existed by the early nineteenth century, and it expanded dramatically after the Civil War. By the early 1900s, servicing the mercantile needs of the black community had become a major enterprise among Eastern European Jewish immigrants, whose meager resources and lack of integration into America's racial culture meant that they had fewer compunctions about dealing with blacks than did white gentile traders. This economic bond continued through the mid-twentieth century. After World War I, the close proximity of black and Jewish neighborhoods — and the shifting boundaries between them — added another key point of contact. Their long history and geographic closeness caused the black and Jewish communities to be more intertwined than elsewhere.

Both conflict and cooperation marked relations between the two groups. From the beginning of the twentieth century, some black leaders accused Jewish store owners and landlords (sometimes justifiably) of exploiting their clientele, yet African Americans also appreciated the positive role that many Jewish businesses played in their communities. The two groups engaged in political turf battles from the era of machine politics to the later years of increased black political power, yet they also formed alliances over mutual interests. Though Jews participated in "white flight" when African Americans began moving into their neighborhoods, they were virtually alone among whites in attempting to maintain integration in districts such as Windsor Hills, Ashburton, and Upper Park Heights during the post–World War II era.

The Jewish stance on racial matters reflected Baltimore's "middle" position between North and South. Until their own social position became relatively secure after World War II, acculturating Jews often felt the need to distance themselves from the stigma associated with blacks. While Jewish Baltimoreans benefited from their status as "white," their exclusion from many clubs, private schools, and other social institutions made clear that they were being denied full participation in the life of the white majority. In response, they sometimes took pains to highlight their whiteness, as US senator Isidor Rayner and Maryland attorney general Isaac Lobe Straus did when they helped lead the fight for black disenfranchisement in Maryland in the early twentieth century. Jewish owners of downtown department stores, leery of being seen as catering to blacks, scrupulously followed Jim Crow policies until the early 1960s despite decades of protest by the local National Association for the Advancement of Colored People (NAACP).

Conversely, from their position just south of the Mason-Dixon Line, Baltimore Jews felt much freer than their counterparts in the Deep South to actively and publicly assist blacks in their quest for equality. From the 1920s to the 1940s, Jewish politicians sponsored anti–Jim Crow legislation (sometimes at the behest of black constituents), and Jewish civic leaders pushed for fair treatment for black people. Jews also played a disproportionate role among local whites in the civil rights movement of the 1950s and 1960s, though not without concern over possible repercussions.

The various ways that Jews navigated the city's racial landscape reveal much about the complexity of race relations and racial politics in Baltimore. Moreover, the fact that immigrant Jews had to forge a civic identity in a context dominated by racial issues; the unusually long history of economic, social, and political interaction between blacks and Jews; and the place that Jews occupied on the fault line of the white-black divide all underscore just how crucial the presence of African Americans was in shaping the worldviews, social strivings, and identity concerns of Jews in Baltimore compared to Jews in other American cities.

Over the years, Baltimore Jews (like other Baltimoreans) developed a strong sense of place, one that persists despite many trends threatening its survival. Baltimore no longer serves as a crossroads with an important national economic role. In today's highly mobile society, regional factors impinge less on daily routines and rhythms since people travel and communicate beyond local borders with ease. As regionalism has weakened as a feature of American life, as racial and ethnic minority groups have become more dispersed throughout the country, and as the rural-urban split has blurred with the growth of suburbs and exurbs, so too has the salience of Baltimore's "middleness" diminished. Given all these trends, can there still be such a thing as a distinctive "Baltimore Jewish" identity?

In his series of Baltimore films, native son Barry Levinson offers an ambiguous view of how successfully Jewish family and group identity weathered the course of the twentieth century. Yet the strong sense of place that comes through in his movies leaves no doubt that the filmmaker has not lost his own powerful attachment to the place where he grew up.[12] Meanwhile, the central role that local Jews continue to play in the life and culture of their city, the tendency of the young to remain in the region, and the close-knit feeling attested to by old-timers and newcomers alike all suggest that their identities as Baltimoreans and as Baltimore Jews remain important to their self-perception.[13]

So what are the features that most distinguish the Baltimore Jewish community in the twenty-first century? It depends on whom you ask. For some, it may be the diverse yet close-knit Orthodox community with its distinctive institutions and bustling gathering places. For others, it may be a cultural scene that stretches from the Owings Mills Jewish Community Center in the far northwest suburbs to Meyerhoff Symphony Hall in central Baltimore. For still others, it might be reviving a Jewish presence in inner-city Baltimore, engaging with urban politics, or giving new life to synagogue buildings that were used by an earlier generation of Jewish Baltimoreans. In fact, it is more accurate to speak of Baltimore Jewish communi*ties* rather than a single, cohesive community. But these various manifestations of Jewish life have their roots in a singular history, recalled by many and influencing all.

1

Baltimore's First Jews

In 1786, the partners of a Baltimore mercantile firm advertised in a Boston newspaper seeking information on Elkin Solomon, a "Dutch Jew," who had recently fled the Maryland seaport, "being largely indebted to several persons there." They suspected that he was either in the Massachusetts capital or in nearby Marblehead, where he had lived during the 1770s under the name Abraham Solomon. The advertisement recalled Solomon's checkered past as a "great traveler . . . much known in the New England states during the war as a smuggler."[1] His notoriety, however, had not isolated him from non-Jewish society: in 1774 he had married a Christian woman, Elizabeth Lowe, and the following year enlisted along with fellow townsmen in the Continental Army. After his discharge, he ran into trouble with the law for illegal currency exchanges and was even accused of spying for the British. Possibly because of these difficulties, he changed his name to Elkin Solomon and followed the army south to Maryland, working as a merchant, currency exchange broker, and dealer in securities.[2]

By 1782, Solomon was established under his new name in Baltimore, where he helped pioneer the brokerage and exchange business. In the colonial era, because of the shortage of cash for large transactions, merchants used bills of exchange drawn on large trading firms abroad. But in smaller cities like Baltimore, where these firms had fewer contacts, such bills were not always honored, leaving the holders in financial distress. Innovators like Solomon helped solve this problem in the postrevolutionary period by purchasing bills of exchange and providing a ready source of currency for local transactions. In helping Baltimore's commerce to expand, however, he and his fellow brokers took on significant risk, and they were often burned by forgeries or worthless notes, which were probably the cause of Solomon's business failure and subsequent flight to Boston in 1786.[3]

Ultimately captured by authorities, Solomon was brought back to Baltimore and confined in the local "gaol," from where he petitioned the legislature to forgive his remaining debts, having handed over all his property to creditors.[4] After his release

> ## *ELKIN SOLOMON,*
> ### BROKER,
> At his Houſe in Gay-Street, near the Bridge, oppoſite to Mr.
> Gerrard Hopkins's Dwelling, and where Mrs. Etting former-
> ly lived,
> ## Carries on the BROKER's BUSI-
> NESS, in aſſiſting Gentlemen to ſell their Cargoes, or Commo-
> dities, to the beſt Advantage, and upon the moſt reaſonable
> Terms. He alſo aſſiſts Gentlemen in the Purchaſe of GOODS,
> WARES and MERCHANDISE. He alſo tranſacts buying
> and ſelling of *Depreciated Certificates, Final Settlements,* and
> *Black Money.*
>   ☞ He returns his Thanks to his old Cuſtomers who conti-
> nue to employ him, and hopes for the Indulgence of the Public,
> in his Occupation, as he doubts not but his Care and Aſſiduity
> in Buſineſs will give general Satisfaction.
>   *N. B.* Caſh diven for *Genſong, Otter* and *Mink Skins.*
>   He has to ſell on Commiſſion, Holland Gin in Caſes, of the
> beſt Kind ; Muſcovado Sugar, of the very beſt Quality ; Coffee ;
> Molaſſes ; Womens' Shoes ; Indigo ; fine Muſlin ; and excel-
> lent Poland Starch.
> *Baltimore-Town, June* 11, 1787.

Advertisement for Elkin Solomon's pioneering brokerage business, published
in the *Maryland Journal and Baltimore Advertiser*, June 12, 1787.

he began to rebuild his business, which once again assumed a position of importance in the city's expanding commercial life. Before long he was able to move his
brokerage house from Gay Street to a more desirable location on the city's main
thoroughfare, Market (now Baltimore) Street, where he also sold on commission
domestic and imported goods, including gin, wine, rum, molasses, coffee, tobacco,
gunpowder, writing and wrapping paper, and a variety of hides and skins. Solomon's
business, however, remained unstable. While he did well in flush times and continued to provide services important to Baltimore's commercial growth, he experienced at least three more bankruptcies before 1809, when he disappeared suddenly
from the Baltimore scene.[5]

As significant as Elkin Solomon was as a commercial innovator in late eighteenth-
and early nineteenth-century Baltimore, he has escaped notice by historians seeking
to document the beginnings of Jewish life in the city, who have usually focused on a
few wealthy, socially prominent, and civic-minded individuals, such as the merchant
Solomon Etting and the lottery entrepreneur and banker Jacob I. Cohen Jr.[6] Elkin Solomon, however, was in many ways more typical of early Jewish settlers in Baltimore
since his career reflected the cycle of boom and bust that made it difficult for most
Jews to achieve the success and stability enjoyed by Etting and Cohen.

Although Jews continually moved to Baltimore from the 1760s to the 1820s to take
advantage of the opportunities it offered, many stayed only temporarily or—like
Solomon—came and went as conditions fluctuated. Solomon's biography, which
conspicuously lacks any mention of Jewish contacts or associations, also reflects

- - - - - - - - - - - - - - -

how the volatile economic environment of early Baltimore prevented the emergence of a stable Jewish community with supporting institutions during the revolutionary and early national periods. Jews who came to the city during these years made the conscious decision that a chance at success was worth forgoing religious and social amenities. Like Solomon, many of them married non-Jews rather than adherents to their own faith.[7] Although Baltimore grew to become the third most populous city in the United States (after New York and Philadelphia) by 1810, its Jewish population remained too transient to sustain a formal religious congregation until almost two decades later, in contrast to those in smaller cities like Richmond, Charleston, and Savannah, which successfully supported synagogues during the same period.[8]

A final insight provided by Elkin Solomon's years in Baltimore is that Jewish settlers contributed greatly to the city's economic development and played crucial roles as innovators, despite the challenges that delayed the growth of a stable Jewish presence. True, the wealth and longevity of the Etting and Cohen families enabled them to make exceptional contributions to the building of the city's roads, canals, and railroads and to the founding of banking and insurance enterprises on which economic growth relied. But Baltimore also benefited in countless ways from the activities of less prominent Jews like Solomon who, despite his repeated failures in the brokerage business, was willing to take risks that helped expand commerce, and like the many shopkeepers and small manufacturers who introduced previously unavailable luxury items and household goods to the city. Even the humble group of recent immigrants from Holland and other European locales who constituted a majority of local Jews by 1810 made a vital contribution as pioneers in pawnbroking and the secondhand trade, both of which had a significant impact on the lives of Baltimoreans.

Jewish settlers of the late eighteenth and early nineteenth centuries never dominated the most important sectors of the city's commercial life, nor did more than a handful leave a meaningful imprint on local society. Still, their presence was significant enough to promote the image of Jews as a vital factor in the growth and development of Baltimore that was palpable in the debates leading up to the passage of the Jew Bill, the law granting Maryland's Jews full civic equality, in 1826. The strength of that image was particularly significant given that as late as 1830, there were only 150 Jews among the city's 80,620 residents.[9] While they struggled for years with the ups and downs of the local economy, over the course of the early national period they were ultimately able to gain a foothold and make their presence felt in ways that were unusually strong for a city where they had not been present at the founding.

The Emergence of Jewish Settlement in Baltimore

Baltimore lagged behind most other East Coast seaports in attracting a significant Jewish presence because the town, though founded in 1729, did not begin to blossom as a major commercial hub until the fifteen-year period preceding the American

Baltimore in 1752. Engraving by William Strickland, 1817, based on an earlier sketch by John Moale. *Courtesy of the Maryland Historical Society, H16.*

Revolution. Until that time, it was smaller and less important than Annapolis, the colony's capital, and Fredericktown (today's Frederick), the center of the backcountry trade. Despite their comparative prominence, these locales also failed to draw a large number of Jews in the era before Baltimore's rise, owing to the fact that the tobacco-dominated economy of these years fostered the use of small river landings, which undermined the growth of market towns.[10]

Still, Maryland was not totally devoid of Jews before the 1760s. Jewish individuals are known to have lived in the colony as early as 1656, only twenty-two years after its establishment by the first Lord Baltimore, George Calvert. Originally founded as a refuge for Catholics, Maryland during its formative years was the scene of intense religious wrangling between the original settlers and later Protestant arrivals. The Act Concerning Religion (the Toleration Act) was adopted in 1649 to protect the rights of Catholic settlers, but it also outlawed blasphemy and the denial of Christianity, leading some historians to argue that Maryland was a hostile setting for Jews during its first century and a half. Indeed, one of the colony's first Jewish settlers, the Lisbon-born physician Jacob Lumbrozo, was charged with blasphemy under the act's provisions. Lumbrozo's brush with the law proved temporary, however,

Engraved for the Newgate Calendar.

Representation of the Transports going from Newgate to take water at Blackfriars.

Jews were among those depicted in the engraving *Convicts at Newgate Prison Awaiting Transport to America. From the* Newgate Calendar *(London), n.d.*

and was probably due more to the assertive expression of his religious views and his unsavory personality—he was also charged with rape—than to any determination on the part of colonial Marylanders to punish nonconformists.[11]

Further proof that Maryland did not exclude Jews on religious grounds is found in the small handful of Jewish merchants who settled in the colony over the course of the seventeenth and eighteenth centuries, setting up shop in Annapolis, Fredericktown, and a few smaller outposts. While most remained for only a short time, two significant exceptions were Fredericktown's bachelor merchants Levi Cohan and Henry Lazarus, who left the budding Jewish community of Lancaster, Pennsylvania, in the 1740s to take a chance on Maryland's backcountry trade. The fact that Cohan and Lazarus lived in the colony for decades and participated actively in commercial and civic affairs demonstrates the acceptance that Jewish settlers could achieve.[12]

Though Maryland enticed few Jewish merchants in this period, one facet of the region's development did bring an unusual group of Jews to the colony in the half century before the American Revolution. Between 1718 and 1775, felons convicted of noncapital offenses in Great Britain were regularly transported to Maryland and Virginia, where they typically worked as servants for a term of seven years. Owing

Baltimore-Town, July 2, 1764.

RAN away from the Subfcribers, Yefterday Morning, a Convict Servant Man named *Solomon Gabrel*, an *Englifhman*, but fpeaks very good *Dutch*, about 5 Feet 3 Inches high, a thick well-fet Fellow, of a down Look, and fwarthy Complexion ; he wears his own Hair, which is of a light fandy Colour, fhort, and curls much, and very thin, almoft bald on the Top ; he is by Trade a Painter, and may pafs for a Butcher, as he is a very good one. He took with him when he went away, a white Shirt and a check one, a brown Broad-Cloth Coat, an old blue Waiftcoat, with Silver Vellum Button Holes, and touch'd in feveral Places with Paint of different Colours, a Pair of Leather Breeches, a Pair of black and a Pair of brown Stockings, high quarter'd Shoes, with yellow Buckles, and a narrow brimm'd Felt Hat.

Whoever brings the faid Fellow to the Subfcribers, or either of them, fhall have, if taken 20 Miles from home, Forty Shillings ; and if further, and out of the County, Five Pounds, paid by

THOMAS JONES,
GEORGE WHITE.

Advertisement for the runaway convict-servant Solomon Gabriel, the first identifiable Jew to live in Baltimore. *Maryland Gazette*, July 2, 1764. *Collection of the Maryland State Archives.*

to the significant number of Jews among the British convict population, particularly in London, no fewer than 250 Jewish malefactors were sent to the Chesapeake during these years. These "transports" were scattered across a vast region, and few remained in Maryland or Virginia after their terms of service ended. Many of them absconded from their masters and fled to Philadelphia or New York with the aim of returning to England.[13]

The bulk of Jewish convict servants arrived in the 1760s and 1770s, when the social problems facing the Anglo-Jewish community were at their height. As a subset of the convict population disproportionately skilled in trades like tailoring and metalwork, these Jews sometimes found themselves sold to masters living in urban settings, where such skills were in the greatest demand. In this way, Baltimore, which by this time had begun to eclipse Annapolis and Fredericktown, received its earliest identifiable Jewish resident, Solomon Gabriel, a London house painter who was sentenced to transportation for the theft of a pocketbook in 1763 and endured a year of servitude before running away from his master.[14] Several other Jewish convicts landed at the port of Baltimore in the two decades before 1783; some of them likely worked in the city, while others labored on plantations in the nearby countryside. The exact number, however, is unknown, since few records specify where they spent their years of servitude.[15]

The end of the Revolutionary War put an end to the transportation of British convicts, but Baltimore's continued rise as a commercial center in the years preceding the revolution had already begun to strengthen the city's appeal to the more conventional type of Jewish settler looking for business opportunities. Beginning in 1760, wheat became increasingly important as a cash crop, and the need for a central marketplace in proximity to the main grain-producing areas had fueled the growth of the port. According to historian Clarence Gould, within a decade Baltimore went from an "obscure village" to "the most important center of Maryland's trade." As a result, the city during the 1760s and 1770s attracted its first significant concentration of Jewish settlers.[16]

At least one of these trailblazing entrepreneurs, Jacob Hart, came directly to Baltimore upon arriving in America in 1768 from his native town of Fürth, Bavaria.[17] Two years later, Mordecai Moses Mordecai, a Talmudic scholar and native of Telz (now Telšiai), Lithuania, relocated his family to the city from Lancaster and established himself as a distiller. Some of the Jewish settlers drawn to Maryland's emerging metropolis came after initial experiences in other towns in the colony. Moses Mordecai (not to be confused with Mordecai Moses Mordecai), who operated a business in Baltimore for at least a short time in 1764, had previously sold buttons and belt buckles in Annapolis and Fredericktown, while Benjamin Levy, the scion of a prominent New York family, had also spent time in Fredericktown as a general merchant and an investor in the backcountry trade with Native Americans during the early 1750s. After suffering severe losses during the French and Indian War, however, Levy moved to Philadelphia, where a long and unsuccessful struggle to win compensation from British authorities left him barely solvent. He came to Baltimore in 1770 in search of a fresh start; within three years he was selling West Indian imports, wines and spirits, fancy groceries, and a wide range of dry goods from a store at Market and Calvert streets.[18]

Fortuitously, the growth that was attracting these Jews to Baltimore received a further boost as protests against exorbitant British taxation began to disrupt patterns of overseas trade in other major port cities. During the 1760s, when the leading merchants of Boston, New York, and Philadelphia signed nonimportation agreements that prevented the landing of British goods, their counterparts in Baltimore resisted such a move, making their city increasingly attractive to those who wished to work around the expanding embargo. Jewish merchants like Michael and Barnard Gratz of Philadelphia, who traded extensively with Native Americans on the western frontier but could no longer bring in foreign goods through their home city, were

Thirty-dollar currency note of the United Colonies, signed by Baltimore merchant Benjamin Levy, 1776. *Levy Family Papers, Collection of the American Jewish Historical Society, New York.*

among the businessmen searching for an alternative location to receive imports. "This place [Philadelphia] is determined on not importing, and it is really dangerous to attempt any such thing," wrote Michael Gratz in a 1770 letter to his older brother, who was tending to business affairs in England. The solution to their problem, the younger Gratz explained, was to "go with a small cargo to Maryland . . . with such goods as is allowed to import there."[19]

After the Revolutionary War began in 1775, Baltimore continued to prosper as one of the few port cities remaining free of British blockade. The wartime economy apparently increased the fortunes of Benjamin Levy, who was asked by the Continental Congress in December 1776 to issue bills of credit bearing the insignia of the "United Colonies" for use as local currency.[20] Not only did many out-of-towners like the Gratzes continue to utilize the port of Baltimore for their overseas trade, but an increasing number of Jews began to settle in the city, attracted by its wartime prosperity.[21] Jacob Hart, who had moved to Philadelphia in the late 1770s, was drawn back to Baltimore by the comparative ease of trade there, and in April 1781 he was among the merchants who advanced money to the Marquis de Lafayette for the purchase of clothing for his soldiers. Hart's brother-in-law, the German-born Isaac Abrahams, moved to Baltimore to join him as a business partner in 1782, and they were soon followed by their father-in-law, Lyon Nathan, who arrived from Philadelphia.[22] The daughter and son-in-law of Mordecai M. Mordecai, Esther and Philip Moses Russell, had settled in the city one year earlier and established themselves in the retail liquor trade.[23]

The budding business careers of some Baltimore Jews were put on hold due to the call of military service. When Lafayette left Baltimore in the summer of 1781 and headed for Virginia, one of the men under his command was Benjamin Levy's eldest son, Nathan. Reuben Etting, a young merchant from York, Pennsylvania, who arrived in Baltimore prior to 1777, put aside his mercantile ambitions to enlist as a private in Captain John Sterrett's Independent Company of the Maryland militia, composed entirely of Baltimore merchants and their clerks. Later in the war, Etting helped suppress an uprising of Loyalists in Somerset County and other parts of the Eastern Shore.[24] Another Baltimore newcomer, Elias Pollock, put down his peddler's pack to enlist in 1778 and served under the alias Joseph Smith in Maryland's Third Regiment. Pollock saw combat up and down the East Coast until 1780, when he received a bayonet wound in South Carolina and was taken prisoner by the British.[25]

All three of these soldiers returned to Baltimore after the conclusion of their military careers to resume their business activities. Etting was joined by his mother's brother, Isaac Solomon, who had fled the Dutch Caribbean island of St. Eustatius upon its invasion by the British in 1781. By the following year, Solomon had established a large ironmonger's shop on Baltimore's Gay Street. Within a few years, their success attracted other family members to the city: Etting's mother, Shinah; her five daughters from York, Pennsylvania; and another of Shinah's brothers, Levy Solomon, who arrived from Lancaster to become a partner with Isaac in the ironware enterprise.[26]

In the immediate aftermath of the war, the end of physical danger and the restoration of free trade in other major centers led many of the wartime Jewish residents of Baltimore to return to their former homes. Despite some new arrivals toward the end of the 1780s, only six or seven Jewish households remained in the city by 1790. Still, the revolutionary period had confirmed Baltimore's place on the American Jewish map, and Jews would begin to move again to the city in significant numbers by the end of the century as it continued to experience phenomenal growth. As many of the new arrivals would discover, however, a boomtown like Baltimore presented both opportunities and challenges, a combination that had uncertain implications for the blossoming of Jewish life.

Boom and Bust:
Jews and Judaism in Early National Baltimore

In 1816, John Myers, a native of Norfolk, Virginia, arrived in Baltimore to open a branch of his father's import-export business, which was one of the largest in the nation. Back in 1786, Moses Myers, John's father, had considered Baltimore as a location for his business but settled instead in Norfolk, where he became one of the first millionaires in the United States and rose to a position of civic leadership as the head of the city's common council. Hoping to succeed as his father had done, John, a veteran of the War of 1812 who was educated in Europe and had traveled widely, arrived in Baltimore with excellent financial backing to open his own import-export firm under the name of John Myers and Company.[27]

Baltimore was then experiencing an economic boom unparalleled in any other American city except New York. The great demand for its wheat exports in Europe and Latin America and its role as a provider of West Indian goods to the markets of Germany and England had combined to make the city a persistent rival of Philadelphia and New York by the early nineteenth century. Its commercial rise had been temporarily interrupted by the War of 1812, but the cessation of hostilities opened the way for continued growth. By 1816, opportunity seekers were pouring in, jobs were plentiful, and new buildings were erected as the city expanded its geographic boundaries.[28] In this setting, Myers quickly prospered. In cooperation with his father's Norfolk firm, he capitalized on Baltimore's strong position in the West Indian trade, importing large quantities of sugar, coffee, and rum from Jamaica and St. Croix and mahogany from Honduras, which he sent on to European customers. He supplemented his import-export business by accepting consignments of freight from other merchants, and he also sold fine linens and carpets imported from Europe and India from a warehouse at the corner of Calvert and Market streets.[29]

Despite this meteoric success, however, the rigors of living in a boomtown environment were driven home to the budding merchant through a series of events that began to unfold in 1817, when he became ill with a fever. Like many of Baltimore's young newcomers, Myers had no family or support network in the city. In increasingly dire straits, he boarded a steamboat for Philadelphia and headed for the home of his sister's friend Rebecca Gratz, where he had lodged during his service in the War of 1812. He was confined to bed for four weeks, his condition so bad that his family was summoned from Norfolk. Gratz, writing to a friend, observed that Myers had been living "in the solitariness of [a] bachelors-hall, [and] had no one to take proper care of him in his illness."[30] Myers returned to Baltimore once he regained his strength, and his business prospered for about two more years. Then, in 1819, a national credit crisis struck, hitting Baltimore harder than the rest of the country because of the mismanagement of local banks. Short on cash because of his extensive speculation in the sugar market and failed business ventures in Panama and Norway, Myers was unable to pay his bills. Not only was he forced to declare bankruptcy and surrender all of his assets, but he also spent several months in a debtors' prison. After his release, he returned to Norfolk, where he worked as a customs collector before his death in 1830.[31]

Myers's short career in Baltimore dramatically illustrates the advantages that drew Jews to the city between 1790 and 1820 as well as the drawbacks that frequently sent them packing. As one of the nation's largest cities, it offered exceptional

----

opportunities for advancement. But flush times were periodically interrupted by depressions, financial crises, and other problems of an economy based on overseas trade. In the 1790s, for example, when protracted warfare between England and France interrupted those countries' trade connections to their colonies, Baltimore benefited exceptionally from its ability to supply foodstuffs to the West Indies and to deliver West Indian goods to the European combatants. But during the intervals of peace, this advantage was lost, and the city's prosperity faltered. Reaping the benefits of wartime trade also invited the interference of the British and French, who frequently seized American vessels and prevented their passage through contested waters. The resulting tensions led to an economically disastrous embargo that closed the port of Baltimore entirely to British vessels during 1807–1808 and ultimately led to the War of 1812, when trade was again halted. Meanwhile, the aggressive style of the city's merchants led to an overextension of credit, fueling a depression that hit Baltimore between 1798 and 1803 and ultimately resulting in the Panic of 1819, which put John Myers out of business along with 150 other leading firms and countless small merchants.[32]

In addition to dramatizing the volatility of economic life in the growing city, Myers's story also illustrates the particular difficulties these circumstances presented for Jews. The cycles of boom and bust that Baltimore experienced in the period before 1820 contributed to a continuous ebb and flow of Jewish settlement in the city, which militated against the growth of cohesive social networks and institutions that Jews typically relied on for aid and support. In turn, the lack of a Jewish community inhibited Jews from putting down roots and made it more likely for them to leave during hard times. For such reasons, Baltimore was a less-than-perfect match for many American Jews during the early national era. Nevertheless, the city did prove to be a good fit for certain types of Jews, especially those whose talent and ingenuity helped them withstand the rigors of its environment and whose particular social and economic circumstances made them feel that they had more to gain than lose by taking a chance on the city.

Thus, the ability of Baltimore to attract Jewish residents during the early national period rested on each potential settler's calculation of the risks and rewards the city offered. This explains the lackluster appeal the city held for many acculturated American Jews, who had no strong motivation to endanger the relatively comfortable status they enjoyed during these years. By 1790, the Jewish population in the United States had begun to attain a degree of stability in contrast to earlier periods when immigration from abroad and geographical mobility were the rule. In the wake of independence, native-born Americans quickly became the dominant force among the country's 1,500 Jews. Living primarily in five or six of the nation's largest cities, where they enjoyed the fellowship of their coreligionists and the amenities of congregational life, they were also increasingly well integrated into non-Jewish society and economically comfortable, factors that reduced the impulse toward movement. The drive to settle the interior of the country remained largely in check before the construction of railroads began in the late 1820s and 1830s, when Jews' penchant for migration would again be stimulated by the growth of new centers like New Orleans and Cincinnati.[33]

Given this context, the Jews from already established American families who did come to Baltimore at the end of the eighteenth century and the beginning of the nineteenth century almost always fell into one of two specific socioeconomic categories. The first consisted of young, single, or recently married men just starting out in their careers, for whom Baltimore offered more opportunity than risk because they had not yet invested years in building up a business, home, or family. John Myers decidedly fell into this group, as did Benjamin Solomon, a brother or close relative of Elkin Solomon, who came from Richmond in 1799 and joined the latter's brokerage business.[34] Another young, single Richmonder who found particular opportunity as an entrepreneur in Baltimore during this period was Jacob I. Cohen Jr., who arrived with his five brothers, one sister, and widowed mother, Judith, in 1808 and would later become one of the preeminent Jewish figures in the city.[35]

The second category of American Jews whose socioeconomic profile made Baltimore appealing consisted of more established individuals who had failed in business elsewhere or were escaping a declining economic environment. Mordecai M. Mordecai, who left Baltimore in the 1770s but decided to return after unsuccessful stints in Pittsburgh, Philadelphia, and Richmond, was representative of this group. So too were the significant number of Jews who came to Baltimore from Lancaster, Pennsylvania, in the 1790s. Lancaster had flourished during the revolution when it briefly had its own Jewish congregation, but the town declined quickly after the war. Reuben Etting's brother Solomon lived there, working as an apprentice and ultimately a partner of his father-in-law, the pioneer merchant Joseph Simon. After the death of his first wife and his marriage to Rachel Gratz, the daughter of Barnard Gratz of Philadelphia, Solomon Etting and his new bride came to Baltimore in 1791 to join his family. They were followed two years later by his uncle Myer Solomon, the family's last holdout in Lancaster. Other Lancastrians who came to Baltimore during this period included Barnard Jacobs, formerly a mohel (ritual circumciser) in the Pennsylvania backcountry, who arrived with two sons around 1790; and Levy Andrew Levy, another business associate of Joseph Simon, who followed his former neighbors to Baltimore in 1799 after an unsuccessful stint in Hagerstown, Maryland.[36]

Although Baltimore's attraction to American Jews was initially limited to these two rather specific sets of individuals, after 1800 the city began to draw a third group of Jewish settlers: recent immigrants from Holland, the German states, and other European points of origin. A few of these arrivals came as indentured servants or "redemptioners," but most were peddlers, small shopkeepers, or craftspeople—among the Dutch Jews in particular were many silversmiths, jewelers, and watchmakers—who generally came to Baltimore after brief stays in New York or Philadelphia. Of modest means, they hoped that the breakneck growth of the city would provide greater opportunity and less competition than the larger urban centers.[37]

Unlike the other Jewish residents of Baltimore, who lived downtown near the harbor or across the Jones Falls in Old Town, these immigrants tended to gather in the working-class neighborhood of Fells Point. They soon began to outnumber the mostly native-born acculturated Jews. Of twelve new Jewish households appearing in Baltimore between 1800 and 1810, eight were headed by recent Dutch or Bohemian immigrants, while only four were headed by native-born or acculturated Jews who had arrived from other cities. This trend intensified in the following decade as the stream of immigrants grew larger. Of thirty new Jewish households appearing between 1810 and 1820, twenty-one were headed by recent Dutch, German, or Polish immigrants, while four were headed by American-born Jews and one by an acculturated Jew who had been born in Poland. The other four new households were headed by recent immigrants from England, two of whom had been born in Poland.[38]

If socioeconomic factors helped determine the types of Jewish individuals who were drawn to Baltimore, a much less concrete set of criteria determined who would succeed and who would fail. Typically the conditions that prevailed in the city during its years of phenomenal growth favored the young, innovative, and well connected; success depended partly on capital but also on talent, persistence, and flexibility. Reuben and Solomon Etting and Jacob I. Cohen Jr. stand out as having brought to their Baltimore ventures the best possible combination of resources and personal qualities, which explains their success and longevity in business.

Between 1794 and 1797, Reuben Etting, in partnership with a non-Jew, Thomas Rutter, was among the merchants shipping Baltimore flour to Curaçao, Santo Domingo, and Jamaica and bringing back coffee, sugar, and other West Indian produce to sell abroad. The Ettings were also active in developing the city's trade in East Indian goods, which became a hallmark of the family's business in both Baltimore and Philadelphia, where Reuben moved in 1804.[39] Like some other Baltimore Jews of the period, including Jacob Franks Levy (a son of Benjamin Levy) and Elkin Solomon, they did not focus on trade exclusively but combined it with activities such as general shipping, real estate investment, and the brokerage and commission business.[40] By 1807, a quarter of those working as brokers in the city were Jewish.[41] For his part, Jacob I. Cohen Jr. popularized lotteries on a previously unheard-of scale, making possible the raising of millions of dollars in capital to finance countless public and private institutions in the city. Others became active in the nascent manufacturing sector: the Revolutionary War veteran Elias Pollock rose from a street peddler to become the owner of a factory making soaps, grooming ointments, and shoe polish.[42]

Yet none of these businessmen—with the possible exceptions of Jacob I. Cohen Jr. and Solomon Etting—escaped episodes of financial ruin. Early in his career, Reuben Etting had all of his merchandise sold at public auction to satisfy his debts. Jacob F. Levy became an insolvent debtor, while Elkin Solomon went through several bankruptcies. Indeed, Solomon's unexplained disappearance from Baltimore after 1809 was probably another case of flight from financial ruin. Pollock lost his factory, became a "bondsman" (apparently for his son-in-law), and had to apply for a veteran's pension to support himself in his old age. Yet despite these often tragic reverses, each of these men enjoyed long periods during which they were able to weather such setbacks successfully.[43]

Other Baltimore Jews were not as resilient, particularly those who came to the city after careers in the backcountry and were unable to adjust to the demands of mercantile life in a burgeoning urban seaport. Levy Andrew Levy struggled as an innkeeper and ultimately declared bankruptcy, while Isaac Mordecai, the son of Mordecai M. Mordecai, failed as a tobacco manufacturer and became a peddler. Barnard Jacobs's son Moses failed as both a shipping agent and a maker of trunks. When he died in 1802, seven of his children were placed in the care of a non-Jewish guardian, while his eldest son apprenticed himself as a "Windsor chair maker."[44]

Less visible in the historical records, but undoubtedly more common than any other type of local Jewish merchant, was the petty trader, peddler, or storekeeper who left Baltimore after only a short foray in business. Judging from the highly transient nature of the Jewish population between 1790 and 1820, it is clear that far more Jewish-owned businesses failed than succeeded, a fact that makes the longevity of the Ettings and Cohens—and even the on-and-off pattern of Elkin Solomon—seem more remarkable. According to demographer Ira Rosenwaike, of the nine householders who arrived between 1791 and 1800, five were gone by 1799 and a sixth by 1803 (a seventh died in 1800). While twelve new householders appeared between 1801 and 1810, four were gone before the decade was even finished, one left in 1812, and four more left in the wake of the Panic of 1819. The panic had an even greater impact on more recent arrivals. A large increase in immigration brought thirty new householders to the city in the 1810s, but an astounding two-thirds of them were gone by 1822, and several of these had not even survived in business during the boom years that preceded the crash.[45]

Baltimore's boomtown setting not only framed the economic decisions and experiences of arriving Jews, but also shaped Jewish social and religious development. In assessing the risks of moving to Baltimore, potential migrants undoubtedly considered the size and stability of the Jewish population, the extent to which Jewish social networks functioned in the city, and the availability of religious amenities, such as a congregation, a ritual slaughterer to provide kosher meat, a ritual circumciser to initiate newborn boys into the covenant, and a functionary capable of performing marriages. Since few if any of these features existed consistently in Baltimore until about 1815, Jews arriving before then had apparently decided that the economic advantages offered by the city outweighed, at least temporarily, their need to live within the context of a formal Jewish community.

The most striking evidence of Jews' willingness to sacrifice the fellowship and support of a Jewish community in favor of Baltimore's opportunities is the unusu-

In 1804, Jane Etting Taylor, daughter of Fanny Etting and the non-Jewish merchant Robert Taylor, embroidered this sampler, as was the fashion among young Baltimore women of the period. *Courtesy of the Maryland Historical Society, BCLM.1994.79.1.*

ally high intermarriage rate. Faced with a paucity of potential Jewish partners, a clear majority of the Jewish men of this period who married during their residence in the city chose to wed local non-Jewish women rather than attempt to find a Jewish bride from outside the city. Benjamin Solomon, for example, despite his membership in Richmond's Beth Shalome Congregation before coming to Baltimore in 1799, married a Christian woman, Harriet Pryse, three years after his arrival. The couple raised their children in the Protestant Episcopal Church.[46] Similarly, Jacob F. Levy, the son of Benjamin and Rachel Levy and the grandson of Nathan Levy, the founding father of Philadelphia Jewry who helped establish the rudiments of Jewish life there in the 1730s, married a non-Jew, Anne Maggs, in 1804.[47] There were also many unions between Jewish women and Christian men. Susan, a daughter of Levy Andrew Levy, married David Olden, while her sister Elizabeth married Olden's business partner Peregrine Falconer.[48] Likewise, two sisters of Reuben and Solomon Etting wed prominent non-Jewish merchants: Frances (Fanny) Etting married Colonel Robert Taylor, and Elizabeth (Betsy) Etting married Robert Mickle.[49]

Not only native-born and acculturated Jews took non-Jewish partners; so did many of the recently arrived Jewish immigrants who clustered in Fells Point. Yet while intermarriage for members of the former group often led them to convert or raise their children as Christians, in the case of the latter group it did not necessarily represent a significant break from their Jewish ties. Solomon Benjamin, a Dutch Jewish jeweler and silversmith, married the non-Jew Catherine (Kitty) Lence in 1809, but they gave their children Jewish names (Samuel, Esther, and Hannah), and Solomon requested in his 1818 will that "my children agreeable to my wish . . . be brought up in the Jewish religion."[50] The Prague-born dry goods dealer Levi Collmus married a Quaker, Frances Williams, in 1812, six years after his arrival in Baltimore, yet he went on to become an organizer of the city's first Jewish communal institutions, the Baltimore Hebrew Congregation (1830) and the United Hebrew Benevolent Society (1834).[51]

Regardless of how intermarriage ultimately shaped each person's social and religious identity, the paucity of prospective Jewish spouses in early national Baltimore left few alternatives for those who wished to marry and have a family. Indeed, no fewer than twenty marriages between Jews and non-Jews can be documented in the city from the 1790s through 1820, and undoubtedly there were several more of which no record remains.[52] For those who were inclined to marry but were unwilling to take a non-Jewish spouse, the only choices were to leave the city or remain single. This at least in part explains the disproportionate number of unmarried Jewish men and women in Baltimore during this period, including many members of the prominent Etting and Cohen families.[53]

The religious compromises demanded by the Baltimore environment in regard to marriage were mirrored in other facets of daily life. Jews who grew up in traditional homes had to adjust to a setting that was less conducive to religious observance. Mordecai Moses Mordecai was well educated in Talmudic literature in his native

Lithuania and was viewed as a religious authority by the members of Mikveh Israel during his residence in Philadelphia, while Solomon Etting had been trained as a shochet (ritual slaughterer) in his former hometown of Lancaster during the 1780s, when a congregation existed there. Yet it is doubtful that either man maintained their strict conformity to halachah (Jewish law) in the fluid social environment of Baltimore, where no Jewish congregation existed. Some Jews did manage to keep kosher in the city despite the challenges. Recipe books preserved in the papers of the Cohen family reveal how its members tried to adapt to the foodways of local elites without sacrificing their religious scruples by using liver and fish to imitate *treyf* (non-kosher) ingredients such as terrapin and lobster.[54]

In the absence of formal Jewish institutions, Baltimore Jews also improvised and made the best use of available resources when it came time to mark a life cycle event or observe a Jewish holiday. When the ship carrying Richmond-bound Westphalian immigrant Zalma Rehiné landed in Baltimore during the high holidays in 1789, he found that worship services were being held in the home of Levy and Isaac Solomon, who invited him to attend.[55] The Cohen brothers are said to have conducted private services in their residence on Saratoga Street for many years.[56]

Jews could also travel to nearby Jewish centers to participate in the formal institutions of community life. Many of Baltimore's acculturated families held membership in Philadelphia's Mikveh Israel Congregation, while recent immigrants to Baltimore often joined the Philadelphia Ashkenazic congregation Rodeph Shalom.[57] Sometimes, however, travel was not feasible, and Baltimore Jews had to make do with the less than ideal resources available in their home city. In 1817, Abraham Lazarus and Elizabeth Cohen, apparently both Jews, had their marriage solemnized by the Reverend Joshua Wells, an elder of the Methodist Episcopal Church in Fells Point, since no Jewish clergyman was available and civil marriage was not yet an option in Maryland.[58] In the 1790s, after Rachel Levy's Philadelphia relatives refused to transfer ownership of a Philadelphia burial plot established by her father, she and her husband, Benjamin, were interred in the cemetery of Baltimore's St. Paul's Episcopal Church, where several other Jews were also buried.[59] Even though records attest to the existence of a "Jews' Burying Ground" in Baltimore as early as 1786, it must have had some features that were unattractive to the Levys, as well as to other prominent families like the Ettings and the Cohens, who established their own private burial grounds instead of using this communal cemetery.[60]

Some of the contradictions and tensions caused by the lack of a religious infrastructure began to diminish during the boom years leading up to the Panic of 1819. In 1818 and 1819, the Dutch Jewish physician Alexander Wertheim, who moved frequently back and forth between Baltimore and Philadelphia, performed eleven circumcisions in the Maryland city.[61] During the same two years, two Jewish marriage ceremonies were solemnized by David Philips, a religious Jew who later became the shammes (sexton) of Congregation Shearith Israel in New York.[62] Unfortunately, the immigrant Jewish population was devastated by the Panic of 1819, and with the vast

Entrepreneur Jacob I. Cohen Jr. identified himself as an American patriot through his
management of the lottery that raised funds during the 1820s to build Baltimore's Washington
Monument. Lithograph by Isidore-Laurent Deroy, c. 1848, based on a drawing by August Kollner.
Courtesy of the Enoch Pratt Free Library, Maryland State Library Resource Center. All rights reserved.

majority forced to leave the city, these rudiments of Jewish communal life ceased to
develop. A small but important core group of immigrant Jews was able to ride out
the crisis, but they would have to wait a decade before the Jewish population could
once again reach the size necessary to make the growth of Jewish community institutions and services possible.

Jewish Citizens of the New Republic

In 1822, George Washington's birthday was marked in Baltimore with a widely pub-
licized drawing organized by the lottery and exchange broker Jacob I. Cohen Jr.,
the proceeds of which benefited the construction of the city's Washington Monument. The monument's board of managers had held lotteries to finance the project
since 1810, but none were as successful as those organized by Cohen. His decision
to combine the drawing with a celebration of the late president's birthday was only
one example of the marketing talent that had convinced the managers to name him

secretary of their board in 1820 and place him in charge of all future lotteries for the project. The excitement surrounding the 1822 drawing was heightened by holding it outdoors on the steps of Cohen's lottery and exchange office at 114 Market Street, where he erected two immense wheels, one holding the lottery tickets and one holding the prize slips. The prizes ranged from small amounts up to a jackpot of $30,000. Although typically lottery winners had to wait several weeks to claim their prizes, Cohen dazzled the crowd by paying the grand prize on the spot and in cash.[63]

The Washington's birthday lottery of 1822 not only revealed Cohen's talent as an entrepreneur, but also reflected how his business career helped him weave his way into the fabric of the city's municipal leadership and identify himself as a symbol of patriotism and civic pride. A devotee of Jeffersonian democracy, Cohen imagined the lottery business as a way for the humble ticket purchaser to contribute to the wide range of public and private improvements that lotteries funded, such as hospitals, schools, firehouses, and roads. Moreover, as his marketing appeals made clear, he believed that his lotteries advanced American ideals by giving working people an opportunity to overcome limitations of class and social background. Reporting on a drawing in 1814 for a $40,000 cash prize—the largest ever offered up to that time by a lottery in the United States—Cohen announced that the winners were "persons in extreme want who, by expending a trifling sum at Cohen's, were thus in a moment put in possession of affluence and *independence*."[64]

Around 1818, anxious to widen his role in political affairs and city government, Cohen took over the reins of the movement to win for Jews the right to hold public office in Maryland, which Solomon Etting had initiated in 1797.[65] Immediately following the passage of what became known as the Jew Bill in 1826, both Cohen and Etting were elected to the First Branch of the Baltimore City Council. Cohen went on to play an important role as the head of the city's Ways and Means Committee and as one of the architects of the public school system.[66]

Perhaps recalling his talent for combining patriotism and entrepreneurship in the 1822 lottery drawing for the Washington Monument, city leaders placed Cohen in charge of the celebration of the centennial of George Washington's birthday in 1832. He organized a massive observance that drew people of all classes with its pageantry and drama. Flags flew from public buildings and from ships in the harbor, businesses closed and churches opened, bells sounded and gun salutes blasted throughout the day. The centerpiece of the celebration was the Washington Monument itself; draped in American flags, it served as the backdrop for a military parade, a series of rousing speeches, and the reading of Washington's Farewell Address. Later that evening, at a public dinner for the city's leaders, Cohen was toasted for having "rendered essential services to this city" and as one who "will always be found at his post, wherever the public interest may call him."[67]

While few other Baltimore Jews of the era made as significant an impact on local affairs, those who remained in the city for more than a short time did mirror Cohen's tendency to see civic integration as a key to success and advancement. Especially considering the modest economic profile and transient nature of much of the Jewish population, Jews made remarkable efforts to identify themselves with movements for civic betterment, with the military, and with organizations that allowed them to interact and demonstrate common cause with their non-Jewish neighbors. In turn, they were often seen by other civic-minded citizens as natural allies in the quest to improve conditions for trade and urban development. Heavily concentrated in mercantile activities, Jews had a vested interest in public projects that strengthened commerce, the lifeblood of the growing port. While histories of Baltimore Jewry have focused primarily on the perceived exclusion of Jews from public life in the years before the passage of the Jew Bill, the truth is that the 1826 constitutional amendment giving Jews the right to hold public office was the result of Jews' already robust civic involvement and represented an acknowledgment by the non-Jewish Baltimoreans who made its passage possible that Jewish participation in the leadership of the city was essential to its continued growth and prosperity.

Baltimore's phenomenal growth and the resulting social fluidity and diversity of its population during the early national period created a particularly welcoming environment for Jews to participate in civic affairs. Even in the colonial days, Baltimore never had a well-entrenched gentry, and as the city grew during the 1790s and early 1800s, civic life remained open to the many German, Irish, Scotch Irish, Dutch, and French Acadian immigrants who arrived in the city.[68] The strength of the German community—about 10 percent of Baltimoreans spoke German in 1790—was a particular boon to Jewish civic integration; Jews like the Ettings and Cohens, whose background lay in German-speaking lands, not only were welcomed into its fold but also became leaders of its most important organization, the German Society of Maryland.[69] Finally, although the decline of slavery over the course of the early national period and a growing free black population continually diminished the clear legal divide between African Americans and whites, racial distinctions remained an important enough measure of civic status in Baltimore that even recent immigrants from Europe enjoyed a standing they would not have had in more northern locales. And those Baltimore Jews who could afford to own slaves—about 50 percent of Jewish households in the years between 1790 and 1810, declining to 27 percent in 1820 and to 16 percent in 1830—or to employ free black people as domestic servants accrued the status of white privilege in a particularly visible way.[70] Solomon Etting and Jacob I. Cohen Jr. also signaled their membership in the white elite by joining the Maryland State Colonization Society, an association founded in 1827 to help relocate free black people to Liberia.[71]

In asserting their strong civic identity, the most prominent Jews in early national Baltimore carved out an important place for themselves in the city's contentious political landscape. Moreover, as Cohen's ongoing tributes to the legacy of George Washington suggest, it was not only the local civic culture with which he and his coreligionists sought to identify. Especially after Baltimore took the spotlight in the War of 1812 and became a symbolic site in the construction of an American patrio-

The first of his distinguished family to settle in Baltimore, Reuben Etting traded with China and the Caribbean and was active in Baltimore politics. Watercolor on ivory by James Peale, 1794. *Courtesy of the Pennsylvania Academy of the Fine Arts, Philadelphia, gift of Frank Marx Etting, 1886.1.5.*

tism, Baltimore Jews seized the opportunity to emphasize their integral role in the nation as well.

In the decades following the revolution, the Baltimore political scene was dominated by the warring Federalist and anti-Federalist camps that characterized the national politics of that era. As Jews took active roles in the emerging political culture, they found multiple reasons to oppose the Federalist agenda and to identify with the Democratic Republicans (usually known simply as "Republicans"). As members of a religious and ethnic minority, they were skeptical of the Federalists' emphasis on a strong centralized government, which was seen as a threat to individual liberties. While nationally Federalists were known as champions of business, in Baltimore many merchants—both Jews and non-Jews—were repelled by the party's pro-British tendencies, since British interference in American commerce during the era's European wars was a major threat to the city's economic survival.[72]

The eldest Etting brother, Reuben, was introduced to local political circles in the early 1790s as an examiner of cargoes in the federal Office of Inspection and as a deputy sheriff of Baltimore County. In these positions he made contacts that helped lead him into the Republican Party when it was organized locally in 1795 in opposition to the Federalist camp. He was apparently among the party loyalists who helped the Republicans seize the dominant position in local politics in the election of 1798.[73] Three years later, when Thomas Jefferson won the presidency for the Republicans, Etting's devotion was recognized with an appointment as the US marshal for Maryland, a post he held until his relocation to Philadelphia in 1804.[74]

Solomon Etting got his start in politics as one of the Baltimoreans who in 1792 protested Secretary of State John Jay's treaty with the British, which he and other merchants felt was insufficient in protecting American trade.[75] Like his brother, Etting became an ardent Republican, serving in 1794 as a member of the standing committee of the Republican Society of Baltimore and in 1796 as one of the leaders of the Republican Fire Company who was deputized to coordinate a citywide emergency plan. That same year, indicating his growing profile in Baltimore politics, he was appointed to the city's committee for health affairs.[76]

The centrality of trade and commerce to Baltimore's growth during the early national period gave Jewish businessmen like Solomon Etting a natural outlet for civic involvement as they helped to build a framework of public and private institutions that were crucial to the city's development. Etting played a key role in founding or managing a string of companies providing fire and marine insurance.[77] He also worked to build Baltimore's banking system, which provided needed capital for business growth. As one of the earliest directors of the Bank of Baltimore, he served on a committee in 1796 charged with issuing its banknotes.[78] After the rise of the Republicans to dominance in local affairs, they desired a separate bank that would pursue Jeffersonian economic principles, so Etting joined in the founding of the Union Bank of Maryland and remained a trustee for decades.[79] Finally, he was involved in many projects to improve the city's infrastructure. He was a founder and director of the Baltimore Water Company (1804) and served on the commission to oversee the construction of new streets and roads when Baltimore expanded its northern boundary in 1816. He was one of the principals in building the Baltimore-Reisterstown Turnpike in 1805 and was among the seven commissioners charged with planning the Susquehanna Canal in 1822.[80]

Younger than Solomon Etting and a later arrival in the city, Jacob I. Cohen Jr. was not as involved as his older colleague in developing the foundation for Baltimore's urban growth. Although he shared with Etting a view of civic life that placed economic development at the center, his own devotion to Republican values led him to pursue a broader, more populist vision of political and civic activism. Already a Republican as a young man in Richmond, Cohen participated in 1803 in a meeting in the Virginia capital at which the election of Thomas Jefferson was hailed as a "restoration of the principles of '76."[81] In Baltimore, while he certainly cultivated ties to the city's business leaders, whose institutions his lotteries helped bankroll, he also built connections to the poorer members of society, who were often the

Solomon Etting and Rachel Gratz Etting. Oval wash drawings by Thomas Gimbrede, c. 1810. After the couple's arrival in 1791, Solomon Etting took part in almost every major civic initiative in Baltimore. *Courtesy of the Maryland Historical Society, 1938.7.99–100.*

purchasers of lottery tickets. One of Cohen's innovations was the introduction of small cash prizes that were given away at the time of grand drawings to customers whose tickets had a single digit in common with the winning number, a practice he heralded as a benefit to many "industrious mechanics."[82] While Etting helped lead the elite Republican Society of Baltimore, Cohen joined the Ancient and Honorable Mechanical Company of Baltimore, a union of Republican artisans that represented the interests of the common person.[83]

Like their civic activism, Baltimore Jews' devotion to military service was informed by their interest in economic development and the freedoms they saw as essential to their own success and integration. In the early national period the ability of the US government to maintain public order, protect its borders and commercial interests, and defend against attack was still being tested. Baltimore Jews had established their willingness to take up arms to protect their interests and liberties during the revolution; in the last decade of the eighteenth century and the first decade of the nineteenth century, many continued to do so by serving in one of the many local militia companies that stood ready to defend the city or be called into action by the state or federal government as the need arose. As an active militiaman, Reuben Etting was among those sent to Pennsylvania in 1794 to put down the Whiskey

Rebellion, and he was later elected the captain of a local volunteer unit, the Baltimore Independent Blues.[84] Simon Magruder Levy, a Baltimorean who became one of the first two cadets appointed to the military academy at West Point in 1802, had begun his US Army career in 1794 as a soldier defending against the efforts of Native Americans to retake their tribal lands in the Ohio Valley, where his father, Levy Andrew Levy, had spent his formative years as a trader.[85]

The most significant example of the enthusiasm of Baltimore Jews for military service came during the War of 1812, when the city became a key locale in the nation's defense against British invasion. Resulting in part from Britain's long-standing policy during its drawn-out naval conflict with France to seize American commercial vessels and impress their sailors into military service, the war drew strong support from the citizens of Baltimore because of the hazard this policy posed to the city's economic well-being. From the commencement of hostilities, and especially after Baltimore became the site of combat in 1814, Solomon Etting was a crucial figure in the city's wartime leadership as a member of the Committee of Safety and Vigilance. Among other tasks, he organized a hospital for wounded soldiers and assisted the quartermaster general in finding homes in which to house soldiers.[86] Most likely acting as a member of the committee, he even corresponded with inventor Robert Fulton about the possibility of building a steam-powered warship to aid in the city's defense.[87]

Meanwhile, the younger generation of local Jews volunteered in significant numbers to take up arms in defense of the city.[88] Mendes I. Cohen, a younger brother of Jacob I. Cohen Jr., was eighteen years old when he joined the Twenty-Seventh Regiment of the Maryland militia, believing it to be leaving to defend Washington, DC. When he learned this was not the case, he transferred to the Baltimore Fencibles, one of the volunteer units stationed at Baltimore's Star Fort (later known as Fort McHenry). Following his lead, Cohen's brothers Jacob, Philip, and Benjamin joined the same unit, as did Solomon Etting's son Samuel. Serving as privates, all were present in 1814 during the bombardment of the fort except for Jacob I. Cohen Jr., who had received a temporary leave to tend to a dying relative in Philadelphia.[89] Mendes I. Cohen later recalled the scene during the British attack when shells rained down on him and his comrades, killing two members of his company who were standing right next to him and his brother Benjamin. The Cohens escaped injury, but Samuel Etting was slightly wounded during the battle.[90]

Not only the sons of acculturated Jewish families, but also some of the city's poor Jewish immigrants answered the call to arms. Two Dutch Jews who appeared on the muster rolls of local militias during the War of 1812 had only been in Baltimore since about 1810: Jacob Moses, later a jeweler in Fells Point, served as a private in the Union Yägers, while peddler Andrew Levy, also from Fells Point, held the same rank in the Maryland Chasseurs. Levi Collmus, who came to Baltimore from Bohemia in 1806, enlisted as a private in the United Maryland Artillery. He was wounded and permanently disabled in the Battle of North Point where, according to his pension

BOMBARDMENT OF FORT MC HENRY.

At least four Jews helped defend the Star Fort (later renamed Fort McHenry) during the
famous 1814 bombardment that inspired Francis Scott Key to write "The Star-Spangled Banner."
Engraving by William Kneass, 1817, after a drawing by William Strickland.
Courtesy of the Yale University Art Gallery.

application, his "exertions . . . in the discharge of his duty as an artillerist were extremely arduous and violent."[91]

The service of Jews in the War of 1812 cemented their identification with both
local and national civic culture and advanced their reputation among non-Jewish
Baltimoreans as devoted citizens and patriots. After the war, many Jewish veterans
maintained memberships in patriotic societies and continued their involvement in
state militias. When construction on the Battle Monument commemorating those
killed in the war was started in 1815, the names of the Cohen brothers, as well as that
of their mother, Judith, who had dotingly sent hot food and coffee to her sons at the
Star Fort by messenger each morning, appeared prominently on the list of donors.[92]

To Jacob I. Cohen Jr., his family's wartime experiences made more galling the
limitation placed on Jewish officeholding by Maryland's constitution, which required public officials to submit to a Christian oath. This requirement was one
of the few barriers to his continued ascent into the ranks of the city's leadership.
Cohen's trademark tendency to build strong ties to Baltimoreans across the economic spectrum reflected not only his business savvy and democratic principles, but
also his ambition to hold political office. This was likely the reason that in the years

Mug used by Private Samuel Etting at the Star Fort in 1814. Fellow members of the
Baltimore Fencibles unit etched their names in the mug as a memento of their service.
Courtesy of the Maryland Historical Society, 1895.1.1.

following the War of 1812, he took over the effort to pass the Jew Bill, which Solomon Etting had directed in its initial, unsuccessful phase.

The restriction that prevented Jews from holding public office in Maryland before 1826 has been described in popular and scholarly accounts as an indication of the low civil status held by Jews in the state during those years. But given the leadership roles played by individuals such as Reuben and Solomon Etting and Jacob I. Cohen Jr. in almost every phase of Baltimore's economic growth, institutional development, and public life, and the participation of more humble Jews in local military units and civic associations, it is clear that the Christian oath requirement in the Maryland constitution had little to do with the attitude of non-Jewish Baltimoreans toward their Jewish neighbors.

Owing to the paucity of Jews in the state at the time of the revolution, the framers of the state constitution had probably not considered the possibility of Jewish elected officials when they mandated a religious test oath for officeholders in 1776. When a few Jews finally did begin to participate actively in Baltimore's civic culture in the 1790s, their non-Jewish neighbors, who recognized them as a great asset for the city's development, would likely have been glad to see them accede to state office. But Baltimoreans had little power to effect a change to the state constitution, given an archaic legislative system that denied the city the same representation in the General Assembly as that enjoyed by each of Maryland's counties, even though it had the population of eight counties put together.[93]

Moreover, Baltimore was denied a city charter until 1796, which meant that until then, there was no city government, and even the most basic decisions regarding local affairs were made by the General Assembly in Annapolis. City politics was the most logical place for Jews to contribute and to pursue their vision for Baltimore's growth and development, but the lack of a municipal government meant that until Baltimore's charter was granted, there were no city offices for Jews to fight for the right to hold. This explains why Solomon Etting first petitioned the legislature to change the Christian oath requirements in 1797, less than a year after officeholding on the local level became possible.

Despite the openness of Baltimoreans to Jews like Etting assuming a role in the city's government, the imbalance in legislative representation that continued even after Baltimore's incorporation as a city stacked the deck against a constitutional amendment that would allow it. Representatives of the state's rural districts, particularly those in the Federalist camp, refused to budge on the issue because they saw their resistance to Jewish civil equality as part of their larger struggle to counteract Baltimore's cosmopolitanism and to contain the city's influence over state affairs.[94] Thus, during successive sessions of the General Assembly following 1797, a delegate from Baltimore City would introduce a bill based on Etting's original petition, and the anti-Baltimore block would defeat it. After several failed attempts, Etting instructed the delegates who were assisting him to cease their efforts.

In 1816, however, Jacob I. Cohen Jr.'s rising ambition for public office led him to

----

send his own proposal to the General Assembly, although the Federalist-controlled legislature failed to take it up for consideration.[95] A slow process of change in the political power structure was beginning, however, due in part to changes in the voting laws, which had expanded the electorate by removing property requirements and other limitations on white men's suffrage. These changes ultimately increased the legislature's cohort of Republicans, who tended to support greater autonomy for Baltimore and, as a result, were also more favorable to the Jew Bill.

One of these new Republican legislators was Thomas Kennedy, elected to the House of Delegates from Washington County in 1817, who heard about Cohen's proposal during his first year in Annapolis and submitted a bill in 1818 to extend to Jews the same rights enjoyed by Christians under the state constitution. A select committee composed of Kennedy and two other delegates, Ebenezer S. Thomas of Baltimore County and Judge Henry Breckinridge of Baltimore City, was appointed to study the measure. But despite the committee's strong support, the bill failed to pass either house of the General Assembly in 1818 or in the next term, even after it was rewritten in the Senate in 1819 as a measure to remove all religious tests, without any special mention of Jews.[96] Circumstances changed significantly in 1821 when Republicans took control of the Senate for the first time. Kennedy reworked the bill to appeal to their Jeffersonian egalitarianism, using the model of the "universal" version that had failed in that chamber on the previous try. Although the actual provisions of this redrafted bill still addressed only the matter of removing religious oaths from use in the state, this time the measure was given a more evocative—if misleading—title: An Act to Extend to All Citizens of Maryland the Same Civil Rights and Religious Privileges That Are Enjoyed under the Constitution of the United States. Kennedy's strategy of repackaging the Jew Bill proved effective, and it was approved by both houses in 1822.[97]

The passage of the bill was an important but insufficient achievement, however. In order for the constitutional amendment to take effect, it had to be confirmed by a second vote in the legislature during the following session. Meanwhile, a flurry of propaganda in the Federalist-controlled parts of the state threatened to derail the effort. In Washington County, these forces succeeded in unseating Kennedy, the amendment's foremost champion.

Despite the initially warm response the bill's universal version had received in the legislature, the license Kennedy took in fashioning the title allowed the Federalists to claim that it would not only extend rights to Jews, but would also open the door to greater freedom for deists, Turks, and free black men. Anxiety regarding the latter group was particularly salient in Maryland politics at the time, since slavery continued to decline, and the resulting increase in the number of free blacks threatened to unhinge the social control whites had long enjoyed. One propagandist inferred that the bill's rationale of bringing the state and federal constitutions into closer agreement on matters of civil rights could be marshaled to argue that "we ought to admit the free negroes to vote or represent us."[98] When the legislature convened again in

SKETCH

OF

PROCEEDINGS IN THE

Legislature of Maryland,

DECEMBER SESSION, 1818,

ON WHAT IS COMMONLY CALLED

The Jew Bill;

CONTAINING

THE REPORT OF THE COMMITTEE

APPOINTED BY THE HOUSE OF DELEGATES

"To consider the justice and expediency of extending to those persons professing the Jewish Religion, the same privileges that are enjoyed by Christians:"

TOGETHER WITH

The Bill reported by the Committee,

AND

THE SPEECHES

OF

THOMAS KENNEDY, Esq. *OF WASHINGTON COUNTY*,

AND

H. M. BRACKENRIDGE, Esq. OF BALTIMORE CITY.

Baltimore:

PRINTED BY JOSEPH ROBINSON,

Circulating Library, corner of Market and Belvidere-streets.

1819.

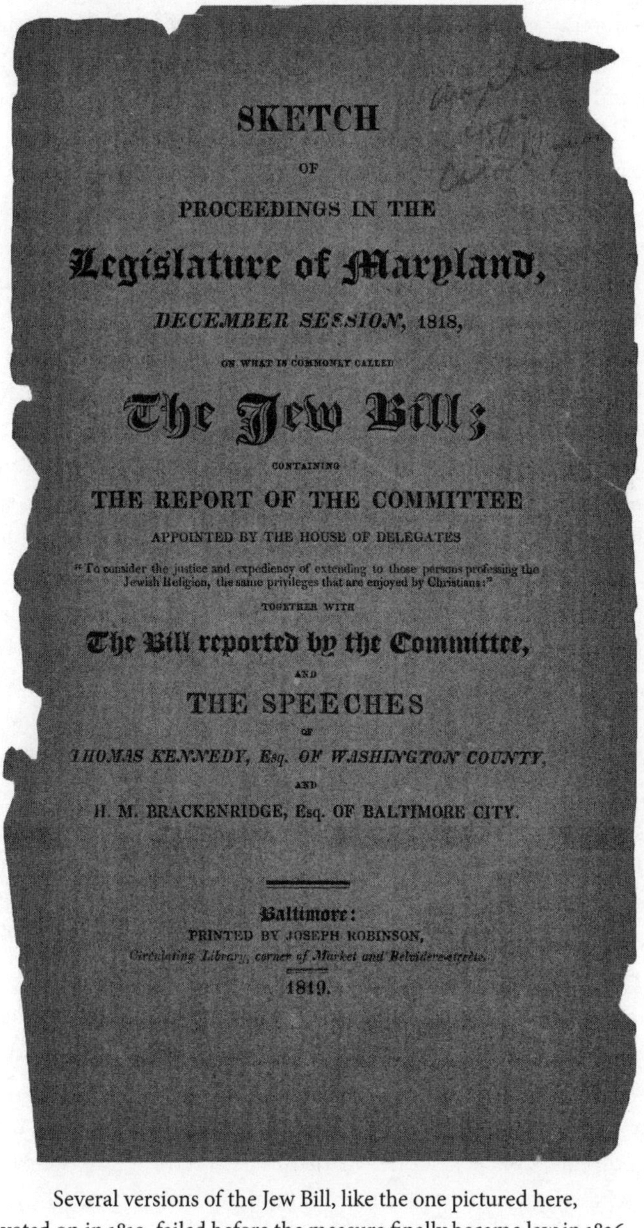

Several versions of the Jew Bill, like the one pictured here, voted on in 1819, failed before the measure finally became law in 1826. *Jewish Museum of Maryland.*

1823, the Republican-dominated Senate confirmed the bill, but in light of the widespread fears aroused by the inaccurate title, the House rejected it.

Despite this turn of events, support for the Jew Bill was not dead. Many of the delegates who had opposed the universal version had nonetheless been convinced by the passionate oratory of their colleagues William G. D. Worthington and John Tyson, both of Baltimore City, and John McMahon of Allegany County that Jewish talent and resources offered great benefit to the state and ought to be courted. With the strong agreement of Jacob I. Cohen Jr., who had long been skeptical that the "universal" approach could succeed, provisions suggesting that the bill might extend new rights to groups other than Jews were removed.[99] The majority in the House soon became satisfied that a reversion to the specific form of the bill would secure the desired advantages for Maryland while avoiding the implications that a broader measure might carry. An additional tweak to the legislation, designed to counter claims that it would give license to "infidels" and "blasphemers," was that Jewish officeholders would have to affirm their belief in an afterlife. Bolstered by the reelection of Kennedy in 1825, these changes were sufficient to win passage of the Jew Bill later the same year, followed by its confirmation as a constitutional amendment in 1826. The final language stipulated that "every citizen of this state professing the Jewish Religion . . . appointed to any office or public trust . . . [shall] make and subscribe a declaration of his belief in a future state of rewards and punishments, in the stead of the declaration now required."[100]

During the many debates over the Jew Bill in the General Assembly between 1818 and 1825, the speeches delivered by its proponents were peppered with arguments provided by Jacob I. Cohen Jr. and Solomon Etting. Cohen in particular played an active behind-the-scenes role in the legislative process, using his business and political connections to cultivate allies. He also kept meticulous track of the votes in each legislative session, information that he intended to use for lobbying efforts and to pursue political payback against the bill's opponents.[101] All this underscores how much the Jew Bill was designed specifically to clear the way for the already highly influential Etting and Cohen to take their places on the Baltimore City Council, rather than as a more general measure to extend civil rights to the larger population of Jews suffering under the ban of civic exclusion, as supporters of the bill usually claimed.

Champions of the Jew Bill were particularly guided by Etting and Cohen in presenting Jews' exclusion from public life in Maryland as more complete than it actually was; they argued that Jews were barred from accepting state military commissions or serving on juries because of the Christian oath required by state law. In practice, however, while Jews were barred from holding elective office on the state and municipal levels, several Jews, including Solomon Etting, had received commissions in militia companies and had served on juries.[102] As information supplied by Etting during the Jew Bill debates made clear, Jewish individuals had routinely been permitted to serve in such capacities "without subscribing to the religious test oath."[103] Since most Jews—like most non-Jews—never dreamed of holding elective office,

Jacob I. Cohen Jr. led the fight for the Maryland Jew Bill during the eight years before its passage in 1826. Later, as a city councilman, he chaired the influential Ways and Means Committee and helped found the city's public school system. *Courtesy of the Maryland Historical Society.*

the fact that these lesser civic roles were open to them suggests that few were ever seriously affected by the test oath requirement or experienced any barriers to participating as they wished in local public life. Viewed in this context, it becomes clear that Etting and Cohen were atypical among Baltimore Jews in their preoccupation with the test oath, just as they were atypical in attaining the degree of wealth and prominence that made public officeholding a reasonable ambition.

As Etting's and Cohen's exclusion from the city council had grown harder to square with the crucial role they had come to play in civic affairs by the 1810s and 1820s, they and their non-Jewish supporters became more convinced than ever that a constitutional amendment was needed to remove the test oath and solve this conundrum. Their legislative campaign, however, would have been unlikely to resonate with lawmakers outside of Baltimore if it had been presented as a practical measure intended to ease the way of two wealthy, influential Jewish businessmen onto the city council. As a result, the Jew Bill proponents described their effort as a fight to obtain basic civil and religious liberties for the Jews of Maryland, rather than as an attempt to propel two already prominent civic leaders into a more formal political role. Placing the issue of civil rights front and center, the proponents also found it expedient to downplay the de facto civic acceptance that most of Maryland's Jews — almost all of whom were in Baltimore — experienced, instead presenting their de jure legal status under the Maryland constitution as if it represented the day-to-day reality of Jewish life in the state.

This strategy was vividly illustrated by a series of events that unfolded just as the debates concerning the Jew Bill were under way in the General Assembly during the 1823–1824 legislative season. In the early spring of 1823, Benjamin Cohen, Jacob's brother, was elected captain of a volunteer military company, the Marion Corps, and given a commission by Governor Samuel Stevens Jr. According to a newspaper notice, he had accepted this commission without incident and by the first week of March was functioning in the role of captain. By the fall of that year, however, when controversy erupted over confirmation of the bill and its future seemed to be in doubt, Benjamin Cohen suddenly claimed that he could not serve as captain because of the state's proscription against Jews holding public office, whereupon the company resolved to operate without a captain until the Jew Bill was brought to a final vote.

The younger Cohen's withdrawal can only be explained as a stunt designed to obscure the *informal* acceptance enjoyed by prominent Jews in many aspects of Baltimore's civic life and as a means of focusing public attention on their *formal* lack of civil equality under the state constitution. Particularly remarkable — and further indicative of the strong civic role Benjamin Cohen and other Jews of his status were already playing — was the extent to which non-Jews cooperated in staging this public spectacle. Governor Stevens, a Republican and a supporter of the Jew Bill, took a starring role in the drama by presenting the leaderless company with a state flag and commending them on their noble behavior in resolving not to replace Cohen.[104]

- - - - - - - - - - - - -

In fairness, the Cohens and Ettings were not wrong to cast their campaign as a fight for civil rights, even if few Jews of the period directly felt the impact of exclusion from officeholding. Although less prominent Jews might not have cared as much about the test oath, its removal did strengthen their ability to serve in many civic roles by codifying this right in state law and removing the need for case-by-case accommodation. Informal accommodation would certainly have lost its efficacy over time, as the processes of acculturation and social mobility led an increasing number of Jews to seek higher-profile roles in government or admittance to the state bar, which had apparently been an unrealized childhood dream of Solomon Etting's son Samuel.[105] Without constitutional protection, Jews pursuing such opportunities would have been subject to the whims of the state legislature, where Baltimore's representation remained too weak to guard their interests.

Clearly, the passage of the Jew Bill helped Jews secure their civil status, but the conventional portrait of Jews as barred from participating in the civic life of their city and state does not accurately reflect the experiences of Solomon Etting and Jacob I. Cohen Jr., nor does it represent the experiences of more modest Jews who served as militiamen and jurors and worked for political parties and civic associations. Understanding how Jewish exclusion from civic life was sometimes exaggerated as a strategy in the legislative battle for the Jew Bill helps clarify the fact that the Jews of Baltimore often took an active part in public affairs during the early national period. It also helps reframe the battle against the Christian oath requirement as one propelled in large part by two prominent individuals who wished to expand their already powerful roles as civic leaders. The non-Jewish Baltimoreans who championed their efforts obviously saw the potential for a growing number of civic-minded Jews to follow in Etting's and Cohen's footsteps as city builders and promoters of the local economy. While the vagaries of state politics and regional rivalries made the struggle for full political equality a long one, the enthusiastic support the Jew Bill received from Baltimoreans and their representatives, and its passage more than a decade before Baltimore City gained proportionate representation in the General Assembly, underscore just how important Jews had become to the life of the city by 1826.

Paradigm Shift: The Birth of a Community

A correspondent calling himself "Philanthropist" reported to a Baltimore newspaper in 1829 that he had been invited to the new synagogue on North Exeter Street in Old Town. "The room is small, as their means are small," he explained, but it was "fitted up with neatness and simplicity." The visitor was particularly struck by "a prayer for our rulers," which had been rendered in English and posted on the wall of the worship room. It petitioned God to protect not only the president and other leaders of the federal government, but also "his Excellency the Governor of the State of Maryland, the members of the State Legislature . . . and the Mayor of our City, the civil authorities, and all inhabitants of Baltimore." Reflecting on the significance of his visit for the city more broadly, Philanthropist heralded the establishment of a synagogue by local Jews as a sign that "here all prejudices are fast wearing away against them."[106]

The appearance of this first Jewish congregation reflected not only an evolution in the religious life of Baltimore Jews, but also a shift in the larger social and economic patterns that influenced Jewish settlement in the city. Ten years earlier, as Jews and others reeled under the impact of the Panic of 1819 and many left the city, few could have imagined that the Jewish population would come to exceed its previous size over the next decade. After all, Baltimore had fallen during the 1820s from its position as a budding trade rival to New York and Philadelphia as the overseas traffic in its port declined. Still, despite its economic reverses, the city continued a pattern of slow growth.[107]

In a scramble to revive Baltimore's competitiveness, political and business leaders invested in a wide range of internal improvements, like canals and railroads, which they hoped would better connect the city to a growing hinterland and once again make Baltimore a center for overseas trade. Among the chief promoters of these improvements were Solomon Etting and Jacob I. Cohen Jr., both of whom served as directors of the Baltimore and Ohio Railroad, founded in 1827. In fact, as members—and, in Etting's case, as the president—of the First Branch of the Baltimore City Council, they had a hand in almost every major aspect of the city's growth during this era. As the council's Ways and Means Committee's chair and as a founder, along with his brothers, of a new banking house in 1831, Cohen was one of the individuals most responsible for returning the city to a state of financial health.[108]

In terms of the growth of Jewish life in Baltimore, however, the most significant developments of the late 1820s and early 1830s did not take place among acculturated Jews like the Ettings and the Cohens, but rather among the immigrant Jews who now overwhelmingly dominated the city's Jewish population. Recent immigrants had outnumbered native-born Jews and immigrants of the pre-revolutionary period as early as 1810, but because many of them stayed only a short time and most left in the wake of the Panic of 1819, the city's Jewish population had not fully evinced an immigrant character. Between 1820 and 1830, however, all but one of the twenty-three new Jewish households that appeared in Baltimore were headed by recent immigrants, mainly from Holland but also from Germany, England, and Poland. Significantly, the number arriving from Germany and other parts of Central Europe was on the rise, a trend that skyrocketed after 1830 as an unprecedented wave of Jewish and non-Jewish migration from that region began to reach Baltimore and other areas of North America.[109]

Compared to the immigrant arrivals of former years, those who came between 1820 and 1830 were less transient; more than half remained in the city long term. This was due in part to the growth of a rudimentary community life, which made it easier for newcomers to stay. But it also resulted from the economic mobility of a core group of immigrants who found success as retailers of dry goods, groceries, and clothing, as well as entrepreneurs who helped establish two new types of business in Baltimore: pawnbroking and the secondhand trade. Despite the low status of both of these undertakings in the popular imagination, each was essential to the changing economy of cities like Baltimore, where a growing working class needed inexpensive goods and short-term loans based on modest forms of collateral.[110] By 1830, the district around Harrison Street near the city's Centre Market was becoming known for its Jewish-owned secondhand stores and pawnshops.

Reflecting their social position, the recent immigrants did not always abide by the rules of polite society as they mingled with their non-Jewish counterparts in working-class sections of the city, like Fells Point and Old Town. The prejudice against Jews that Philanthropist noted was actually a new phenomenon in Baltimore, part of the anti-immigrant sentiment that became more and more common as the ranks of newcomers—particularly Irish and Germans—swelled. It also stemmed from the poverty of some recent immigrants, whose desperation sometimes led them to commit crimes of property, and from the less-than-respectable nature of Jewish trades like pawnbroking, which could place even successful businessmen in the position of unknowingly (or knowingly) receiving stolen goods.[111]

The growth of religious life and the emergence of community institutions among the immigrants mitigated the impact of disadvantageous social conditions by providing a network of support and cooperation for Jews, which in turn blunted—as the remarks of Philanthropist suggest—the negative perception of the newcomers. While Baltimore had lost its mohel and Jewish marriage officiant in the mass exodus of 1819, by 1830 there was again someone to perform Jewish marriages: Joseph Jacobs, a chemist listed in a city directory of the period as "priest of the Jews." There is also evidence that an informal minyan (prayer quorum) was operating in the city as early as 1823, since in that year a Dutch Jewish emissary seeking contributions for his charitable work in the Holy Land addressed a solicitation letter to "The President and the Congregation in Baltimore."[112]

Public Jewish worship was formalized by 1829, and the following year the small congregation on Exeter Street, Nidchei Israel (The Scattered of Israel), applied to the Maryland General Assembly for incorporation under the English name Baltimore Hebrew Congregation. Reminiscent of the politics of the Jew Bill, the application was initially denied by a legislature still empowered to micromanage Baltimore's local affairs, but it was subsequently approved. As Ira Rosenwaike has explained, the ability of Jews to maintain a synagogue for the first time in Baltimore's history resulted directly from the emergence of a core group of leaders whose financial success enabled them to put down more or less permanent roots in the city. Three of the men whose names appeared as incorporators of the Baltimore Hebrew Congregation in 1830 (Levi Benjamin, Moses Millum, and John M. Dyer) had been in the city for more than a decade, and the other two (Joseph Osterman and Lewis Silver), though more recent arrivals, would remain in Baltimore for more than a dozen years.[113]

While the rudiments of Jewish community life were finally in place by 1830, dramatic changes that would further transform the city and its Jewish population later in the century were imperceptibly on the horizon. Even as the city's role as a leader in overseas trade continued to diminish, the railroads and other internal improvements that city leaders built to reverse this trend became crucial to the emergence of Baltimore as a manufacturing center and supplier of goods to the country's interior. These developments in turn fueled the large wave of immigrants that poured into the city in the middle decades of the nineteenth century, ushering in a remarkable period of growth for Baltimore Jewry.

2

A "City and Mother in Israel"

On December 15, 1880, more than 600 guests gathered at the Concordia Opera House to celebrate the twenty-fifth anniversary of the Hebrew Benevolent Society, Baltimore's oldest and largest Jewish philanthropic organization. The evening's cere- monies were carefully crafted to express the members' commitment both to their Jewish heritage and to the values of the larger, non-Jewish world. American flags surrounded a display of gas jets shaped to spell out the Hebrew word "tzedakah" (charity). The society's president sat strategically between Mayor Ferdinand Latrobe and Benjamin Szold, rabbi of the Oheb Shalom Congregation and the senior mem- ber of the local Jewish clergy.[1]

Also apparent amid this meld of themes was the connection of Baltimore's Jews to the city's prominent German American population. The Concordia was both the major gathering place of Baltimore's Germans and the principal meeting spot for Jewish banquets, fairs, and celebrations. Rabbi Szold gave a speech in German, and Har Sinai's younger and more progressive rabbi, Samuel Sale, spoke in English, followed by an address by the mayor. The evening culminated in the opening of hun- dreds of envelopes containing charitable pledges, each of which was made known to the audience. By night's end, more than $8,000 in contributions had been an- nounced.[2]

The anniversary celebration followed what had become by 1880 a fairly predict- able program. Yet it also provided a snapshot of the development of Baltimore's Jewish community since the founding of its first synagogue, Baltimore Hebrew Congregation, more than five decades earlier. At the time of the Jew Bill debates in 1826, only about 150 Jewish individuals resided in the entire state of Maryland. But within a few years, political and economic changes in Central and Eastern Europe caused a surge in Jewish immigration to the United States, just as Baltimore's rising fortunes made it the second-largest city in the United States. No longer a volatile boomtown with limited appeal to permanent Jewish settlers, the city had about 1,000 Jews by 1840 and between 5,000 and 7,000 by the outbreak of the Civil War, allowing it to vie with Philadelphia for the distinction of being the largest American Jewish center outside New York.[3] By 1880, Baltimore had fallen behind several other leading cities: its Jewish population was surpassed by those of San Francisco, Brooklyn, Philadelphia, and Chicago. Still, the city had one of the largest Jewish communities in the United States with 10,000 Jews.[4] Most important, Baltimore stood out as a place known for its distinguished Jewish leaders and for the variety and vibrancy of its congregations and communal institutions. By this measure in particular, nineteenth-century Baltimore was what in Jewish tradition is called a "city and mother in Israel."[5]

In addition to reflecting the dramatic growth and importance of the city's Jewish population, the 1880 banquet revealed the thorough cultural transformation that had occurred among Baltimore Jews. Though most had arrived in the city as poor immigrants raised in a traditional Jewish environment, they had experienced significant social and economic mobility, displaying along the way a decided openness to American culture. Born into societies where Jews had few legal rights and were largely confined to occupations like peddling and cattle dealing, many had risen to become successful retail merchants and clothing manufacturers. As they embraced the promise of America, they reshaped their communal organizations and style of religious worship to fit their new surroundings. While Baltimore's Jews, like those in other American locations, pursued acculturation in different ways and often disagreed on the terms of change, overall they shared the experience of trying to balance tradition and communal loyalties with their pursuit of success and acceptance in the larger non-Jewish world.

From Europe to America

When Henry Sonneborn and his brother Jonas set out for America in 1849, their family had lived in the small Hessian town of Breidenbach for at least a century. Their grandfather Loew Aaron (the name Sonneborn was not adopted until 1808) received a letter of "safe conduct" (*Geleitbrief*) from the grand duke in Darmstadt in 1749, allowing him to reside in Breidenbach as a livestock dealer, fruit broker, and butcher. The Sonneborns were typical of the *Dorfjuden* (village Jews) who lived in small clusters across the German countryside and filled the marketing and service needs of a society otherwise made up of Christian landowners and peasants. In Breidenbach they were one of eight Jewish families who remained distinct from their neighbors not only by virtue of their legal status and their occupations, but also in their practice of traditional Judaism, their manner of dress and deportment, and their preference for Yiddish over High German.[6]

The traditional lifestyle of Jews in rural Hesse seemed on the verge of change as Henry and Jonas Sonneborn approached adulthood, especially after the Grand Duchy of Hesse extended full legal equality to Jews in 1848. Yet the daily lives of Jews in Breidenbach did not significantly reflect a trend toward modernization or integration. Their father, Moses, continued to carry on the livestock trade that his family had followed for generations, and the boys were trained to enter the family business. Although the expansion of rights should have paved the way for social and economic mobility, the deterioration of the rural economy under the impact of urbanization meant that the circumstances of many small-town Jews declined rather than improved. To supplement the family income, Henry and Jonas were sent to wander the countryside as peddlers of skins and pelts.[7]

While their economic difficulties mounted, Jewish merchants and artisans became a focus for the growing resentment of the German peasantry, who suffered greatly from the decay of feudal society and saw Jews not only as competitors for new economic roles, but as beneficiaries of the changing political order. Only months after the Jewish emancipation law passed the Hessian parliament, peasants' frustration erupted in a series of antigovernment riots that included the looting of Jewish property in Breidenbach and several nearby towns.[8] Perhaps anxious to deflect anger against the government by blaming the Jews, local officials grew more rigid in their oversight of Jewish economic activities. This had dire consequences for the Sonneborns in 1849: conducting business in a neighboring town, Henry and Jonas were accosted by a constable, who accused them of stealing. Having been drinking, the constable was aggressive with the boys, who fended off his attack and fled home. Advised by his Jewish neighbors that such a brush with the law spelled certain prosecution, Moses Sonneborn quickly arranged for his sons to leave the country. They fled to Holland, boarded a ship, and landed several weeks later in New York. They had heard of Baltimore from friends, who described it as a promising location for new immigrants, but with funds sufficient only for a single train ticket, they decided that Henry would proceed alone while Jonas would remain, at least temporarily, in New York.[9]

Like Henry Sonneborn, most Jewish immigrants who arrived in Baltimore after 1830 hailed from small towns and villages in German-speaking regions of Central Europe, where their families had been economic middlemen since the Middle Ages. Ultimately the combined processes of political reform and industrialization and the rise of new urban centers would benefit Central European Jews; by the 1880s, they had undergone a dramatic social transformation that greatly improved their economic position. But because these developments were drawn out over many decades and because they were accompanied by social turmoil that sparked reactionary movements among the disaffected non-Jewish population, their impact was not uniformly positive. Moreover, the uneven pace of change meant that Jews in many Central European towns and villages in the first half of the nineteenth century still found themselves barred from certain trades and crafts, hemmed in by limits on settlement, and unable to take advantage of new opportunities.[10]

As a burgeoning population of young Central European Jews faced these obstacles to building a secure life, the impetus toward emigration took shape. Beginning as a small but noticeable stream after 1820, it grew by the 1840s and did not slow even as political emancipation extended its reach. Ever since the Jews of the Rhineland gained civil rights under French rule in the late eighteenth century, only to lose them when the territory transferred to Prussia in 1815, the process of Jewish emancipation had been full of contradictions. In Bavaria, the point of origin for the largest number of Baltimore Jews through the 1870s, the government technically extended citizenship to Jews in 1813 and supported Jewish secular education. But these reforms came with increased restrictions on social and economic life that lasted into the 1860s, including the dreaded *Matrikel* laws, which allowed Jews to pass on the right of residence in their localities only to eldest sons, thereby preventing others from legally marrying and establishing families. For Jews who were allowed to taste the fruits of emancipation, only to have them withdrawn or kept just out of reach, emigration and the freedoms it promised became even more attractive than it was before the era of emancipation began.[11]

Despite the broad impact of these frustrations, the movement to America was a selective one. First and foremost, emigration proved attractive to the young and single. While it is not hard to find evidence of families like Jonas and Merle Friedenwald, who arrived in Baltimore in 1832 with three children and Jonas's elderly father, Chaim, much more typical were young men or women traveling alone or with siblings, cousins, or neighbors.[12] This was because declining economic opportunities and legal restrictions like the *Matrikel* disproportionately affected the unmarried and those not yet established in business. Emigrants also tended to come from the ranks of poorer Jews, who were less able to withstand the economic and legal restrictions than were members of better-situated families. Despite occasional anti-Jewish riots, such as those that erupted in 1848, no widespread fear of violence or repression existed; most Jews believed that, eventually, the promise of emancipation would be fully realized. Those who were well settled and employed were therefore less motivated to leave.[13]

Emigration was also shaped by geography, since the ups and downs of the emancipation process and the imposition of legal restrictions differed from place to place. The naturalization records of Baltimore Jews up to 1851 reveal that almost half came from the kingdom of Bavaria, where Jews had suffered under some of the most frustrating and contradictory policies claiming to offer them "civic betterment." Smaller numbers came from other German states: 10 percent from Baden-Württemberg and almost 5 percent from Hesse. Some 17 percent simply stated their place of origin as "Germany."[14]

Just over 80 percent of Jewish immigrants arriving in Baltimore before 1851 hailed from one of the German states, a higher percentage than those settling in other American cities during the period.[15] However, there are good reasons to refrain from terming Baltimore's nineteenth-century immigrants "German Jews," at least as a description of their culture of origin. First, as naturalization records make clear, the notion of a cohesive "Germany" in the decades before political unification in 1871 was weak: immigrants were more likely to think of themselves as coming from particular regions or states, each of which presented a distinct social, economic, and political context for Jewish life. Moreover, small but significant numbers came from outside the German-speaking heartland: 5 percent from Holland, 4 percent from England, and slightly smaller percentages from Prussia's eastern provinces, Poland, and Bohemia.[16] The number of Jewish immigrants from more eastern locales increased in the decades after 1851. By the end of the Civil War, Baltimore was home not only to a growing number of Prussian Jews (many from the formerly Polish province of Posen) but also to an expanding population of Jews from the Russian Empire. By 1875, well before the onset of what is normally considered the period of Eastern European Jewish migration, the city already had three synagogues identifying themselves as "Polish" or "Russian."[17]

The most profound reason to refrain from considering this immigration to be German, however, is that even among emigrants leaving the German states, few had experienced a degree of integration or acculturation that might have caused them to part with a traditional Jewish self-conception and begin to think of themselves as members of a larger "German" society and culture. True, a vanguard of secularizing Jews had started to break down social barriers and immerse themselves in the language and culture of the non-Jewish world. Some, led by a small but growing cadre of liberal rabbis, had begun to consider religious reforms. Even in smaller towns and villages Jews had begun to alter some traditional cultural and religious practices. Overall, however, such changes were piecemeal before 1871, when the unification of Germany finally cleared the way for comprehensive Jewish emancipation and when increased urbanization sped the pace of acculturation. During the peak years of Jewish immigration before the Civil War, most Jews leaving Europe for Baltimore were *Dorfjuden*, like the Sonneborns, who still practiced distinctively Jewish trades, were strongly rooted in Jewish tradition, and had not forged significant social or cultural ties with non-Jews.[18]

Indeed, most of the immigrants who later styled themselves as the "German Jews" of Baltimore would have thought of themselves primarily as Jews rather than as Germans at the time of their arrival. As discussed below, the claiming of a German identity became an attractive way to adapt to Baltimore, with its large community of non-Jewish Germans and its many German-language associations and clubs. After 1880, the desire to distance themselves from the wave of Jewish immigrants arriving from Eastern Europe would further encourage this group's tendency to fashion themselves as "German Jews."[19]

While Jewish newcomers of the mid-nineteenth century settled in all parts of the growing United States, there were particular reasons to choose Baltimore. First, its accessible harbor and strong trade connections with the ports of Liverpool and Bremen stimulated its emergence as a major immigrant port of arrival. By 1834 the Baltimore-Bremen connection had made the city a major destination for German immigrants, who often arrived on ships making return voyages after unloading Maryland tobacco in Europe. By the outbreak of the Civil War, at least a quarter of Baltimore's population was of German descent, including Jews from German-speaking lands who followed the same emigration routes as their non-Jewish neighbors. Jewish emigrants from more eastern points of origin also frequently departed from German ports, but because they were more likely to leave from Hamburg than from Bremen, they were less likely to end up in Baltimore.[20]

If the strong ties between Baltimore and Bremen landed many immigrants in the city, it was Baltimore's rapid growth and expanding economy that convinced such a large number to stay. The city's thriving industrial sector offered ready employment to skilled and unskilled immigrants, as well as to migrants from rural areas and from other cities in the United States. The dramatic population increase, in turn, fueled further growth. In such an auspicious economic environment, Baltimore was able to hold its position as the nation's second-largest city from about 1830 through the mid-1850s.[21]

Most attractive for Jews, however, was the city's strategic position as a supply center for retail goods. Strongly focused on retail trade and composed disproportionately of peddlers during the years of heaviest immigration, Jewish newcomers benefited from Baltimore's location between the manufacturing centers of the North and the untapped markets of the South. Its connection by turnpike to the National Road and its position as the starting point of the Baltimore and Ohio Railroad also gave the city unparalleled access to developing midwestern regions. In 1853, when Jewish immigration was at its height, the railroad reached the Ohio River, creating a lucrative vehicle for the flow of merchandise sold by Jewish entrepreneurs. As the commercial hub for a vast hinterland stretching from southern Pennsylvania to Virginia and the Carolinas, and from the Atlantic to the Ohio River and beyond, Baltimore provided an ideal arena for Jewish immigrants to apply their commercial skills in ways that yielded much more significant rewards than they had in Europe.[22]

Gaining an Economic Foothold

When the young immigrant Simeon Hecht arrived in Baltimore in the late 1840s, his relatives supplied him with a pack of dry goods and notions to peddle along Belair Road, where he became known to local inhabitants as "Jew Sam the Peddler." As Hecht's ambition grew, he ventured into Virginia and peddled through the Shenandoah Valley, and he was soon taken under the wing of Baltimore dry goods dealer William S. Rayner, who sent him with merchandise to the Eastern Shore. Rayner then set up Hecht in business back in Baltimore, where he opened Hecht's Red Post Store, a small dry goods establishment on the corner of Orleans and Eden streets, in a neighborhood of mostly native-born Americans. With Rayner's support, Hecht prospered and eventually brought from Germany his brothers and several members of his wife's family, all of whom he started in business as peddlers. Soon, he was supplying not only this large group of relatives but also a number of other Jewish peddlers in need of a first job, overseeing their careers much as Rayner had overseen his. Hecht helped these peddlers become retail merchants by renting them stores, paying the initial expenses, and supplying them with merchandise at cost in return for a share of the profits. By 1854, he was supporting at least nine stores in the city.[23]

Simeon Hecht's story illustrates how a Jewish economy took shape in Baltimore and its hinterland during the years of Jewish immigration from Central Europe. At every step along his path, Hecht relied on networks that forged ties of kinship and ethnic loyalty into powerful tools of economic advancement. In an age when immigrant Jews had few other sources of credit, and before an array of Jewish organizations emerged to look after the welfare of the community, such networks were the only structures to which immigrants could turn to gain a foothold in new and unfamiliar surroundings. In Europe, kinship and ethnic networks had long bound together Jews across geographical expanses, sustaining them in sometimes hostile environments. In the free and comparatively dynamic setting of the United States, Jews were able to exploit these traditional connections in unprecedented ways. By allowing immigrant Jews to connect Baltimore to markets across several states and to nurture the demand for manufactured goods that drove innovation in America's growing industrial economy, family and ethnic networks proved to be a crucial factor in the dramatic social and economic transformation that accompanied their adaptation to American life.[24]

As Hecht's story shows, the commercial success of Baltimore Jews was tied to the activities of immigrants who spread out across a sizable hinterland, selling goods supplied by their contacts in the metropolis and laying the foundation for their own eventual settlement in the city. Many of Baltimore's most prominent Jewish merchants—men like department store founder Moses Hutzler and nationally known clothing manufacturers Levi Greif and Henry Sonneborn—spent their initial years in America traveling in wagons or with packs on their backs. Some graduated to work in small shops in towns like Cumberland, Frederick, or Hagerstown before circling back to Baltimore and investing in larger enterprises. When Greif arrived in Baltimore as a fourteen-year-old immigrant in 1852, his uncle sent him to Shepherdstown, Virginia, where he had arranged a position as a clerk. Sonneborn peddled through the Pennsylvania Dutch country before opening a general store in Fairmont, Virginia, which he parlayed into a chain of stores in locations as far flung as Janesville, Wisconsin, and Cleveland, Ohio. In 1853, he returned to Baltimore and began to manufacture clothing, which he sold to country merchants, including two of his brothers, whom he had established in business in Cumberland and Wheeling.[25]

Like Hecht, most Jews who graduated from peddling went into some sort of retail business after settling in the city. Sixty-four percent of Jews in the 1845 Baltimore city directory ran retail establishments. Of these, the largest number, representing 20 percent of Jewish householders, were clothiers; 17 percent owned dry goods establishments; and an equal percentage owned groceries. An additional 10 percent of Jewish householders were distributed in less common retail enter-

"The Peddler's Wagon," *Harper's Weekly*, June 20, 1868. *Courtesy of the Library of Congress.*

prises: half of these owned taverns, and the other half owned confectionery stores, pawnshops, furniture stores, and a tobacco shop. Thirty percent of Jewish house-holders were craftspeople: two-thirds of these were tailors and makers of boots, shoes, and caps, while the other third were distributed in endeavors including watchmaking, painting and glazing, locksmithing, carpentry, and butchering. Only 3 percent of the city's Jews were listed as peddlers, although there were probably many others who were too mobile to be listed in the city directory. A handful were employed by Jewish institutions as religious functionaries, teachers, and a "keeper of the Jews Synagogue," while only one Jew was listed as a manual laborer. Whether retailers or craftspeople, the largest concentration—40 percent—were involved in some aspect of the clothing business, and this number rises to 57 percent when we include dry goods dealers who sold textiles, lace, and other trimmings.[26] While clothing and dry goods were never exclusively Jewish businesses in Baltimore, Jews had carved out a significant presence in these areas that would become even more pronounced after the outbreak of the Civil War.

Because commercial success meant reaching out to customers of all back-grounds, Jews established businesses across the city, wherever the opportunities for trade were best. The two most popular locations were Fells Point and the downtown

The intersection of Baltimore Street and Centre Market, c. 1850.
This area was a hub of Jewish commercial activity during the mid-nineteenth century.
Courtesy of the Maryland Historical Society, MC711-3.

Moses Wiesenfeld's Wholesale Clothing House on West Baltimore Street, opposite Hanover Street, was one of the largest firms of its kind in Baltimore. *From the* Baltimore Almanac, *1858.*

Samuel Kahn and his mother, Amelia, in front of their secondhand clothing store, 74 Harrison Street, c. 1880. *Jewish Museum of Maryland.*

Centre Market area, both of which had been trading centers since the eighteenth century. Fells Point was the port for arriving immigrants until after the Civil War and was the city's major shipping and shipbuilding center. After 1867, when many of these functions shifted to other parts of the harbor, Fells Point retained importance as the site of waterfront industries, such as canning and packing. Jews established businesses on Bond and Camden (later, Fleet) streets and especially along Broadway surrounding the Broadway Market, where they found a steady flow of customers. Similar conditions attracted them to the three-block strip between Baltimore and Pratt streets around the Centre Market, Baltimore's oldest. There, Jews selling clothing, boots, and shoes came to constitute a substantial proportion of the merchants. Harrison Street, which ran north from the market, became the most densely Jewish street in the area, home to dozens of pawnshops, secondhand stores, and other relatively low-grade business enterprises.[27]

As Jewish immigration to Baltimore increased during the 1840s, Jewish business enterprises—and, with them, residences—spread to other commercial districts. Gay Street, running north from Centre Market and northeast across Jones Falls, became a favorite area for dry goods, millinery, and furniture stores. Like the two older hubs, Gay Street had a city market house, the Belair Market. Jews who opened up shops nearby were the first to venture into the area known as Old Town. West Baltimore Street, the city's "great promenade . . . containing many handsome shops and stores," became a magnet for higher-end dry goods emporiums and clothing establishments, which ran from the Centre Market area far into West Baltimore and spilled over onto surrounding streets. Closer to the harbor, Pratt Street became a major location for the same types of Jewish-owned business, though only as far west as Eutaw Street.[28]

The varying qualities of these different business districts—the rough-and-tumble of Fells Point and Harrison Street, the upscale feel of West Pratt and Baltimore streets—indicate that not all Baltimore Jews met with equal success. Considering the modest beginnings of most Jewish immigrants to the city, the rise of merchants like Moses Hutzler and Joel Gutman, who opened dry goods emporiums on North Howard Street near Lexington Market in the 1850s, or clothing manufacturers like Benjamin Burgunder, Moses Wiesenfeld, and Isaac Hamburger, who joined Sonneborn and Greif as pioneers in the ready-made clothing industry, was astonishingly rapid.[29] Such men have loomed large in the collective memory of Baltimore Jews, but most Jews were decidedly more modest in their attainments. Secondhand dealers and pawnbrokers were more plentiful than were merchant princes.

Whether they owned a small shop or a large emporium, Baltimore's Jews found that family and ethnic networks remained as crucial to economic life in the city as they had been in the countryside. Like Simeon Hecht, many young merchants could not have opened their first retail establishments without the backing of friends or relatives. They could also rely on organizations such as the United Hebrew Benevolent Society, which was founded in 1834 to provide local Jews with a means of "affording relief to each other . . . in the event of sickness, distress, or death."[30] This organization, along with the Hebrew Assistance Society, founded in 1846, and B'nai B'rith, which appeared in Baltimore in 1844, embodied the principle of mutual assistance in a more structured version of the economic support and cooperation that Jewish immigrants routinely offered to one another less formally.[31]

The investment in family and ethnic networks did not diminish as immigrant Jews gained wealth and status. Merchants understood that their ongoing success relied on regular contact with far-flung relatives and friends, who could help maintain and widen the market for their goods. Merchants also saw relatives as the safest and most reliable business partners, and they often increased the efficacy of their networks by bringing trusted young business associates into the family circle, as happened when Betsy Friedenwald, a daughter of junk dealer and grocer Jonas Friedenwald, married her father's ambitious clerk Moses Wiesenfeld, and when Moses Hutzler's daughter Theresa married dry goods wholesaler Elkan Bamberger.[32]

In Europe, Jews' roles as petty traders in small towns and villages marked them as marginal, a remnant of a feudal past that was fading from the scene. Peddling and the reliance on ethnic networks were strategies for survival in the face of declining conditions. In the United States, an expanding economy and a vast territory in need of consumer goods allowed Jews to use the skills and strategies they had learned in their homelands to take full advantage of American opportunity. While not every Jew who arrived in Baltimore became a department store owner or clothing manufacturer, Jewish immigrants were able to experience a degree of economic mobility that would have been unimaginable had they remained in Europe. It was this firm economic foundation that paved the way for immigrant Jews' strong identification with American civic life and their embrace of American culture.

Demanding Civic Inclusion

In 1848, just as revolutions threatened to overturn monarchies in France, the German states, and the Austro-Hungarian Empire, Baltimore Jews took part in a mass meeting held in Monument Square to celebrate the advance of republicanism in Europe. Organized largely by local Germans, the event drew the participation of important officials, such as Mayor Jacob G. Davies and US senator Reverdy Johnson. For prominent Jews on the organizing committee and for those in attendance, the event's German framework gave them a significant role in the kind of citywide meeting in which they might otherwise not have been able to participate. It also provided a rare public opportunity to identify themselves with themes of American citizenship and democracy, since the participants cast themselves as "a free people . . . in convention on one side of the Atlantic, to do honor to those, newborn to freedom, on the other."[33]

The scene was repeated in 1851, when Jews took conspicuous part in a parade honoring the visit of the Hungarian revolutionary Lajos Kossuth to Baltimore.

As the Jeschurun Lodge No. 3 of the Jewish fraternal order B'nai B'rith marched along the parade route, members carried three large banners: one of Moses, one of Kossuth, and one of George Washington. With this display, these immigrant Jews not only claimed a place in American civic life, but also asserted that American democracy was broad enough to embrace them as Jews and immigrants.[34]

Although the processes of social and cultural change unfolded over several decades, civic and political culture was an aspect of American life with which Jewish immigrants identified even before they arrived on American shores. Democracy, which guaranteed freedom of religion and relieved Jews of the debilitating economic restrictions under which they suffered in Europe, was the key feature that led European Jews to see the United States as the place where they might most successfully overcome their otherwise insoluble problems. While they would sometimes struggle with the repercussions of living in a democratic society, these immigrants never questioned their belief in the superiority of the American legal and political system and its ability to positively transform their lives. They experienced its benefits long before they learned to speak, dress, or act like Americans. Indeed, after just five years of residence, they could formalize their status as US citizens who were entitled to the equal protection under law that had so long eluded them in Europe.[35]

While Baltimore's early Jewish settlers Solomon Etting and Jacob I. Cohen Jr. had formally entered political life directly after the passage of the Jew Bill in 1826, the civic involvement of the more humble Jewish immigrants who followed them dates to 1834, when John M. Dyer, the first president of the Baltimore Hebrew Congregation, won a special election to replace a deceased Fourth Ward alderman on the First Branch of the city council. Dyer had come to Baltimore in 1812 from Mainz, a city then under French rule, and soon became prominent in both Jewish and non-Jewish affairs. As the builder of one of the city's largest meatpacking firms, he was a leader in the Butchers' Association, a role that propelled him into city politics. Although he failed to win reelection when his term as alderman expired, he remained a force in ward politics as a loyalist to the Whig Party, which favored a modern, market-oriented economy.[36]

Dyer's son Leon played a more contentious role in municipal affairs. He became a police magistrate in 1834 (one year after becoming a US citizen) and served as a member of the local Whig Party's standing committee, which voiced outrage at federal monetary policy.[37] During the bank riot of 1835, the younger Dyer came under intense investigation when it was charged that he had led the mob that attacked and burned the homes of several Union Bank of Maryland directors. While he admitted to having accompanied the mob, he claimed his role had been to restrain rather than encourage violence. Despite widespread belief in his guilt, he avoided prosecution when his allies published testimonies exculpating him in the press.[38] Perhaps to ensure that the charges would not resurface, Leon Dyer soon left Baltimore and embarked on a wide-ranging career that included fighting Seminoles in Louisiana and serving as a volunteer in the Texas war for independence. He returned around

1840 and served a seven-year tenure as the president of the Baltimore Hebrew Congregation, after which he left the city again to settle in San Francisco.[39]

The Dyers were unusual for their involvement in politics at such an early stage of Jewish immigration to Baltimore, as well as for their support of the Whig Party, which did not have a strong appeal among immigrants. As the city's Jewish population swelled in the 1840s and 1850s, most Jews, like the German and Irish immigrants who arrived during the same period, gravitated to the Democratic Party. Like the earlier generation of Baltimore Jews who had strongly supported the Democratic Republicans, the Jewish backers of Andrew Jackson's party were drawn by its devotion to religious liberty, its anti-elitism, and its embrace of immigrants as valued contributors to American life. Immigrants of the era saw the Democrats as defenders against a virulent new nativist strain in American political culture, which was propagated by a series of secret societies and short-lived political parties and which reached its apogee with the founding of the American (Know-Nothing) Party in 1855. Within a short time, the Know-Nothings became the dominant force in Baltimore City politics, and clubs of rowdies who supported their nativist agenda created a culture of street violence that left foreigners and political opponents open to physical attack.[40]

Jews were not singled out as a target of the Know-Nothings, who focused broadly on foreigners and reserved their harshest invective for Catholics. Still, Jews felt the impact of the nativist sentiment sweeping Baltimore even before the consolidation of the Know-Nothings as a major political party. In 1850, worshippers who gathered for the conclusion of the Sabbath at the Fells Point Hebrew Friendship Congregation, the city's second synagogue, were "assaulted by loud hootings and revileings, disturbing the worship and ending by the breaking of several windows by the rowdies in the street." The following night, the assailants returned and attacked some of the worshippers.[41] In the years that followed, similar gangs of nativist street roughs regularly disturbed Jewish balls and picnics.[42] Jews and other immigrants were particularly in danger from violence and intimidation at election time: in 1857, for example, dozens of Jews were among those complaining that their access to the polls had been impeded by the menacing presence of Know-Nothing mobs. In a few cases Jewish voters were beaten or forced to vote for the Know-Nothing ticket against their will. In 1859, at least two elderly Jews were assaulted while trying to cast their ballots.[43]

The tendency of nativists to articulate a vision of America as a Protestant country also troubled Jews since it threatened to exclude them as well as Catholics from the national culture and to invalidate rights essential to their success and integration. Jews grew even more concerned when the nativist view was bolstered by the growth of Protestant missionary activity aimed at the conversion of Jewish immigrants. While the American Society for the Melioration of the Condition of the Jews (ASMCJ) had operated in Baltimore since the 1820s, it had previously focused on raising funds for overseas missions rather than on local conversion efforts. Its

Know-Nothing rowdies were a force on the streets of Baltimore in the 1850s, often threatening immigrants, including Jews, with violent attacks. Pen and ink drawing, c. 1858.
Courtesy of the Maryland Historical Society, 1967.30.1.

goals shifted, however, as its leadership began to see Baltimore's swelling Jewish population as an attractive target. In 1844, the ASMCJ started sending to Baltimore traveling agents, such as Siliam Bonhomme, a French Jewish convert who affiliated first as a Methodist and then as an Episcopalian. Posen-born John Neander (né Marcus Hoch), who had trained as a rabbi before becoming a minister in the Dutch Reformed Church, founded a permanent ASMCJ mission in Baltimore in 1845 with assistance from local Protestant clergy.[44] Building on these early efforts over the next decade and a half, as Jewish immigration reached its peak, a continual stream of missionaries from a variety of Protestant denominations came to Baltimore to attempt to convert the city's Jews.[45]

These missionaries aggressively courted local Jews, approaching them in the streets, visiting their homes, and calling upon them in their stores. They distributed conversionary tracts and published articles in local newspapers, particularly the *Baltimore Clipper*, a Know-Nothing organ.[46] They gained at least a few converts, among them the twenty-one-year-old immigrant Solomon Fuld, who had studied philosophy and languages in Europe and advertised in the *Sun* seeking employment as a teacher or translator. Perceiving an inquisitive young man who might be open to persuasion, Bonhomme answered Fuld's ad and apparently won his loyalty. In a desperate attempt to intervene, Fuld's brother had him arrested on a trumped-up charge, but he was unable to prevent the young scholar from complying with Bonhomme's suggestion to enroll in the Episcopal seminary in Alexandria, Virginia.[47]

Anxious to counter the threats posed by nativist politicians and street gangs who sought to shut foreign-born people out of American politics and by missionaries who encouraged the view of the United States as a Protestant country, immigrant Jews developed a visible presence within the Baltimore Democratic organization during the 1840s. In this regard, they were no different than the masses of Irish and German immigrants in the city, who were adamant in their opposition to nativism.[48] While immigrant groups were courted by the Democrats, however, they were not readily welcomed into the party hierarchy. Jewish activists, therefore, aligned closely with their non-Jewish German counterparts, who were numerous enough to create their own Democratic organizations and publications.

Jews and non-Jewish Germans cooperated politically as early as 1843, when Joseph Simpson, a Jewish engraver born in Vilna, Lithuania, but thoroughly German in cultural orientation, represented the German Democrats at a reception honoring President John Tyler's visit to Baltimore. Undoubtedly to the delight of his German compatriots, Simpson's remarks elicited from the president a response that welcomed immigrants as a vital part of American society and "recognized fully the equal civil rights of all naturalized citizens."[49] The same year, Simpson financed *Der Demokrat*, one of the earliest German-language party publications in Baltimore, in collaboration with the German editor Samuel Maclea.[50] In 1849 Dr. Moritz Wiener, a Jewish physician who had gained fame as a novelist and litterateur in his native Berlin, began a twelve-year tenure as the managing editor of *Der Deutsche Corre-*

spondent, which became the most popular German-language newspaper in Baltimore and a major force in galvanizing the city's large German-speaking population to oppose the Know-Nothing agenda.[51]

Even as they mobilized as part of the German community and wrote in the German language, Jews like Simpson and Wiener spoke not as foreigners but as US citizens defending core constitutional principles. Given the social barriers that prevented their participation in the political clubs and newspapers of native-born Americans, their membership in German clubs was less a statement of cultural or national affinity than it was an assertion that US citizens could come together across ethnic and religious boundaries in support of shared civic values. In flaying missionaries and nativist politicians in their articles and speeches, they ceded not one inch to the argument that non-Christians or citizens of foreign birth were in any way less entitled to full membership in American society.

Der Deutsche Correspondent reflected the importance of the German press as a transitional space for Jews anxious to articulate an American civic identity and participate in civic culture. Baltimore Jews during the 1850s and 1860s made the *Correspondent* their newspaper of choice. Not only did the paper mirror their political perspective, but many of the immigrants read German more easily than English. More important, the paper included articles and editorials by members of the Jewish community, sermons by local rabbis, and news of Jewish organizational and social life—all integrated and given a place of respect in the paper's broader treatment of political and cultural affairs.[52] The *Correspondent* provided Baltimore Jews with a sense of inclusion in the civic life of the non-Jewish German community that would have been unimaginable in their homelands and that they hoped might presage their eventual integration into the larger, English-speaking American world.

Even as they stressed their status as Americans and highlighted their links to non-Jewish Germans, Jewish activists in Baltimore did not believe that staking their claim to membership in the broader civil society necessitated the downplaying of their ethnic and religious distinctiveness as Jews. When missionary Louis C. Newman published a conversionary interpretation of Yom Kippur in the local English press, for example, Simpson responded with a lengthy English-language pamphlet portraying missionary efforts as inimical to American ideals, styling himself proudly on the cover as "a Citizen of the United States of the Hebrew Confession."[53] Similarly, in 1846, Simpson and several other Baltimore Jews had no qualms about mingling their Jewish and national identities in organizing the First Baltimore Hebrew Guards, a Jewish militia unit that volunteered to fight for the United States in the war with Mexico.[54] Nor did fear of being labeled a special-interest group inhibit Baltimore Jews from taking the lead among American Jewish communities in protesting an 1857 treaty with Switzerland that failed to guarantee free passage through the country for American Jews as it did for American Christians. Two years later, a local Jewish delegation was equally bold in urging President James Buchanan to pressure the papal government to return Edgar Mortara, an Italian Jewish child abducted from his parents and baptized by his Catholic nurse.[55]

While Jews could not realistically hope to stop the forces of nativism or expect the US government to routinely respond to their requests, their consistent demands that America live up to its values of inclusion and equality made a strong impression on many members of the dominant society, who frequently expressed support for Jewish rights and civic belonging. After the attacks on the Fells Point Hebrew Friendship Congregation in 1850, for example, the *Sun* declared the mob action to be a "great outrage" deserving of "the condemnation of every citizen."[56] The paper likewise supported local Jews in their efforts on behalf of Edgar Mortara, denouncing his abduction in Italy as an "outrage against humanity" and "a violation of the first principles of right and justice."[57]

If such expressions of support gave Jews some measure of security, so did their sense that other groups on the local scene were targeted more consistently than they were. They knew, for example, that the nativists held far more animus for Catholics than for Jews. This was apparent during the Mortara affair, when James M. Harris, a Baltimore Know-Nothing who served in the US Congress, aligned with Jewish leaders in introducing a resolution asking the president to intervene with papal authorities on Mortara's behalf.[58] Even more significantly, the continuing importance of the color line in framing local politics and culture provided a counterbalance to nativist agitation. Despite the measure of success enjoyed by the Know-Nothings in their attempt to make the native-foreigner divide the most crucial one in Baltimore society, the division between blacks and whites remained palpable enough to provide Jews and other immigrants with a claim—albeit a contested one—to membership in the dominant culture.

This does not mean that immigrant Jews were invested in the slave system or that they embraced the Democrats' focus on white supremacy with any particular vigor. Compared with immigrants of many other backgrounds, Jews were rather unaggressive in their approach to issues related to slavery and the status of free African Americans. As an upwardly mobile group disproportionately involved in retail trades, Jews did not compete with free black people for jobs or housing, as did many Irish and German laborers.[59] Neither did Jews have much in common with Baltimore's shrinking slaveholding class, since Jewish economic endeavors rarely if ever involved slave labor. The available records suggest that after 1840, few if any Baltimore Jews—even members of older, native-born families—owned slaves, and only a handful employed free black people as domestics, preferring to hire European servants who were more familiar with their culinary and housekeeping practices.[60]

Some Central European Jews of Baltimore did have extensive contact with free blacks in their commercial dealings, especially those who ran pawnshops and secondhand stores that attracted a large African American clientele. On occasion these merchants fell into disrepute as receivers of stolen goods brought to them by black customers. While, of course, crimes of property were common among the poor of all backgrounds, Baltimore's culture of racial division meant that law enforcement and the press cast disproportionate suspicion on African Americans and the merchants who were willing to serve them.[61] More commonly, however, the commercial relationship between African Americans and Jews reinforced the latter group's higher social status and their image among white Baltimoreans as responsible citizens. Jewish merchants, for example, were frequently mentioned in the press as victims of African American theft, and they often took care to portray themselves as helping to police black criminal activity by publishing notices that they had foiled the attempt of a "colored" man or woman who had tried to sell them stolen goods.[62]

While Jews of this period had fewer reasons than other immigrant groups to embrace the platform of white supremacy, they generally toed the Democratic line on race because they understood that this would continue to win them the party's loyalty and protection. Nativism, not racial politics, was their primary concern, but they knew that it was the Democrats' strong commitment to white supremacy that caused the party to reach out to European immigrants so warmly.[63]

Although Jews in antebellum Baltimore understood the need for continued vigilance in civic matters, the support and approval they received from certain sectors of non-Jewish society, as well as their awareness that many groups held a less advantageous position in the social hierarchy, served to confirm their faith that they could enjoy the protections of American democracy without downplaying their Jewish loyalties and that ultimately Jewish rights would be upheld even by those who did not view Jews as social equals. Social acceptance, however, would remain a more complicated goal, one that would take much longer to achieve, entail a greater compromise of Jewish tradition, and inspire significant disagreement among different Jewish factions. Moreover, as nativism receded and slavery and sectionalism became more divisive issues in the years leading up to the Civil War, Jews would have to reposition themselves to adapt to a changing political landscape.

Acculturation and Its Limits before the Civil War

In 1839, a member of Baltimore Hebrew Congregation presented a petition to the synagogue board. Receiving no response, the man attended a subsequent meeting and asked the president what had happened to his petition. The president indelicately replied that it had been thrown under the table. Affronted, the petitioner denounced the board members as "a pretty set of men, to elect for a president a man who had sold rabbit skins in Germany." As the Baltimore *Sun* described, "the taunt seemed peculiarly cutting, for . . . they rushed on him like tigers and would have eaten him up or swallowed him whole had it not been for the witness who kept them off while the little man made his escape."[64]

The fierceness with which the board members responded to their critic's insult underscores how seriously immigrant Jews of the mid-nineteenth century took the issue of social status. By reminding them of their pasts as *Dorfjuden*, the petitioner was challenging their ability to transform themselves into people of standing in the United States. Yet it was precisely this humble European past that drove Jewish immigrants to identify with American culture and the status it represented. Most had arrived as young people, unaccompanied by parents or grandparents who might have encouraged them to cling more tightly to traditional patterns. Moreover, their tendency to settle in different parts of the city in search of business opportunities, rather than in a single Jewish residential enclave, placed them in frequent contact with non-Jews and maximized their opportunities for acculturation.[65] Shortly after their arrival, their determination to become Americans was visible in new habits of dress, linguistic patterns, and leisure practices.

As Jewish immigrants changed their personal behavior and deportment, they also looked to their community organizations to advance the dual processes of Americanization and social mobility. Early on, Jewish associational life was dominated by mutual benefit societies designed to support new arrivals in gaining an economic foothold. By the 1850s, as success made many less reliant on mutual aid, communal organizations shifted their focus to helping poor Jews—mostly widows, orphans, and those handicapped by illness or disability—and to responding to catastrophic events, such as epidemics and natural disasters. Typical of this new focus was the Society for Educating Poor and Orphan Children, founded in 1852. Four years later, the Hebrew Assistance Society, founded in 1846 on the mutual assistance model, was rechartered as the Hebrew Benevolent Society of Baltimore and quickly became the city's premier Jewish charity.[66]

Charitable activities were well rooted in Jewish religious tradition and had been crucial to the survival of Jewish communities for centuries. But in the context of nineteenth-century Baltimore, as in other American Jewish communities of the period, philanthropy also became a vehicle for Jews to assert their place in local civic affairs and highlight their role as responsible citizens. They took special pride in the fact that Jewish charities prevented members of their community from becoming charges on the resources of local government. Some wealthier Jews also made a point of donating to non-Jewish philanthropies as a way of demonstrating their broad-mindedness and humanity. This record of generosity led the *Baltimore American* to remark admiringly in 1856 that "the Jews take care of their own poor and contribute to poor of all religions."[67]

In addition to reflecting civic-mindedness, philanthropy was a powerful vehicle for acculturating Jews to demonstrate their rising social and material status. The ability to make substantial contributions toward helping the poor was, for most Jewish immigrants, a dramatic departure from their humble beginnings. By participating in philanthropy, they affirmed to themselves and others just how significantly they were being transformed and elevated in America. Furthermore, the many fairs, balls, and dances held to support the work of Jewish charities allowed participants to showcase their adoption of American modes of fashion and sociability.

The world of Jewish philanthropy also reflected the immigrants' embrace of

Masquerade Ball of the Harmony Circle, 1866. Jewish Museum of Maryland.

American gender norms. While women played crucial roles in traditional Jewish society and had always embraced charitable work as part of their religious obligations, acculturating Jewish women very much wanted to forge a more public identity, as they saw their Protestant counterparts doing in Christian missionary and charity organizations.[68] As a result, in 1856 Jewish women in Baltimore founded the Hebrew Ladies' Sewing Society, which made garments and linens for the poor and served unofficially as a women's auxiliary to the male-dominated Hebrew Benevolent Society. In 1862, its members produced more than 1,800 items for distribution, including ladies' and children's dresses, underwear, stockings, and blankets.[69] The following year, the society elected as its leader Betsy Friedenwald Wiesenfeld, who retained her post for more than a quarter century and proved to be a powerhouse in charity management. Under her leadership, clothing and other necessities were provided not only to local victims of floods and epidemics, but also to distant sufferers, such as those burned out in Chicago by the fire of 1871. In addition to this work, the society also organized entertainments to raise money for the Hebrew Benevolent

Betsy Friedenwald Wiesenfeld was the longtime president of Baltimore's
Hebrew Ladies' Sewing Society and a major force in Jewish philanthropy in the city.
Photo, c. 1865. *Jewish Museum of Maryland.*

Society and sponsored an annual Calico Dress Ball, at the conclusion of which the members donated the dresses they had worn to charity.[70]

Education offered another way for acculturating Jews to build an associational life that enhanced their social and civic status. Given that most immigrants had received little if any secular schooling in Europe, gaining exposure to the literature and culture of the non-Jewish world was considered a significant marker of social transformation. Several Jewish associations of the 1840s and 1850s stressed education as a core aspect of their platforms. B'nai B'rith founded multiple branches in Baltimore that not only promoted Jewish fellowship, but also encouraged members to develop their intellectual lives through the creation of libraries and reading rooms. By the 1850s and early 1860s, the Hebrew Young Men's Literary Association, the Mendelssohn Literary Association, and the Cliosophic Hebrew Literary and Dramatic Society were among the organizations pursuing similar goals.[71]

While these organizations all aimed to broaden the perspective of Baltimore's Jewish immigrants and allow them to absorb more fully the culture and values of the non-Jewish world, their approaches differed depending on the ages and outlooks of their organizers and the time period in which they were established. The B'nai B'rith founders, for example, had apparently received some exposure to secular education in their German homelands and saw German culture as an attractive vehicle for the education of their fellow immigrants. Although most Jewish newcomers spoke Yiddish at home and were not experienced in reading or writing High German, they often had a sufficient capability in the language to follow the lead of the more educated immigrants. Meanwhile, some of the rabbis who arrived in Baltimore during the 1850s had been trained in German universities and preached to their congregations in German—though their regular use of sermons departed from the European model, where synagogue worship was a less formal affair. Since these sermons added to the educational and cultural enrichment that Jewish fraternal and literary associations provided, they were a welcome innovation.[72] Mirroring the trend in politics, the size and status of Baltimore's non-Jewish German population made the German language attractive to Jews, who were happy to see their rabbis and community leaders quoted in *Der Deutsche Correspondent* and to imagine themselves as part of a larger cultural setting. For immigrants who had not yet mastered English, then, the use of High German in Jewish associational and congregational life was a first step to participating in a bourgeois American public sphere.[73]

As a vehicle of social and cultural change, the use of German in Jewish settings was seen as complementary rather than antagonistic to the process of learning English and incorporating it into the Jewish repertoire. While rabbis capable of lecturing in English were scarce before the 1880s, many Jewish associations, especially those founded by the youngest immigrants, embraced English early on. A group of recent arrivals between the ages of eighteen and twenty, for example, founded the Hebrew Young Men's Literary Association in 1853. They carried on their activities and kept their minutes in English from the beginning. The association's facility on North Charles Street featured a library, gymnasium, and special rooms for reading, conversation, and playing chess. To hone their English, members organized classes and lectures on literary topics and held regular debates on questions such as "Do Circumstances Justify Crime?" and "Is Eloquence a Gift of Nature or Is It Acquired by Art?"[74]

The enthusiasm with which immigrant Jews embraced and adapted to the broader culture around them, however, was not accompanied by a thorough integration into the intimate social circles of their non-Jewish neighbors. True, some Jews did become members of non-Jewish fraternal orders, such as the Masons and Odd Fellows, although they generally joined lodges made up mostly of fellow Jewish immigrants.[75] A few also took active roles in the social and cultural institutions of Baltimore's German American community. During the 1850s and 1860s, Leopold Blumenberg, a former Prussian military officer who would become a major in the Union army during the Civil War, participated in German athletic and shooting clubs, while Otto Sutro, trained as an organist in Brussels, was prominent in German musical circles. Some wealthy Jewish families sent their sons to schools run by German teachers, such as Heinrich Scheib, the pastor of Zion Lutheran Church, and Frederick Knapp, whose German and English Institute courted students of all faiths and even included Hebrew in its curriculum.[76]

But such cases were exceptions to the general pattern in which Jews carried on social, charitable, and educational affairs largely apart from their non-Jewish neighbors. Most children attended Jewish schools, such as those run by Rabbi Aaron Guinzburg and by *Lehrer* Jonas Goldschmidt, where they studied religious and secular topics and learned Hebrew, English, and German.[77] Their parents devoted their energies to the Hebrew Benevolent Society and the Ladies' Sewing Society, and men spent their leisure hours at the club rooms of the B'nai B'rith and the Hebrew Young Men's Literary Association. One factor limiting the interactions between Jews and non-Jews was the exclusion practiced by clubs and organizations populated by white native-born Americans. The Henry Clay Lyceum, a literary society composed of young, native-born men, for example, drew publicity in 1856 when it denied entry to a Jewish applicant.[78] Such outright discrimination was less common in German American associations. Overall, however, the separateness of Jewish social and cultural activities during this period was less the result of prejudice than a reflection of the simple fact that despite their great desire to identify with all things American (and in some cases, German American), immigrant Jews were neither ready nor able to forgo the comfort and support they derived from socializing and organizing primarily within their own ranks.[79]

The persistence of social lines between Jews and non-Jews is made particularly apparent by the extremely low incidence of intermarriage in these years. In contrast to the revolutionary and early national periods, when intermarriage was a fact of life for local Jews, after 1830 it occurred only among a handful of Baltimore Jews who had been propelled into close social contact with non-Jews by virtue of an unusual

- - - - - - - - - - - - -

European background or professional path.[80] The rarity of interfaith unions among the immigrants also reflected how their social contact with non-Jews was regulated by gender. Whatever intermingling occurred through lodges and associations was largely limited to men, because those contacts were understood as an extension of business and civic activities. Similarly, mainly Jewish boys attended the German schools of Scheib and Knapp, because those institutions were considered training grounds for the pursuits they would take up as businessmen or professionals. When it came to the more intimate setting of a dance or a ball, where men and women socialized together, Jews were careful to organize such activities separately.[81]

Thus, in the decades before 1870 Baltimore Jews can best be described as vigorously pursuing acculturation but not yet seeking entry into the social circles of their non-Jewish neighbors. While they insisted on their equality as US citizens and strongly identified with non-Jewish cultural patterns, they typically spent their leisure time with other Jews, married other Jews, and saw Jewish organizations as their main social outlets. Not until the dramatic economic and social transformations that would come in the wake of the Civil War would these relatively clear lines between Jews and non-Jews begin to erode.

Toward an American Judaism

In 1842, Jewish members of the Masons and Odd Fellows appeared at the funeral of Jacob Ahrens, a charter member of Baltimore Hebrew Congregation, and performed fraternal rituals unfamiliar to the congregation's rabbi, Abraham Rice. Rice was the first ordained rabbi to arrive in the United States and had been in the country for only two years. Viewing the fraternal rituals as *chukat ha-goyim* (Christian customs forbidden to Jews), he refused to officiate at future burials where they were performed.[82] Consequently, seventeen men, viewing Rabbi Rice's ruling as an obstacle to their embrace of American culture, broke away from the city's pioneer congregation and formed the Har Sinai Verein (Mount Sinai Association). On Shavuot, six months after Ahrens's death, the group began to conduct separate religious services. They read from a printed Bible, since the parent congregation refused to lend them a Torah scroll. They soon ordered prayer books from the Hamburg Temple—one of the first congregations in Europe to adopt liberal reforms to the liturgy—and also introduced the use of an organ during worship, which traditionalists like Rice saw as a serious violation of Jewish law.[83]

The founding of Har Sinai is generally interpreted by historians as the beginning of the Reform movement in American Judaism.[84] Viewed against the background of Jewish religious life in Baltimore and across the United States from the 1840s to 1860s, however, the changes instituted by the new congregation are less of a clean break from traditional Judaism than an example of immigrants wrestling with loyalties to both tradition and the process of cultural adaptation. Despite a proliferating number of congregations and the arrival of rabbis with conflicting worldviews, Bal-

America's first ordained rabbi, Abraham Rice, was hired to head the Baltimore Hebrew Congregation in 1840, shortly after arriving from Bavaria. He later broke with the synagogue over its embrace of religious reforms. *Jewish Museum of Maryland.*

timore Jews during this period cannot be said to have divided into clear ideological and institutional camps.[85]

In getting past the conventional view that the founding of Har Sinai represented a clear ideological rift between traditional Jews and a newly self-conscious liberal group, it is helpful to note that there was nothing approaching a "traditional" consensus among Baltimore Jews before 1842; intense debates and controversies over religious customs and practices had taken place within the Baltimore Hebrew Congregation long before Har Sinai emerged, and they continued long after. Especially before the arrival of Rabbi Rice in 1840, the absence of any clear religious authority encouraged individuals to make their own decisions and compromises in regard to Jewish practice, paving the way for dissension and debate to become the rule rather than the exception in Baltimore and other American Jewish communities.

Locally, such dissension was apparent from the very beginning of organized congregational life. In 1830, just one year after the founding of Baltimore Hebrew Congregation, its officers found themselves in civil court defending their decision to deny burial in the main part of the congregation's cemetery to the infant son of member Emanuel Semon because the child had a non-Jewish mother and had not lived long enough to undergo the rites of conversion or circumcision.[86] In 1842, the same year that Har Sinai's founders broke away from Baltimore Hebrew, another synagogue was similarly divided over questions of religious ritual. The trustees of the United Hebrew Benevolent Society, a mutual aid organization founded in 1834 that had evolved into an independent religious congregation serving Jews in Fells Point, had to defend themselves in court against charges of theft after they removed the Torah scrolls from the sanctuary to prevent disturbances by an angry member who did not agree with how services were being conducted. The exact nature of the plaintiff's grievance was not specified, but the acrimony forced the trustees to discontinue public worship and return to holding services in private homes until the Fells Point Hebrew Friendship Congregation (Oheb Israel) was founded the following year.[87]

Nor did the founding of Har Sinai end the recurrence of religious controversy within Baltimore Hebrew. The lack of rigorous ritual observance on the part of the members, particularly their tendency to violate the Sabbath, increasingly angered Rabbi Rice, who resigned in disgust in 1849, taking a small group of loyalists with him to worship in his home on North Howard Street. After Rice's departure, the congregation continued to define itself as Orthodox, but intense wrangling over a host of practices—the introduction of English sermons, the confirmation of girls, changes to the liturgy—remained the norm for decades. Through the Civil War, the synagogue went through a series of rabbis of differing religious outlooks. Moderate reformer Henry Hochheimer, who left in 1859 to become the rabbi of the Fells Point Hebrew Friendship Congregation, was followed by staunch traditionalist Bernard Illowy. When Illowy departed in 1862, the congregation invited Rice to return to his former post, which he did briefly before his death later the same year. Through all these changes, the religious identity of the congregation remained conflicted, with dramatic assertions of Orthodox practice occurring alongside considerable departures from tradition.[88] While historical accounts have painted Baltimore Hebrew as an Orthodox holdout amid a growing trend toward reform during the 1840s and 1850s, the contradictions that characterized religious life within Baltimore's oldest synagogue suggest that its members were not so different in outlook from those of the new congregations founded during these decades.

Indeed, the newer congregations often emerged more for practical reasons than as a result of ideological concerns. The Fells Point Hebrew Friendship Congregation, for example, served those in the eastern reaches of the city for whom the trek to Baltimore Hebrew's downtown location was too burdensome. Some accounts claim that Oheb Shalom Congregation was founded in 1853 by those who wished to introduce moderate reforms, but its early history tends to contradict this narrative, since its religious practices were decidedly traditional and its members did not exhibit any tendency toward innovation during the first five years. Geography may have been a factor here, too, since Oheb Shalom's initial location was on Gay Street, west of Jones Falls, more convenient for Jewish residents who likely felt disadvantaged by the move of Baltimore Hebrew from downtown to East Baltimore in 1845.[89] Still another motivation was that the young founders were traveling clothing merchants whose frequent absences from the city prevented them from obtaining choice seats at the existing congregations. To some extent, the proliferation of congregations during the 1840s and 1850s simply reflected a realization that the city's growing Jewish population could not be contained in only one or two houses of worship. When the Fells Point Hebrew Friendship Congregation built a synagogue in Old Town in 1848 just blocks from Baltimore Hebrew's new location, the two synagogues, which had few religious differences and were served at different times by the same rabbi, settled into a cooperative relationship reflecting an understanding that there were more than enough congregants to go around.[90]

Regardless of their ritual practices, Baltimore's Jewish congregations had much in common before 1870 thanks to a nearly universal focus among the city's Jews on the importance of acculturation. Although Har Sinai instituted a greater number of reforms than did other congregations, and Oheb Shalom embarked on a moderate path of reform after building its Hanover Street synagogue in 1858, members of Baltimore Hebrew and Hebrew Friendship were no less adamant in their embrace of American culture. Baltimore Hebrew counted among its ranks some of the most acculturated and civically prominent Jews in the city, including politicians John and Leon Dyer, philanthropist Jonas Friedenwald, and his son-in-law, the clothing manufacturer Moses Wiesenfeld. While these men did not favor major ritual changes, they believed strongly in identifying the synagogue as a place imbued with American values and customs.[91]

To affirm this goal while maintaining a commitment to traditional practices was not easy, which accounts for the continual rancor over ritual policy at Baltimore Hebrew through the nineteenth century. But despite carrying the Orthodox banner in the years before 1870, the congregation enacted a number of innovations aimed at asserting its status as modern and acculturated, including the removal of lattice from the women's gallery, the abolition of sitting on the floor in "stocking feet" on Tisha B'Av, the introduction of planed coffins and German prayers at funerals, the use of family cemetery lots, and the omission of readings from special scrolls, such as Ruth, Lamentations, and the Song of Solomon, on holidays.[92]

Baltimore Hebrew displayed its acculturationist tendencies most visibly with the construction of the Lloyd Street Synagogue, which represented a deliberate effort to leave behind the unsavory Harrison Street location that had served the congregation during its formative years. Built in 1845 at substantial cost and designed in the popular Greek Revival style by architect Robert Carey Long Jr., the new synagogue had an impressive brick façade, granite steps, and imposing columns, all carefully designed as a statement of the community's material success and the congregation's place in the landscape of Baltimore's houses of worship. No less attentive to American style was the synagogue of the Hebrew Friendship Congregation, whose new

Carte de visite of the Lloyd Street Synagogue, by D. R. Stiltz and Co., c. 1864. The Greek Revival synagogue was home to the Baltimore Hebrew Congregation from 1845 to 1889. *Ross J. Kelbaugh Collection, Jewish Museum of Maryland.*

"church" on Eden Street drew praise in 1848 from a local journalist for its beautiful chandelier, red velvet ark curtain embroidered with gold thread, and an eastern wall painted with a faux marble finish.[93] Members of both congregations also signaled their growing social aspirations by establishing residences near the new East Baltimore synagogues, demonstrating that they could now afford to live apart from their places of business in the city's major marketing districts.[94]

Membership in one of the more traditional congregations did not always mean that daily life was lived according to the dictates of Jewish law and tradition. While some members of Baltimore Hebrew and Hebrew Friendship maintained a high standard of religious observance, the repeated discussion in surviving synagogue minutes about merchants keeping their stores open on the Sabbath and festivals, the complaints of rabbis about laxity in observing the laws of kashrut and ritual purity, and descriptions in the press of the lively social gatherings held at Jewish clubs on Friday nights all suggest that many of their congregants differed little in their personal behavior from those at Har Sinai and Oheb Shalom, even though they preferred a more traditional synagogue experience. According to one report, even the Orthodoxy of the sixteen or so Jews who left Baltimore Hebrew Congregation in 1849 to worship with the rigidly traditional Abraham Rice was "not so much a matter of conviction as it [was] the offspring of whims."[95]

The perceived gaps between the various congregations narrow even further when one considers not only that the "traditional" congregations were more modern and progressive than is typically recognized, but also that the so-called reform-minded congregations were more traditional than standard accounts convey. Har Sinai introduced an organ and altered the liturgy, but the congregation continued during its early years to enforce head coverings for men, and the observance of the second day of festivals was not abandoned until 1856. Even after women were allowed to leave the elevated gallery and be seated on the main floor of the congregation's new High Street Temple in 1849, they continued to sit separately from the men for another two decades. Abram Hutzler, who grew up in Har Sinai during this period, recalled the services as "almost orthodox."[96]

In their private lives, too, Har Sinai members preserved many traditional practices. Several members continued to use a "Shabbos goy" to light fires so as to avoid violating the Sabbath, Hutzler noted.[97] Brit milah (ritual circumcision) remained a standard practice for newborn males. Although one of the congregation's leading lights, Dr. Abram B. Arnold, expressed reservations to his medical colleagues about the safety and advisability of circumcision, he nonetheless conducted the procedure for local Jews more than 800 times between 1850 and 1869.[98] When the Cincinnati rabbi Isaac Mayer Wise visited Baltimore in 1858, he found that while it was common for Har Sinai congregants to "eat terefah and chametz on Passover, smoke cigarettes and write on [the] Sabbath," many at the same time "keep a kosher house [and] are partly orthodox."[99]

Similar contradictions existed at Oheb Shalom. While the West Baltimore con-

Even after the 1849 construction of Har Sinai's High Street Temple, men and women continued to sit separately during worship for two decades. *From Charles A. Rubenstein,* The History of Har Sinai Congregation of the City of Baltimore *(Baltimore: Kohn and Pollock, 1918).*

gregation introduced an organ and a mixed choir and adopted Isaac Mayer Wise's abridged prayer book, *Minhag America*, in 1858, it used the traditional Roedelheim siddur on holidays until 1864. The congregation also continued to observe the second day of festivals and required head covering by men. Despite the laxity with which Baltimore Jews across the congregational spectrum treated Sabbath observance, Oheb Shalom officially maintained the standard of denying honors to those who kept their stores open on the Sabbath, a practice that Baltimore Hebrew had dispensed with the year that Oheb Shalom was founded.[100]

The rabbis who began to occupy the pulpits of Baltimore congregations during the 1840s and 1850s fought these contradictory tendencies and sought to impose greater order and consistency on Jewish religious life. Through sermons and articles, they carved out distinct ideological positions on the process of change. Har Sinai's radical reformer David Einhorn and Oheb Shalom's more moderate Benjamin Szold exchanged a series of polemics in 1859, the year that Szold arrived in Baltimore from his native Hungary. Szold promoted a "historical" approach to Jewish religious innovation—a precursor to what would later be called Conservative Judaism—as an al-

Oheb Shalom's Hungarian-born rabbi Benjamin Szold advocated a moderate
path of religious innovation. Photo, c. 1860. *Jewish Museum of Maryland.*

ternative to Einhorn's more aggressive brand of reform. Einhorn had been called to
Har Sinai in 1855 from Bavaria, where he had established a reputation as a religious
firebrand. In 1856 he began to publish a German-language journal, *Sinai*, which
addressed a national audience and laid out his view that ethical monotheism, rather
than traditional ritual practice, was the true essence of Judaism.[101]

Einhorn and Szold both introduced new liturgies to push their congregants
toward greater theological precision. Einhorn's *Olat Tamid* (1855) was mostly in
German and deleted references to a return to Zion, the sacrificial system, and the
resurrection of the dead. Szold's *Abodath Israel* (1864) made some of the same
changes, but preserved more of the traditional Hebrew text alongside a German
translation.[102] Baltimore rabbis also combated inconsistency by debating the status
of Jewish law and the veracity of the Talmud, hoping to clarify for their congregants
which Jewish practices were important to maintain and which were not. In 1855,
Baltimore Hebrew's Bavarian-born Henry Hochheimer and Hebrew Friendship's
Aaron Guinzburg, a native of Bohemia, were among the signatories calling for a
rabbinical conference in Cleveland, Ohio, which was designed to bring traditionalists and reformers together in search of common ground. Although neither of the

rabbis attended the subsequent meeting, those assembled issued a public statement affirming not only that the Bible was of divine origin but also that the Talmud was an authoritative legal code. Einhorn, who had only recently arrived in the United States at the time of the conference, vehemently protested in a circular published by his congregation, denying that the "Talmudic exegesis of the Bible" was either "legal or obligatory."[103]

The efforts of these rabbis had some impact on their congregants and led, over time, to Jews gravitating to synagogues based on their degree of comfort with ritual innovation. But in assessing the development of Judaism in Baltimore (and elsewhere in the United States) it would be wrong to place too much emphasis on the influence of rabbinic leadership or to underestimate the time it took for clear divisions between ideological camps to crystallize. True, congregants often praised their rabbis and defended them in the press when they clashed with their rivals, but their loyalty had little to do with ideology. When Julius Stiefel, the president of Oheb Shalom, defended Szold against Einhorn's polemics, he said nothing about the content of the debate, but simply praised his rabbi as "a scholar and a gentleman in every sense of the term" and took Einhorn to task for conduct "unbecoming a Gentleman and particularly a Minister."[104] Einhorn had enlisted members of his congregation to sign his protest of the Cleveland Conference in 1855, but it is doubtful that many of them really cared about the fine points of Talmudic authority. Years later, in a tribute to Einhorn that included memories of his rabbinate in Baltimore, Har Sinai members recalled his "force of character" and his "vibrant and persuasive" voice, but said little about his reformist ideas.[105]

Har Sinai did have a few highly educated members who grasped the details of Einhorn's Reform ideology. William S. Rayner, for example, had been a Hebrew teacher before immigrating to Baltimore, and he helped Einhorn translate and edit his Reform prayer book. Overall, however, the inconsistency of Har Sinai's laity in their approach to reform and tradition suggests that few saw these issues through an ideological lens. This was true for the more traditional congregations as well. In 1845, when Abraham Rice offered his acculturation-minded congregants a chance to shorten the worship service by removing the piyyutim (medieval religious poems), a change he found acceptable from the perspective of halachah, they rejected his proposal and expressed their desire—apparently for sentimental reasons—to retain these traditional prayers. Rice could not understand how they could "eat foul food and desecrate the Sabbath in public," yet refuse to remove aspects of the service that were not required by Orthodox standards. Unlike their rabbi, the members' approach to Judaism was not governed by a concern for halachic consistency. Even as they allowed Rice's successor, Henry Hochheimer, to introduce minor reforms that were more controversial from a halachic standpoint, they would not part with the piyyutim until 1860.[106]

Such examples demonstrate that the differences among Baltimore's Jewish congregations before the Civil War did not represent clear divisions concerning tradition and change as much as they reflected different versions of a common attempt to navigate between those two impulses. If we take into consideration inconsistencies in personal behavior alongside the contradictions in public worship evident in virtually every synagogue, it becomes clear that congregational affiliation was less about ideology than about how individuals apportioned, often in a haphazard manner, the trade-offs that almost all Jews were making as they adapted to their environment. The particular changes people preferred—and whether they were to be made in private behavior, public worship, or both—were determined not by any easy formula but by a confusing mélange of pressures and opportunities that all Jews faced in their encounter with a new, open society. While it is tempting to look for the roots of the denominational divide that would deepen by the end of the century, what is more significant in this period is that Jews across congregations were changing their personal behavior in ways that clashed with traditional religious practices, while changes in public worship remained modest and mostly cosmetic. Even the most "reformist" congregations—Har Sinai and Oheb Shalom—avoided changes such as the adoption of family pews, where men and women sat together, and the discarding of head covering for men, neither of which would be instituted until the end of the 1860s. Not until Baltimore Jews experienced a heightened level of social mobility in the wake of the Civil War would religious change begin to take place on a more significant scale.

Navigating the Civil War

At 10 a.m. on October 17, 1864, guards bearing orders from the military governor of Washington, DC, surrounded eight large dry goods, hardware, and clothing stores in Baltimore, five of which were owned by Jews. The guards arrested the proprietors and their clerks, while military officials seized the keys to their establishments and confiscated their goods, papers, and books. The men were marched to the Camden Street depot and taken by train to Washington, where they were confined in the Old Capitol Prison.[107]

In Washington, the charges against the men were explained. According to the testimony of a blockade runner, Pardon Worsley, their firms had sold him goods that they knew to be intended for the benefit of the Confederacy, including military uniforms and buttons. One Jewish prisoner, Abraham Friedenreich, was released after it became clear that he was no longer associated with the firm bearing his name, which was owned by his nephew. Several others were tried, sentenced to prison terms of between one and five years, and fined up to $15,000, despite the exertions of prominent Baltimoreans on their behalf. After languishing in jail for four months, however, most of the men were released when President Abraham Lincoln requested leniency from the military commission. The only one forced to remain incarcerated was clothing manufacturer Moses Wiesenfeld, one of Baltimore's most prominent Jewish citizens, who had made the mistake of trying to bribe a judge ad-

Clothier Moses Wiesenfeld was a longtime president of the Hebrew Benevolent Society and a strong Union supporter during the Civil War, but he ran afoul of federal occupying authorities for trading in contraband. *Jewish Museum of Maryland.*

vocate in order to influence the case. That Wiesenfeld had publicly identified himself as a "Friend of the Union" at the outset of the conflict did him little good. He spent the duration of the war in the federal penitentiary in Albany, New York.[108]

Wiesenfeld's fall from grace was emblematic of how the Civil War shook the foundations of Baltimore's Jewish community, which had prospered over the previous two and a half decades. The city's Jewish residents, heavily concentrated in clothing and dry goods businesses, had built their success on an ability to leverage ethnic networks stretching into the southern states. This success had been threatened by the growing drumbeat toward war that began with the election of Lincoln in November 1860, and was further undermined when federal troops, fearing that Baltimore's southern sympathies would make it an outpost of the Confederacy, took control of the city and brought business to a halt. Once martial law was declared and daily life became more stable, business resumed. But the outlawing of trade with the Confederacy and the imposition of restrictions by military authorities sapped much of the energy of the city's formerly vibrant commercial life.[109]

Faced with such challenges, Baltimore Jews had to think strategically about how best to navigate the potentially destructive impact of sectional conflict. Their position in a border city made it difficult for them, as it did for other Baltimoreans, to identify fully with the interests of either North or South. While a minority of Jews did enthusiastically adopt a Union or Confederate stance, most responded in more complex ways that were informed by local experiences—for example, their history of struggle against the Know-Nothings—and designed to protect their immediate interests, particularly in the business realm. The fact that Wiesenfeld opposed secession but supplied goods to blockade runners is a case in point. Viewed from the perspective of national politics, his behavior seems contradictory, but from a local Jewish perspective it was consistent as a strategy for economic survival.

Although the war disrupted the social and economic advancement initiated by Baltimore's Jews during the 1840s and 1850s, ultimately the skill with which they responded to the challenges of war served them well. The tendency of most Jews to oppose secession while affirming local racial mores; to adjust their political allegiances and cooperate with former adversaries; and to cope with a Union blockade without fully sacrificing the benefits of southern trade allowed them not only to mitigate wartime setbacks, but also to place themselves in a stronger position than many other American Jewish communities to take advantage of postwar trends. In short, they successfully turned the problems of life on the middle ground into advantages.

Wiesenfeld's personal drama stands out as one of the more agonizing twists of a story that began four years earlier, during the tumultuous election season of 1860. As the Democratic Party split into northern and southern factions, the majority of Baltimore Jews—like most of the city's Democrats—lined up behind presidential candidate John Breckinridge, whose southern rights ticket carried the city by a slim majority. As in former years, the Democrats' pro-immigrant orientation reinforced Jewish support for the party and its proslavery agenda. In fact, the allegiance of Jews to the party was at a high point because of the large role Democrats had played in finally ousting the nativist Know-Nothings from leadership in recent municipal elections (a campaign that was officially conducted under the auspices of a nonpartisan Reform Association). Even though Breckinridge's supporters were in the forefront of the pro-southern agitation that was pushing the country closer to war, the ouster of the Know-Nothings confirmed the view of Baltimore's Jews that the proslavery Democrats were the surest antidote to the violence and rowdyism that had so long plagued the city's immigrants.[110]

While most Jews affirmed their ties to the local Breckinridge Democrats, a small group threw their support to the Republican ticket. The local Republican Party was weak—Lincoln garnered less than 4 percent in the city's presidential election—but because it drew most of its local support from German freethinkers who opposed slavery, it attracted the handful of Jews who participated in their circles. These included men like Dr. Abram B. Arnold, who in 1860 sat on the executive committee of the state's Republican Party, and Leopold Blumenberg, a manufacturer who had led members of the Baltimore Turnverein in forming the Wide-Awakes, a paramili-

Leopold Blumenberg was decried as a "Black Republican" for his support of Lincoln in 1860. He distinguished himself as a Union officer during the Battle of Antietam, and after the war he was elevated by brevet to the rank of brigadier general. Portrait by unknown artist, 1864. *Jewish Museum of Maryland.*

tary organization charged with keeping order at Republican rallies and repelling the attacks of angry mobs.[111] The most prominent Jewish spokesman for the Republican cause was Har Sinai's rabbi, David Einhorn, whose universalist outlook included passionate support for the abolition of slavery. He expressed his views in his German-language journal, *Sinai*, whose editorial line followed that of Baltimore's liberal German daily, *Der Wecker*. Although these Jewish liberals were also animated by an aversion to the hateful legacy of the Know-Nothings, they differed from the vast majority of their coreligionists in viewing anti-black racism as an evil equal to anti-immigrant prejudice.[112]

The support of most local Jews for the status quo on slavery was clear in the weeks after South Carolina's declaration of secession on December 24, 1860. On January 4, which had been declared a day of fasting and reflection by outgoing President James Buchanan, Bernard Illowy, the rabbi of the city's largest synagogue, Baltimore Hebrew Congregation, delivered a sermon vigorously condemning any attempt to forcibly dismantle the slave system in southern states. Claiming that ancient Jewish leaders did not understand slavery as an unqualified evil and did not see its abolition as a moral imperative, he argued that "we have no right to exercise violence against the institutions of other states or countries, even if religious feelings and philanthropic sentiments bid us disapprove of them."[113] A similar sermon delivered on the same day in New York by Rabbi Morris J. Raphall gained widespread publicity and soon appeared for sale in pamphlet form in Baltimore bookstores.[114] When David Einhorn published a denunciation of Raphall's piece, Baltimore Jews quickly organized an "indignation meeting" to make clear to the proslavery public that the liberal rabbi in no way represented Jewish opinion in the city.[115] As Einhorn later recalled, even a segment of his own congregation held the prevailing local view that to oppose slavery constituted "unheard of daring, bordering on madness."[116]

But even though most Baltimore Jews affirmed Illowy's views on slavery, they were less prepared to accept another aspect of the rabbi's sermon—his justification of secession. "Who can blame our brethren of the South," the rabbi had asked, "for seceding from a society whose government cannot, or will not, protect the property rights and privileges of a great portion of the Union?"[117] This was a view that frightened many local Jews, given that the question of secession now loomed over all discussions of Maryland's future and threatened to unleash chaos on the state. The city's two other prominent rabbis publicly denounced secession. Oheb Shalom's Benjamin Szold based his opposition on universal religious themes, trumpeting the ideals of peace and conciliation and praying that, like Joseph and his brothers, the states of the Union would soon be "reconciled [and] reunited in love and good faith."[118] The Hebrew Friendship Congregation's Henry Hochheimer, who spoke against disunion on the same day Illowy delivered his sermon, explicitly discussed the importance of the Union for his congregants. "This is the land that gave us freedom as a birthright, liberty as a just claim, and equality as the inalienable privilege of humanity," the rabbi explained. It was incumbent upon immigrant Jews to pray for the Union that had delivered them from a "mournful past" of closed opportunities and had "so hospitably opened . . . the wealthiest resources."[119]

The chaotic events of January and February 1861 confirmed the antisecessionist stance of most Baltimore Jews. Like Baltimoreans in general, during the winter and early spring they feared the upheaval that secession and war might bring to Maryland. Several prominent Jews, particularly those who had actively supported Breckinridge, aligned themselves with a movement calling for a "Convention of the People" to discuss the state's role in the unfolding crisis. They hoped such a meeting would avert disunion by applying pressure on federal officials to moderate their stance toward the South.[120] More significant was the willingness of at least a dozen Baltimore Jews to break ranks with the southern rights camp and participate in a nonpartisan mass meeting of "Friends of the Union" at the Maryland Institute on January 10, with Moses Wiesenfeld serving as a vice president of the organizing committee. The resolutions adopted at the meeting urged sectional conciliation and condemned secession—but not slavery—as inimical to American liberty and prosperity. Here the particular interests of the Jewish community, alluded to by Hochheimer, came into play. To a greater extent than most in the Democratic fold, Jews were threatened with economic devastation should secession bring the city's trade to a halt. The fact that many former Know-Nothings also participated in the meeting demonstrates vividly how the prospect of secession and war was transforming the political landscape and bringing unlikely partners together in common cause.[121]

While fears of secession caused many Jews to reevaluate their pro-southern stance in early 1861, the beginning of hostilities and the arrival in Baltimore on April 19 of Massachusetts militiamen on their way to Washington, DC, to enter federal service pushed some back toward traditional loyalties. As Jews joined other Baltimoreans across the political spectrum in their shock at the presence of northern troops in their city, members of at least a few leading Jewish families declared themselves to be active secessionists, including Isaac, Moses, and Joseph Friedenwald, brothers-in-law of Moses Wiesenfeld. Joseph Friedenwald was among those arrested for assault during the Pratt Street riot, when protesters attacked the Massachusetts troops with bricks, paving stones, and gunfire during their march across the city and the troops responded with deadly force. Isaac Friedenwald left Baltimore to join the Confederate army, as did Edward Cohen, the son of Benjamin I. Cohen and the nephew of banker and civic leader Jacob I. Cohen Jr.[122] While only a minority of Jews took such active stands in defense of the southern cause, in the immediate aftermath of the riot many who had expressed adamant opposition to secession recoiled from their strong pro-Union stance, placing blame for the violence on those who had seemingly pushed their anti-southern grievances too far. When an angry mob destroyed the offices of both *Sinai* and *Der Wecker*, causing Rabbi Einhorn to flee to Philadelphia, his congregation made it clear that he was not to return to Baltimore unless he was willing to forgo any further antislavery statements from the pulpit or in the press, a limitation he rejected.[123]

But the arrival of a federal occupation force and the declaration of martial law in Baltimore in May 1861 helped remind local Jews why so many had opposed secession in the first place. Since the riot, trade had come to an absolute halt, giving local merchants a taste of what the future might hold if they angered federal officials into isolating the city. In such an environment, even Jews with strong southern sympathies understood the need to blunt their anti-Union sentiments. Once order was restored, trade lines reopened to points north, even as a blockade was established along the state's border with Confederate Virginia.[124]

As the difficulties encountered by Wiesenfeld and the other Jewish merchants arrested in 1864 suggest, some Jews adapted to the less-than-ideal commercial environment under federal occupation by combining legal trade with occasional blockade running, which allowed them to keep their ties to the southern market alive. The city's proximity to the border made it a center for blockade runners, who smuggled uniforms, buttons, medicines, and even weaponry south to Richmond. "In this business," recalled William E. Doster, who served as the provost marshal of Washington during the war, "Baltimore Jews excelled."[125] In truth, most of the Jews who actu-

Joseph Friedenwald was the only known Jewish participant in the Pratt Street riot, which marked the beginning of hostilities in Baltimore during the Civil War. *The Lexington of 1861,* lithograph by Currier and Ives. *Courtesy of the Maryland Historical Society.*

ally ran the blockade were traders who came to Baltimore from the South, where their fortunes had been dashed by the onset of hostilities. Their dire circumstances led them to conclude that the financial benefit of satisfying Confederate needs was worth the tremendous risk of crossing the border illegally.[126] And the willingness of a well-established merchant like Wiesenfeld to work with blockade runners despite his Union loyalties demonstrates that illicit trade was more a matter of economic survival than an expression of sectional allegiance.

If the risk of arrest was an occupational hazard of illegally trading with the South, an even more daunting feature of economic life during the war years was the difficulty of managing debt and credit. Like other border states, Maryland passed a "stay law" in 1861 that tried to keep money in the state by allowing individuals and corporations to cancel their debts to out-of-state creditors. While this move aided some Jewish businessmen, it also imperiled some of the more established merchants, like Simeon Hecht, who served as a middleman between northern suppliers and the many Jewish retailers—including several of his own relatives—whom he had set up in business over the years. When his agents canceled their debts to northern wholesalers, Hecht felt obligated to pay those firms for the $60,000 worth of merchandise

- - - - - - - - - - - - -

that he had helped his associates obtain. He soon found himself in bankruptcy.[127] In this manner, the regional politics of the war destroyed many of the family and ethnic networks upon which the success of Baltimore Jews had been built.

Politically, federal occupation weakened the ability of Democrats to retain their influence over municipal affairs, opening the way for the ascent of the Unionists, a loosely organized political group that included many former Know-Nothings and pro-Union Democrats who were not prepared to join the Republican Party. As the Unionists asserted control over local government, they also attracted a few Jews who previously had moved in Republican circles, like Leopold Blumenberg, who joined former Know-Nothing Henry Winter Davis to campaign for Unionist congressional candidates in 1861, and William S. Rayner, who helped organize a mass meeting of the Unconditional Union Party in 1863.[128]

Meanwhile, the majority of Baltimore Jews whose roots were in the Democratic Party generally remained aloof from active political involvement during the years of federal occupation. Even those who had participated in pro-Union meetings during the opening months of 1861 shied away from public involvement in Unionist politics. Still, most continued to believe in the efficacy of the Union and tried to navigate the changing political landscape as best as possible, aiming to keep the peace with the former Know-Nothings who had resumed their positions of power. In this environment, it became possible for a former Know-Nothing organ like the *Baltimore Clipper* to support the appointment of Jewish chaplains in the Union army, abandoning the nativist tendency to see the United States as a solely Christian nation.[129] In 1862, when "Parson" William Ganaway Brownlow, a Methodist preacher and journalist in Knoxville, Tennessee, attacked Jews in his articles, the *Clipper* defended their honor as a "great religious and national people."[130]

The healing of these old divisions was significant, especially because in many locations in both the North and South, Jews frequently became scapegoats for wartime social and economic turmoil. This did not happen in Baltimore, partially because its status as a southern city under northern control limited the potential for partisan warfare and created a set of civic and business interests that were shared by individuals across the political spectrum. Federal officials may have stereotyped Jews as blockade-running opportunists, but among Baltimoreans, merchants such as Wiesenfeld were viewed with sympathy and respect. When he and his fellow merchants were arrested in 1864, many prominent residents of Baltimore protested, and they continued during Wiesenfeld's imprisonment to advocate for his kind treatment, explaining through an intermediary that "he was looked upon by his fellow citizens as a man of the strictest integrity."[131]

In other locales Jews were castigated as avoiders of military service in both the Confederate and Union armies, but in Baltimore avoidance of the draft was widespread among citizens of all faiths and backgrounds. A few Jews fought for the Union and Confederate forces, but men like Blumenberg, who helped form the Fifth Maryland Infantry Regiment and led troops as a Union colonel at Antietam, were atypical. Overwhelmingly, the city's Jewish men stayed put and, if drafted into the Union army, followed the lead of many other white Baltimoreans of their class who took advantage of the state law permitting the hiring of substitutes, resulting in a local Union fighting force made up disproportionately of free black men and poor Irish immigrants.[132] In short, a period that was a low point for the security of American Jews on a national level, and which had threatened to undo decades of Jewish success in Baltimore as well, ultimately became a time of growing acceptance and integration for local Jews.

The Impact of Postwar Prosperity

The increasing civic integration of Baltimore Jews paid its largest dividend at the end of the war, when a rejuvenated economy not only made up for the tensions and losses of the previous five years, but also set the scene for Jews to play a vital role in the dramatic growth of the city's commercial and industrial life. Baltimore did not emerge in the post–Civil War period as a top industrial city like New York, Philadelphia, or Chicago; it dropped from the nation's second-largest city in 1850 to the fourth-largest in 1860 and to the sixth-largest in 1870. Yet the city still grew significantly in the postwar years, capitalizing on its important role as a supply center to southern markets, which expanded as the South embraced urban and commercial development. Even before the end of hostilities, Baltimore's Jewish merchants had begun sending representatives to southern cities as they came under Union control, and the number of these agents increased dramatically after the war ended. Soon, the system of Jewish economic networks was rehabilitated and expanded to serve a new and open field. By the 1870s, with the aid of improved rail connections, Baltimore firms were supplying clothing, dry goods, and other items throughout the South.[133]

Although Baltimore lagged behind several other American cities in industrial development, the field in which the city did excel—clothing—was one in which Jews were crucially involved. Despite the traumas experienced by clothing manufacturers like Moses Wiesenfeld, the Civil War proved to be a boon to the industry. The production of military uniforms during the conflict forced manufacturers to perfect their ability to make ready-made clothing, for which a huge demand emerged in the postwar years. Henry Sonneborn was among those who pioneered in the large-scale manufacture of men's suits, which he successfully sold to the southern and midwestern markets. Levi Greif followed a similar trajectory, and by 1877 the firm he founded with his brother was producing suits from a large factory building. The clothing boom even turned around the fortunes of Wiesenfeld, who regained his position as a top manufacturer; at the time of his death in 1868, he was considered the preeminent layman of Baltimore Jewry. When Wiesenfeld's firm closed two decades later, it was described as "the leading establishment of its kind in the South," having reached an unprecedented $1.5 million per year in business.[134] By 1870, due

נארדדייטשער ללאיד.

דירעקטע רייטשע פאסטראמפפשיפפאהרט

פאן   נאך

ברעמען   אמעריקא

נאך נעוו־ארלעאנס:	נאך באלטימארע:	נאך נעוויארק:
דאמפפער האננאפפער	ד. ברוינשווייג 11. אקטאבער.	יעדען
18. אקטאבער.	ד. נירנבערג 25. אקטאבער.	זאננאבענד.
דאמפפער פראנקפורט	ד. לייפציג 8 נאוועמבער.	I. קא׳. 500 מארק
6. דעצעמבער.	ד. ברוינשווייג 2? נאוועמבער	II. קא׳. 300 מארק
קאייטע 630 מארק .	קאייטע 400 מארק	צווישענדעקק 120 מארק
צווישענדעקק 150 מארק .	צווישענדעקק 120 מארק	

צור ערטייהלונג פאן פאססאגעשיינע פיר אביגע דאמפפער זאווי־א פיר דיאעניגע
יעדער אנדערען ליניע צווישען אייראפא אונד אמעריקא זינד בעפאללמעכטיגט
Johanning und Behmer, Berlin, Louisenplatz 7.

Advertisement for passage to Baltimore on the North German Lloyd shipping line, from the Hebrew newspaper *Ha-magid*, published in East Prussia for a Russian Jewish reading audience, Oct. 11, 1876.

in no small part to the efforts of Jewish entrepreneurs, some 7,000 Baltimoreans were employed in the men's clothing business. The industry developed in a central district west of downtown bounded by Pratt, Howard, Baltimore, and Paca streets. As it grew, it diversified to include the production of sleepwear, underwear, and other cotton goods.[135]

The commercial and manufacturing successes of the postwar years led to a dramatic influx of Jewish newcomers to the city. Immigration had declined during the war, but soon resumed at a rapid pace. Some came from familiar points of origin, like fifteen-year-old Hessian-born Max Hochschild, who arrived in 1870 and, after stints as a clerk and a jobber of ribbons in small-town Maryland and Washington, DC, opened a dry goods store on Gay Street that would grow into one of Baltimore's leading emporiums. More commonly, Jews arriving from abroad after the war came from eastern locales, such as Posen, a former Polish territory under Prussian rule. Among these Poseners was Michael S. Levy, who would become Baltimore's leading hat manufacturer.[136] A small but swelling group of immigrants also began to arrive from the Russian Empire. By 1865, Baltimore had its first congregation of Russian and Polish Jews, Bikur Cholim, and by 1876, immigration from Eastern Europe was significant enough for the North German Lloyd shipping

The firm founded by Isaac Strouse (*second from right*) and his brothers
(*left to right*) Abraham, Benjamin, Saul, Eli, and Leopold exemplified Baltimore's rise as a center
for clothing manufacturing in the post–Civil War decades. *Jewish Museum of Maryland.*

line to run advertisements for its Baltimore route in the Hebrew newspapers read
by Jews in Russia.[137]

Most Jewish newcomers during the late 1860s and 1870s, however, arrived from
other parts of the United States rather than from abroad. Southern Jews who had
suffered reverses during the war saw Baltimore as a place to get a fresh start. Lazarus
and Susannah Fels came in 1866 from Yanceyville, North Carolina, to establish a
soap manufacturing business. A decade later, their son Joseph acquired a Philadelphia firm and went on to produce the famous Fels-Naptha brand. Moses Cohen
Mordecai, a former South Carolina state senator and the most prominent Jewish
resident of antebellum Charleston, revived his failed shipping and importing firm by
moving it to Baltimore around 1865. In partnership with his brother David and other
family members, he also established a steamship line with routes to southern cities
and Havana, Cuba. Baltimore's expanding dry goods trade and its emerging role as
a clothing manufacturing center drew many to the city. Isaac Strouse had immigrated to the United States in 1850 from a small town near Heidelberg and had owned
businesses in Virginia, Illinois, and Washington, DC, before arriving in Baltimore in
1867 to invest his savings in the manufacturing and wholesaling of clothing. Within

a decade, he and his brothers built one of the city's largest clothing businesses, with a six-story stone and brick factory at the corner of Paca and Lombard streets.[138]

For newcomers and older residents alike, opportunities for upward mobility during the late 1860s and 1870s were bountiful. Although ongoing immigration from abroad meant that there were always Jews in Baltimore who were just beginning the process of adjustment to the American setting, the majority of Jews, who had already been in the country for a decade or more, increasingly succeeded at entering economic, social, and cultural arenas that had previously been inaccessible to them.

While most Baltimore Jews remained concentrated in trade and commerce, the postwar era saw many branch out into new occupations. David Bachrach, who emigrated from Hesse as a child and settled in Connecticut, came to Baltimore during the Civil War as an apprentice photographer and soon opened his own studio, where he perfected a method for making photo prints on painter's canvas. The Bohemian-born brothers Louis E. and Max Levy also pioneered in photography, discovering a process for making halftone photo engravings suitable for publishing, which they patented in 1875. After two years in Baltimore they moved to Philadelphia and founded the Levytype Company. David Binswanger established a job-printing business, and Isaac Friedenwald founded a publishing house. Moses Wolf left the clothing business in 1867 to become the first Baltimore Jew to open an insurance brokerage, specializing in coverage against fire.[139]

Although Jewish involvement in the professions remained rare before the 1880s, a few young men entered the medical field, adding to the small number of Jewish doctors—some with German training—who had settled in Baltimore in earlier decades. Among these new physicians was Samuel L. Frank, an eye, ear, nose, and throat expert who trained at the University of Maryland and in Würzburg, Germany, before starting work in Baltimore hospitals during the 1860s. Aaron Friedenwald received his MD from the University of Maryland just before the Civil War and, like Frank, augmented his education with studies in Germany. By the 1870s he had become one of Baltimore's leading ophthalmologists.[140] Four young Baltimore-born Jews who graduated from law school in the late 1860s and early 1870s became the first attorneys to emerge from the Jewish community. Daniel Greenbaum, son of a Bavarian-born clothier, was named the valedictorian of Central High School (later City College) in 1866 before embarking on a career as a real estate lawyer. Charles J. Wiener, son of the physician and journalist Dr. Moritz Wiener, studied under a local judge and began to practice law by 1869. After graduating from the University of Maryland law school in 1874, Lewis Hochheimer, son of Rabbi Henry Hochheimer, directed his legal efforts toward aiding children and prisoners. Isidor Rayner, son of the dry goods merchant and philanthropist William S. Rayner, trained in law at the University of Virginia and was admitted to the Maryland bar in 1871.[141]

The younger Rayner was also among the first Baltimore Jews to be elected to public office in the post–Civil War era, helping to initiate a chain of Jewish officeholding that has continued to this day. Although Solomon Etting and Jacob I. Cohen Jr. had enjoyed distinguished careers on the Baltimore City Council, and Jacob's younger brother Mendes I. Cohen had represented Baltimore in the House of Delegates in Annapolis in 1847, the only Jewish immigrant to hold public office before the Civil War was the short-term councilman John M. Dyer. The rise of Jewish officeholders in the 1870s, therefore, marked a new level of integration into local civic culture. Colonel Marcus S. Hess, who had fought with Maryland governor Oden Bowie in the Mexican-American War and served for many years as the president of the German-dominated Concordia Association, started the trend in 1876 when he was elected to the House of Delegates. He was followed by Rayner, who took a seat in the House in 1878. Rayner went on to become a state senator, state attorney general, and a US senator. As Jews became more conspicuous in state and local politics, the basic pattern of party affiliation that prevailed during the war years continued: a small number belonged to the Republican Party, while the overwhelming majority were Democrats.[142]

As Baltimore Jews began to see members of their community ascend to elected office, they increased their activism regarding local issues that directly affected Jewish social and economic standing. Top on their agenda was the fight against the Sunday laws, which mandated the closure of most businesses and limited options for public recreation on the Christian Sabbath. Jews had complained about Sunday laws since the 1850s, but in the days of Know-Nothing political control, there was little chance of changing these provisions. In 1866, however, when the Maryland legislature considered adopting a comprehensive state law mandating Sunday closures, Baltimore Jews were in a better position to protest. Holding a series of public meetings and sending a petition signed by hundreds to the General Assembly, they claimed that the proposed law infringed on their rights, describing it as an inappropriate establishment of religion and an unfair economic measure, since it forced those who observed the Jewish Sabbath to close their businesses for two days. In some cases, Jews joined forces with local Germans, whose Sunday leisure practices included the consumption of alcohol at local gathering spots and who therefore saw the laws as a threat to their cultural autonomy. Ultimately, the Sunday laws remained on the books well into the twentieth century, but the confidence and visibility of the Jewish effort against them demonstrated the rising stature of Jews in the local civic order.[143]

Philanthropy remained a central arena for Jews to demonstrate their economic and social mobility and their responsibility as citizens, but in the late 1860s and 1870s their philanthropic achievements outstripped anything the Jewish community had accomplished before the war. The growing wealth of Baltimore Jews was reflected in the expansion of the budget of the Hebrew Benevolent Society. By 1872, the society was distributing more than $4,000 per year to disadvantaged recipients and had built a sizable reserve fund to meet unforeseen needs. It was also becoming known as a significant factor in charitable giving outside Jewish circles. When a

The Hebrew Hospital and Asylum, pictured here in 1880, was built on East Monument Street in 1868. Along with the Hebrew Orphan Asylum, founded in 1872, it reflected the expansion of Jewish philanthropic endeavors in Baltimore during the postwar economic boom.
Jewish Museum of Maryland.

major flood struck Baltimore and surrounding towns in 1868, the society donated $3,600 to the city's relief efforts, to be distributed without regard to religious affiliation. As impressive as this charitable support was, the annual budget continued to grow dramatically, more than doubling in the next three years. By 1875, the Hebrew Benevolent Society was distributing the unprecedented sum of $10,000 annually.[144]

Even more remarkable, this sharp increase in charitable funding occurred as Baltimore Jews poured their resources into two new major philanthropic efforts. The first was the Hebrew Hospital and Asylum, conceived as a project of the Hebrew Benevolent Society in 1866 and established as an independent institution two years later with the construction of a handsome building on East Monument Street. Reflecting Jews' fear of missionary overtures, to which Jewish patients in Christian hospitals sometimes fell victim, as well as the desire to demonstrate that Jews "took care of their own," the hospital soon became a fixture in Baltimore's medical and charitable communities. It also provided employment for the growing number of young Jews who were training as physicians.[145] The second major focus of Jewish philanthropy in the postwar years was the Hebrew Orphan Asylum, founded in 1872 when William Rayner used $50,000 of his personal funds to purchase and renovate Calverton, a former county almshouse located on the outskirts of town, where thirty-two Jewish orphans were soon housed. The building burned in 1874, but the community immediately replaced it with an even grander structure. As architectural landmarks that were often depicted in overviews of the city's institutions, the hospital and the orphan asylum vividly signified the civic ascent of Baltimore's Jews.[146]

While such philanthropic activities were financed by the wealth of businessmen like Rayner and Wiesenfeld, who headed the Hebrew Benevolent Society for ten consecutive terms, they were also supported by an ever-expanding program of fairs, balls, and bazaars. Baltimore's Jews had long sponsored such fundraising events, but in the postwar decade they became more lavish, drew greater public notice, and were designed more consciously to show off the social standing of the participants. So important were these events as rituals of Jewish acculturation and self-fashioning that in 1864 a group headed by Charles G. Hutzler organized the Harmony Circle, a social club that sponsored annual balls as an aim in itself, detached from any larger philanthropic purpose.[147] Others preferred to keep sociability and philanthropy intertwined, even as they understood these events as opportunities to assert their material success and social status. In 1868, for example, several Jewish community leaders headed by Goody Rosenfeld founded the Purim Association, which held an annual Grand Carnival and Bal Masque to benefit the Hebrew Hospital and the orphan asylum in alternating years. These events featured lavish costumes and humorous publications printed just for the occasion. "Why is this Ball Room to-night like a fine, large and ripe peach?" asked the *Purim Gazette Extra* of 1869. "Because it is full of juice (Jews!)."[148]

Adding to the prestige of Jewish balls, fairs, and bazaars was the fact that most of them took place at the Concordia Opera House, a grand hall constructed in 1865 on the west side of the city, which hosted not only operas, but also dramatic presentations, concerts, and assemblies of all sorts. Jews' preference for this venue demonstrates that they continued to see their acculturation as linked at least partially to German American institutions, since the hall was built by the Concordia Association, a society founded in 1847 to promote literary and cultural events for German-speaking immigrants. Before the Civil War, few Jews had connections to the Concordia Association, but an increasing number joined after the war. Attending theater and opera in its hall was a sign of their rising social status, since, as one newspaper report explained, the members included "many of the most refined and wealthy of our German fellow citizens."[149]

While the Concordia's fashionable surroundings served Jews' need to mark their rising status, the fact that it functioned less as a closely knit association and more as a venue for public amusement allowed Jews to attend performances without interacting on an intimate basis with the German American attendees. The Concordia also enabled groups to rent its space for their own separate events. Thus, Jews could hold the masquerade ball of the Baltimore Purim Association and annual dances of the Hebrew Young Men's Literary Association in the same stately rooms where the

German American Arion Singing Society and the Liederkranz Society held their galas, without sacrificing the Jewish focus of their celebrations.[150]

Though ties to the Concordia Association reflected their increased social mobility in the postwar years, Baltimore Jews did not limit themselves to the German-language cultural sphere. The era saw an increasing identification with English as the language of everyday life and community activity. The rising group of second-generation Baltimore Jews naturally gravitated toward English, forcing Jewish institutions to accommodate this change if they wished to remain vibrant. Many of the city's rabbis clung to German as a language of religious instruction, but the tide was against them, a fact that became obvious as early as 1867, when Hebrew Friendship's rabbi Henry Hochheimer and Solomon Deutsch, Einhorn's successor at Har Sinai, were the only two speakers at the opening of a new communal religious school who did not deliver their remarks in English.[151]

A watershed came in 1871, when improvements in the public school system and the adoption of German as an elective course led to the closing of the city's German and Jewish private schools. With most Jewish children now receiving a public education in English, German had little chance of surviving. The same year as the school reforms, Rabbi Benjamin Szold began to lecture in English every other week at Oheb Shalom. By the end of the decade, other synagogues had instituted English sermons, and Baltimore Hebrew Congregation had changed its bylaws to require that all meetings be conducted in English. In 1875, the city's first Jewish newspaper, the *Jewish Chronicle*, was published in English, and synagogue services and special events, such as confirmations, increasingly shifted to English as well.[152]

Inevitably, the shift in language, the entry of Jewish children into the public schools, and the growing tendency of young Jews to pursue nontraditional occupations meant that among the young, the long-standing social isolation of Baltimore Jews began to diminish. While their parents may have avoided intimate social contact with non-Jews when visiting the Concordia Opera House, younger Jews who now regularly interacted with gentiles in their classrooms, in leisure venues, and in professional settings no longer took the social barriers between Jews and non-Jews for granted. As a result, while intermarriage remained rare, it began to occur more frequently than before. Young professional men whose education and training took them out of familiar Jewish social settings were particularly prone to marrying non-Jewish women. Aspiring attorneys Charles J. Wiener and Isidor Rayner, for example, were immersed in non-Jewish society as law students, as associates in non-Jewish law firms, and as rising stars on the Baltimore political scene; both married non-Jewish women they met through their new networks.[153]

The increasing social status of Baltimore's acculturated Jews was also reflected in the accelerated changes to synagogue life. The most acrimonious struggles took place within the city's oldest congregation, Baltimore Hebrew, where the pulpit remained empty between 1862 and 1868, probably because disputes among the members over issues of acculturation and ritual innovation made it impossible for them

The junk dealer and grocer Jonas Friedenwald led the fight against religious reform at Baltimore Hebrew Congregation. In 1871 he and others formed a new Orthodox synagogue, Chizuk Amuno (Strengtheners of the Faith). *Jewish Museum of Maryland.*

to agree on a leader. Finally, in 1868 the reform-minded camp prevailed with the election of Rabbi Abraham Hoffman who, within two years, approved the establishment of a mixed choir and an abridged liturgy, changes similar to those made several years earlier by Har Sinai and Oheb Shalom.[154]

The dissidents who rejected reform, led by Jonas Friedenwald, sued to prevent these changes, and when they lost in court in 1871, they seceded from Baltimore Hebrew to form their own more traditional congregation, Chizuk Amuno (Strengtheners of the Faith), which maintained Orthodox religious standards but did not lack in identification with American culture. Hiring the city's first American-born rabbi, Henry Schneeberger, in 1876 and replacing German with English before some of the reform-oriented congregations did, the leaders of Chizuk Amuno wished to demonstrate that one could be a fully acculturated American without abandoning Jewish religious traditions.[155] A similar outlook animated the founders of Shearith Israel, an Orthodox congregation made up mostly of Jews from southern German villages who had worshipped in a series of smaller synagogues (really, informal prayer meetings) in the western part of Baltimore before consolidating in 1879. Although Shearith Israel was of more modest stature than the other congregations, according to one account its members were "Orthodox Jews who were as cultured and Americanized as the Reform Jews."[156]

As the distinctions between Reform and Orthodox congregations increased in the postwar years, Baltimore Judaism became much more segmented. The congregations that had embraced religious reforms in previous decades had limited their agendas to mostly cosmetic changes, but between 1869 and 1873, Baltimore Hebrew, Oheb Shalom, and Har Sinai all pushed beyond their previous boundaries by instituting family seating. Changes to the worship service and rituals continued through the 1870s and 1880s, leading to the crystallization of Reform Judaism as a distinct movement with a coherent set of beliefs and practices.[157]

The segmentation of Jewish religious life in Baltimore also increased with the establishment of new congregations by Jews from Eastern Europe, who had started to arrive in small but significant numbers after the war. In addition to the pioneering Eastern European congregation Bikur Cholim (Visiting the Sick), two additional congregations emerged in the postwar decade. B'nai Israel, colloquially known as the "Russishe shul," served mainly Lithuanian Jews, who were the largest single Jewish group immigrating to Baltimore and other American cities by the 1870s. Anshe Chesed Bialystok (Compassionate People of Bialystok) represented immigrants from the well-known textile-producing town in eastern Poland.[158]

The members of these early Eastern European Jewish congregations lived mostly in the unsavory neighborhood around Harrison Street and in Fells Point, where many earlier Jewish immigrants had started out before they began their social and economic climb.[159] This group was the vanguard of a much larger influx of Eastern European Jews who would begin to arrive in Baltimore and other American cities during the 1880s. Because of their large numbers, their demographic profile, and changes in the American economy, these newcomers would find a much different context for acculturation than their predecessors had. The differing experiences of the two groups and their often conflicting approaches to forging a Jewish life in the United States would form one of the central themes of the American Jewish experience during the closing decades of the nineteenth century and the opening decades of the twentieth.

3

The Great Wave Hits Baltimore

On the morning of Wednesday, August 19, 1891, employees at the Canton immigrant pier, where the packet liner *Slavonia* had arrived from Hamburg, noticed an unusual commotion. Crowded near the ship were fifty-four Russian Jewish men, women, and children who had been detained after immigration inspectors judged them "likely to become a burden on the resources of this country."[1] A recent directive from the Immigration Bureau in Washington, DC, had urged officials to be more exacting in screening for indigent arrivals. As word spread about the plight of the detainees, the Jews of Baltimore—both the older community of Central European origin and the growing population of more recently arrived immigrants from Eastern Europe— scrambled to prevent the group from being deported. The more established Jews used their influence to secure the release of twelve detainees and generously offered to put up the assets of the Hebrew Benevolent Society and other communal charities as bond for the rest. But the Immigration Bureau refused to accept the community's money, stating that only personal bonds would be accepted. Despite the daunting task of raising thousands of dollars in a very short time, leaders among the newer immigrants worked with wealthier "German" Jewish benefactors to pull together the necessary funds. Less than a week after the *Slavonia*'s arrival, the bonds were paid, and the Jews of Baltimore breathed a collective sigh of relief. Still, they knew that they could not rest for long. They needed to quickly find employment for the new arrivals or the bonds they had posted would be lost and the immigrants sent back.[2]

The drama surrounding the arrival of the *Slavonia* provides but one example of the pressures and difficulties experienced in Baltimore during the post-1880 wave of Eastern European Jewish immigration to the United States. Baltimore's ongoing transition to an industrial economy offered opportunities to new immigrants, but it also produced many social and economic hardships that had not afflicted Jewish settlers of previous generations. Moreover, the massive size of the migratory wave made the process of adjustment to American life slower and more difficult than it had been for earlier arrivals. Aware of these challenges, the city's acculturated Jews,

104

A ship filled with immigrants docks at Baltimore's Locust Point, c. 1904.
Courtesy of the Maryland Historical Society, MC7433-3.

Immigrants in a detention pen awaiting inspection at Locust Point, c. 1904.
Courtesy of the Maryland Historical Society, MC7433-4.

who were already outnumbered by the Eastern European immigrants at the time of the *Slavonia* incident, feared that the newcomers might imperil their social standing and deplete the resources of their charitable institutions. With no end to the massive influx in sight, however, it soon became clear that the immigrants were a force to be reckoned with and that they would permanently alter the tone and character of Baltimore Jewry.

A Golden Door to the South

Eastern European Jews had come to North America during the colonial and early national periods and had grown in number during the major wave of Jewish immigration in the mid-nineteenth century. Baltimore was no exception: it had attracted the Lithuanian Jewish distiller, Mordecai M. Mordecai, as early as 1770 and was home to a congregation of Russian and Polish Jews by 1865. But only after 1880 did social, political, and economic forces combine to unleash an exodus from Eastern Europe massive enough to define an entirely new era of American Jewish history.

Although the post-1880 arrivals had not experienced the beginnings of political emancipation or social integration in their homelands to the extent that previous Jewish immigrants had, neither had they been totally sheltered from the forces of modernization. Far from the stagnant and tradition-bound society often depicted in popular culture, the world of Eastern European Jews became increasingly fluid and dynamic during the nineteenth century. Institutions of Jewish communal self-government in the Russian Empire—the point of origin for about 75 percent of the Jews who came to the United States in the post-1880 period—began to crumble in the 1820s as new forms of political activism emerged and as new leaders, many of them endowed with secular knowledge, challenged the rabbinate and communal oligarchy. As the century progressed, urbanization and internal migration intensified, bringing many small-town Jews to larger centers like Warsaw, Kovno, and Odessa. Statistics collected at ports of entry suggest that Jewish immigrants to the United States were, on the whole, more skilled and literate than those who remained behind, an indication that many had already been exposed to urban living. Finally, during the years of social and political unrest at the opening of the twentieth century, when immigration to America was at its peak, movements like socialism, Zionism, and Bundism reshaped Jewish identity. Overseas immigration both grew out of and reflected the much larger set of social and demographic revolutions that were transforming the face of Eastern European Jewry.[3]

Most Eastern European Jewish immigrants of this period left their homes for the same reasons that had propelled earlier arrivals, including the decline of the rural economy, which undermined Jewish occupational stability; the fear of military conscription; and government-imposed legal and residential restrictions that eroded their ability to make ends meet. (The pogroms that periodically convulsed parts of the Russian Empire after 1881, though unique in their furor, played a smaller role in encouraging emigration than is normally assumed and were far less significant than chronic economic and social problems.) Nevertheless, the movement of Jews from Eastern Europe differed in important ways from earlier migrations. Certainly, the post-1880 arrivals fled more dire circumstances. While the Central European Jewish immigrants of previous decades had arrived mostly young and unmarried, post-1880 immigrants were more diverse in age and often came as whole families, sometimes with the husband, father, or son arriving first to prepare the way for the others. This pattern of family migration indicates that even those well rooted in Eastern European Jewish society found the mounting social and economic crises unbearable. The comparatively desperate situation from which post-1880 immigrants escaped was also reflected in the sheer size of the human movement, which dwarfed all previous migrations of Jews to America. And even though most Jews were not directly affected by the pogroms, these terrifying events left a profound psychological imprint on Jews across the region. Because episodes of anti-Jewish violence increased in frequency and intensity as Russia confronted the processes of social and political change, many Jews came to believe that there was little future for them in Russia, no matter what new regime might come to power.[4]

The most important distinctions between the pre- and post-1880 migrations, however, had less to do with conditions in Europe than with dramatic changes in America that created a very different setting for the new arrivals. By the end of the nineteenth century, the United States had emerged as a major industrial power. Cities offered both new kinds of work opportunities and poorer, more segregated living conditions for Jewish immigrants, who now overwhelmingly chose the largest urban centers as their first, and often permanent, places of settlement.[5] This shift did not mean, however, that the Jewish presence outside the major population centers dwindled. An 1887 report from Baltimore, for example, revealed that "almost every town of any size in Maryland and Virginia contains one or more Russian [Jewish] store-keepers."[6] Still, compared with earlier trends, a greater proportion of Jewish immigrants were now settling in major industrial cities, where factory jobs were plentiful and large Jewish enclaves were emerging. This new environment and the large size of the "great wave" created a much different context for Jewish life than had existed for previous immigrants.[7]

As the nation's commercial and industrial powerhouse, New York attracted at least half of all Jewish immigrants who arrived from Eastern Europe in the post-1880 period. Remarkably, although Jews never constituted more than 2 percent of the US population during this era, by the time World War I sharply curtailed mass immigration, 25 percent of New York's population was Jewish. Because New York loomed so large in American Jewish life, even the most important secondary Jewish communities—Chicago, Philadelphia, Boston, and Baltimore—were much smaller. In 1900, for example, New York was home to more than 500,000 Jews, while the two competitors for the second largest community, Chicago and Philadelphia, each had only 75,000. Baltimore, the fifth-largest at 30,000–35,000, had been recently surpassed by Boston, home to 40,000 Jews.[8]

These second-tier Jewish communities had much in common. To some extent they offered smaller versions of the New York experience: all were industrial centers, all had burgeoning clothing industries where many Jews worked, and all contained significant enclaves where immigrant Jews crafted a cultural and institutional life that distinguished them from the native-born population, other immigrant groups, and the older, more acculturated Jewish community. All except Chicago were major ports where immigrant arrivals took their first steps on the soil of the United States. In the 1880s and 1890s, Baltimore's railway connections to the West allowed it to jockey with Philadelphia for the position of second-largest immigrant depot, although it fell behind both the Pennsylvania city and a rising Boston in the early twentieth century. At that time, an average of 5,400 Jewish immigrants came through Baltimore each year, with the largest number—almost 11,000—arriving in 1906 on the heels of the first Russian Revolution and a series of disastrous pogroms.[9]

All the second-tier immigrant centers also resembled New York in the types of Eastern European Jews they attracted. Jews from historical Lithuania (which included parts of contemporary Poland, Latvia, and Belarus) dominated the immigrant stream in the 1880s and 1890s. Because Lithuania had a higher concentration of Jews than did other parts of the Russian Empire's Jewish Pale of Settlement, and fewer major cities to absorb those looking to escape from declining small towns, it was the region where Jews struggled the most with problems of economic competition and lack of opportunity.[10] Pogroms were less typical in Lithuania than in southern Russia, confirming that the rise of mass migration was motivated more by socioeconomic conditions than by direct experience with physical violence.[11] The predominance of Litvaks in Baltimore's Jewish community during this early period was reflected in the background of the city's most prominent rabbinic figures, immigrant businessmen, and presidents of Jewish organizations. It was also apparent from the many synagogues founded on a landsmanshaft (hometown society) model that were associated with Lithuanian locales.[12] As immigration peaked during the early twentieth century, however, Baltimore—like other Jewish centers in the United States—received an increasing number of arrivals from other parts of Eastern Europe, including Russia's Polish and Ukrainian provinces, Romania, and the Hungarian and Galician regions of the Austrian Empire.[13]

Despite the ways in which the second-tier Jewish centers resembled New York and each other, there were also factors that distinguished each location and created different contexts for Jewish life. One quality that set Baltimore apart was its smaller size. While New York, Philadelphia, Brooklyn, Chicago, and Boston were the five largest cities in the United States when the period of mass immigration began in 1880, Baltimore, despite having the sixth-largest Jewish community, had fallen behind St. Louis in overall population to become the seventh-largest city. By 1920, despite the incorporation of Brooklyn into New York City, Baltimore dropped even

A member of the Kardinsky family and her two children pose
in Shavli (now Šiauliai), Lithuania, before departing to join their husband and father
in Baltimore, c. 1905. *Jewish Museum of Maryland.*

further to the position of eighth-largest US city due to the rising fortunes of Cleveland and Detroit.[14]

More striking is the fact that Baltimore had a much lower proportion of foreign-born residents than any of the other leading Jewish centers. Despite the city's status as a major immigration port, by 1910 foreign-born residents constituted only 14 percent of Baltimore's population, compared with 25 percent in Philadelphia, 36 percent in Chicago and Boston, and 41 percent in New York.[15] Partly, this can be explained by the unique 1867 agreement between the B&O Railroad and the North German Lloyd shipping line, to which Baltimore owed much of its status as a port of entry. While this partnership guaranteed a regular flow of immigrant traffic into the city from North German Lloyd's home port of Bremen, it was specifically designed to place passengers arriving at the Locust Point immigrant depot onto B&O trains departing for locations in the American interior.[16] As a result, compared to other port cities Baltimore more often served as a transit center than as a final destination. Also limiting the city's prominence as an immigrant hub was the crucial economic role played by African Americans, who during the entire period of mass immigration constituted a greater proportion of the population in Baltimore—about 15 percent—than in any northern industrial center.[17] Because black workers filled much of the city's demand for unskilled labor and domestic service, immigrants looking for jobs of this type found Baltimore to offer comparatively fewer opportunities.

To some degree, Baltimore's failure to attract a larger share of immigrants after 1880 constrained the growth of its Jewish population and diminished its status as a premier American Jewish center. By 1910, both Boston and the burgeoning manufacuring city of Cleveland had surpassed Baltimore in Jewish population. Overall, however, Baltimore stands out during this period not for its waning appeal among Jews, but for the remarkable degree to which it continued to attract Jewish immigrants despite its decline in popularity among immigrants more broadly. Indeed, in 1910 Jews were a larger proportion of the foreign-born population in Baltimore than in any American city except Philadelphia and New York. Over the next decade the city's Jewish population rose to more than 60,000, and Russian Jews alone came to outnumber Germans as Baltimore's largest immigrant group.[18] By 1920 only New York, the undisputed capital of Jewish America, had a larger proportion of Jews among its foreign-born residents.[19] Clearly, Baltimore offered something significant to Jews that it did not offer to other immigrant groups.

Baltimore's appeal to Jewish immigrants was undoubtedly rooted in the city's strength in garment manufacturing, an industry that attracted large numbers of Jewish workers in all the major Jewish population centers of the period. The production of clothing had been Baltimore's single largest industry ever since the economic boom that followed the Civil War. About 20 percent of all industrial workers were employed in the manufacture of garments in 1905, and the industry retained its top position in the city's economy until the 1920s. Baltimore was never the largest center for garment manufacturing in the United States; it was outstripped by New York,

Chicago, and Philadelphia even when the local production of men's clothing—Baltimore's specialty—was at its height during the golden age of 1916–1920. But the city's garment industry thrived because of its strategic position near the Mason-Dixon Line and its lock on the important southern market, allowing Baltimore to offer a steady source of employment for Jewish laborers and a chance for the most ambitious to move into jobs as custom tailors and manufacturers. As a 1911 government study revealed, the garment trades held unusual sway over Baltimore Jews, who worked in the manufacture of clothing in greater proportion than did their counterparts in other major cities.[20]

By contrast, the city offered comparatively few economic opportunities to the non-Jewish immigrants of this period. Although non-Jewish Lithuanians, Poles, Bohemians, and Italians did find employment in local garment factories, members of these groups more typically sought work in heavy industries, like mining, meatpacking, and steel production, none of which figured significantly in Baltimore's economy. In fact, no industry other than clothing production engaged more than a small percentage of the city's workforce before the Bethlehem Steel Company developed its plant at Sparrows Point beginning in 1916. In 1905, for example, the largest concentrations of industrial workers outside the garment trades were employed in canning (6 percent), tobacco processing (5 percent), railway car construction and repair (5 percent), and foundry work (5 percent).[21]

The concentration of Baltimore's Jewish immigrants in the garment trades not only provided them with an occupational niche in a city otherwise lacking in industrial opportunities, but also shielded them from job competition with African Americans. Because non-Jewish immigrants generally arrived in the United States with little previous experience in industry or urban living, they often gravitated to unskilled jobs, which in Baltimore were the mainstay of the large African American population. The garment industry, with its higher proportion of skilled workers, engaged few African Americans before World War I.[22] Moreover, as the only immigrant group with a significant presence in peddling and other forms of petty commerce, Eastern European Jews—or at least the businesspeople among them—saw African Americans as a potential customer base that could help propel their community toward its goals of success and mobility, much as earlier Jewish arrivals in Baltimore had seen them.[23]

If Baltimore's distinctive geographical, industrial, and demographic setting created economic circumstances that drew Eastern European Jews, the city also placed its distinctive stamp on the immigrants' social and cultural experiences as they adapted to their new home. The salience of race in Baltimore was a result of the city's position straddling North and South. There were major contests over segregation and African Americans' legal status, which provided a much different context for the pursuit of citizenship and social standing than the one experienced by Jewish immigrants in other major Jewish centers of the era. Baltimore's southern temperament, reinforced by the traditions of its native-born white majority, was also reflected in

Israel Denaburg (*right*), a native of Borisov in Russia's Minsk Province (now Barysaw, Belarus),
set up shop in Baltimore as a tailor in 1904. He was followed a year later by his brother-in-law
Harry Feldman (*left*), who became a presser for Henry Sonneborn and Company.
Photo, c. 1905. *Jewish Museum of Maryland. Courtesy of Eric L. Goldstein.*

its social conservatism, its suspicion of cosmopolitanism, and its reputation as an intensely religious city.[24] These aspects of the city's character reinforced the strength of Orthodox Judaism, which had already been apparent during the previous wave of immigration, and also worked against the vibrancy of socialist and radical movements that were so crucial to Jewish life elsewhere.

In many respects, then, Baltimore's distinctive qualities were bound up with its middleness — more industrial than cities to the south, yet lacking the heavy industries of the North; an immigrant port of entry with a historically large black population; a large city with a small-town, socially conservative culture. These qualities would give rise to the peculiar blend of opportunities and limits that defined the Jewish experience in Baltimore as the nineteenth century came to a close and the twentieth century opened.

Jews in the Eyes of Baltimoreans

When Hutzler Brothers opened the doors of its new store on Howard and Clay streets in 1888, observers hailed the five-story structure as an achievement for the city as well as for the prominent retailing family. Constructed of gray stone, it featured an imposing turret, a waving flag emblazoned with the Hutzler name, and carvings of Napoleon, the goddess Justice, and even the firm's founder, Bavarian immigrant Moses Hutzler, embedded in the façade. As a commercial "palace," the store offered an entirely new shopping experience. Average Baltimoreans could peruse its elaborate window displays and shop in luxury while choosing from a jaw-dropping variety of clothing, household items, fabrics, and lace. "It is one of the largest and best arranged buildings of its kind in the United States," declared a writer for the *Sun*. "[It] is a credit to Baltimore and her workmen and a monument to the enterprise and industry of her proprietors."[25]

In addition to marking a watershed in Baltimore's commercial history, the opening of Hutzler's palace reflected the impressive strides made by the city's Central European Jewish immigrants and their offspring since they began to arrive in large numbers more than a half century earlier. While few other members of this now thoroughly acculturated group achieved the success of the Hutzlers, on the whole they continued to experience the dramatic economic mobility that had begun in the post–Civil War years. Even more remarkable was the profound influence they had come to exercise on economic and civic life. As the owners of major retail stores, including Gutman's, Hecht's, and Hochschild, Kohn, and as the most significant force behind the city's flourishing clothing industry, Central European Jews had proven crucial to Baltimore's growth and development. The cohort of Jews entering the professions continued to grow, with the founding of Johns Hopkins University in 1876 providing a welcome home to Jewish students and faculty members. The role of Jews in politics also expanded. While it had once been rare for Jews to hold public office in Baltimore, they now routinely served on the city council, in the

The Hochschild, Kohn department store, built in 1897 at Howard and West Lexington streets, was one of Baltimore's commercial showplaces. Hutzler Brothers' "palace," built in 1888, is visible to the right. Photo, c. 1903. *Jewish Museum of Maryland.*

state legislature, and as judges on local courts, typically representing the Democratic Party but in some cases affiliating with the Republicans. By the first decade of the twentieth century, Maryland even had a Jewish attorney general, Isaac Lobe Straus, and a Jewish US senator, Isidor Rayner.[26]

Beginning in the 1880s, however, the exhilaration of success was tempered by the sting of social discrimination, which cast a cloud over the aspirations of Baltimore's Central European Jews. While Jewish immigrants of the mid-nineteenth century had typically avoided socializing outside their ethnic and religious community, the economic and cultural transformations of the ensuing decades had ignited a desire to move beyond the limits of their tightly knit fellowship. Members of the younger, American-born generation were particularly hopeful that the ties they were forging to white elites in the business and civic arenas would translate to acceptance in fashionable society.

Ironically, the social transformations that fostered a spirit of expectation among acculturated Jews created apprehension among the elite Baltimoreans whose acceptance they sought. These leaders of society perceived the shifting class boundaries of the period as a threat to their own dominance, and they began to fortify their

Founded in 1858, L. Greif and Brother eventually became the second-largest men's clothing manufacturer in the United States, while Henry Sonneborn and Company became the largest. Both firms were major employers of Eastern European Jewish garment workers in Baltimore. Photo, c. 1915. *Courtesy of the Maryland Historical Society.*

status by closing ranks and drawing distinctions between themselves and those they deemed the crass nouveaux riche. Jews were hardly the only group whose mobility threatened elites' standing, but as a particularly visible population experiencing an unusual economic climb, Jews served as a convenient scapegoat for the fears of the establishment.[27] It became common practice to prevent prominent Jews from entering high-toned gathering places like the Maryland and Athenaeum clubs. Beginning in 1889, following the pattern in many other American cities, elite Baltimoreans began to publish the *Society Visiting List*, which announced publicly who was welcome in their circles and—by omission—who was not.[28]

The same process was reflected in residential patterns. When Henry Sonneborn built a fine home in Northwest Baltimore's prestigious Eutaw Place neighborhood in 1878, he doubtlessly felt he was marking his ascent into Baltimore society. As other Jews began to follow him, however, wealthy non-Jews in the area responded by moving away, leaving the district to become a gilded ghetto by the century's end. There were even signs of unwelcome in the German American community, where Jews had long found an open door. As Jews became a greater force in the Concordia Association, once the focus of the city's German cultural life, non-Jewish members sought other outlets for their leisure activities. The change was so dramatic by 1889 that when the Concordia gave a banquet marking the centennial of George Washington's inauguration, the organization was referred to in the press as being "composed largely of prominent Hebrews."[29]

Although gentile elites largely succeeded in preventing Jews from gaining access to their society institutions, the barriers they erected did not prove completely impenetrable. During the late nineteenth and early twentieth centuries, a few Jews of unusual wealth and influence—figures like Senator Rayner and his father, William, who had made a fortune in real estate investing; civil engineer Mendes Cohen, whose roots in the United States went back to colonial times; and whiskey baron Alfred J. Ulman—were admitted to exclusive clubs and won inclusion on the *Society Visiting List*.[30] So too did a handful of Jewish faculty members at Johns Hopkins— the English-born mathematician James Joseph Sylvester; Fabian Franklin, who later became the editor of the Baltimore *News*; and Sanskrit expert Maurice Bloomfield— whose status as intellectuals eased their entrée into non-Jewish circles.[31] But these were rare exceptions; despite the public recognition Jews often received for their contributions to business and civic affairs, white gentiles' insistence on social exclusivity was so great that even Jewish families as highly regarded as the Hutzlers, Strouses, and Sonneborns could not overcome it. Moreover, those who did break through these barriers often acquiesced to pressure to attenuate their Jewishness and to intermarry, compromises that most Jews—even the wealthiest and most prominent—were unwilling to make.[32]

For the acculturated Jews of Baltimore who were confronting this confusing and contradictory situation regarding their status in the larger non-Jewish world, the great wave of Jewish immigration from Eastern Europe that began during the late

Isidor Rayner, the scion of a wealthy German Jewish family, served in the Maryland legislature, as the state's attorney general, and from 1905 until his death, as a US senator from Maryland. *Courtesy of the Library of Congress.*

nineteenth century could not have come at a worse time. Already struggling to understand why they were not receiving the full embrace of Baltimore's social elites, they feared that the influx of poor, foreign Jews would cast negative attention on the Jewish community and undermine even further their ongoing drive for status and recognition. Whatever sense of security the acculturated, uptown Jews of Baltimore drew from praise they received for their business and civic contributions, they worried as Eastern European Jews became a frequent topic of discussion among Baltimore's white, mostly Protestant opinion makers.

By the early 1890s, Eastern European Jewish immigrants were sometimes linked in the local press and in government reports to social ills, such as the spread of slum conditions, unhygienic sweatshops, and labor unrest.[33] Leaders of craft unions worried that an influx of poor Jewish laborers would introduce unfair competition and degrade working conditions. Other observers described in mournful terms the physical and social transformation of East Baltimore, where most of the immigrants settled. The *Sun* noted the great change on Lombard Street, where the former home of Charles Carroll of Carrollton, a signer of the Declaration of Independence, now housed a Russian Jewish synagogue. The same paper dubbed the Shot Tower, a city landmark on East Fayette Street, "Baltimore's Tower of Babel"

Sweatshops operated by immigrant Jews were labeled a major problem by social reformers, journalists, and government officials. The strict enforcement of a 1902 inspection law led to the disappearance of many such enterprises by 1910. *From* Thirteenth Annual Report of the Bureau of Statistics and Information of Maryland *(1904). Collection of the Maryland State Archives.*

because of the polyglot "jargon"—meaning Yiddish—increasingly spoken in its environs.[34]

Some public figures, reflecting Baltimore's social conservatism and its role as an ecclesiastical center for both Catholics and Protestants, perceived Jewish immigrants as a threat to the city's moral order. The police and members of the judiciary, for example, saw public meetings of Jewish socialists as an affront to local religious values, and they targeted organizers for arrest and prosecution.[35] Eastern European Jews were also frequently charged as violators of the Sunday laws, and when Jewish organizations argued for loosening the restrictions on work and leisure on the Christian Sabbath, clergymen like the Protestant Episcopal bishop William Paret pushed back by issuing a call to preserve the Christian nature of American society.[36] Other Protestant denominations established missions to convert the newcomers.[37]

But if immigrant Jews were occasionally cast as contributors to urban decay, promoters of radicalism, and antagonists to Christianity, this was hardly the overriding view among the white gentiles who guided public discourse. Alongside these negative images were many positive assessments of the new wave of Jewish arrivals, and on the whole Baltimore's opinion makers seem to have perceived the influx of Eastern European Jews—and of non-Jewish Southern and Eastern European immigrants—as presenting the city with more advantages than disadvantages. Leading Baltimoreans recognized that their burgeoning economy needed workers. Though

newspaper editors sometimes advocated restricting the entry of anarchists and socialists, suspected disease carriers, and those unable to read or write in their native
languages, they consistently described the arrival of "intelligent and industrious immigrants" as a crucial factor enabling the city's growth as a manufacturing center.[38]
This recognition of the need for immigrant labor helped prevent a resurgence of
the nativism that had gripped Baltimore and shaped its political culture during the
period of Know-Nothing rule that preceded the Civil War. Although ethnic and
national hatreds had not vanished from local politics, the major parties were now
more likely to cater to the interests of immigrants in order to cultivate the loyalty of
this rapidly growing constituency.[39]

Baltimore's leading spokesmen not only welcomed Eastern European Jews as
part of a broader immigrant workforce, but also singled them out as a particularly
desirable group. An 1889 report on "Russo-Polish Hebrews" in the city, for example,
described them as an "enterprising, thrifty people" who displayed a love of learning,
a strong devotion to their religion, and "moderation in everything, including true
temperance in drinking." Far from suggesting that Jews detracted from the Christian character of local society, the article described how, when forced by economic
necessity to work on Sundays, the immigrants did so without "wanton ostentation"
and with "as little disturbance of the general quiet . . . as possible."[40]

Such glowing assessments continued to surface even after the number of Jewish
arrivals from Eastern Europe peaked during the early twentieth century. In 1911, a
writer for the *Sun* pointed to Jewish immigrants as model citizens, arguing that they
constituted 75 percent of those naturalized annually by local courts and that their
superior knowledge of the Constitution stood in sharp contrast to the neglect of the
"basic principles of the government" among the Irish.[41] And if the image of Eastern
European Jews often suffered from their association with sweatshops and slum conditions, social reformers and journalists typically credited these problems not to the
character traits of the immigrants but to the inadequacy of city government and the
corruption of machine politics. Ultimately, the negative impact that descriptions of
poverty-stricken Jewish immigrants had on the public's perception was substantially
offset by frequent accounts of them in the press and in public discourse as sober,
patriotic, charitable, industrious, and good material for the American melting pot.[42]

Undoubtedly, the city's culture of race played a significant role in bolstering this
positive assessment of Eastern European Jewish arrivals. Because white civic leaders, journalists, and politicians focused so intently on the black-white divide and
saw African Americans as the group that most threatened the stability and success
of local society, they were less animated than their counterparts in northern industrial cities by concerns about immigrants. In fact, commentators often stressed the
importance of sustaining European immigration to the city in order to counteract
what they saw as the harmful impact of "undesirable Negroes" streaming in from
rural areas.[43]

The black-white divide, however, does not explain why Jews often received warmer

----

praise than other European immigrant groups did. In part, this can be credited to a reverence frequently articulated by spokesmen of the Protestant majority for Judaism as part of the Western religious heritage. Public perceptions of Jewish immigrants were also influenced by the newcomers' social and economic profile: their unusual concentration in skilled work and commerce, their high literacy rates, and their disproportionate role in the city's largest industry. These factors allowed Eastern European Jews to attain economic mobility, take advantage of educational opportunities, and imbibe the culture and habits of the dominant society more quickly than many other immigrant groups could.[44]

No less important in promoting a positive image of Eastern European Jews was the popular perception of the immigrants as refugees from violent pogroms, whose life experiences vividly illustrated the contrast between Russian tyranny and the blessings of American liberty. The power of this narrative was on display in 1903, when Baltimoreans of different religious backgrounds organized one of the largest protest demonstrations held in the United States following the Kishinev pogrom. As featured speakers, the mayor and a former governor set the tone by intertwining denunciations of Jewish oppression and praise for Jewish character traits with patriotic appeals. As an adjunct to the demonstration, sermons reproving the Kishinev "horror" were delivered in several Protestant congregations, including the Immanuel Baptist Church, whose pastor, Rev. Madison Peters, was so stirred by the persecution of Russian Jews that he became a student of Jewish history and went on to lecture and write widely about Jewish contributions to civilization.[45]

Such outspokenness came not only from Protestant clergy but also from Catholic eminences. James Cardinal Gibbons, who forged close ties to the Jewish community during his long tenure as Baltimore's archbishop, had condemned anti-Jewish brutality in Russia as early as 1890, arguing that Christians owed much to the originators of the Old Testament and the kinsmen of Jesus. Though he could not attend the Kishinev protest meeting, he sent a written statement describing the pogrom as a "blot upon civilization."[46] The city's newspapers—the *Sun*, the *American*, the *News*, and the *Herald*—also took an active part in denouncing the Kishinev massacre and decrying the barbarity of tsarist oppression. Despite the growing social cleavage between acculturated Jews and prominent German Americans, the city's leading German organ, *Der Deutsche Correspondent*, remained a strong opponent of antisemitism throughout the pre–World War I period.[47]

The fact that Baltimore's most influential figures articulated, on balance, a positive view of Eastern European Jews should not be misconstrued as evidence of a culture of philosemitism. Though often contested or discredited, negative opinions about the new arrivals remained a salient feature of the city's public discourse throughout the period of mass immigration. More important, as genuine as many opinion makers may have been in lauding Jewish civic and economic contributions, they certainly did not see Jewish immigrants as potential social peers. In many cases the very same individuals who limited the access of acculturated "German" Jews to the city's fashionable clubs, neighborhoods, and places of recreation, these leaders undoubtedly saw the Eastern Europeans as even more unfit for entrance into polite society. If these reservations rarely registered in their public discussions of the immigrants, it was only because they took the social distance between themselves and the newcomers for granted. Indeed, the hyperbole to which public figures sometimes resorted in praising the character of Eastern European Jews was only made possible by the fact that the immigrants represented less of a threat to their social dominance than did the wealthier and more acculturated Central Europeans.

If the large social gulf between white elites and immigrant Jews created an opening for positive opinions, it follows that less-privileged Baltimoreans, who often saw the immigrants as social and economic rivals, were more likely to harbor hostile attitudes. Despite the efforts of prominent ethnic leaders like the Irish American cardinal Gibbons and the editors of *Der Deutsche Correspondent* to oppose anti-Jewish prejudice, their working-class constituents, many of them Catholic immigrants, often expressed antisemitic sentiments bred from anger over their own marginal position in local society and their resentment of Jewish economic success. Drawing on traditional ethnic and religious hatreds, which were refracted through the lens of contemporary struggles with urban life, these groups made Jews the scapegoats for a host of modern problems. Sometimes their frustrations were vented in publications like the German Catholic *Volkszeitung* or the official diocesan paper, the *Catholic Mirror*, which reflected the viewpoint of its largely Irish readership. They also boiled over onto the streets of East Baltimore, where immigrant Jews and their children occasionally encountered physical violence at the hands of Irish, Polish, and German toughs.[48]

The views of the African American community were a bit more complex, because blacks sometimes identified Jews as kindred sufferers of oppression or as role models for economic development. Still, compared with the discourse of middle-class whites, articles and editorials in the *Afro-American* were more likely to portray Jews as economic competitors and to express anger at how they exercised white privilege, edged African Americans out of business opportunities, and adopted the racist outlook of the majority culture.[49]

Whether embracing, condescending, or downright hostile, the sentiments of Baltimore's non-Jewish population affected the city's two Jewish communities— the uptown "German" Jews and the downtown Eastern European immigrants— differently. The ambition of acculturated Jews to achieve social acceptance in gentile society made them highly sensitive to any public discussion that marked Jews as different or linked them to social ills, even though such discourse focused disproportionately on the new arrivals and rarely confused the immigrants with their more Americanized counterparts. Condemnations that lumped Jews together as a single group came mostly from aggrieved working-class Catholics and African Americans, who had little power to negatively affect Jews' standing. In their constant anxiety over the Jewish image, uptown Jews often failed to appreciate just how positively their immigrant counterparts were viewed by white gentile opinion makers. Ironically, it was the uptown Jews' own success and mobility, not the poverty and foreignness of the immigrants, that threatened the dominance of the gentile establishment seriously enough to activate discriminatory practices. In short, the immigrants were less of a real liability than they were a foil for acculturated Jews as they experienced the pain and rejection of their exclusion from non-Jewish society.

The strong sense of insecurity felt by Baltimore's uptown Jews during this period had two principal outcomes. The first was an intensified effort to assert their social status on several fronts. Resigned to their exclusion from the social circles of prominent white gentiles, they determined to build a parallel elite culture, complete with its own fashionable neighborhood and outlets for leisure. Even as white gentiles fled the increased movement of wealthy Jews into Eutaw Place, the district's Jewish denizens strove to enhance its air of respectability. In addition to the imposing residences that multiplied during the 1890s and early 1900s, they built two grand clubhouses—the Phoenix Club on Eutaw Place and the Clover Club on Madison Avenue—that replaced the now-defunct Concordia Association and rivaled non-Jewish clubs in opulence.[50] To pursue countrified pastimes such as swimming, tennis, and golf, which took place at restricted gentile country clubs outside the city, they founded the Suburban Club, which opened its $75,000 facility on Park Heights Avenue in 1901.[51]

The push among acculturated Jews to mark their social prestige also included a thorough remaking of their synagogues. There, the assertions of status were apparent not only in the building of lavish new uptown edifices, but also in the adoption of further ritual reforms, which were often designed to reduce the foreignness of Jewish practice and manifest greater cultural kinship with non-Jewish society. In 1891, Baltimore Hebrew Congregation opened its Madison Avenue Temple, a Byzantine granite and sandstone structure with a large dome and two imposing towers, which, according to press reports, evinced an air of "dignity and repose, the massive proportions suggesting grandeur in simplicity." It welcomed a new rabbi, Adolph Guttmacher, who shortened the service, introduced more English prayers, discontinued the wearing of head coverings and prayer shawls by men, and brought the congregation into formal affiliation with the Reform movement. The opening of Oheb Shalom's magnificent Eutaw Place Temple in 1892 coincided with the forced retirement of the moderate reformer Rabbi Benjamin Szold, who was replaced by the young "English-speaking" (though German-born) Rabbi William Rosenau. According to one description, Rosenau "bleached away the traditional flavor of services" at Oheb Shalom not only by replacing Hebrew prayers with English translations, but also by reducing congregational participation in favor of "more performance by rabbi and cantor." In 1906, Rosenau influenced his flock to replace Szold's *Abodath Israel* with the more radical *Union Prayer Book*.[52] Around the time that Har Sinai built its Bolton Street Temple in 1894, its rabbi, Tobias Schanfarber, approved the holding of religious services on Sundays,

The Eutaw Place neighborhood, c. 1910. The dome of Oheb Shalom, built in 1892, is visible to the right of the fountain. *Jewish Museum of Maryland.*

The Suburban Club on Park Heights Avenue, eight miles from Baltimore. *From Isidor Blum,* The Jews of Baltimore: An Historical Summary of Their Progress and Status *(Baltimore: Historical Review Publishing Company, 1910).*

making it the congregation that most significantly reshaped its ritual to mirror Christian practice.[53]

While the congregations led by Guttmacher, Rosenau, and Schanfarber pushed ritual innovation to new heights, the path of acculturation taken by members of Chizuk Amuno and Shearith Israel demonstrates that in Baltimore, Jews hoping to conform to the cultural codes of non-Jewish society did not see Reform Judaism as their only option. Indeed, to a greater extent than in other Jewish centers of the period, Orthodoxy remained a feasible option for many of Baltimore's acculturated Jews, with no less than one-quarter of this group continuing to identify as Orthodox at the turn of the twentieth century. Even though Chizuk Amuno joined the United Synagogue—the national umbrella organization for the nascent Conservative movement—in 1913, it continued for decades to describe itself as Orthodox, a practice revealing how indistinct the line remained between Orthodox and Conservative Judaism during this period.[54]

The continued viability of Orthodoxy, even among Jews who felt strong pressure to conform to the manners and mores of the larger society, was facilitated by the traditional tone of Baltimore's culture, with its reverence for religious authority and for practices, such as Sabbath observance, that cut across religious communities. As the seat of a Catholic archdiocese and a major center for many Protestant denominations, the city provided a setting that allowed at least some Jews to believe that strict adherence to their religious customs did not place them out of step with the values of their non-Jewish neighbors. Why some acculturated Jews came to this conclusion while others did not can only be explained by the variety that characterizes any group's perception of and response to societal pressures. What is clear is that Orthodox Jews of Central European origin were no less concerned than their Reform counterparts with emphasizing their class status and their credentials as Americans. Chizuk Amuno had established itself decades earlier as a leader in the movement toward Americanization with its refined, American-born rabbi, Henry W. Schneeberger. In 1892, Shearith Israel made a similar statement by installing Schepsel Shaffer, a Russian-born, German-educated rabbi who held a PhD from the University of Berlin and who, like Schneeberger, could ably lecture in English.[55] Moreover, between 1895 and 1903, both Orthodox congregations built impressive uptown synagogues that showcased the wealth and prominence of their members and asserted their civic belonging.[56]

The second result of the insecurity of the established Jewish community during this period was its complex, often tortured relationship with the Eastern European Jewish immigrants. The anxiety with which uptown Jews approached the newcomers was most palpable in the first years of the immigrant influx, when they urged aid societies in New York to cease sending refugees to Baltimore and debated whether to use communal funds to send needy immigrants back to Russia rather than help them settle in the city. They also financed two agricultural colonies— one in Virginia and one in southern Maryland—where they hoped immigrants

The 1903 design of Shearith Israel's McCulloh Street synagogue reflected its members' embrace of American cultural and aesthetic standards. *From Isidor Blum,* The Jews of Baltimore: An Historical Summary of Their Progress and Status *(Baltimore: Historical Review Publishing Company, 1910).*

could engage in productive work at a comfortable distance from Baltimore.[57] Such attempts at curtailing immigration into the city diminished by the mid-1880s, however, as it became clear that the stream of new arrivals was too powerful to stop. As reality set in, acculturated Jews decided that to protect their own image, they needed to shift their energies toward seizing control of the immigrants' adjustment process and Americanizing them as quickly as possible. Although this goal was neither based on an accurate reading of public opinion nor attainable given the strength and independence of the immigrant population, it would nonetheless shape the relationship between the two groups for decades to come.

Meanwhile, the immigrants themselves worried little about their public image. Though they bore the brunt of the hostility expressed by rival ethnic groups and had the most to lose from the negative judgments of law enforcement officials, social reformers, and other critics, the large size and social isolation of the immigrant population made the newcomers less sensitive to the opinions of others. Acceptance by social elites was far from their minds, and because they typically viewed their non-Jewish fellow immigrants as occupying a lower social and economic plane than themselves, they felt no need to impress them. Of course, immigrants were anxious to claim their status as Americans, and concern with their image would grow— especially among the young—as they acculturated. But for most, the immediate goal was to overcome the serious material and economic challenges they faced and to build the basic support networks that would allow them to pursue their dreams of America.

Holding America to Account

In 1913, a labor action among garment workers at the L. Greif and Brother factory at German and Eutaw streets produced an unlikely hero in Lena Schlossberg. Along with 300 of her comrades, Schlossberg walked off the job to protest Greif's practice of taking on scab work for New York clothing firms whose workers were on strike. Workers at Greif, organized locally by the United Garment Workers of America (UGWA), had gone on strike many times before, but this demonstration stood out as different. It was more militant and determined than previous actions and was directed not by the skilled workers who controlled the union, but by Jewish immigrant women from East Baltimore, whose commandeering of the protest reflected their frustration with the UGWA's chronic inability to win concessions for the rank and file. As their demands broadened to include a union shop, increased wages, and a nine-hour workday, the strikers gained the support of hundreds of garment workers from other Baltimore firms, who left their posts to join the picket line. Due to Schlossberg's rousing speaking ability and the vitriol she so effectively hurled at the police, she soon was unanimously recognized as the leader of the strikers. A Baltimore *Sun* reporter captured the spirit of this "Joan of Arc . . . of the garment workers" as he described her shaking a fist at her former supervisor, yelling: "We fight to the last blood; labor always wins!"[58]

Schlossberg and her fellow workers failed to win agreement to their demands from Greif in 1913. Though their actions laid the groundwork for future gains, for the time being they continued to endure low pay, long hours, and poor conditions, not to mention insulting treatment by their employers and the disregard of union leaders who were supposed to represent them. Like many of their fellow Jewish immigrants, they had dreamed in their homelands of a *goldene medine* (golden land) across the ocean, only to find an America that violently clashed with their expectations. Schlossberg's story underscores the obstacles faced by Jewish immigrants, as well as the resolve they displayed in confronting their difficulties.

The challenges that Eastern European Jewish immigrants encountered resulted from the dramatic changes wrought by industrial capitalism on the economic, social, and physical landscape of urban America in the decades after the Civil War. In Baltimore, these changes included the industrialization of downtown and the bifurcation of the city's neighborhoods along racial, ethnic, and class lines, with immigrants and African Americans pouring into the areas closest to the central manufacturing district, and middle- and upper-class white residents fleeing to less developed areas more distant from the burgeoning center.[59]

Eastern European Jewish immigrants gravitated to the East Baltimore neighborhood adjacent to downtown, just across the Jones Falls. Although there had been a Central European Jewish presence in this area since the 1840s, and many of the "German" Jewish congregations had built synagogues there, the district became much more of a Jewish enclave with the arrival of the newer immigrants who, according to an 1891 report, quickly made the area from Front Street to Broadway and from Pratt Street to several squares beyond Baltimore Street their "colony."[60] This change reflected not only the much larger size of the Eastern European wave, but also the immigrants' occupational profile. Because most were laborers rather than retail merchants, they did not need to spread out around the city to reach a customer base, as the Central European Jews had in the pre–Civil War era. Instead, they could enjoy the advantages of living together with those who shared their language, culture, and religious customs.

There were some exceptions: immigrant Jews who did work in the retail sector developed business and residential clusters in other parts of the city, such as in the African American district along Pennsylvania Avenue or in South Baltimore, where Lithuanian Jews gathered in the area around Hanover, Hill, and Charles streets. A small group of Jewish clothing workers settled southwest of downtown, close to the city's large clothing factories, where they founded their own synagogue, the Moses Montefiore Hebrew Congregation.[61] But despite the existence of these satellite communities, East Baltimore remained the undisputed residential and cultural center of the city's Jewish immigrants.

The identification of East Baltimore as an Eastern European Jewish enclave was

An enclosed court in the "tenement district" of East Baltimore, c. 1905.
Courtesy of the Wisconsin Historical Society, WHi-26710.

furthered by the departure of the older residents—native-born Americans, Irish and German immigrants, and Central European Jews—who had settled there in the mid-nineteenth century. By 1895, most Central European Jews had relocated to the new Eutaw Place hub; the few who remained were generally poor, aged, or widowed. As the population shifted, Eastern European Jews placed their distinctive stamp on the district, opening numerous businesses catering to the tastes and needs of their fellow immigrants and dotting the landscape with their religious, educational, and charitable institutions. As Ida Porges recalled, by the first decade of the twentieth century, "one could walk through blocks and blocks of the Jewish section and not see one store with other than Yiddish or Hebrew signs, or one street without a synagogue or . . . Hebrew school."[62] Yet immigrant Jews were not totally isolated in East Baltimore, since many Irish Americans had remained in the section east of the Jewish settlement, while Polish, Lithuanian, and Italian immigrants lived just to the south and southeast. Meanwhile, African Americans inhabited alleys and small courts interspersed among the immigrant neighborhoods.[63]

As immigrant Jews poured into East Baltimore, poverty and overcrowding led to a visible deterioration of the physical environment. North Exeter, a major Jewish residential street, was described as "a crowded place of tenement houses, saloons, filthy shops, foul odors, [and] hideous noises."[64] While Baltimore had no hulking tenement structures like those of New York's Lower East Side, it did have many two- and three-story dwellings where three or more families shared a total of six to eight rooms. A 1907 investigation revealed that East Baltimore residents lacked not only privacy, but also indoor plumbing and space for recreation. Crowded conditions forced children to gather on their front stoops and play in alleys and courts where they were subjected to the hazards of overflowing privies. Poor sanitary conditions were compounded by the fact that the few open yards were used for the kosher slaughtering of chickens. On a single block of Albemarle Street, two houses had a "fence, yard, and house wall all coated with layers of coagulated blood" with "flies and feathers everywhere." In the summer heat, the report noted, "the smell from such yards is sickening."[65]

Unregulated workshops and small factories, where many immigrants found their first jobs, posed an even greater menace to public health and safety. Abe Gellman worked with 200 men in a crowded room where tobacco was stripped for the making of cigars and cigarettes. The process created great quantities of dust, which covered everything and caused severe respiratory ailments. Gellman recalled that he would reach home at the end of each day "with the tobacco dust sticking to me; my face was the color of a cigar and my mouth and throat [were] full of tobacco."[66]

Most Jewish laborers found work in one of the East Baltimore sweatshops that constituted a major sector of the city's clothing industry. In 1894, a government survey identified more than 200 sweatshops in the district bounded by Lexington Street, Eastern Avenue, Caroline Street, and the Jones Falls. These shops owed their existence to the notorious contracting system, which allowed large manufac-

Interior of the Henry Sonneborn and Company clothing factory, 1902. Jewish immigrant
women were a substantial part of the workforce in Baltimore's garment industry.
Courtesy of the Maryland Historical Society, Z9.703.PP8.

turers to cut costs by engaging contractors to produce piecework for them at their
own expense. Though a few East Baltimore sweatshops were owned by Lithuanian
or Bohemian non-Jews, most contractors were Eastern European Jews who had
been in the country several years and wished to better themselves economically.
To maximize their profits, they hired fellow Jewish immigrants who were willing
to accept low wages and endure poor conditions in exchange for the ability to work
in a Yiddish-speaking environment and, in many cases, to observe the Sabbath
and Jewish festivals.[67] According to the 1894 report, most shops contained "a large
number of persons of both sexes . . . crowded into second story and attic rooms,
surrounded on all sides by piles of clippings from the garments upon which they
are engaged." In addition to the lack of light and ventilation, the mingling of living
space and work space created a particularly hazardous and unsanitary environment. At Jacob Novick's pants-making shop on North High Street, for example,
trash and stagnant water filled the alley near the entrance, and working girls toiled
in a crowded bedroom, where they also slept at night. Novick's five young children
were kept home from school so they could help the family in "the almost hopeless
task of making a living."[68]

Samuel and Albertina Harrison on the steps of their grocery at 1216 McElderry Street, c. 1890. *Jewish Museum of Maryland.*

Members of the Hendler and Sachs families pose outside Isaac Hendler's dairy,
3738 Bank Street, c. 1890s. In 1905 Isaac's son L. Manuel Hendler (*on white horse*) founded the
Hendler Creamery Company, which became Baltimore's largest manufacturer of ice cream.
Jewish Museum of Maryland.

Even the most skilled workers put in fourteen to sixteen hours per day under
these egregious conditions, and most employees barely made a living wage. The
contractors did not fare much better. With sewing machines bought on the installment plan and the risk of default constantly looming, explained the investigators, "it
is only by constant self-denial and hard labor that [they] can even live."[69] After the
turn of the twentieth century, garment workers were increasingly able to escape the
sweatshops and find work in one of the "inside shops" managed directly by the manufacturers, such as Henry Sonneborn and Company, L. Greif and Brother, Strouse
and Brothers, and Schloss Brothers. Though cleaner and safer than the sweatshops,
the inside shops were not without their own hazards, and the problems of low wages,
long hours, and poor job security persisted.[70]

Overall, however, Eastern European Jews in Baltimore, as in other cities in the
United States, were usually better able than other immigrant groups to overcome
economic hardship. Unlike Slavic or Italian newcomers who had been peasants and
farmers in Europe, many Jews arrived in America with experience as urban dwellers
and with skills that suited them well for trade and industrial life. Thus, they entered
the occupational pool at a higher level than did most new arrivals, and they were

EPHRAIM MACHT

Real Estate and Banking

MACHT BUILDING, BALTIMORE, MD.

Ephraim Macht became one of Baltimore's wealthiest real estate moguls.
From Isidor Blum, The Jews of Baltimore: An Historical Summary of Their Progress and Status
(Baltimore: Historical Review Publishing Company, 1910).

able to use their skills to rise more quickly on the social and economic ladder. In addition to those working in the garment and tobacco industries, Baltimore's Jewish immigrants included painters, carpenters, cabinetmakers, paperhangers, watchmakers, jewelers, and plumbers. There was also a small but influential group that became members of the professional class, often working multiple jobs and studying at night in order to receive a medical or law degree.[71]

More common than craftspeople or professionals were those who became small business owners. With its expanding economy and growing population, Baltimore provided a receptive environment for the opening of groceries, saloons, bakeries, butcher shops, dairies, junk and scrap yards, and even movie theaters. While many business owners struggled, some made great strides. Among other success stories, Baltimore's foremost producers of umbrellas (Simon and Harry Ades), artificial flowers (Charles Ledvinka), and ice cream (L. Manuel Hendler) and one of the city's largest suppliers of coal, wood, and ice (Charles Hoffberger) all started as humble immigrant entrepreneurs.[72]

The largest number of Jewish entrepreneurs remained in clothing-related businesses. Some struggling contractors in crowded tenement houses went on to open ladies' tailoring shops in fashionable districts. Others became significant manufacturers of pants, shirts, neckties, cloaks, shoes, and suspenders. Solomon Ginsberg began in the men's clothing business in 1891, and by 1910 his firm was described as "one of the largest wholesale clothing manufacturing establishments in Baltimore." While large firms owned by Central European Jews continued to control the production of men's clothing, which made up the largest part of the Baltimore market, by the early twentieth century Eastern European Jews were the city's leading manufacturers of women's suits and coats.[73]

The most successful immigrant businessmen, like the Central Europeans before them, played a significant role in Baltimore's development. Ephraim Macht came to the city from his native Kovno in 1887. Beginning as a humble laborer, he amassed sufficient capital to found a real estate and banking business, which thrived due to the availability of cheap property following the Baltimore fire of 1904. By 1911, Macht was one of a few major builders vying to dominate the construction and sale of Baltimore row houses. His homebuilding activities would help shape the growth of the city over the next several decades.[74]

Fellow Lithuanian Jacob Epstein had a substantial impact on Baltimore's role as the commercial gateway to the South. Epstein arrived in the city as a teenager in 1879 and peddled in rural Maryland and Pennsylvania for two years. Returning to Baltimore in 1881 to open a housewares and general merchandise business, he built a thriving wholesale firm by sending fellow Jewish immigrants to peddle his goods throughout the southern states. Expanding beyond this ethnic network to become a major supplier of southern retailers, by 1904 his Baltimore Bargain House was shipping more than $1 million of goods per month and employed almost 1,000 workers. In 1910 the press reported the firm's payroll to be larger than that of any other local business except the B&O Railroad and described Epstein's purchase of an entire city block for a coming expansion as "the largest real estate transaction in the mercantile history of Baltimore." His activities brought Epstein credit as the leading promoter of Baltimore's southern trade. "You spread the fame of Baltimore and Maryland throughout the nation, particularly the South," noted Maryland governor Austin Lane Crothers in one tribute. "Whenever there was a movement by business men of the state to do something to promote its markets or its products, we could always be sure that you, Mr. Epstein, were furnishing the 'horsepower' to make the machinery run."[75]

As Epstein's story shows, previous experience as skilled workers and urban dwellers made up only part of the recipe for Jewish mobility. Also crucial was Jews' history as a persecuted minority and their role as middlemen in the European economy, which made them adept at forging ethnic networks and evolving strategies for mutual aid, skills that many other immigrants had to learn for the first time after arriving in America. Jewish peddlers and small merchants knew they could turn to other Jews for assistance when trying to gain a foothold in the business world or when they needed merchandise or credit. Eastern European Jews quickly developed

Hebrew Friendly Inn, 111 North Aisquith Street.
From Isidor Blum, The Jews of Baltimore: An Historical Summary of Their Progress
and Status *(Baltimore: Historical Review Publishing Company, 1910).*

their own web of mutual aid societies, loan societies, and charitable organizations
that rivaled the organizational structure of the established Jewish community.

Landsmanshaften (hometown societies) like the Zager Protective Association,
Posvohler Friendly Society, and Bobroisker Beneficial Circle represented Jews from
a host of different Eastern European locales. Members often housed newly arrived
countrymen, helped them find employment, and continued to provide various
forms of assistance as they became established.[76] Many Baltimore landsmanshaften
also functioned as building and loan associations, which paved the way for their
immigrant members to become homeowners or landlords.[77] Because not every new
arrival had a network of *landslayt* on which they could rely, many immigrants to
Baltimore joined the local branches of national Jewish fraternal organizations, like
Independent Order B'rith Abraham and Independent Order Free Sons of Judah.
These societies paid death benefits that were often crucial in helping members' families take care of final expenses.[78]

Because lodges often experienced financial troubles and tended to provide a nar-

The founders of the Hebrew Free Loan Association, including Jacob Epstein
(*center, seated at table*), 1898. *Jewish Museum of Maryland.*

row range of benefits, immigrants also organized local mutual aid societies to provide a wider safety net for their communities. The earliest organization of this type in
Baltimore was the Hebrew Young Men's Sick Relief Association, founded in a South
Baltimore cap-making shop in 1888. The association not only paid death benefits,
but also provided sick benefits, free use of a medical doctor, access to cemetery plots,
and the services of a *khevre kadisha* (burial society) when a death occurred.[79] In the
1890s and early 1900s the number of mutual aid and charitable associations among
the immigrants rose dramatically. In 1890 the Hebrew Friendly Inn was established
for recent arrivals and wayfarers (usually peddlers traveling through Baltimore) who
needed temporary lodging and meals. In 1898, some of the most successful among
the immigrants launched the Hebrew Free Loan Association to assist "the deserving
needy by loaning money upon reasonable security and without interest."[80] Three
years later, to address the rising problem of families who were temporarily unable to
care for their children because of sickness or financial distress, the immigrant community established the Hebrew Children's Sheltering and Protective Association,
which housed children in a small facility on South High Street.[81]

While these lodges, mutual aid societies, and charitable associations were led by
men, the women of the Jewish immigrant community established a parallel set of
organizations. Some were ladies' auxiliaries, which supported institutions like the
Hebrew Friendly Inn and the Hebrew Children's Sheltering and Protective Association by holding fairs, dances, and other fundraising events.[82] Other women's organizations were based on the model of old-country *hevrot*, which worked informally
to distribute funds to individual families to meet their daily needs. These included

the Beth Rachel Society, founded in 1892, whose members each paid five cents per week for the purpose of sick relief, as well as the Maskil El Dol (Sympathizers of the Poor) Society and the Ladies Protective Relief Association, both incorporated in 1902.[83] A few women's organizations, however, branched out in new directions to meet the specific challenges of immigrant life. In 1900, the large number of single immigrant women struggling to make a living led six of them to found the Young Ladies Benevolent Society to care for "girls who are handicapped physically, morally, or financially." Also around the turn of the century, another group established the Hebrew Ladies Consumptive Aid Society to assist those with tuberculosis, a common occupational hazard affecting garment workers.[84]

The founding of mutual aid and charitable societies came naturally to the immigrants because they had often participated in similar groups in Eastern Europe. Labor unions, with their focus on strikes and protest, were a less familiar form of association, but their leaders nonetheless forged them into powerful tools for challenging the garment industry's poor working conditions and low wages by utilizing the same strategies of self-help and ethnic networking that animated the more traditional community organizations. As early as 1889, the employees of Ulman and Company began to contribute monthly dues of five cents to finance an organization that allowed them to carry out a successful strike for higher pay.[85] The union lasted only a few months, but in the years that followed, Baltimore's Jewish garment workers began to build a more durable labor movement of independent Yiddish-speaking unions that agitated for better pay and improved working conditions in the industry. The most influential of these was the Baltimore Cloakmakers' Union, which organized in 1890 and two years later joined the UGWA, an affiliate of the American Federation of Labor.[86]

The UGWA, still headed by the skilled German and Irish American workers who had dominated the industry before the late nineteenth century, did not always champion the interests of the Jewish immigrants, who comprised a majority of shop-floor employees by the 1890s. Nevertheless, Eastern European Jews maintained the most active locals in the union, reflecting both their well-honed skills at ethnic networking and their commitment to fighting injustice. Jewish clothing workers were exceptionally motivated to persevere in the battle for improved labor conditions because, with rare exceptions, returning to their European homes was not an option, as it was for members of other immigrant groups.[87] The smaller factions of non-Jewish Lithuanians, Bohemians, and Italians in the industry had their radical elements, and their members often participated alongside Jews in labor actions, but Jewish unionists played the largest role in combating the unfair practices of Baltimore's garment manufacturers. Jews took the lead, for example, in convincing workers of various backgrounds to leave the UGWA and seek the more determined leadership of the Jewish-controlled International Ladies' Garment Workers' Union (ILGWU) and the Amalgamated Clothing Workers of America (ACWA). Between 1913 and 1918, these unions helped transform the Baltimore garment industry, organizing strikes in both

Shopping on East Lombard Street. *Ross J. Kelbaugh Collection, Jewish Museum of Maryland.*

the men's and women's branches of the trade that forced most of the major manufacturers to sign arbitration agreements and become union shops.[88]

Whether Jewish immigrants were business owners or garment workers, their greater economic mobility allowed them to improve their standard of living more quickly than other immigrants and to more vigorously embrace the central symbols of American freedom and opportunity. Although the need to work and help support their families often remained an obstacle, Jewish youths attended public schools at a higher rate than the children of any other immigrant group in the city.[89] Immigrant Jews also stood out as particularly active participants in America's commercial culture. Whatever economic struggles they experienced, their access to the wide array of goods in the commercial district of East Baltimore, particularly along East Lombard Street, stood in sharp contrast to the conditions of scarcity they had experienced in their homelands. Indeed, the ready availability of foodstuffs, such as the salamis and smoked fish purveyed by a growing number of delicatessens, marked their new home as a place of relative abundance.[90] Meanwhile, the proliferation of movie houses, dance halls, and other places of commercial amusement, both along the thoroughfares of East Baltimore and in the city at large, helped feed a sense of possibility and excitement about America among Jewish immigrants young and old.[91] Although initially shocked by the gap between their expectations of the *goldene medine* and the real world they found upon arrival, Eastern European Jewish immigrants were eventually able to overcome material setbacks and affirm their faith in the United States as a land of promise.

Between Two Worlds

As Jewish immigrants gained a foothold in their new homes, they discovered that material deficiencies were not the only challenging aspect of their adaptation to American life. They also struggled with a daunting cultural dilemma: how to square the values and priorities of their new surroundings with their most deeply held commitments as Jews. Like those arriving in the nation's other urban centers during the late nineteenth and early twentieth centuries, Jewish immigrants to Baltimore found a social and cultural environment at odds with the standards they had been used to in Eastern Europe. Many of the jobs available to new arrivals took time away from religious obligations and required the violation of the Sabbath. Economic privation required daughters as well as sons to go to work, and unlike the home-centered crafts and occupations that often prevailed among Jews in small-town Poland, Lithuania, and Ukraine, work in factories and sweatshops meant hours away from the security of family. Children who became wage earners soon expected to make their own decisions and to keep at least a portion of their income for their own use, often creating intergenerational conflict.

As they imbibed the culture of democracy and capitalism, Jewish immigrants increasingly pursued independence and self-fulfillment, but often struggled when these goals conflicted with the pull of obligations to family, community, and religion. The Yiddish stage actress Bessie Thomashefsky, recalling her childhood in the mid-1880s, described how her mother would give her a few pennies every Shabbos to visit Baltimore's dime museum or attend a downtown theater. Because she spent all the other days toiling as a tobacco stripper and later as a worker in a stocking factory, Saturdays were the only time the young immigrant had for leisure. "All week long I only lived and waited for Shabbos," Thomashefsky recalled, not to attend synagogue or enjoy a restful day at home, but "to run to the Masonic Temple, [where] I saw . . . *Macbeth, Hamlet, King Lear*, and many more plays."[92] Even for those who otherwise observed many of the strictures of Orthodox Judaism, Friday evenings and Saturdays became times to enjoy the city's commercial leisure outlets. In 1895, when a tragic fire at the Front Street Theatre caused the deaths of more than twenty Jewish immigrants and injured countless others, a local journalist was surprised that so many members of a presumably Orthodox community had been spending their Sabbath eve attending a Yiddish drama.[93]

The emphasis on independence and self-fulfillment also informed new attitudes toward love and marriage. Since no step was more determinative of one's future path than marriage, how could young people embrace the possibilities that America

The wedding of Mendel and Ida Glaser, 1894. *Jewish Museum of Maryland.*

had to offer if they allowed their parents to choose their life partner? The freedom to realize one's potential required that love, not duty, be the guiding force in such a decision. Baltimore courts during the late nineteenth and early twentieth centuries heard dozens of cases in which Jewish immigrants sought to escape marriages or engagements that had been forced upon them by their parents, either before or after arriving in the United States. While members of the older generation often saw such efforts as an affront to the sanctity of the Jewish family, these cases reflected the resolve of young immigrants not to sacrifice the promise of American life to the demands of traditional mores.[94]

At worst, the influence of the American environment threatened to lead immigrants—particularly youths—into drug and alcohol abuse, crime, and prostitution. Juvenile delinquency had become a concern in East Baltimore by 1907, when it was estimated that twenty-one Jewish boys were being brought before the local juvenile court each month. "Many a Jewish father has beheld with despair the corruption of an honest and obedient boy by influences felt for the first time in America," opined Louis H. Levin, the editor of the *Jewish Comment*. "There is no greater problem that we have to deal with than the development of the ghetto boy." Orthodox rabbis, municipal social workers, and leaders of the uptown Jewish community all expressed the need to combat the unwholesome influences present in the immigrant district, lobbying especially for the removal of several "disorderly houses" located near two major synagogues on Lloyd Street.[95]

Those at the helm of religious life in the immigrant community understood that they needed to defend against the secularizing forces in American society if they wished to preserve traditional values and practices. Congregational leaders, for example, created bylaws that demanded ritual observance and punished religious laxity. The constitution of B'nai Israel, the city's leading Russian congregation, excluded "anyone who violates the Sabbath" from holding office.[96] Shomrei Mishmeres, a congregation founded in 1890 by Hasidic Jews from Volhynia, was even more rigid, specifying that any member who continued to violate the Sabbath or holidays after three written warnings was to be excluded from membership.[97] Isador Terrell, who grew up attending Shomrei Mishmeres, recalled one member who suffered excommunication for opening his business on the Sabbath. Even after the offender reversed his practice, his fellow congregants continued to keep him at arm's length.[98]

Early on, advocates of Jewish observance created a free school to allow children to obtain a Jewish education regardless of their ability to pay tuition. Founded in 1889, the Baltimore Talmud Torah offered boys a curriculum of Jewish history and study of the Bible, Talmud, and Shulchan Aruch (Code of Jewish Law). The guiding force behind the school, Tanchum Silberman, had come to Baltimore as a religious functionary but later entered business and became a successful dry goods merchant. He spearheaded the raising of funds for the Talmud Torah and devoted much of his own wealth to its development. As an entrepreneur, he was more willing than other Orthodox leaders to introduce innovations addressing the needs of the younger generation. In 1899, the school began limited classes for girls, and around 1904 the language of instruction changed from Yiddish to English. Five years later, with the help of uptown philanthropists, the school moved from its modest home on North High Street to a renovated facility on East Baltimore Street. The new building featured a worship space, a lecture hall, and a library designed to provide an intellectual focus for youths who would otherwise spend "their evenings, Saturdays, and Sundays on the street corners." With fourteen classrooms capable of seating 1,000 students, the Talmud Torah also became a fully coeducational institution.[99]

While Orthodox Jews met with some success in enforcing religious observance within their congregations and promoting Jewish learning among the poor, influencing the broad masses presented a more daunting challenge. Coming from many different regions in Eastern Europe, immigrants embraced disparate sets of customs and practices, making it difficult to mobilize them around a common religious agenda. Moreover, few leaders possessed sufficient education, status, or authority to bridge these differences and unite the various factions in common action. Most of the religious leaders among the immigrants were not properly ordained rabbis; they were "reverends" who could conduct worship services, officiate at marriages, and perform or supervise kosher slaughter, but their knowledge and training were limited, and they generally wielded little influence outside their own closely knit circles.[100]

To remedy this situation, lay leaders continuously tried to attract to Baltimore eminent rabbis who could provide the leadership necessary to create a bulwark against secularization and the abandonment of tradition. In the late 1880s, two prominent congregations, Bikur Cholim and B'nai Israel, recruited noteworthy figures—the Lithuanian-born scholars Simon Isaac Finkelstein and Moses Simon Sivitz—to occupy their respective pulpits. Each rabbi stayed only a few years, however, before moving on to occupy important positions elsewhere.[101] A more stable period of Orthodox leadership began in 1891 with the arrival of Rabbi Aba Chaim Levinson. A native of Kovno, Lithuania, Levinson came to Baltimore from Rochester, New York, where he had served a leading Orthodox congregation for eight years and made a name for himself as an expert on Jewish law. In Baltimore, while he was formally hired to replace Sivitz at B'nai Israel, his broader charge was to serve as the halachic authority for a number of Estern European congregations, which agreed to accept him as the city's "chief rabbi."[102]

Levinson's presence strengthened Orthodox institutions and made Baltimore a more attractive destination for other prominent rabbis, such as Abraham N. Schwartz, a fellow Lithuanian who came to Baltimore from New London, Connecticut, in 1908 to head Shomrei Mishmeres.[103] While Levinson addressed a variety of religious concerns, his primary focus was the maintenance of strict kashrut standards, viewed by many as the key responsibility of a communal rabbi.[104] During the 1890s he arranged for special facilities to grind flour for the production of matzoh for Passover, and he created the Federation of Orthodox Congregations to oversee

Talmud Torah Hall, 1029 East Baltimore Street, soon after its opening in 1909.
After 1930 the building housed the Progressive Labor Lyceum, operated by the Workmen's Circle.
Jewish Museum of Maryland.

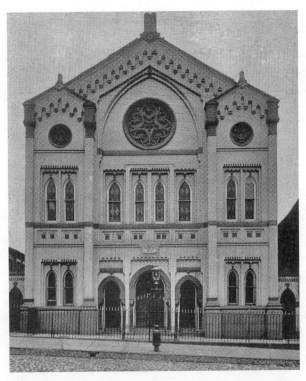

Chizuk Amuno's synagogue, built in 1876 at 27 Lloyd Street,
became the home of the "Russian shul" B'nai Israel in 1895. *From Isidor Blum,*
The Jews of Baltimore: An Historical Summary of Their Progress and Status
(Baltimore: Historical Review Publishing Company, 1910).

and standardize the work of the city's shochtim (ritual slaughterers). This proved
controversial among local kosher butchers, who had previously supervised the work
of the shochtim without undue interference from rabbinic leaders. The new regu-
lations drove up the price of kosher meat, pushing some butchers to abandon local
suppliers in favor of a source in Chicago that could meet their needs at lower cost.
In order to secure its authority, the federation issued a ruling in 1908 forbidding this
practice and requiring all butchers to sell only meat slaughtered by locally approved
shochtim.[105]

Although Levinson and the other federation leaders believed their rigidity would
help preserve the authority of Orthodox Judaism in Baltimore, their narrow focus
on kashrut reflected an inability to understand and respond to the much larger set
of social and cultural changes that were transforming and challenging the immigrant community. To the rabbis, Jewish and American values seemed to be in such
great opposition that they could not imagine the possibility of reconciling the two.
According to Ida Porges, this was the dilemma faced by her father, Max Slotovsky,
the rabbi of the Vishayer Congregation. "America was not the Golden Land for my

Nathan London in the doorway of his kosher butcher shop, 1165 East Lombard Street, c. 1910.
Jewish Museum of Maryland.

father," she recalled. As his congregation grew in material success, "all he saw was the increasing indifference to religion, and the terrible time Orthodox Jews had in adjusting to a new, and quite godless, civilization."[106]

This negative outlook was shared by many of the Orthodox rabbinic and lay leaders in the city, who ceded little ground to the advocates of acculturation in their midst. In 1904, presumably after the directors of the Baltimore Talmud Torah announced the innovation of introducing English as the language of instruction, a group of protesters founded a rival school, the Talmud Torah Ve-Emunah, for the express purpose of "teach[ing] the principles of Orthodox Judaism in Yiddish."[107] In 1917, under the leadership of Rabbi Abraham N. Schwartz, the same group launched the Yeshiva Torah Ve-Emunah (known in English as the Hebrew Parochial School), the first boys' yeshiva outside of New York to offer an all-day curriculum combining secular subjects (taught in English) and Jewish subjects (taught in Yiddish). This educational model was designed not only to strengthen religious studies beyond what part-time instruction could provide, but also to remove Jewish youths from the influence of the public schools, which Orthodox leaders saw as a chief culprit in leading young people away from Jewish tradition.[108] Although the Hebrew Parochial School provided a bulwark against change that helped Orthodoxy to survive as a significant factor in Jewish communal life, overall the Orthodox leadership's refusal to accommodate acculturation reflected the increasing distance between their outlook and that of the larger Jewish population they wished to influence.

This sense of alienation from tradition was most apparent among young Jews, whose daily experiences were most at odds with the priorities of the Orthodox world. While the Talmud Torah enjoyed a measure of success in influencing its pupils, it served only a small fraction of East Baltimore's Jewish youth. The majority, who were taught by tutors or attended private hedarim, had a less affirming experience with Hebrew education. Robert H. Brotman recalled that he and his friends were simply taught to read Hebrew by sight, repeating the words until they could remember them, but never understanding what they meant.[109] Congregations were similarly obtuse about the needs of children. On Sabbaths at Shomrei Mishmeres, for example, it became customary for the boys of the congregation, including Rabbi Schwartz's son, to gather on Lloyd Street to play softball during the reading of the Torah. One of those boys, Louis Shecter, recalled that while Schwartz was highly respected among his flock, his sermons were "uninspiring to the younger listener." The public school, rather than the synagogue, became the focus of Shecter's life. As he described it, the "charm of the fascinating American environment" drew him away from the influence of traditional Jewish values.[110]

The increasing distance of young Jews from Orthodoxy was part of a natural process of acculturation and caused them little anguish. For adults, however, the dissonance between their traditional allegiances and their growing investment in the American values of independence and individualism could be troubling. This tension was readily apparent during the struggle over kosher supervision that erupted in 1909–1910. Most of Baltimore's immigrant Jews were committed to observing the laws of kashrut, but as the price of kosher meat soared during the standoff between the Federation of Orthodox Congregations and Baltimore's Jewish butchers, consumer frustrations boiled over. At a mass meeting in the Monumental Theatre, 3,000 East Baltimore residents protested the "unwarrantable assumption of rights" by religious authorities. Jewish women took to the streets to enforce a boycott of kosher meat outlets, blocking the entrances to butcher shops and in some cases even pouring gasoline or coal oil on the purchases of those who dared to cross their picket line. When the federation refused to relent, the protesters set up their own cooperative stores where they proceeded to defy the rabbis' ban on meat sent from Chicago. In the end, the recalcitrance of the rabbis and their inability to understand the needs of average Jews diminished, rather than enhanced, their religious authority.[111]

- - - - - - - - - - - - - -

The bar mitzvah of Louis Stein, 1908. *Jewish Museum of Maryland*.

Rabbi Abraham N. Schwartz of Shomrei Mishmeres Congregation
assumed the role of "chief rabbi" for Baltimore's Orthodox Jews after the death
of Rabbi Aba Chaim Levinson in 1912. *Jewish Museum of Maryland.*

Despite its troubles, Orthodoxy retained a notable pull on Baltimore's immigrants during the pre–World War I period, one that it exercised in few other American Jewish centers. Rabbis like Levinson and Schwartz commanded respect even
among the nonreligious. In New York the chief rabbi, Jacob Joseph, who like Levinson had tried to assert control over his city's shochtim, became a sad, even marginal
figure in the years before his death in 1902. In Baltimore, Schwartz, concerned that
employees of the Sonneborn clothing factory would lose their jobs because they
refused to desecrate the Sabbath, intervened with Henry Sonneborn's rabbi at Oheb
Shalom, William Rosenau, to help ensure that the workers retained their posts. Such
involvement of a leading Orthodox figure in a labor dispute would have been unimaginable in most other cities.[112]

This deference toward Orthodox leadership was a sign of Baltimore's position as
the smallest and most socially conservative of the five major Jewish immigrant hubs
in the United States. Its size meant that Jews were both more interconnected and less

able to avoid the oversight of family, friends, and neighbors, making it difficult to partake in the anonymity of urban life as was possible in New York, Chicago, Philadelphia, and Boston. Eastern European immigrants who "made it"— even those who chose to acculturate—often retained close ties to the Orthodox institutions in which they had grown up. Moreover, immigrant religious life benefited from the significant segment of the uptown Jewish community that had remained Orthodox, a trend that further reflected Baltimore's conservative religious culture. In a city that was less hospitable to secularization than other major centers, the synagogues of East Baltimore remained vital institutions well into the twentieth century, with large attendances on Sabbaths and holidays, well-stocked study halls, and a host of auxiliary societies and *hevrot* that made them community centers as much as houses of worship.

When measured against the desire for Americanization and the exigencies of daily life, the claims Orthodoxy continued to make on Baltimore's immigrants meant that families and individuals often struggled with conflicting impulses and engaged in a host of contradictory practices. Quite common were homes devoted to the synagogue and to kashrut, where social or economic pressures caused individual family members to violate the Sabbath or holidays. Just as families divided on these issues along lines of age, they often divided on them according to gender. Since immigrant men more commonly worked outside the home, they often felt the pressures of economic survival and the pull of the wider world more profoundly. Avrum Rifman described poignantly how his pious mother, Zeesla-Baile, carried an immense burden because her husband, Chaim-Shemon, had worked in a sweatshop on the Sabbath when the couple first came to Baltimore. Years later, when they lost a twelve-year-old daughter during the flu epidemic of 1918, she was convinced that the death was a punishment for "not having restrained [her husband] from . . . Sabbath violations."[113]

Some immigrants remained haunted by their past ties to tradition years after they formally broke with religious practice. Rubin Goldstein, a paperhanger and confectionery store owner in the neighborhood around Patterson Park, came to the United States in 1905 from Odessa. Although possessed of a traditional Jewish education, Goldstein did not affiliate with a congregation in Baltimore, choosing instead to join a Workmen's Circle lodge. When each of his sons became thirteen, however, he felt compelled to take them to a neighborhood synagogue for a weekday service and have them called to the Torah for an impromptu bar mitzvah. Later, when his eldest son married a non-Jewish woman, Goldstein confided to a family member that according to the Talmud, a divorce could be effected if the wife failed to give her husband any offspring within the prescribed time frame.[114] As this strange mix of logic reveals, immigrants like Goldstein were unable to neatly synthesize their traditional religious background with the values of America. Instead, Eastern European Jews had to function as best they could in a world of sharp contrasts and frequent contradictions.

- - - - - - - - - - - - -

Politics and Culture on the Middle Ground

One Sunday in 1889, Samuel Garson, a Russian Jew recently arrived in Baltimore, set out to explore what cultural opportunities the city offered for immigrant workers. He discovered that an organization called the Isaac Bar Levinsohn Hebrew Literary Society gathered every week in Harugari Hall on Baltimore Street near Exeter to hear lectures on various topics. The society, founded a year earlier by a group of maskilim—young Russian Jewish intellectuals who valued both the Hebrew language and secular knowledge—aimed to spread "enlightenment" among the uneducated Jewish masses of Baltimore. Garson, who had spent time in New York and Boston and was active in radical circles, hoped to hear something of interest regarding the cause of Jewish labor. As he sat down, he discovered that a member of the acculturated Central European Jewish community was delivering a lecture in English about the work of a Jewish woman poet. Garson tried to focus, but he had no interest in the topic. Finally he could stand it no longer. "*Vos hakt er mir a tshaynik?!*—Why are you bothering me about a Jewish poetess?!" he muttered to himself in frustration. "This poppycock has no value for the popular masses." Garson left the meeting in disgust, determined to fix what he considered a deplorable situation.[115]

As Garson's reaction indicated, the literary society's lectures reflected the accommodationist agenda of its leaders, who encouraged among the immigrants respect for Jewish tradition and acculturation to middle-class American norms. Along with regular guest speakers from the local "German" Jewish community, they urged their audience to embrace the political institutions of the United States and to see English and Hebrew as complementary vehicles for Jewish cultural expression. In Garson's view, however, such an approach only distracted struggling Jewish workers from their true social and economic interests. What Baltimore needed, he thought, were fiery lectures of the type given by Jewish radicals in New York and Boston to educate workers about their plight and inspire them to fight back against their oppressors. He contacted his friends at the Pioneers of Liberty, a Jewish anarchist organization in New York, who sent him copies of their Yiddish newspaper and arranged for several speakers to come to Baltimore. In preparation for their arrival, Garson rented Canmaker's Hall and announced the formation of the Workingmen's Educational Society.[116]

Soon a fierce rivalry emerged between the two organizations, which fought for the allegiance of the city's Jewish immigrants by holding competing lectures each week. The Workingmen's Educational Society succeeded in attracting a sizable attendance, owing to the intense curiosity the group's oppositional rhetoric inspired among those who had never before been exposed to radical ideas. Once they gained an understanding of the society's goals, however, many who attended the meetings came to express their opposition rather than their support. Meanwhile, the leaders of the Isaac Bar Levinsohn Hebrew Literary Society often fulminated against the radicals in their meetings and in the national Hebrew press, helping to whip up concern and fear about their activities.[117]

Tensions reached a fever pitch by the fall of 1890, by which time Garson had left the city and the leadership of the Workingmen's Educational Society had passed to Michael Cohn, a devotee of the Pioneers who had moved to Baltimore to attend medical school at the College of Physicians and Surgeons. Cohn, a masterful orator, shocked his audiences with antireligious attacks. One night, when audience members challenged him, he proposed a debate with those who wished to defend the Orthodox viewpoint. The following week, more than 1,000 people packed the hall. When Cohn asked his opponent for proof of God's existence, screams came from the audience and a riot broke out. The police arrested ten people—mostly Orthodox protesters—and hauled them off to the local station. Cohn remained under surveillance for several months until the police finally arrested him following another incendiary speech, which they interpreted as a call to violence.[118]

While this tale of two dueling societies may at first glance seem to capture the rich ideological ferment among various factions of Jewish immigrants during the late nineteenth century, the fact that both of these organizations failed after a few years suggests that neither one was really very attractive to Baltimore's Eastern European Jews. Garson was right about the Isaac Bar Levinsohn Hebrew Literary Society: lectures about a Jewish poet may have been of interest to a small circle of immigrant intellectuals, but the average unsophisticated Jewish laborer found little that was exciting or edifying in such talks. Garson miscalculated, however, about the same audience being interested in anarchist theory and antireligious propaganda. Such lectures were either over the heads of listeners or, as the 1890 riot revealed, offensive to their traditional sensibilities. These topics might have made sense in New York, where there were plenty of Jewish radicals who were used to such things, but Baltimore was not New York. Jewish immigrants in Baltimore wanted to learn about and experience the vast new world around them, but as Jewish cultural life over the next few decades would reveal, they needed to pursue this goal in a way that spoke to the interests and values of the smaller, more conservative, and tightly knit community in which they lived.

In navigating the unfamiliar terrain of American urban life, Baltimore's Jewish immigrants had a burning need for sources of instruction and guidance in their own language that would give them a basic knowledge of science and literature, of which they had learned very little in their Eastern European homes, and familiarize them with the practical dimensions of American life—the manners, mores, and customs to which they would have to adapt if they wished to take full advantage of their new surroundings. In New York, immigrants had access to a thriving Yiddish press, which already by the 1890s had become the largest in the world, since Yiddish publications in Russia were restricted by government censorship before 1903. The smaller size of Baltimore, however, made it difficult to support a regular Yiddish publication. In 1890, Alexander Harkavy, a pioneering Yiddish linguist and lexicographer who later be-

Der Baltimorer vegvayzer (Baltimore Guide), May 8, 1902. The city's longest-running Yiddish
newspaper, *Der vegvayzer* was founded about 1895 and appeared for more than a decade.

came a well-known writer of popular textbooks for immigrants, founded in Baltimore
the *Yidisher progres* (Jewish Progress), which declared as its goal the "awaken[ing of]
our Jewish immigrant brothers to climb higher and higher on the rungs of the ladder
of science." The periodical failed after only nine issues.[119]

   After two other unsuccessful efforts, the city's first long-running Yiddish newspaper finally appeared in 1895, when printer Moses Silberman, in whose High Street
shop all of the previous newspapers had been printed, stepped into the role of publisher and engaged a young immigrant medical student, Maurice Chideckel, as editor.[120] Called *Der Baltimorer vegvayzer* (Baltimore Guide), the paper suited well the
needs of the city's immigrant readers, providing general news, editorials, stories of
Jewish interest, and a serialized novel—usually a translation of one of the European
classics—in every issue. Some editions also featured poetry, biographies of notable
figures, and popular science articles. Unlike some earlier local Yiddish publications,
Der vegvayzer's aim was more educational than political. According to Chideckel, it
was "truly independent," catering "not only to the natural thirst for news, but also
to the ever-insistent . . . intellectual needs of its readers."[121] As its title suggested, the
periodical was an ideal vehicle to guide Baltimore's immigrant Jews toward a greater
knowledge of the world and a better understanding of American life.

   Der vegvayzer ran until Silberman's death in 1908, and thereafter Baltimore was served by a few other Yiddish papers, including the short-lived *Baltimor Ameri-kaner* (Baltimore American, 1908–1909), edited by rabbi and politician Abraham S. Schochet, and a local edition of the nationally marketed *Yidishes tageblat* (Jewish Daily News), which appeared just before World War I.[122] Baltimore Jews also regularly read New York newspapers, including the *Forverts* (Jewish Daily Forward) and the *Morgn zhurnal* (Jewish Morning Journal). During this time, another cultural institution—the Yiddish theater—took root in Baltimore and became an additional source of comfort and guidance, providing a means for the immigrant population to explore topics as diverse as fashion, love, and the history and culture of foreign lands. The theater was also a place to relax, enjoy, and escape—if only for a while—the dissonance of the immigrant experience.

Traveling Yiddish theater companies appeared in Baltimore beginning in the mid-1880s, and by the opening years of the twentieth century the city had become a regular stop for leading performers from the New York Yiddish stage, including Jacob Adler, Keni Liptzin, and David Kessler.[123] Baltimore got its own permanent Yiddish troupe in 1907, when the Frank Brothers Stock Company set up shop at the Baltimore Theatre on East Baltimore Street, boasting a company of forty actors and offering a different play every night. On its busiest evenings the theater attracted crowds of 1,200 people. Frank Brothers left by 1912 but was replaced by a stock company that performed regularly at the Monumental Theatre (also known as the Orpheum), located on Baltimore Street just east of the Jones Falls, until the venue became a burlesque house in 1917.[124]

As some Jewish immigrants in Baltimore tried to ease their encounter with American society by taking advantage of a growing number of Yiddish cultural resources, many also began to experiment with the newer, more modern definitions of Jewishness that were taking hold in Eastern Europe and America. Movements like Zionism and Jewish socialism first emerged in Russia as a response to the disillusionment brought on by the pogroms of 1881, and they grew in popularity after the renewed wave of anti-Jewish riots in 1903 and 1905. Some immigrants who came to Baltimore in the early years of the migration wave had been exposed to these movements in their formative stage, while many who came after the convulsions of 1903–1905 had absorbed more refined or ideologically specific versions. No matter which group they belonged to, immigrants faced the question of whether these movements would complement the Americanization process by bringing a more modern perspective to Jewish life or introduce goals and concepts that clashed with the values of the American environment.

Zionist activity in Baltimore began in 1889, when a branch of the Hovevei Tsiyon (Lovers of Zion) society was founded in the city, followed three years later by a branch of Shovei Tsiyon (Returners to Zion), an association encouraging colonization in Palestine. Neither group lasted more than a year. In 1894, the Hevrat Tsiyon (Zion Association), a more enduring organization, was established under the leadership of Reuben Aaronsohn, with members including Solomon Baroway,

Moshe Falk Mervis, and Israel Fine, all of whom were devotees of Hebrew culture. Also participating were four rabbis from East Baltimore congregations. These initial activities mark Baltimore as one of the earliest American cities with a significant Zionist presence.[125]

The convening of the First Zionist Congress in Basel, Switzerland, in 1897 resulted in heightened attention to the Zionist movement in the United States, and Baltimore was particularly in the spotlight because one of its rabbis, Schepsel Shaffer of the Shearith Israel Congregation, was the only official delegate sent by a Zionist society in the United States.[126] The following year, the establishment of the Federation of American Zionists in New York encouraged the creation of another Baltimore society, the Ezras Chovevei Zion (Help of the Lovers of Zion). Unlike the elite Hevrat Tsiyon, it was conceived as a large membership organization and soon became the anchor for the Baltimore movement. The organization raised funds to support colonization and encouraged its members to purchase shares of the Jewish Colonial Trust. One novel fundraising scheme was undertaken by Adolph Sauber, who purchased 200 bottles of wine from Palestine and distributed them throughout the city with donation envelopes attached. The society enhanced its visibility by staging frequent mass meetings featuring local Jewish leaders, like Rabbi Shaffer, and out-of-town dignitaries, like the renowned folk orator Rabbi Zvi Hirsch Masliansky. By 1903, three additional Zionist societies were founded: Daughters of Zion, Children of Zion, and Agudas B'nai Zion, leading to the creation of an umbrella organization, the United Zionists of Baltimore.[127]

The varieties of Zionism continued to expand as new ideologies were imported from Europe. One of the city's younger Zionist leaders, Dr. Herman Seidel, organized a meeting in Baltimore in 1905 that launched the American arm of Poale Zion (Workers of Zion), a movement that combined Jewish nationalist and socialist aims.[128] Aitz Chaim Congregation's rabbi, Moses Romanoff, brought Mizrachi, the religious Zionist movement, to Baltimore in 1915 when he hosted the organization's national gathering, which ended with an enthusiastic mass meeting at the Eden Street Synagogue.[129] As World War I approached, Baltimore Zionism generated an increasing number of societies, events, rallies, and conferences. In many ways, the movement and its symbols became woven into the fabric of the immigrants' broader communal undertakings and celebrations.

From the beginning of Zionist activity in Baltimore, a recurrent theme promoted by many of these societies was the compatibility of the movement with US citizenship. Rallies and demonstrations routinely combined the display of American and Zionist flags and the singing of "My Country, 'Tis of Thee" and "The Star-Spangled Banner" with that of the Zionist anthem, "HaTikvah" (The Hope). At a mass meeting of Ezras Chovevei Zion in 1902, Rabbi Shaffer denied that Zionism prevented Jews from loving the United States and its ideals. He predicted that America's strong humanitarian principles would result in its lending crucial assistance in the creation of a Jewish state, just as it had aided Cuba in becoming independent from Spain.

Labor Zionists from several American cities met in Baltimore to create a national movement in 1905. *Jewish Museum of Maryland.*

The following year, to make a similar point, the United Zionists of Baltimore sent a Zionist flag, along with an explanation of its meaning, to President Theodore Roosevelt at his summer home in Oyster Bay, New York.[130]

The compatibility of Zionism and Americanism was underscored by the participation of a small but prominent group of acculturated Baltimore Jews, who were "converted" to the Zionist movement by their immigrant acquaintances and went on to play major leadership roles nationally and internationally. This group included Henrietta Szold, the daughter of Oheb Shalom's longtime rabbi, who gained prominence as an essayist and editor for the Jewish Publication Society of America before founding the women's Zionist organization Hadassah in 1912; and the ophthalmologist Harry Friedenwald, scion of a prominent family of physicians and communal leaders, who served as the national president of the Federation of American Zionists from 1904 to 1911. Among the many other uptown Jews who joined Baltimore's Zionist ranks were Judge Jacob M. Moses; Chizuk Amuno's rabbi, Henry W. Schneeberger; and Oheb Shalom's cantor, Alois Kaiser. For these members of the Jewish establishment, Zionism provided a sense of authenticity and relevance that the version of Judaism prevalent in their own circles failed to embody. While they remained a minority among the city's acculturated Jews, their ties to Zionism belie an image of the movement as one that hopelessly divided the uptown and downtown communities.[131]

- - - - - - - - - - - - -

Although the participation and leadership of acculturated uptown Jews lent Zionism legitimacy, it was ultimately the rank and file of Eastern European Jewish immigrants who propelled the movement's rapid ascendance. Zionism spoke powerfully to both their past experiences and their aspirations for the future. It not only affirmed the notion of Jews as a people, which had been crucial to their self-perception in Eastern Europe, but also offered a version of Jewish identity that was responsive to the challenges of contemporary life. As Zionism's ability to incorporate American themes demonstrated, the movement balanced the immigrants' impulses for particularism and universalism in compelling ways. Above all, it helped bridge the gap for those immigrants struggling with conflicts between tradition and modernity. While not all of Baltimore's Orthodox rabbis and institutions embraced Jewish nationalism, many of them did, making the traditional world of East Baltimore seem less out of touch with pressing issues of the day.

Among both immigrant and acculturated adherents, Zionism seemed to find a particularly auspicious environment in Baltimore. It is doubtful whether any American city had an organized Zionist movement earlier, and few produced more Zionist leaders or hosted more national conferences and meetings. The reason for the city's rise to leadership in Zionist circles is unclear, but certainly once Baltimoreans like Friedenwald, Szold, and Seidel achieved national prominence in the movement, momentum was created that made it natural for many other locals to seize similar roles.

Compared to Zionism, socialism did not find as fertile a field among Baltimore's Jewish immigrants despite the success it enjoyed in New York and several other major American cities. As shown by the violent reaction to Michael Cohn's antireligious speeches at Canmaker's Hall in 1890, radical movements attracted fewer devoted followers in Baltimore's comparatively traditional community and faced continual opposition from broader forces in the city, including Christian leaders, the police, and the political establishment. True, one of the activists who established a local branch of the Jewish Workers' Bund in 1897 called Baltimore a "great radical city."[132] Viewed through the lens of historical data, however, this judgment seems to have been wishful thinking. Having failed to understand that the tone of Baltimore society was much more conservative than that of New York, Cohn had damaged the prospects for Jewish socialism with his fiery rhetoric more than he had helped them. The police, alarmed at the unrest Cohn had caused, were determined to prevent a recurrence. For years after his departure from the city, officers vigilantly watched the immigrant quarter for signs of radical activity and even kept tabs on individuals who had attended or helped plan the lectures in Canmaker's Hall.[133]

In 1901, Jewish radicals finally began to emerge from the shadows when they incorporated the Young Men's Progressive Labor Society, which opened a small reading room for Yiddish-speaking workers in East Baltimore. But the following year, when the fledgling organization affiliated with a new national group for Jewish laborers, the Workmen's Circle, a report spread that the police believed it to be a nest of anarchist agitators. The group's leaders vociferously denied this charge, issuing

Library card from the Young Men's Progressive Labor Society, which became a branch of the Workmen's Circle in 1902. *Jewish Museum of Maryland*.

an invitation to the press to attend one of its meetings to verify its character. A *Sun* reporter took them up on their offer and concluded that the Workmen's Circle was just an "ordinary beneficial society." The president of the branch, Morris Miller, explained that "we sometimes discuss social questions, frequently using the *Sun* as a textbook, but this association has no object beyond provision for sick and death benefits." In a parting shot at law enforcement, he concluded: "We are not an anarchistic society, nor have we any relations with any such society, with the provisional exception of the police of this city who wish to make our acquaintance."[134]

This exchange is interesting both for the way that Miller portrayed the Workmen's Circle and for the reasons he felt it necessary to do so. Technically the organization, founded in New York in 1900 and known in Yiddish as the Arbeter Ring, was a fraternal and beneficial society similar to the lodges that had long existed among Eastern European Jewish immigrants. Aside from providing sick and death benefits to its members, its main goals were social and educational. In Baltimore, for example, five local branches pooled the resources of their 800 members in 1912 to open a hall at the corner of Aisquith and Lexington streets, with space for meetings and recreation and a library with a variety of periodicals and 4,000 books in English, Yiddish, and Russian.[135]

Yet while the national group had no formal ties to any radical political party or movement, it was generally understood by its members to be an organization that supported socialist causes and ideals. In New York, members of the Workmen's Circle proudly wore their socialist affiliations on their sleeves, but in Baltimore the socialist connection was highlighted more selectively, given the city's hostility to radicalism and the fact that the Workmen's Circle was not, in any case, a propagandistic organization of the type that concerned the police. This may explain why the leaders who had worked so hard to establish a central meeting place for the organization avoided officially placing the hall under Workmen's Circle auspices, but instead created a separate governing board for the facility and gave it the somewhat innocuous name Progressive Labor Lyceum.[136]

This is not to suggest that the Baltimore Workmen's Circle failed to play a meaningful role in the lives of its members. Quite to the contrary, it provided a strong sense of community and, much like Zionism, mediated the tensions of immigrant life by allowing its members to maintain a strong sense of Jewishness that was also in conversation with modern trends and ideas. Its naturalization bureau assisted members in obtaining US citizenship. At its secular Sunday school, children learned how to read and write in Yiddish and were taught Jewish history "in a modern way." Despite the pressure it faced to downplay its socialist moorings, the Workmen's Circle in Baltimore did host speakers who advocated for socialist causes, including revolution in Russia, and it counted among its members a small number of Jewish activists who perennially ran as socialist candidates for municipal and state offices. It also lent crucial support to labor unions, particularly by giving its hall free of charge for use by striking workers.[137]

- - - - - - - - - - - - - -

Still, without detracting from the strides that local Jewish radicals did make under inauspicious conditions, it is fair to say that compared to the strength of similar activities in larger centers, socialist undertakings among Jews in Baltimore were circumscribed in ways that reduced their effectiveness, limited their importance and visibility, and prevented radical organizations from multiplying or growing larger. The city's daily press, for example, hardly ever mentioned any efforts at political agitation by Jewish socialists. One rare report tells of a 1908 meeting of "Hebrew Socialists"—likely the local branch of the Bund—held in the Princess Theater to rally "those unemployed Hebrews of East Baltimore of socialistic tendencies." The gathering was held to protest the Jewish community's method for giving charitable assistance, which, one speaker argued, "degrades a man and ultimately ends in the man becoming a tramp."[138] The newspapers occasionally published profiles of colorful socialist figures, portraying them as eccentrics rather than as serious political operatives. One of these men, known in East Baltimore as "Old Man" Sokolow, ran a "notion, dry good, delicatessen and soda water emporium" on the corner of Caroline and Pratt streets, where he regaled customers with pearls of socialist wisdom.[139]

Unlike New York, which sent socialist Meyer London to the US Congress in 1914, Baltimore never gave the handful of socialist candidates that appeared on the ballot each election year—even the immigrant Jews among them—more than a few votes.[140] Similarly, although socialists were active in the unionization movements and strikes of Baltimore clothing workers, they did not dominate these efforts as they did in many other cities. Israel Silverman, the founder of the ILGWU in Baltimore and the guiding spirit of its most active local, was a Democrat, as was Israel Levin, the vice president of the local American Federation of Labor branch, who quit his post to lead the 1914 secession movement that allowed the ACWA to gain a foothold in Baltimore.[141] Although the new union did elevate many socialists to leadership positions, election returns of the period suggest that exceedingly few of the rank and file were formally associated with the Socialist Party.[142]

If most local immigrant Jews remained reticent about identifying with socialism, they did enthusiastically participate in mainstream US party politics, often through membership in specifically Jewish political clubs. Understanding their Jewishness as an all-encompassing identity rather than a strictly religious matter, immigrant Jews firmly believed that they shared political interests as a group. In this regard, they were similar to other immigrants, including Irish, Italians, and Germans, who organized political clubs along ethnic lines. This type of organization was encouraged by the machine politics of the era, because political bosses found it a useful tool to harness the group loyalties of immigrants and to turn ethnic rivalries to their advantage. Thus, during the 1890s, when a critical mass of Jewish immigrants passed the milestone of becoming naturalized citizens, clubs for Jewish voters began to proliferate and quickly became a factor in the city's political life.[143]

- - - - - - - - - - - - - -

Because neither Democrats nor Republicans had a complete lock on city or state politics around the turn of the twentieth century, Jews did not affiliate as a block with one party or the other. And because immigrant Jews constituted a large population and owned more property and business establishments than any other immigrant group, their support was vigorously courted by the city and state organizations of both parties. In 1903, the Republicans elected two immigrant Jews—Joseph Seidenman and William Weissager—to the First Branch of the city council, and the Democrats sent Lithuanian-born cigar manufacturer Myer D. H. Lipman to the Maryland House of Delegates in 1904.[144]

Immigrant politicians were most frequently elected on the ward level, where they generally sought to advance the interests of the Eastern European Jewish constituencies that elected them, with of course some variation based on party affiliation. To effectively represent Jewish concerns, they found it essential to forge close alliances with native-born party leaders and politicians representing other ethnic communities. These relationships helped Jewish immigrants to win appointments to bodies such as the Board of Supervisors of Elections and the state Democratic and Republican central committees. Eastern European Jews were also appointed with some frequency to the position of police justice (sometimes known as justice of the peace or police magistrate) in some Baltimore Municipal Court districts. Police justices wielded significant powers, including the ability to issue summons, fine, and jail residents of their districts and to rule on disputes that came before them. Adolph Sauber, the owner of a cloth-sponging business and a leader of many institutions in the Jewish immigrant community, was appointed justice of the northwestern police district in 1902, after having served for two years as a justice-at-large. Between 1909 and 1912, Sauber's fellow Democrat, the rabbi and Yiddish newspaper editor Abraham S. Schochet, served as a police justice in the Third Ward in the heart of Jewish East Baltimore.[145]

While immigrant politicians brought Jewish concerns into the political arena, they also brought politics into the Jewish arena, particularly through a dynamic organization founded in 1902 by the city's best-connected immigrant leaders: the Independent Order Brith Sholom of the City of Baltimore. Though initially conceived as a fraternal organization similar to B'rith Abraham or the Central European Jewish order B'nai B'rith, Brith Sholom ultimately embraced a different mission than its older counterparts: consolidating the influence of acculturating Jews in civic life and advancing Jewish political interests on the city and state levels.[146] Because of their focus on local politics, Brith Sholom's leaders resisted attempts to expand the organization's geographical reach. Indeed, when a group of Jewish Philadelphians launched a national order using the name Brith Sholom in 1905, the Baltimore organization adamantly refused to merge with the new group.[147] Though the Baltimore-based Brith Sholom did ultimately establish a few lodges in other Maryland cities and in Virginia, Baltimore remained the focus of its activities. Thus, while it displayed the trappings of a more traditional fraternal order, its primary function

- - - - - - - - - - - - -

Brith Sholom Hall was the headquarters for the Baltimore-based Jewish
fraternal organization that encouraged Jewish civic activism. Photo, c. 1914.
Jewish Museum of Maryland.

was to serve as "one of the representative bodies of the city to deal with Jewish
questions."[148]

The political nature of Brith Sholom infused almost every aspect of the organization. The men who served as its grand masters were generally prominent in local
politics, like the Democrat Adolph Sauber and two leading Republican activists, real
estate developer Isidore Kres and insurance broker Morris Selenkow. The bipartisan
nature of the organization affirmed that the political activism of the immigrants
privileged Jewish interests over party platforms and agendas. In addition to bringing
together seasoned Jewish politicians and activists in common cause, the order created lodges specifically designed for younger men, which they hoped would provide a
training ground for the next generation of Jewish political leadership. The political
mission of Brith Sholom was evident at its conferences and mass meetings, many
of which featured addresses by the mayor, the governor, and other state and local

officials. And while Brith Sholom looked after Jewish charitable concerns and occasionally expressed opinions on matters of international Jewish interest, it asserted itself continually as the Jewish voice in discussions about city planning, development, and boosterism.[149]

The Eastern European Jews of Baltimore may not have lived in the most cosmopolitan of immigrant centers, but they managed to forge a cultural life that made much of their existing resources and alleviated the tension and dissonance of the immigrant experience. They also shaped a distinctive political profile that reflected the particular possibilities and limitations of the local setting. If Baltimore's culture discouraged the radicalism that was a hallmark of Jewish politics in other urban centers, it fed the growth of Zionism and involvement in party politics, movements that would propel the immigrants to greater status and influence in both the Jewish and non-Jewish worlds. As this process unfolded, however, one of the most significant challenges immigrants faced was navigating their relationship with the more acculturated Jews of Central European background, who sometimes aided them and sometimes stood in their way.

"Germans," "Russians," and the Politics of Americanization

From rocky beginnings in the 1880s, relations between the city's "German" and "Russian" Jews—or, as they were sometimes called, the "uptown" and "downtown" communities—evolved through a painfully slow set of negotiations. Among the factors driving this struggle were the continual growth of the immigrant population, the increasing economic mobility and sophistication of the immigrants, and the emergence of leaders who could challenge the older establishment's monopoly on Jewish communal stewardship. Meanwhile, uptown Jews often were afraid that the newcomers would soil their reputation in the non-Jewish world and desperately tried to suppress the immigrants' influence. As members of the Central European Jewish power structure in Baltimore were forced to confront the rising stature of the immigrant community and to deal with its leadership on key issues, some began to develop a sense of respect and admiration for the "Russians." Still, it took many years for the fears of the established Jewish community to fully subside and for the two camps to be able to work together as equals in a trusting and cooperative relationship.

The resolve of Baltimore's Central European Jews both to aid their immigrant coreligionists and to transform them was expressed in the burgeoning network of schools, settlement houses, and social service agencies that emerged beginning in the 1890s. Although the Hebrew Benevolent Society continued to provide financial assistance to needy Jews of all backgrounds, the leaders of the acculturated community understood that if they wished to encourage Americanization among the Eastern Europeans and safeguard the good name of Baltimore Jewry, they needed to move beyond simply aiding the poor and begin to create institutions that would shape the character and outlook of the immigrants. They made a conscious effort to focus communal energies and resources on young people, who were thought to be the most receptive to such efforts. "We need not attempt the hopeless task of moulding the character of the old man and woman," editorialized Louis H. Levin in the *Jewish Comment* in 1896, "but our best efforts are required for influencing the young and elevating them above the groveling life and sordid surroundings which are theirs."[150]

Among the first steps toward this goal was creating more Americanized alternatives to the options for Jewish education available in the immigrant community. The Hebrew Education Society opened in 1895 at the Orthodox but acculturated Chizuk Amuno—still located at that time on Lloyd Street in the heart of the immigrant district—where American-born rabbi Henry Schneeberger emphasized the importance of good conduct among the students and where English replaced what the organizers called "the jargon" (Yiddish) as the language of instruction. The school later hired the young educator Samson Benderly, who would go on to modernize Jewish education nationally.[151] At the Reform-oriented Frank Free Sabbath School, poor immigrant children gathered on Saturdays for lessons in "morality from the Bible, tidiness and . . . the manners of cultured people in an enlightened country." The managers of the school hoped that such offerings would "keep the children off the street, and . . . let them become more interested in the teachings of their faith."[152]

The linchpins of the acculturated community's Americanization efforts were two organizations established to conduct settlement work among the youths of East Baltimore. The Daughters in Israel, founded in 1891, envisioned itself as a Jewish version of the King's Daughters, a Protestant women's service organization. The platform of the Daughters in Israel involved the creation of small "circles" or "bands" of acculturated Jewish women, each of which undertook a different social service project, such as teaching immigrant girls to sew or training young mothers in modern parenting methods. In 1897, the Daughters created a home for working girls, where young women who had come to the United States without their parents could live for a modest weekly charge and take advantage of the society's many classes and activities.[153] The men's counterpart to the Daughters in Israel, the Maccabeans, focused on providing wholesome recreation for young immigrant men and boys. Founded in 1896 by fifty recent Jewish graduates of Johns Hopkins University, the group opened a reading room and library where visitors could gather to browse the latest titles or play chess. By 1898, the Maccabeans offered industrial training, lectures on citizenship and "good government," and clubs devoted to physical culture, debating, and the singing of patriotic songs.[154]

The work of these schools and settlement houses undoubtedly benefited thousands of Baltimore's Jewish immigrants and reflected a true desire on the part of acculturated Jews to help their less fortunate coreligionists. Yet the volunteers who led and staffed these institutions were often heavy-handed in pursuing what Levin had termed the "moulding" of their clientele. Despite assertions that they treated

Like many organizations managed by uptown Jews, the Hebrew Orphan Asylum sought to acculturate its Eastern European Jewish clientele through athletics, manual training, and other Americanizing activities. Photo, c. 1911. *Jewish Museum of Maryland*.

their charges with "equality" and "a sincere friendly interest," the volunteers often described their role in imparting "enlightenment," "refinement," and "uplift" in ways intended to contrast their own high level of civilization with the backwardness and ignorance of those they sought to aid.[155] This attitude of superiority suggests that they were motivated by insecurity about their own social status as much as by altruism and that they aimed to assert their position as proper, civilized, middle-class American men and women as much as they wished to help the immigrants.

A similar paternalism characterized the relationship between acculturated Jews and Eastern European Jewish immigrants in the political arena. By the closing years of the nineteenth century, Jews of Central European background had made significant inroads into local politics on both the city and state levels. Yet Jewish politicians were not always embraced by the political establishment, and like the city's acculturated Jews more broadly, they often felt their acceptance to be tenuous. Against this backdrop, they frequently looked to the immigrant Jews of East Baltimore as a large and growing constituency whose votes they might corral in order to bolster their own position.

The immigrants were happy to be courted by prominent politicians who could aid them in their own fight for political influence. The election of Myer D. H. Lipman, a Lithuanian Jewish cigar manufacturer, to the Maryland House of Delegates in 1904, for example, owed much to the support of Isidor Rayner and his allies, who needed to put a loyalist in the House to aid in securing Rayner's election as US senator the following year (at that time, US senators were elected by state legislatures, rather than by popular vote). Lipman not only fought for Rayner as promised, but became a dutiful mouthpiece for the senator among the Jews of East Baltimore in the years that followed.[156]

Sometimes, however, the immigrants were not so compliant. In 1903, East Baltimore politician Joseph Seidenman angered the uptown Democratic Party activist Joseph Friedenwald, who fancied himself as having influence among the "Russians," by running for the Fifth Ward city council seat as a Republican. Friedenwald desperately tried to convince the ward's Jewish immigrant voters to support the non-Jewish Democratic candidate, even bringing the famed Yiddish poet Morris Rosenfeld and the folk orator Zvi Hirsch Masliansky from New York to campaign for his ticket. In the end, Friedenwald's influence was not enough to overcome the desire of immigrant voters to elect a Jewish candidate, irrespective of party.[157]

A more crucial attempt at courting the immigrant vote came in 1909, when Democrats sought support to ratify an amendment to the state constitution that would disenfranchise most African American voters. A similar amendment had failed to win approval in 1905, largely because immigrant voters, including Jews, believed that some of the measure's provisions threatened their own franchise rights. Two years after the 1905 defeat, Democrats crafted a new version of the bill, this time written by the state's Jewish attorney general, Isaac Lobe Straus, and supported by Senator Rayner. African Americans were highly aware of the historical irony of two Jewish politicians supporting black disenfranchisement and lost no opportunity in scoring them for their racism, condemning Straus in particular as a "latter day Haman" and the "Persecuting Attorney of the Colored Race in Maryland." Aside from their stated argument that the franchise was not safe in the hands of illiterate African Americans, the Democrats were anxious to see the amendment pass because it would remove from the rolls a significant part of the Republican voting base in the state, ensuring the dominance of their party for the foreseeable future.[158]

The Straus amendment, as the proposed measure became known, passed the Democratic-controlled legislature in 1908, but needed to be confirmed in the following year's general election. Rayner became the chief spokesman for the amendment in the months leading up to the vote, and he and other party representatives made East Baltimore one of their chief battlegrounds, since they knew that the support of immigrant voters would be crucial to their success.[159] While the new amendment did not include some of the threatening language that had troubled foreign-born citizens during the previous campaign, Straus had been unable to remove a provision requiring those who would be naturalized in the future to pass an additional state-administered citizenship test in order to secure the right to vote.

This caused considerable fear among the immigrants, and debate raged in East Baltimore during the election season. Rayner received loyal support from his protégé Lipman, who implored his fellow immigrant Jews to help remove the "illiterate and unthrifty negro" from the electorate. While a few other Jewish immigrant leaders supported the party's effort, the amendment failed to pass, due in large part to the continued opposition of the majority of Baltimore's foreign-born voters.[160] Despite the influence and favors they had to offer, the uptown Jewish politicians involved in the campaign could not control the downtown vote.

The outcome of the amendment controversy was one of many signs that Baltimore's Jewish immigrant population was asserting its independence from the leadership of acculturated Jews. Certainly the growing organization of Jewish labor, culminating in the successful unionization of Henry Sonneborn and Company and Strouse and Brothers by the ILGWU and ACWA between 1909 and 1916, sent a message to the uptown Jews that the immigrants were a force to be reckoned with and that the power differential between the two groups was shrinking.[161] The same could be said of the Zionist movement, which continued to grow and become more influential despite vocal criticism from several Reform rabbis, including Baltimore Hebrew's Adolph Guttmacher, Oheb Shalom's William Rosenau, and—perhaps most vehemently—Har Sinai's Charles A. Rubenstein.[162]

Perhaps the most explicit declaration of independence on the part of Baltimore's immigrant Jews came in the charitable arena, which had been a point of tension between the uptown and downtown communities since the two groups first locked heads over the control of philanthropic efforts in the 1880s. In 1906, the leaders of the uptown charities voted to create an umbrella agency, the Federated Jewish Charities, which would raise money for its constituent organizations through direct appeals for funds, rather than the much less efficient methods used in prior years. The "Federation," as the agency became known, was the brainchild of its first president, economist Jacob H. Hollander, a Johns Hopkins University professor who believed that poverty could be eliminated through the application of modern, scientific methods of philanthropy. As a condition of membership in the new agency, Hollander insisted, each beneficiary organization had to agree not to "give a ball, banquet, dinner, bazaar, or any sort of entertainment to raise money" that might interfere with the Federated's annual appeal.[163] He also believed that an effective charitable organization needed the oversight and stability of a professional director (the "secretary"), a position for which he recruited Louis H. Levin, an attorney by training who had become prominent in Jewish community affairs through his editorship of the *Jewish Comment* and soon became one of the pioneers of modern Jewish social service. The Federated was an instant success, raising its annual income in the first year alone from $46,682 to $70,734.[164]

In 1914, the United Hebrew Charities founded the Hebrew Home for
Incurables as an adjunct to the Hebrew Friendly Inn and Aged Home. Mindel Smolowitch,
pictured here at age 106, was one of the new home's oldest residents. Photo, c. 1915.
Jewish Museum of Maryland.

Following the practice of Jewish federations recently founded in cities across the
United States, the Federated Jewish Charities did not include philanthropic organizations managed by the downtown Jewish community. As one of its subsequent
presidents, Eli Frank, later explained, by 1906 the charities of the immigrant community had "not yet reached the stage of development in the . . . methods of their
conduct or of their support that would have then warranted their inclusion." Not
wanting to be branded as disorganized or behind the times, the leaders of the downtown charities decided in 1907 to create their own federation, the United Hebrew
Charities.[165] Led by the prominent garment manufacturer Solomon Ginsberg and
a board that included Eastern European business leaders Jacob Epstein, Ephraim
Macht, and Israel Levinstein, the "United" adopted the same practice of direct solicitation used by the Federated, doing away with the practice of "making collections

at social gatherings [and] at synagogues, and selling tickets for balls, picnics, or concerts."[166] The United Hebrew Charities is noteworthy as the first charitable federation established by Eastern European Jews in the United States. Having started with an initial fund of only $6,000, the organization raised an impressive $26,746 in its second year.[167]

In founding the United Hebrew Charities, Eastern European Jewish leaders did not intend to supplant the efforts of Central European Jews and their philanthropies to aid the immigrant population. On the contrary, they understood well that the acculturated Jews, because of their relative wealth and influence, still had a major role to play. When Jacob Epstein wished to establish a home for Jewish consumptives in 1908, for example, he gave $25,000 not to the United but to the Federated, since he knew it would be better equipped to inaugurate such an institution.[168] Nor did the Federated leadership view the creation of the United as a hostile move. Hollander, Frank, and other uptown spokesmen hailed it as a victory for progressive philanthropy, and they frequently offered their support and encouragement. In the final analysis, that was the outcome the Eastern Europeans wanted most: the respect and recognition of the broader Jewish community for having achieved a position of leadership in communal affairs.[169]

As the city's Eastern European Jews asserted their status and leadership in the broader Jewish community, they benefited from the strong bonds they had forged over the previous decades with a small group of acculturated Jews—mostly from the Zionist camp—who had rejected the paternalism and condescension of the Central European Jewish establishment and had encouraged the immigrants to become more independent and self-confident. Rather than seeing work with the immigrants as an opportunity for self-aggrandizement, figures like Henrietta Szold and Harry Friedenwald understood it as a chance to forge a stronger connection to Judaism and Jewish peoplehood. In their view, the immigrants were not misguided charges in need of remaking, but rather authentic Jews from whom they had much to learn. To Szold, the members of her father's middle-class congregation had "the souls of bookkeepers," while the immigrants had "the souls of Jews."[170] This feeling is what attracted her to meetings of the Eastern European–led Isaac Bar Levinsohn Hebrew Literary Society when it was founded in 1888 and, later, encouraged her to help its leaders establish the Russian Night School, the first institution in the city designed to teach English to foreign-born adults.[171] It was also what inspired her and Friedenwald to embark upon their lifelong support of Zionism and to become deeply involved in the emerging Conservative movement in Judaism, which reflected their desire to create an Americanized religious tradition infused with the authenticity and spiritual engagement they perceived among their "Russian friends."[172]

Other acculturated Jews who became firmly attached to the immigrant community included the lawyer and politician Jacob M. Moses, who first encountered Baltimore's Eastern European Jews as a law student interested in the labor movement. In 1902, as a member of the Maryland House of Delegates, he successfully

Henrietta Szold credited her "Russian friends" with bringing
her to Zionism. She later founded Hadassah, the Women's Zionist Organization
of America. Photo, c. 1885. *Jewish Museum of Maryland.*

championed an inspection law that held sweatshop owners accountable for health
and safety violations and led to the disappearance of sweatshops from much of East
Baltimore by 1910. As he told an interviewer later in life, he associated the "wage
slavery" of Russian Jews with the servitude of the ancient Israelites in Egypt and
believed that in drafting the 1902 act, he was "helping the new immigrants to become free from their bondage."[173] Moses was also the lead arbitrator in negotiations
between the Jewish unions and the leading clothing firms between 1913 and 1915,
which resulted in improved wages and working conditions for the immigrants. Like
Szold and Friedenwald, Moses's encounters with the immigrant community led him
to embrace Zionism, which he described in a 1901 speech as the only movement of
vitality among contemporary Jews. Having found his spiritual home with the immigrants, Moses was a regular speaker at East Baltimore meetings and rallies. While
he played a role in uptown institutions, he was also one of the officers of the United
Hebrew Charities.[174]

The United was conspicuously aided by another wealthy uptown Jew, William
Levy, who served as the second president of the immigrants' charitable federation.
The son of immigrants from Posen who remained devoted to their Orthodox tradi-

Candidate for State Senate, 1899.

מר · דזשייקאב מ· מאזעס

דעמ. קאנדיראט פיר סטייט סענאט לעגזשיכלייטיוו דיס כרי נ

Yiddish handbill for the state senate campaign of Jacob M. Moses, 1899.
Moses, an acculturated Jew of German background, championed anti-sweatshop legislation
and later became a Zionist. *Jewish Museum of Maryland.*

In 1910, Americanization activities for immigrants were consolidated with the
founding of the Jewish Educational Alliance, which became a magnet for East Baltimore youth.
Courtesy of the Maryland Historical Society.

tions despite their economic success, Levy felt particularly strong ties of kinship to the Eastern Europeans. As a young man, he had lived among the immigrants in East Baltimore because his family wished to stay within walking distance of their synagogue, Chizuk Amuno, which remained on Lloyd Street until 1895. Admiring the Eastern Europeans for their maintenance of traditions that he regretted were being lost among Jews of his own background, Levy channeled much of his philanthropy to the immigrant community in order to ensure that its institutions thrived.[175]

The level of identification with the immigrant cause displayed by Szold, Friedenwald, Moses, and Levy remained rare among the city's acculturated Jews in the period before World War I. But the efforts of such individuals to bolster the Eastern Europeans and their institutions gradually helped foster within Baltimore's Central European Jewish establishment a more respectful attitude toward the immigrants and a greater appreciation of their talents and cultural resources. Nowhere was this growing respect and appreciation more apparent than in the activities of the Jewish Educational Alliance (JEA), founded in 1909 through a merger of the Daughters in Israel and the Maccabeans. The JEA employed modern methods of social work and dispensed with the self-congratulatory rhetoric about "civilizing" the immigrants that had infused the work of the earlier institutions. Fittingly, this enterprise was housed after 1912 in a new building on East Baltimore Street funded by a generous gift from William Levy.[176]

Though the JEA did aim to make Americans of the immigrants, it did so in a way that honored their backgrounds and traditions, bringing, for example, the immigrant physician and activist Herman Seidel to lecture on citizenship.[177] The JEA's "head workers" (the term used for the early executive directors), many of whom were of Eastern European background, formed close personal bonds with the youths they served. They opened the institution's meeting rooms to groups like the Ha-Techia Zionist Society, which held an impressive ceremony at the JEA in 1915 to commemorate the eleventh yahrzeit of Theodor Herzl, the founder of political Zionism.[178] Most important, they fashioned a program that gave immigrant youths the chance to experience American-style recreation and to engage in activities like debating and mock elections on their own terms, without imposing external criteria or lecturing them on manners or deportment. The freeing and empowering environment created at the JEA was exemplified by a drama class where small children were encouraged to develop their own understanding of the parts they were given, rather than rely on direction from the teachers. "Oh, Mrs. Nathan!" exclaimed a young girl as she leaped in the air in a fairy costume. "The soul of me is all set free!"[179]

Like the United Hebrew Charities, the JEA reflected the maturing of the relationship between Baltimore's two distinct Jewish communities in the decade before World War I. The immigrants had demonstrated their status and independence in politics and philanthropy, and their cultural endeavors were now gaining greater respect beyond the small circle of admirers who had long supported them. In many ways, they still relied on the acculturated Jewish establishment for aid and leadership, but they

----

were poised to assert themselves in more significant ways as the coming war and the rise of a new generation promised to further transform Jewish life in Baltimore.

A Wartime Shift

The problems and tensions surrounding immigrant adjustment continued to dominate the lives of Baltimore Jews as long as the flow of new arrivals continued unabated and the majority of the Jewish population remained foreign-born. This began to change, however, with the outbreak of World War I in Europe, which set in motion a number of processes that would alter the ground on which Jewish life in Baltimore was built.

First and foremost, the beginning of hostilities led to a precipitous decline in immigration. During the war, the number of Jewish immigrants arriving in the United States each year plummeted to about 14 percent of the previous yearly average. Although there was a slight increase in the immediate postwar years, the number again declined dramatically after 1921, when the US Congress adopted the first of a series of laws restricting immigration. The situation in Baltimore clearly reflected the national pattern. In 1914, the year the war broke out, 2,448 Jews from Europe were recorded as heading to Maryland. In 1916, Jewish arrivals destined for the state dropped to only 58. After the war, the number never again exceeded 161 Jewish immigrants in a single year, and in 1921 not a single Jewish immigrant to the United States declared Maryland as a final destination.[180]

While the decline in immigration began to transform Baltimore Jewry into an increasingly native-born group, the war provided opportunities for young immigrant Jews and the children of immigrants to display their strong devotion to the United States through military service. Given that Eastern European Jews far outnumbered their Central European counterparts, undoubtedly most of the 1,596 Jewish servicemen from Baltimore were of Eastern European background. However, the most distinguished Jewish servicemen came from the ranks of Baltimore's Central European Jewish families—men like Brigadier General Charles H. Lauchheimer, who became the highest-ranking member of the US Marine Corps shortly before US entry into the war and oversaw its Adjutant and Inspector's Department throughout the conflict. But Jews of recent immigrant origin also achieved recognition. Sergeant Nizel Rafalsky, an army physician whose Russian-born parents owned a confectionery store on South Charles Street, received the Distinguished Service Cross for attending to wounded soldiers under heavy shelling and machine gun fire near Verdun, France.[181] In addition to those serving in the US military, some 80 young members of Baltimore's Eastern European Jewish community expressed their patriotism—as well as their Zionism—by joining the Jewish Legion, which helped the British drive the Turks out of Palestine. The *Sun* offered approving coverage of their determination to "fight the Hun and his allies."[182]

On Tu B'Shevat, members of the Jewish Legion in Palestine plant trees beneath an American flag, c. 1918. *Jewish Museum of Maryland.*

While shared wartime service did not efface the social distinctions between up-town and downtown Jews, the public recognized and mourned the sacrifices of the 271 Jewish Baltimoreans wounded in battle and the 54 killed in action, irrespective of their origins. The city's most-honored Jewish war hero was Lieutenant Merrill Rosenfeld, a lawyer and the son of a prominent German Jewish clothing manufacturer, who was killed in 1918 while leading an expedition against enemy machine gunners in the Argonne. When his body was returned for burial in 1921, Mayor William F. Broening and US senator Joseph I. France were among those who delivered eulogies at the Baltimore Hebrew Congregation's Madison Avenue Temple. The funeral of Russian-born private Frank Berger was a more modest affair, conducted before a gathering of downtown Jews at the Jack Lewis Funeral Home. Still, it was noted with reverence in the *Sun*, and a detachment of servicemen from Camp Meade accompanied Berger's casket on its journey to the Hebrew Mount Carmel Cemetery.[183]

On the homefront, the mobilization of the Jewish community in response to war conditions reflected the still-dominant role played by acculturated Central European Jews in shaping philanthropic efforts, but also revealed the rising influence of Eastern European Jews in the circle of leadership. When a Baltimore branch of the Jewish Welfare Board was founded in 1917 to aid Jewish soldiers in Europe and care for the religious and social needs of Jewish soldiers stationed at Camp Meade, the organizers included not only uptown figures, such as Oheb Shalom's rabbi, William Rosenau, and Hochschild, Kohn partner Walter Sondheim, but also immigrant notables, such as the Baltimore Bargain House magnate Jacob Epstein.[184]

Another nationally organized wartime effort that allowed Baltimore's immigrant community to assert local leadership was the American Jewish Relief Committee (AJRC), founded in 1914 to help relieve the suffering of Jews in the European war zone. An outgrowth of the American Jewish Committee, a defense organization dominated by the German Jewish elite, the AJRC became the focus of political acrimony between acculturated and immigrant Jews in cities across the United States.[185] In Baltimore, however, the local affiliate emerged as a model of cooperation between the two groups.

The co-chairs of the Baltimore relief effort were the longtime Zionist activist Harry Friedenwald, a native Baltimorean and the son of German Jewish immigrants, and Rabbi Reuben Rivkin, the spiritual leader of East Baltimore's Aitz Chaim Congregation. Rivkin, who immigrated to the United States in 1905 and came to Baltimore a few years later, represented a new style of Orthodox leadership. While in training and appearance he had all the credentials of a traditional rabbinic figure, he was also a gifted orator who had adapted his preaching to the needs of mass political meetings and rallies. He and Friedenwald addressed huge crowds at the Hippodrome and other Baltimore locations, and he followed the English-language speakers with rousing Yiddish speeches that combined themes of American patriotism with emotional calls to aid suffering Jews in the war zone. The joint leadership of the campaign, as well as the growing importance of mass participation in philanthropic efforts, marked the first time that Eastern European Jews played such a central role in shaping the agenda of the broader Jewish community.[186]

The most significant sign of the reorientation of communal priorities toward the concerns of the Eastern European group came with the increasing influence of Zionism. As the Jewish refugee problem, the recognition of Jewish rights in postwar Europe, and the prospect of securing a Jewish homeland in Palestine became significant questions of international discussion, Zionists played an ever-increasing role in establishing the priorities of the American Jewish community. In Baltimore, as in other Jewish centers, the top Zionist leadership positions were often held by Jews of Central European background like Friedenwald, who were chosen because of their perceived ability to represent the movement to the non-Jewish world. Overall, however, the movement was driven by Eastern European Jews, who dominated the membership and held most of the secondary leadership positions. The war had · greatly increased support for the Zionist cause, and by 1918 Baltimore had 5,000 organized Zionists and many more sympathizers who did not belong to any formal organization or movement.[187]

The dominance of the Zionists and, by association, Eastern European Jews over the larger agenda of the American Jewish community had become clear after 1916, when the Zionist-oriented American Jewish Congress emerged as a vehicle to represent American Jewish interests in postwar international negotiations. The movement to convene a Jewish congress was largely dismissed in its first year of existence by the Central European communal elite, but in 1917, when it was evident that the new organization would play a significant role in the crucial events unfolding abroad, uptown leaders agreed to participate in a community-wide election to determine who would represent Baltimore at the upcoming national meeting. With voters casting their ballots at locations as diverse as the JEA, East Baltimore synagogues, and fashionable Reform temples, the final result was an overwhelming victory for downtown and Zionist forces.[188]

While the results were criticized by Rabbi Rosenau—one of the unsuccessful candidates—and his colleague at Har Sinai, Rabbi Charles A. Rubenstein, the congress election demonstrated vividly the shrinking role of the Central European Jewish establishment as the arbiter of communal affairs. Unwilling to relinquish their traditional position of authority, Rosenau and Rubenstein went on the offensive, initiating a major campaign to denounce the Zionists as a destructive element in American Jewish life. Seizing an opportunity to take over the local Jewish newspaper, the *Jewish Comment*, whose longtime editor, Louis H. Levin, had resigned due to illness, the rabbis turned the weekly into an anti-Zionist organ. When Rosenau, who was serving as the president of the Reform movement's Central Conference of American Rabbis, hosted the group's national gathering in Baltimore in 1918, he and Rubenstein tried to convince their colleagues to banish all Zionist rabbis from the organization and to adopt the *Comment* as their publication.

Their effort backfired, however. In response to the grandstanding of Rosenau and Rubenstein, a large number of Reform rabbis, including the young Morris Lazaron, who had recently taken over the pulpit of Baltimore Hebrew Congregation, declared their loyalty to the Zionist movement. In a short time, the *Jewish Comment* folded for lack of readership. Rubenstein, who would resign from Har Sinai for undisclosed reasons in 1920 and become an insurance salesman, retained some influence: he became the editor of a new weekly publication, the *Jewish Times*, in 1919. But his experience with the *Comment* had taught him that he could not press his anti-Zionist agenda too far. He pledged in his opening *Times* editorial that the paper would not favor "any particular movement or group," acknowledging that "only on such conditions can a Jewish paper asking for the support of the entire Jewish community exist."[189]

A dramatic transformation of communal life was obviously afoot. Though the wealth and resources of Baltimore's established Central European Jews allowed them to retain a disproportionate role in community leadership, the ongoing acculturation of Eastern European Jewish immigrants and their American-born children was quickly altering the traditional balance of power. As Jews of Eastern European background continued their social and economic rise in the post–World War I years, their priorities and concerns would increasingly guide the affairs of the Baltimore Jewish community.

4
Bawlmer Jews
THE INTERWAR YEARS

- - - - - - - - - - - - -

As 1921 began, Maurice Bisgyer, the resident director of the Jewish Educational Alliance, fretted about how the beloved East Baltimore settlement house would serve the astounding 18,000 children and adults who passed through its doors each month. "Coming from Northwest, South, Southwest, and far East Baltimore," he reported, "they have taxed our building beyond its limit." He also despaired over the "great gap" between immigrant parents and their children. In the "typical East Baltimore home," fathers toiled long hours at the factory or store while mothers labored over household drudgery. Preoccupied with making ends meet and guided by a rigid Old World morality, they had lost influence over their children, who were enticed by the city's pool rooms, dance halls, and other urban temptations. Without effective intervention, he feared, these youths would become a lost generation.[1]

Bisgyer did not realize it, but everything was about to change. Just four months after he lamented the gulf between immigrants and their children, the US Congress enacted the first of two laws establishing quotas that would bring Jewish immigration to a virtual halt.[2] After a century of Jewish life influenced by a continual stream of arrivals from Europe, the children subject to the pull of the pool room and the dance hall now had the responsibility of forging a truly American Jewish community. Ironically, although the quotas hastened the Americanization of the nation's Jewish population, the legislation—aimed specifically at barring the entry of Southern and Eastern Europeans—foreshadowed a period of rising antisemitism that would place significant limits on Jews' integration into mainstream American life. Even as they made rapid economic strides and moved beyond the immigrant milieu, they would face discrimination that affected where they could live, work, socialize, and attend school.

These national trends played out in ways that reflected Baltimore's geography and culture. As a less cosmopolitan and more southern-tinged city than America's largest urban centers, Baltimore continued to evince a greater degree of social conservatism and religious traditionalism across the ethnic and denominational spectrum. Secularization proceeded more slowly than in larger Jewish hubs, and communal institutions retained a stronger hold. Economic conditions particular to Baltimore also had important ramifications. The rise of steelmaking and shipbuilding during World War I launched the city as "a modern industrial complex, vital to the American economy," as author Sherry Olson puts it.[3] The following decade provided ample opportunity for Jews to get ahead, despite being shut out of some industries. Meanwhile, the city's unique position as a meeting ground between African Americans and European immigrant groups continued to offer both advantages and disadvantages as Jews carved out their place in the evolving social order.

Baltimore's industrial boom caused the population to surge more than 53 percent from 1910 to 1940 and prompted a major extension of the city's boundaries. In 1918, to make room for its swelling workforce and to gain control of the expanding harbor, the city annexed a large swath of surrounding land, tripling in area from thirty to ninety-two square miles. The largely undeveloped new territory underwent a residential building boom that had consequences for the entire city. Suddenly, people of all income levels were on the move: the wealthy and the middle classes to the spacious new homes and row houses of the annex, the less well-off to the places they left behind.[4]

Discriminatory real estate practices decisively shaped the racial and ethnic landscape as the expanded city developed. African Americans, barred from the annexed area and the suburbs beyond, became concentrated in the city center. As their numbers grew, they moved into areas vacated by white immigrant groups whose improved circumstances enabled them to move to the next rung of better housing, though they too faced exclusionary policies.[5]

Jews kept pace with Baltimore's population growth despite the halt in fresh-off-the-boat arrivals. With their numbers rising to around 73,000 by 1937, they made up 8–9 percent of the city's residents through the interwar era. Jewish immigrants enthusiastically joined in the mass exodus of foreign-born residents from the city's core. Following their Central European coreligionists, they abandoned East Baltimore for a succession of northwest neighborhoods. Change came quickly: by 1925 more than half of the Jewish population lived in Northwest Baltimore. Meanwhile, as it shed its immigrant status and grew in numbers, the Jewish community grew in confidence as well.[6]

The wholesale resettlement of Jews to Northwest Baltimore informed every aspect of Jewish life. As historian Deborah Dash Moore noted, such second-generation Jewish neighborhoods across the United States offered a safe place for the children of immigrants to experiment with becoming Americans. The densely Jewish environment enabled them to hold onto their Jewish identity even as the influence of religion and Yiddishkeit diminished and the influence of American culture grew stronger. "American and Jewish components" became "woven into a matrix of local activity" in a "natural, informal, almost invisible" way, writes Moore.[7] In other words, these neighborhoods allowed Jews to forge an American Jewish culture.

Hanging out in Northwest Baltimore: Gilbert Sandler (*front row, left*) and buddies in the early 1930s. *Jewish Museum of Maryland. Courtesy of Gilbert Sandler.*

In Baltimore, as elsewhere, this new culture reflected the influences of the local environment.

The emergence of Northwest Baltimore as a Jewish space greatly influenced how Jews related to the surrounding society. The new Jewish district served as a launching pad for entrepreneurs, who could then reach beyond the ethnic economy with the kinds of businesses that characterized a new era of consumerism. And though having their own turf served in some ways to isolate Jews, it offered a strong base of support that allowed Jewish politicians and community leaders to play major roles in city politics and urban affairs. The new proximity to West Baltimore, the city's largest African American district, heightened tensions between the two groups but also offered possibilities for cooperation.

Indeed, contradictions abounded as the Jewish community remade itself during the interwar period. Leaders committed to Jewish unity achieved success in bringing together different segments of Baltimore Jewry—with their signal accomplishment being the 1921 merger of uptown and downtown charities into the Associated Jewish Charities—even as the community splintered over a variety of issues from Zionism to conditions in the garment industry. Americanization continued to undermine traditional religious practice even as a strong undercurrent of religious revival took hold among a significant segment of young people. Jewish neighborhoods, Jewish social life, and a preoccupation with pressing Jewish affairs (local, national, and international) reinforced a tendency toward insularity. Nevertheless, Jews embraced the local culture wholeheartedly and intensified their participation in the life of their city as they reconstructed themselves as Jewish Baltimoreans.

Northwest Passage:
Geography and Identity in Jewish Baltimore

When upwardly mobile Jews sought to escape the overcrowded, rundown housing of their immigrant enclaves in the years following World War I, they were "excluded from so many areas that the only direction [they] could go was northwest," asserted Leon Sachs, the longtime head of the Baltimore Jewish Council. Though many cities had well-defined Jewish neighborhoods, Baltimore Jews "had been herded into the northwest section of the city to such an extent that we were labeled everywhere as probably the most ghettoized community in the country." Sachs, who was in the thick of battles to combat antisemitism in the mid-twentieth century, spoke from experience. Indeed, by the time he joined the Baltimore Jewish Council in 1941, four out of five Jews in the city lived in Northwest Baltimore, and discrimination had played a critical role. But forces both within and outside the community combined to cause Baltimore Jewry's unusually high residential concentration.[8]

Sachs placed most of the blame on the Roland Park Company, which, he claimed, made residential restrictions popular. Certainly he was right to emphasize the major role played by the city's premier residential developer. The Roland Park Company's founder, Edward Bouton, firmly believed that selling to Jews resulted in depressed property values because gentiles would not buy homes in Jewish areas. Since his company developed much of North Baltimore, its strict ban kept upwardly mobile Jews out of a large swath of the city's new residential districts, including Roland Park, Guilford, Homeland, and Northwood.[9]

The methods developed by the Roland Park Company to bar Jews were copied by other firms. Because only a handful of companies controlled large tracts of land, their combined efforts effectively circumscribed the Jewish population. The process went as follows: First, the companies carefully screened the initial buyers. Then, to ensure that these homeowners did not later sell to Jews, the companies relied not on deed restrictions (which were used primarily against African Americans) but on a potent mix of advertising, signage, and a "gentlemen's agreement" with the city's real estate board, which enforced discipline among realtors through control of the multiple listing service. Northwood was advertised as an "ideal location for discriminating people," while a sign at the entrance to Homeland proclaimed it to be "restricted." A 1930 brochure assured buyers, "you probably know" the "kind of people" who "can be found in Homeland–Guilford–Roland Park." Such market-

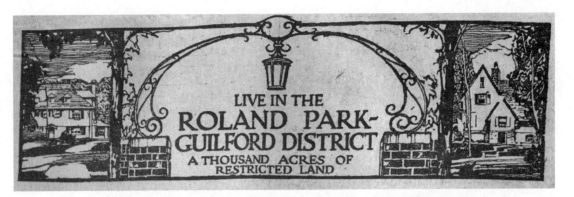

Roland Park Company ads in the early 1920s laid claim to "A Thousand Acres of Restricted Land." The company developed much of North Baltimore, effectively shutting Jews out of many neighborhoods. *Courtesy of Johns Hopkins University Special Collections.*

ing techniques signaled to Jews that they were not welcome even if not explicitly banned.[10]

Jews who missed the warnings or slipped through the screening process found that the implicit could quickly become explicit. In 1941, thirty-five Ruxton residents signed a letter to Mr. and Mrs. Robert E. Hecht Sr., who had recently purchased a lot in the upscale North Baltimore community. "You have had an offer to take the lot off your hands without any loss to yourselves," the letter pointed out. "We respectfully, but urgently, request you to accept." A real estate company canceled Israel Saffron's contract to buy a home in Northeast Baltimore's middle-class Ednor Gardens when it was discovered that he was Jewish. The agent told him he "could not sell the property to a Jew" but would be "very glad to sell him any home in a Jewish neighborhood."[11] Discrimination in housing was not yet illegal, so the agent faced no penalty for being honest. But according to the social conventions of the day, subtlety was preferred in enforcing barriers against Jews, Italians, and other European ethnic minorities. Jews were, after all, "white," and many had attained a degree of civic or economic accomplishment.

These two episodes aside, the mechanisms to bar Jews operated largely on an impersonal level that enabled developers to focus on their economic rationale rather than the bigotry that was behind it. Indeed, prominent Jewish real estate developers also discriminated against Jews. Joseph Meyerhoff, for example, partnered with the Roland Park Company during the depths of the Depression and scrupulously followed Bouton's anti-Jewish policy. Though he later stated that he "wasn't happy about it," he and other Jewish developers accepted Bouton's claim that gentiles would not live near Jews and saw the restrictions as simply a good business practice.[12]

Meanwhile, racial politics and white Baltimore's concern to prevent the advance of African Americans into white residential districts may have played as large a role as antisemitism in channeling the Jewish population's movement to the northwest. With a historically large black population, Baltimore had long led the nation in efforts to segregate blacks. Jews, like the city's other European ethnic groups, gained from the city's racialized housing market, which made the color line the most important factor in determining where people lived. However, in the eyes of native-born whites, Jews were implicated in the attempts of African Americans to break out of their confined areas. As Antero Pietila points out in his groundbreaking study of housing discrimination in Baltimore, the opposition to Jews' encroachment into non-Jewish areas was heightened by the fact that Jewish neighborhoods often became "transitional zones where sellers ultimately tapped the black market."[13]

While this pattern could be found in other cities, it was particularly significant in Baltimore, the only American city at that time with sizable concentrations of both blacks and Jews. In 1920, the city was roughly 15 percent black and 9 percent Jewish; in contrast, other cities with large Jewish communities had very few African Americans during this early stage of the Great Migration of southern blacks to the North.[14] Thus, in addition to the typical anti-Jewish tendencies of real estate brokers, housing developers, and gentile homeowners that existed elsewhere, the large percentage of black people in Baltimore made the white establishment especially determined to limit the spread of Jews, who might later sell their houses to African Americans.

In fact, during the interwar years the city's Jewish neighborhoods did continuously give way to expanding black settlement, which could no longer be contained in the traditional African American district in West Baltimore. To escape overcrowding, black people looked to the heavily Jewish neighborhood to the north rather than to the white, non-Jewish neighborhood to the west, where they faced greater resistance. As Leon Sachs later observed, Jews did not "throw bricks and break windows when blacks moved in." Moreover, Pietila points out, "the Real Estate Board did not generally accept Jews to membership. As a result, the board lacked capacity and will to enforce segregation in predominantly Jewish districts."[15]

Nor were Jews as likely to participate in the anti-black campaigns pursued by elite homeowner associations. When Harry Friedenwald was approached by segregationist William Marbury in 1929 to sign a petition for "the protection of our neighborhood from Negro invasion," he refused. "Our people have had such a long experience in the particular question of segregation . . . that I would never actively promote such a movement," he told Marbury, who replied that "nothing was going to arouse the animosity against the Jews more than this attitude of aligning themselves with the Negroes."[16] Some Jews did join homeowner associations aimed at keeping out blacks, either because they agreed with the goal or because they wanted to fit in. But more commonly, they simply moved farther northwest.

The racial dynamics and anti-Jewish prejudice that steered Jews into a single section of the city were reinforced by the choices made by Jews themselves. After decades of hard use, East Baltimore's cramped immigrant district had greatly deteriorated. Many homes still lacked indoor plumbing; public parks and private yards were few and far between. At first, many families chose to move nearby: the neighborhood directly to the east offered larger row houses, the green space of Patterson Park, and proximity to familiar synagogues, institutions, and the Lombard Street market. But the eastern extension of the immigrant enclave lasted only a few decades. The expansive precincts of Northwest Baltimore beckoned as an ideal place for tight-knit networks of family and friends not only to enjoy better housing, parks, and other amenities, but also to build new, more modern institutions and create commercial districts that would cater to their evolving needs. The eagerness of Jews to cluster together and re-create their community was demonstrated by the seven congregations that sprang up in Northwest Baltimore between 1918 and 1921, with many more to come.[17]

While Northwest Baltimore came to include almost the entirety of Baltimore Jewry, it was nevertheless a place where diversity reigned. In the annex, new residential developments for the affluent featured detached homes and large yards; within the old city limits, blocks of 800-square-foot row houses with tiny front porches drew the working class; and a growing middle class found plenty of options in between. Eutaw Place in the early 1920s still housed the Central European Jewish elite in gracious mansions and elegant apartment buildings. Upwardly mobile Eastern European Jews settled nearby in the blocks adjacent to Druid Hill Park. Working-class immigrants tended to settle in Lower Park Heights and west along the North Avenue corridor toward Easterwood Park. The more well-off Eastern European families moved to the annex neighborhoods of Upper Park Heights and Forest Park, where substantial homes mixed with blocks of spacious row houses.[18]

"German" Jews were on the move as well, motivated by the development of suburban-style housing in newly annexed Upper Park Heights, Mount Washington, and Windsor Hills—and also by the encroachment of Eastern European Jews and blacks into the Eutaw Place district. Wealthy Jewish families had previously maintained summer homes in the "sylvan village" of Mount Washington, which bordered Upper Park Heights. "Never restricted, in spirit or letter," it became a mixed Jewish and gentile neighborhood after annexation. Prominent Jewish families had discovered the wooded (and gentile) Windsor Hills as early as 1910, when the future judge Joseph Ulman and his wife moved in. Their arrival, followed by the Hutzlers, Hamburgers, and Hollanders, "caused almost as much excitement as the arrival of blacks many years later," stated a local history. But the gentiles of Windsor Hills did not flee, and the neighborhood, located just below Forest Park, remained mixed. "German" Jews also pioneered in settling outside the city boundary in the northwest suburb of Pikesville, where some took up residence in an exclusive new development, Dumbarton. Legend has it that Dumbarton *was* restricted: Eastern European Jews were barred by "gentlemen's agreement."[19]

Who remained behind in East Baltimore? The immigrant district was "still thickly populated" with Jews in 1925, noted a Hebrew Benevolent Society worker, but its residents were older and poorer than those who had moved out. By 1930 Jews shared the original enclave with Italians and blacks as families continued their

Left: Lower Park Heights was Baltimore's quintessential interwar Jewish neighborhood. Here, Carol Eckhaus stands at Park Heights and Spring Hill avenues, 1934. *Jewish Museum of Maryland*. *Right*: Berney Katzenberg Jr. in Forest Park, an upscale alternative to Lower Park Heights, late 1930s. *Jewish Museum of Maryland*.

march northwest or spread farther east. Yet the Lombard Street market continued to thrive, increasingly patronized by customers who had moved away but returned regularly, drawn by its familiar vendors and foodstuffs and its Old World ambience. Shoppers would also stroll over to Baltimore Street to take in the Yiddish theater or dine at kosher restaurants, such as the New York Dairy Lunch Room, Silverman's Dairy Restaurant, and the Vienna Restaurant (for meat eaters).[20] The smaller immigrant enclave in Southwest Baltimore also persisted, its families sustained by employment in the nearby clothing factories. Known as Little Jerusalem, the area was described by former resident Barnett Berman as an "island of *Yiddishkeit* in a Christian sea," with its own shuls, a Talmud Torah, and a small JEA branch. The decline of the garment industry, however, would cause its residents, too, to succumb to the pull of the northwest through the 1930s.[21]

While the eastern and southwestern Baltimore enclaves hung on during the interwar years as reminders of the immigrant past, Northwest Baltimore saw the development of a culture that was distinctly Jewish yet decidedly American. It too had kosher butcher shops and bakeries, but its commercial strips also offered modern gathering places, including drugstores, movie theaters, and bowling alleys. Public areas were extensions of family and community space where residents could comfortably construct a mixed American and Jewish lifestyle. Sachs Drug Store was a "second home" for youths who lived near Druid Hill Park. Popular spots in Lower Park Heights included the Hot Shoppe (known for its milkshakes), White Tower Hamburger Shoppe, and Lapides Delly. "Your whole life revolved around the neighborhood," recalled Marcia Smith Keiser. Gil Sandler described Park Heights Avenue's "street corner society" as "a way of life" where young people showed off their American style and met their future spouses. Public libraries, schools, and even streetcars became part of the communal landscape. As one person told Sandler, "We knew every conductor and every motorman, and they knew us."[22]

This hybrid American Jewish culture spread quickly, if not evenly. As families of similar income clustered together, they created distinct Jewish neighborhoods, each with its own character. Half of the members of the Labor Lyceum relocated to Lower Park Heights, according to a 1925 community study. Traces of the immigrant lifestyle lingered in such working-class areas. In the alleys of Lower Park Heights, shochtim operated in garages "with feathers flying." Nat Youngelson's local *Yiddish Hour* radio show was so popular that "in warm weather when windows were open you could walk down the street, pass house by house, and not miss a word."[23]

The delicatessens of Northwest Baltimore catered to residents in different stages of acculturation. Jews and non-Jews rubbed shoulders at Nates and Leons, where a diverse clientele included politicians, businesspeople, couples out on the town, racetrack denizens, and numbers runners. Ballow's, meanwhile, advertised only on a Yiddish radio program and attracted an all-Jewish crowd. The tumult of Yiddish conversation and the pungent smell of cooked meats contributed to the deli's Jewish atmosphere. But even Ballow's was not immune to change: its decision to open on Saturdays cost the restaurant its kosher certification. It may have been the "Headquarters of Good Luck Herring," but its Jewishness was becoming more kosher-style than kosher.[24]

American pastimes came to dominate neighborhood life. Druid Hill Park served as "Jewish Baltimore's green oasis," a place to picnic, engage in sports, or simply hang out. The park's clay tennis courts were especially popular, while the renowned softball leagues of Easterwood Park captivated boys who lived farther west along North Avenue. Phil Sherman noted that Hebrew school was "the only recognized reason" to miss a game. The Jewish community even had an amusement park in its midst, Carlin's Park in Lower Park Heights, where young people could stroll the midway and take advantage of the attractions, including a roller coaster, an arcade, and a popular skating rink.[25]

Adults looked askance at the freedom of young people to create their own culture as they roamed the streets and sampled the offerings of American consumer society. Too many gathering places were unwholesome, they feared. Social workers warned against the dance hall at Carlin's Park, where Jewish boys went to "'pick up' girls."

Sports played a key role in youth culture in Baltimore's Jewish neighborhoods in the interwar period. *Jewish Museum of Maryland.*

Parents worried about the influence of Pimlico racetrack, located in the midst of Park Heights. Harry London recalled, "We were forever being reminded that people having anything to do with the racetrack around the corner, especially Jews, were undesirables, criminals, gangsters; bums at least." The rough-edged social life of the era spilled over into unlikely places. Candy stores and drugstores served as centers for the numbers racket, according to a JEA worker, while "the many newly formed mushroom political clubs" enticed neighborhood youths with gambling and drinking. Yet these clubs provided the infrastructure of a neighborhood power base that would soon translate into heightened political influence for the Jewish population.[26]

Indeed, the societal discrimination that helped herd Jews into Northwest Baltimore ended up empowering them. Having their own space gave them the opportunity to develop the confidence and the resources to make their mark economically, politically, and culturally. Jewish upward mobility owed much to connections people made in the everyday course of neighborhood life. As Gil Sandler notes, on the "back-lot playing fields" of Northwest Baltimore, "young men met the men-

The dance hall at Carlin's Park was a popular spot for Jewish youth. *Courtesy of the Enoch Pratt Free Library, Maryland State Library Resource Center. All rights reserved.*

tors who would lead them into distinguished careers in medicine, law, business."[27] Just as port-of-entry neighborhoods provided economic and cultural resources that enabled immigrants to get a start in the United States, Northwest Baltimore's second-generation neighborhoods became a strategy for rising in American society.

Beyond the Sweatshop:
Branching Out in the New Baltimore Economy

Having emerged as an industrial power during World War I, Baltimore flourished in the 1920s. The port rose from the nation's seventh most active to third. Steel and shipbuilding dominated while other manufacturers opened large branch plants. Baltimoreans of all sorts saw their fortunes improve. In particular, "working people enjoyed rising living standards," notes historian Ken Durr. "Home ownership rates rose, families bought radios, and a few could even afford cars." Motorists could travel along the miles of newly constructed roads and viaducts that reached into the annex, the epicenter of a residential building boom that was adding 6,000 new homes to the city per year.[28]

Jews looking to find their place in the post–World War I economy confronted challenges, however. In an era of consolidation, small family businesses faced competition from ever-larger companies and chain stores. Jews who abandoned entrepreneurial ambitions to seek employment in large firms were often stymied in their attempts to find work outside the Jewish community. Many companies discriminated against them, from the spice manufacturer McCormick to insurance firms such as the Maryland Casualty Company. Classified ads often specified "gentiles only."[29]

To make matters worse, the one industry dominated by Jews—clothing manufacture—fell into an unexpected and rapid decline. The needle trades had surged during World War I as the city's location proved ideal for shipping uniforms, blankets, and other items for military use. Wartime labor shortages had helped local garment unions to win pay raises, better conditions, and an arbitration system that became a national model. By the war's end, 60 percent of needle trades workers were organized compared with 15 percent in other Baltimore industries, and the Amalgamated Clothing Workers of America (ACWA) had become the city's largest union. In 1919 it won a forty-four-hour week as employment and unionization reached all-time highs, with 27,000 workers (almost half of them women) employed in men's clothing production alone, Baltimore's specialty.[30]

But only a few months after a December 1919 *Baltimore Sun* article recognized the ACWA as a real power in the city's economy, the clothing industry found itself reeling. A delayed postwar depression that hit garment manufacturing nationally proved especially ruinous in Baltimore, partly because firms such as Sonneborn and Company had focused on military needs and had difficulty regaining customers after the war. More than 10,000 jobs disappeared in 1920 alone, mostly in men's clothing, the branch where Jews were concentrated. Membership in the ACWA plummeted as Baltimore slipped from third to fifth in men's clothing production by 1922.[31]

Companies large and small shut down or slashed hours and wages, with some 60 percent of jobs lost even before the Great Depression. The first large firm to close was Strouse and Brothers—a blow to unionized workers, since the company had developed a good relationship with the ACWA. Sonneborn, which had also taken a progressive stance on labor, worked with the ACWA through the 1920s to find a way back to profitability. But then the Depression hit, and in 1931 the city's largest clothing manufacturer shut its doors. Other companies took the opposite approach. As wages plunged, local garment workers became among the lowest paid in the nation, giving manufacturers a competitive advantage they did not care to relinquish. Already anti-union, they became even more hostile to workers' attempts to improve pay and conditions.[32]

Management and labor fought a series of bitter, often violent battles through the 1920s and 1930s. In the '20s, charges of radicalism isolated unions locally and nationally, but the '30s saw public opinion swing in the ACWA's favor, helped along by a citizens' committee led by Har Sinai rabbi Edward Israel and Johns Hopkins economist Jacob Hollander, whose investigation exposed "shameful" conditions at J. Schoeneman's, one of the city's largest firms. After hitting "rock bottom" around 1930, the ACWA regained its footing with a risky 1932 general strike led by women, who outnumbered men in the workforce. The fiery leader Sarah Barron was arrested thirteen times, and union lawyer Jacob Edelman was often "summoned in

Union women, including Sarah Barron (*seated, third from left*),
at a banquet, 1940s. *Jewish Museum of Maryland.*

the middle of the night to secure her release" from jail. The strike brought several companies under union contract and the labor-friendly administration of Franklin D. Roosevelt helped solidify union gains. But the Schoeneman company refused to accept a union victory and "stole away in the middle of the night," moving its jobs to Pennsylvania.[33]

The industry's layoffs and labor turmoil, combined with the pull of new opportunities available to the younger generation, depleted the ranks of Jewish garment workers. By the mid-1930s, Italians and other non-Jewish immigrant groups outnumbered Jews in the workforce. The number of African Americans in the needle trades also rose, their presence aided by New Deal reforms championed by the Jewish garment unions. The manufacturers' profile changed as well. The disappearance of firms that had long dominated the industry led to more out-of-town ownership, but also provided openings for a new breed of Eastern European Jewish entrepreneurs. For example, Israel Myers, son of Polish immigrants, took over the faltering clothing firm where he had started as a teenage stenographer. Years later he would achieve success with an innovative raincoat he called London Fog.[34]

Though some Jews remained as owners, workers, and union leaders, the garment industry nevertheless lost its primacy in Jewish economic life. An expanding consumer market benefited other traditional Jewish businesses while creating whole new fields of commercial activity. Eastern European Jews and their progeny avidly pursued these opportunities while also advancing in the professions. As a result, the interwar period was one of growing occupational diversity for Baltimore Jews, while Eastern Europeans made economic gains and emerged as the dominant economic force within Baltimore Jewry.

For traditional businesses and upstarts alike, modernization was key to success in the new era. Aaron Straus built on a rising business model, the chain store, to turn his Reliable Stores Corporation into a national conglomerate. New production and marketing techniques helped Baltimore firms dominate US umbrella manufacturing. Gans Brothers ("Born in Baltimore—Raised Everywhere") led the way, though rival Polan Katz ("Reigning Beauty") surged after introducing the first colored umbrella that did not bleed when rained on. Not all innovations proved beneficial, however; retailer Hess Shoes brought the newly invented "shoe fitting fluoroscope" (an X-ray machine) to Baltimore. It proved quite popular but was retired after scientists discovered the dangers of routinely exposing customers and salespeople to radiation.[35]

Some businesses applied modern technologies to the traditional Jewish horse-and-cart operation, often under the stewardship of the second generation. In 1928 the Hoffberger family built one of the nation's first cold storage facilities, helping to expand their modest coal and ice delivery business into a diversified empire that would later include three iconic Baltimore products: Pompeian Olive Oil, National Bohemian beer (the ubiquitous "Natty Boh"), and the Baltimore Orioles.[36] World War I turned the once-lowly junk trade into a booming scrap industry, to the benefit of several entrepreneurs. Latvian immigrant Morris Schapiro, who started his career hauling refuse out of the ruins of the Baltimore fire of 1904, became adept at scrapping obsolete naval vessels. He prospered as Baltimore became a leading center for this activity.[37]

Wholesalers contended with the rise of chain stores and the growing ability of retailers to deal directly with manufacturers, but Baltimore's domination of the southern market kept the industry viable. Jacob Epstein's Baltimore Bargain House, renamed the American Wholesale Corporation in 1919 to reflect its national stature, employed 2,500 people in its manufacturing and wholesale operations and mailed 2 million catalogs per year.[38] Around Epstein's West Baltimore empire congregated smaller wholesalers, almost all Jewish-owned. As older firms struggled with new market realities, Eastern European immigrants jumped in, often targeting niche markets, such as Askin Brothers' hosiery and underwear firm. Wholesaling was especially attractive to religiously observant entrepreneurs because, unlike retailers, they did not have to stay open on the Sabbath.[39]

Hutzler Brothers boasted of being the first department store in Baltimore to provide parking space for customers, 1925. *Jewish Museum of Maryland.*

As crowds thronged the downtown shopping district in the consumer-driven 1920s, the Jewish-owned department stores entered their heyday. They, too, innovated to keep up with the times. Recognizing its customers' growing use of the automobile, in 1925 Hutzler's opened downtown's first store parking lot. Gutman's introduced the escalator to Baltimore in its eight-story addition built in 1929. The department stores served as a significant source of employment for Jews; Hutzler's alone had around 1,200 employees in the 1920s. With a largely female workforce, the stores offered particular opportunities for women, who could rise to upper-level positions as buyers and managers in some (though not all) departments. Hutzler's company newsletter, *Tips and Taps*, was run largely by women, from the editor in chief to the staff artist.[40]

Small family businesses remained a cornerstone of Jewish economic activity, but the most successful changed with the times, using modern methods to move beyond their ethnic base. In a new era of urban nightlife, Nates and Leons "Always Awake" deli enticed customers by staying open all night, attracting patrons reluctant to go home after the nightclubs closed. Ike and Dora Silber, who had failed with two previous bakeries, found success in 1922 with a shop on Monroe Street. While Ike did the baking, Dora was the entrepreneur, encouraging her husband to try new recipes

Louis Israelson and his children Reuben and Annetta in their grocery store on
Pennsylvania Avenue, c. 1929. The store typified the small Jewish family business of the era.
Jewish Museum of Maryland. Courtesy of Glenda Goldberg and Susan Grott.

and buy modern equipment. Together they built a popular chain that would grow
to some thirty stores.[41]

The small size and narrow profit margin of family stores made them vulner-
able, however. Even during the prosperous 1920s, a sudden rise in costs or another adverse circumstance could spell failure. Like the Silbers, some families
kept trying until they succeeded, opening under new names or in new locations
after shutting down or going bankrupt. Wives played integral roles as owners,
managers, salespeople, bookkeepers, and helpers. Some, like Dora Silber, were
the driving force behind their store's success. Others worked just to keep from
failing. Bess Fishman recalled that her father was often ill, so her mother kept the
store going: "She did what had to be done and that was it." Children also contributed. "We kids grew up working in the store," said Leon Albin, whose family lived
above their secondhand clothing shop on Pennsylvania Avenue. "It was impossible to separate family life from business life." Indeed, the family store was all-
consuming. "When we ate in our dining room in back of our store my mother sat
so she could see what was going on," stated Jonas Yousem. "No matter what she

was doing—cooking, eating or whatever—if she saw a customer, she would go wait on the customer."[42]

Though many family-run stores found success serving Northwest Baltimore's growing Jewish community, others reached out to a non-Jewish clientele. Jewish businesses large and small lined commercial strips such as South Charles, East Monument, and Gay streets. Jews also operated countless corner groceries in non-Jewish neighborhoods.[43] The African American population remained an important customer base, especially in West Baltimore. Despite severe discrimination, African Americans benefited from the World War I boom years: purchasing power increased, and the community supported a growing black middle class of professionals and service providers. But by all accounts, most of the district's merchants were Jewish. This was not unusual; in cities across the nation, Jewish entrepreneurs of limited means found opportunity in black districts. The economic relationship was especially significant in Baltimore, where commercial ties had developed over decades of interaction. During the interwar period, the proximity of African American and Jewish neighborhoods only intensified this interaction, while also fostering Jewish ownership of real estate in nearby black areas.[44]

The housing boom helped make real estate an important economic growth area for Jews, not only enabling established builders, such as Ephraim Macht, to expand their activities, but also launching a new generation of developers, property owners, and realtors. Some, like the Meyerhoff brothers, headed straight for the undeveloped annex. Others, like Victor Frenkil, got their start as skilled building tradesmen and small contractors. Still others began as small investors, benefiting from the cheap prices, tax sales, auctions, and foreclosures of the Depression. As these entrepreneurs established themselves, they laid the groundwork for the breathtaking expansion of Jewish involvement in Baltimore real estate that would occur after World War II.[45]

The post-World War I period was also an "era of autos and radios," and some Jewish entrepreneurs moved beyond clothing and grocery stores to become early purveyors of these modern consumer goods. As rising incomes, greater access to credit, and lower costs put car ownership within reach of more Americans, the auto dealership came into its own. Abe Legum opened a small garage in 1920; his Park Circle Motor Company eventually grew into one of the largest Chevy dealerships in the country. Its chief local competitor was also a Jewish-owned firm, Fox Chevrolet, formed in 1933 by Louis Fox at the tender age of twenty-one.[46] By the early 1920s, American Oil Company founders Louis and Jacob Blaustein had already pioneered in the business of fueling automobiles when they developed the first high-octane gasoline, which they called Amoco, by adding benzol, a by-product of Baltimore's Bethlehem Steel coke ovens. Using the techniques of the new advertising age, they turned Amoco into a recognizable brand, not simply an ingredient needed to operate a car. They scored a public relations coup when Charles Lindbergh used Amoco to fuel the *Spirit of St. Louis* during his historic

The Zamoiski family pioneered in Baltimore's radio industry. *Jewish Museum of Maryland.*

transatlantic flight from New York to Paris. Despite their national profile, they remained in Baltimore and invested a chunk of their profits in downtown real estate.[47]

Meanwhile, the entertainment industry underwent a revolution in the 1920s. Radio and feature-length movies began to outpace vaudeville, while spectator sports became widely popular for the first time. Ben Glass capitalized on both of the era's major trends: starting out as a car mechanic, he soon specialized in repairing car radios. He then opened a radio repair shop, which gradually turned into a record store. His son, the future composer Philip Glass, would benefit from the musical exposure the store gave him. Joseph Zamoiski, the owner of an electric supply firm, pioneered in selling radios with the help of his son Calman, who started Baltimore's first radio station in the family home in 1921. By the time it went off the air in 1923, WKC had done its job: thousands of Baltimoreans had bought radio sets, other local stations had started up, and the Zamoiskis were on their way to owning one of the nation's largest wholesale radio firms.[48]

Jews operated many of the era's new theaters and nightclubs and promoted numerous sporting events. Harry "Heinie" Blaustein (no relation to the Amoco Blausteins) guided several boxers to world titles as Baltimore's most respected trainer. Isadore Rappaport earned the nickname "Mr. Showbiz" as the owner of the Hippodrome Theatre, where he alternated old-style vaudeville shows with new feature-length films and popular big band acts. In 1928 Emanuel Davidove and Harry Goldberg purchased a former (white) church in West Baltimore, which they transformed into the palatial Harlem Theatre, "a 1,500-seat motion picture theatre for Negroes" that

The Harlem Theatre brought "a semblance of Broadway glamor" to West Baltimore, enthused the *Afro-American*. Its grand opening in October 1932 drew a crowd of 30,000 and featured a parade with brass bands and floats. *Courtesy of the* Afro-American.

"Wildcat" Izzy Rainess was one of several Baltimore Jewish boxers who found success during the interwar era. *Jewish Museum of Maryland.*

featured a "celestial ceiling" of "twinkling electrical stars and projected clouds," the *Afro-American* newspaper reported.[49]

From bandleaders to boxers, Jews also earned their livelihoods as performers. Nationally, boxing offered opportunity to working-class kids from tough backgrounds, which meant blacks, Jews, Italians, and members of other ethnic groups. Among Baltimore's many Jewish boxers, one standout was the former newsboy Jack Portney, a welterweight who learned to fight to protect himself from bigger newsboys who wanted his turf. In his twelve-year boxing career he recorded 150 wins and 15 losses. Izzy Rainess, a parking attendant at Pimlico racetrack, was discovered by a jockey's agent impressed with his prowess in fights with other attendants. A local star whose style earned him the nickname "Wildcat," the five foot seven, 145-pound brawler won 26 of 28 pro fights.[50]

Jewish entrepreneurs played a key role in transforming "The Block," a stretch of downtown lined with vaudeville and burlesque houses, theaters, and clubs. As live acts struggled to compete with movies and radio, The Block lost customers. One club owner hit upon a solution: legend has it that Max Cohen introduced striptease to The Block at his nightclub, the Oasis, a "bottle bar" that offered ice and entertainment to patrons who supplied their own alcohol during Prohibition. Cohen's hostesses would sit and chat with customers until the music began, when they would get up, peel off their evening gowns, and dance in scanty costumes. Other establishments soon offered their own striptease shows along with more conventional comedy and musical acts. From chic clubs to downscale burlesque joints, most of these venues were owned by Jews — if not always enthusiastically. In financial straits during the Depression, Ben Livingston took over the Clover Theater after his brother Isaac, a pawnshop owner, acquired it in a loan default. "He hated it but made good money," Ben's son Bernard recalled. Known as a "scratch house" because of the insects that plagued its patrons, "the place was always packed."[51]

Cohen's bottle bar and Livingston's Clover Theater provide examples of how Jewish businesspeople adapted to the two defining events of the interwar period: Prohibition and the Depression. Prohibition was universally disliked and universally disregarded in Baltimore, the longtime home of many breweries, a thriving liquor industry, and a German-influenced culture that saw drinking as a natural part of social life. H. L. Mencken railed against Prohibition in the *Evening Sun*, and the political establishment sided with the "wets." Most American Jews opposed Prohibition as well. As Rabbi William Rosenau of the prestigious Eutaw Place Temple told the *Sun* in 1930, "the sooner [P]rohibition is done away with the better it will be." He may have felt freer to speak out than rabbis in more "dry" cities, but his fervent opposition might also have had to do with the frequency with which Jews appeared in the newspaper as Prohibition violators. Engaging in criminal behavior — even in opposition to a dubious law — did not reflect well on a people striving to enter the mainstream. Indeed, Jewish leaders in many cities feared that reports of Jewish liquor law transgressions would stoke antisemitism.[52]

For first- and second-generation immigrants struggling to gain an economic foothold, Prohibition offered enticing ways to earn a living. The rougher precincts of East Baltimore provided the backdrop for numerous *Sun* articles about Jewish lawbreakers. Samuel Paper's bakery was raided in January 1922 after a still exploded and caught fire in the rear of his shop. Nearby, lawmen found twenty-five barrels of wine at Abraham Levine's restaurant. As an angry crowd gathered, Levine's wife struck a sergeant over the head with an alarm clock, and their twelve-year-old son told an officer that "if he had a pistol he would shoot him." Most of Jewish East Baltimore apparently shared this unrepentant attitude. When federal agents destroyed a distillery in the rear of 119 North High Street, some 500 jeering onlookers "thronged surrounding roofs and fences and at times threatened violence."[53]

Though newspaper articles revealed transgressions by other ethnic groups, the heavy Jewish participation in bootlegging was a matter of "general knowledge," states historian Phil Kahn. Even women were not immune to temptation. One *Sun* article reported on a single day's worth of raids in 1923 that netted five Jewish women for selling liquor out of the family store.[54] But while such examples suggest the typical mom-and-pop Jewish business, bootlegging was far from a cozy enterprise. Bootleggers engaged in bribery, extortion, and violence to protect their turf, employing Jewish toughs who used weapons as well as their fists and moved easily between the worlds of bootlegging, gambling, and political hooliganism. When a neighbor showed up at bootlegger Milton Glaser's Pennsylvania Avenue confectionery and threatened to "squeal if he didn't get cut in on the action," Glaser's enforcer punched him in the face, sending him down a long flight of steps. The family memoir hints that the young enforcer was none other than Jack Pollack, the future boss of the city's Democratic machine.[55]

Prohibition fostered a shadow economy that did not disappear with the law's repeal in 1933, when the Depression raged and jobs were scarce. Jews continued to find opportunity in the underworld, especially in various forms of gambling. Baltimore gambling czar Ike Sapperstein ran a numbers syndicate from the 1930s to the 1950s; his career had begun in the 1920s when he was jailed on weapons charges and imprisoned for five years for second-degree murder. Yet the press often portrayed members of the "sporting fraternity" in colorful, Runyonesque terms. The *Sun* quoted boxing promoter George Goldberg's views on upcoming matches even after he was indicted for numbers running and bribery in 1936.[56]

The semi-legitimate status of such figures during the interwar years indicates how Prohibition invited a certain disrespect for the law, while the Depression encouraged Baltimoreans to look on illicit activity as an inventive—even admirable—response to hard times. Indeed, some Jewish families counted on their shady relatives for financial support. Proceeds from Buck Offit's bookie business helped his brothers' shirt-making company survive the 1930s. The family always treated him with respect though his profession was never discussed. Upward mobility would later reduce the need for Jews to resort to unsavory ways to make a living and would isolate those who still did so. But in the interwar era, bootleggers, burlesque owners, bookies, and gamblers were often part of the family.[57]

In retrospect, the Great Depression posed a temporary setback in the economic trajectory of American—and Baltimore—Jewry. Before the crash, even the immigrant strongholds of East and Southwest Baltimore had seen rising incomes and greater diversity in employment, while the new immigration quotas ensured that boatloads of penniless newcomers would no longer arrive daily to replenish the ranks of the poverty-stricken.[58] Their steady rise out of the working class in the 1920s meant that Jews did not suffer as severely as other groups in the 1930s. But to people living through it, the Depression was a time of anxiety, insecurity, and hardship, with the future far from assured.

The collapse of the US economy meant the collapse of many family businesses. Louis Katzenstein's clothing firm had survived the industry's 1920s decline, but could not outlast the Depression. "Everywhere downtown you could see long lines of men applying for jobs that weren't there," his son Alvin recalled. "The customers had no money to buy and so the stores stopped ordering. It wasn't long before my father was out of business." Sydney Cohen's father opened a "gorgeous" downtown delicatessen in 1931, but soon found that hard-pressed customers would "bring their own sandwiches in and just order a soda." The deli lasted one year before going bankrupt. One out of six Baltimore families entered the relief rolls; among African Americans, the unemployment rate neared 50 percent. More than ever, residents relied on credit at neighborhood stores, straining the finances of Jewish shopkeepers.[59]

The economic crisis was a blow to families that had only recently achieved a comfortable middle-class lifestyle. Many survived by retrenching. Ruth Surosky's parents moved their butcher shop into their home on Whitelock Street, near Druid Hill Park. The family crowded into two rooms behind the shop while Ruth's aunt, uncle, and cousin moved into a third back room. Such doubling up was a common strategy. "Three families would sell two of the houses they owned and all move into the third," recalled Alvin Katzenstein.[60]

The Associated Jewish Charities provided indigent Jewish families with food, clothing, and coal, and it negotiated lower rents with landlords. By 1930 the agency faced "unprecedented" demands for emergency relief, and worse was yet to come: relief expenditures doubled in 1931 and doubled again in 1932. The Jewish Educational Alliance opened an employment bureau, hoping to counter the effects of long-term unemployment on Jewish youths. "These young people must have jobs for their morale . . . unless they are to be public charges for the rest of their days," an Associated official wrote.[61] When the New Deal came along, unemployed Jews young and old enrolled in work relief, from laid-off tailors to struggling artists like Aaron Sopher, who worked as an illustrator with the Works Progress Administration's Writers Project. Meanwhile, communal workers themselves struggled: as donations fell, the Associated cut the salaries of its overworked staff. During the 1932 high holidays, the *Jewish Times* asked its readers how they could "pray with a clear conscience, knowing that their rabbis have such a hard struggle. Make a good New Year resolution—PAY YOUR RABBI."[62]

The Jewish elite did not escape unscathed. Some lost fortunes in the stock market. Others struggled to hold onto long-established businesses. The venerable Levy Straw Hat Company suffered a steep decline from which it never recovered. The Hochschild, Kohn department store saw its sales volume drop by half, provoking layoffs and salary cuts. Having recently spent $1.2 million on an expansion, Gutman's found the early '30s "very, very rough going," according to Arthur Gutman. "For awhile, we could only buy merchandise C.O.D."[63]

But the downtown department stores not only managed to survive, they provided a bright spot to help Baltimoreans through the dark days. Hutzler's expanded into a new art deco building beside its existing location in 1932, at the height of the Depression. More than 50,000 people attended the opening festivities. Gutman's recouped by searching far and wide for low-cost merchandise to pass along to customers. Its monthly "$1 Day" sales drew huge crowds, Arthur Gutman recalled. As customers' dollars flew through a pneumatic tube to a central room, "the money would

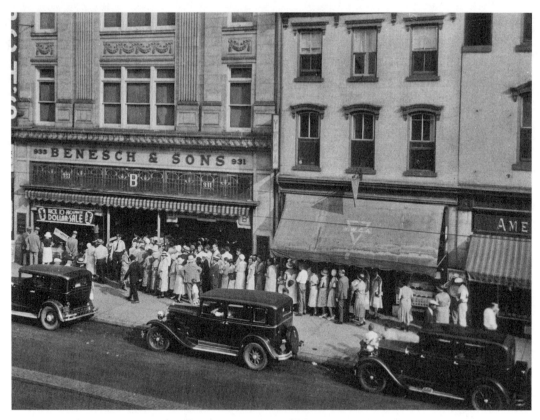

A dollar sale draws crowds to the Benesch and Sons department store on Gay Street during the Depression. *Jewish Museum of Maryland.*

come in so fast we had to stuff it in wastebaskets." Hochschild, Kohn staged its first Thanksgiving Day Toytown Parade in 1936 to entice the Depression-weary populace downtown. The parade became an annual Baltimore tradition.[64]

Some businesses that Jews had traditionally pursued were, if not Depression-proof, at least built to withstand tough times. Pawnbrokers and installment businesses, of course, saw increased demand, though they faced a high risk of customer default. One entrepreneur opened a small loan company in the midst of the Depression and managed to succeed in a nontraditional way. Rose Shanis Glick focused on lending to women, serving a market that "other financial institutions weren't willing to serve," a local banker recalled. Her firm would later become the city's largest locally owned consumer loan company. Others too found success in hard times. Ben Cohen and his brother became liquidators. "Where a store would go out of business, they would go in, assess the stock, and auction it off," his daughter Rosalee Davison recalled.[65]

Although the Depression disrupted upward mobility, it did not disrupt long-term trends toward economic diversity and professional employment. In fact, it accelerated them: the Depression's impact on small family stores and on the already-damaged clothing industry meant that those two mainstays of the past could no longer be relied upon. Instead, young people looked elsewhere, from the underground economy to New Deal agencies to emerging fields of opportunity. The dearth of jobs also encouraged them to stay in school if at all possible, training for professional careers. They could not know it at the time, but their actions during those bleak years would position them well for the future.

Perhaps the most distinctive change in the economic profile of American Jewry during the interwar period was the tremendous increase of Jews in the professions. The nation's system of free public education enabled even the poorest Jewish children to envision careers in law, medicine, education, and the arts—and in fields that had not existed before, such as advertising, social work, and an expanding public sector. Driven to escape the drudgery of the sweatshop and the constant anxiety of the small storekeeper, the sons and daughters of Jewish immigrants ardently pursued opportunities unknown to their parents. Many young people scraped their way through school, attending classes during the day and working at night (or vice versa), searching out loans and scholarships, living as frugally as possible. Herbert Goldstone entered the University of Maryland's medical school in 1930 thanks to a loan from the Central Scholarship Bureau, a Jewish agency. During one term he had to pawn his father's watch to buy food.[66] Butcher's daughter Rose Zetzer overcame more than just poverty. Despite being confronted with "whoever heard of a woman lawyer?" from everyone she knew, she earned a law degree in 1924 at the age of twenty-one. One of only a handful of female lawyers in Maryland, she opened the state's first all-women law firm in 1940 and became the first woman member of the Maryland Bar Association in 1946.[67]

For children of Jewish immigrants to enter the professions was nothing new. The sons of Baltimore's Central European Jewish community had become prominent doctors, lawyers, and educators in the decades after the Civil War, and Eastern European Jews had joined them by the early twentieth century. But these individuals made up a small minority within their fields. In contrast, the professionals who emerged from the largest second generation in American Jewish history changed not only the Jewish occupational profile, but the ethnic makeup of the professions themselves. Almost half of the fifty-five newly minted lawyers admitted to the Baltimore bar in November 1923 were Jewish men and women. By 1936, half of the nation's medical school applicants were Jewish, *Fortune* magazine reported.[68]

The growing number of Jews trained as doctors and lawyers provoked a backlash as elites bemoaned a threat to upper-class culture and traditional Protestant "Anglo-Saxon" leadership. Medical and law schools from Harvard to Stanford began instituting quotas in the 1920s to limit the number of Jews admitted. The medical schools at the University of Maryland and Johns Hopkins University followed suit in the 1930s even though prominent Jewish scholars and professionals had long been associated with both institutions. (Judge Eli Frank, for example, taught at Maryland's law school and became a Hopkins trustee in the 1920s.) The Baltimore Jewish Council found that starting in 1936, Jews made up exactly 15 percent of the incoming class every year at the University of Maryland's medical school, after previously constituting 25–45 percent of new students. Discrimination at Hopkins was harder to document, though BJC head Leon Sachs dated the problem to the administration of President Isaiah Bowman, which began in 1935.[69] Faced with a kind of antisemitism that their parents—shielded by working in traditionally Jewish occupations—had not experienced, some young Jews pushed forward while others adjusted their expectations. Many who could not get past the medical school quotas earned pharmacy degrees instead, leading to a sharp rise in Jewish pharmacists. (A pharmacy degree was also more affordable, another important consideration.)

After receiving professional training, job discrimination loomed as the next obstacle. For many, whether to conceal one's Jewish identity became an issue. There were "no jobs in engineering" during the Depression, "and even if there were, Jewish boys would never have gotten them," recalled Willard Hackerman, who was fresh out of Hopkins in the mid-1930s. He managed to land a job at Whiting-Turner. "They didn't ask me and I didn't tell 'em," he explained. "So I was always terrified. . . . [Hiring Jews] just wasn't done." Faced with a payroll form that asked his religion, he thought, "Oh, I am dead." He responded simply that he was Orthodox. The firm later became the state's most influential contractor under Hackerman's leadership.[70]

Hospitals that limited the number of Jewish staff doctors and residents "inadvertently contributed to the fine quality of Sinai Hospital," observed Philip Kahn. Indeed, as Jewish institutions grew in the 1920s, a sort of professional "ethnic economy" developed that mitigated the impact of discrimination. Sinai opened a new building on East Monument Street in 1926, doubling in size. It began training interns and residents and opened a social services department. While some Jewish women overcame gender barriers (on top of antisemitism) to become doctors and lawyers, many others joined the growing ranks of social workers, nurses, and teachers. Some achieved high positions in Jewish agencies; nurse Ada Rosenthal, for example, served as Sinai's superintendent from 1920 to 1940.[71]

The professional ethnic economy was not limited to health and social services. The advertising industry grew partly out of the promotional activities of department stores and came into its own in the consumer-driven 1920s. Many Jews in Baltimore's ad industry started out in the marketing departments of such stores. Joseph Katz, a clerk at the Hub, worked his way up to ad manager and established his own successful agency in 1920. Louis Shecter worked for Katz and for Hecht's before opening an agency in 1931; his brother-in-law Jack Levin later joined him. These kinds of networks eased Jews' entry into white-collar careers.[72]

With its strong and growing Jewish professional contingent, Baltimore conformed to nationwide trends in American Jewry. Despite the Depression's hardships, historian Henry Feingold notes, it was clear that "the Jewish sojourn in the working class would not last beyond the next generation." By the end of the 1930s,

Sinai Hospital offered employment to Jewish doctors and nurses, who faced discrimination else-where. Here, residents and nurses pose with young patients, 1920s. *Jewish Museum of Maryland*.

as the nation emerged from the Depression and mobilized for the next war, the city's Jewish workforce was much changed from what it had been at the end of World War I: more educated, more white collar, and engaged in a more diverse range of occupations.[73]

However, one trend noted by Feingold does not resonate with the Baltimore experience. As Jews nationwide embraced the professions, he asserted, individual goals became valued above "group identity or religious belief," causing a "dilution of ethnic identity."[74] The view from Baltimore looked quite different. Success in the professions had a strong communal component not only because professionals found employment in Jewish institutions, but because of the networks—rooted in Jewish neighborhoods—that helped Jews get ahead, from friendships forged on the softball diamonds of Easterwood Park to the patronage jobs meted out by the political machine that grew out of Northwest Baltimore's political clubs. The degree to which the neighborhood remained at the center of Jewish life is, perhaps, another example of how small-town Baltimore differed from more cosmopolitan cities.

Individuals who became doctors, lawyers, nurses, and pharmacists stayed intensely loyal to their neighborhood-based Jewish community. Reunion groups such as the JEA Alumni, the Easterwood Park Boys, and the East Baltimore Boys helped to bind Baltimore Jewry even as their members found success outside the ethnic economy. Vibrant Jewish professional clubs—formed partly in response to the discrimination Jews faced in their careers—bolstered Jewish social and cultural life and served as a vehicle for members to get involved in Jewish causes. The Sinai Nurses Alumnae (though not exclusively Jewish), the Alpha Zeta Omega pharmacists' fraternity, and AZO's women's auxiliary, the Azoans, are just a few examples.

In close-knit Jewish Baltimore, individuals could straddle many worlds. Dentist Samuel Neistadt led the socialist Workmen's Circle; physician Herman Seidel was the city's most active Zionist; Rose Zetzer, lawyer and feminist, was active with Hadassah and the Jewish Big Brother League. Like other strivers of the interwar era, garment worker and union leader Jacob Edelman attended night school to earn his law degree. His career as a labor lawyer and city councilman did not preclude him from devoting much of his time to Jewish organizations. Such people connected different strands of the Jewish community, reinforcing a dynamic communal scene.

Building an American Jewish Community

On December 19, 1919, Baltimore's fledgling *Jewish Times* unveiled a new column, "The Chronicler," which promised brief reports on local events of "more than ordinary significance." The debut column featured a mass meeting of young Zionists, a theater production staged by the Young Women's Hebrew Association, a lecture sponsored by the Amalgamated Clothing Workers of America, and a meeting of the new Society for the Promotion of Sabbath Observance. In a single page, this first

"Chronicler" captured the diversity of Jewish communal life at the dawn of the interwar era. The *Jewish Times*'s editor, Charles Rubenstein, had deliberately selected a wide range of events to give readers a "comprehensive view of the activities that are carried on in their midst." Though Rubenstein had played a divisive role in battles over Zionism as the managing editor of the *Jewish Comment*, he vowed that his new newspaper would show "a sympathetic interest in every movement affecting Jewish life and thought" and would promote mutual understanding, "with the hope of removing the discord that has unfortunately arisen in many Jewish communities." The *Jewish Times*, he promised, would serve as a platform to build unity from diversity.[75]

This would remain a challenge. Even as Eastern European immigrants became Americanized, divisions between them and Jews of Central European descent remained strong. Socially the two seemed worlds apart. They continued to clash in fierce garment industry disputes while the immigrants' Orthodoxy and the earlier arrivals' American Reform Judaism provoked mutual scorn. Other communal disagreements took on lives of their own: Zionist versus non-Zionist (not to mention the warring factions within Zionism), secular versus religious, Yiddish versus English. Meanwhile, young people exhibited interests and priorities that baffled the older generation, "Germans" and "Russians" alike.

Such divisions, evident nationwide, caused historian Henry Feingold to conclude that in the interwar period, "the term community no longer adequately described American Jewry. . . . Both Judaism, the binding religious culture, and Jewishness, the secular ethnic culture of the immigrant generation, lost much of their power to reinforce communal cohesiveness." Instead of one community, there were "several Jewish communities that lived in an uneasy relationship." Most seriously, he asserted, this lack of cohesion would lead to a failure to mount "effective community action for the rescue of European Jews" from Nazism.[76]

Feingold, however, overstated the unity that existed before 1918 and underestimated the forces promoting solidarity in the new era. In Baltimore, certainly, the existence of dense second-generation Jewish neighborhoods fostered group cohesion; as Deborah Dash Moore points out, simply living in such neighborhoods made one a member of the Jewish community.[77] Even as neighbors engaged in different communal pursuits, collectively they created their own local version of Jewish American culture and social life in the row houses, streets, and gathering places of Northwest Baltimore. This was community on an informal level, and it was powerful.

On an organized level, the years following World War I saw an explosion of activity as the Baltimore Jewish community created new institutions and reorganized old ones to respond to changing times. Diverse as these efforts were, a network of leaders, male and female, connected many of them. Undoubtedly some attempts to promote solidarity failed. The rifts that had surfaced during the 1917 American Jewish Congress election continued to hinder efforts to advocate for Jewish causes. Sometimes, Jews came together across lines of generation, religion, and class; at other times, factions seemed to work at cross-purposes. Baltimore Jews could in no way be described as one big happy family, yet their myriad activities and even their conflicts created a vital Jewish community life.

The most important communal development happened at the dawn of the interwar era, when uptown and downtown leaders finally succeeded in unifying the community's charities. The impetus came from the influential contingent within Baltimore's Jewish elite gathered around the Levy, Friedenwald, and Szold families. Ever since Henrietta Szold encountered the immigrant intellectuals of the Isaac Bar Levinsohn Hebrew Literary Society in 1888, these prominent families had embraced Jewish cultural diversity. They continued to push for unity in the post–World War I era, joined by allies such as Jacob Epstein (a Lithuanian with "German" sons-in-law); labor sympathizer Jacob Moses and his wife, Hortense; and Sadie and Emil Crockin (who demonstrated Jewish unity through their own "German" and "Russian" mixed marriage).

Significant joint undertakings emerged in the mid-1910s. In 1915 the B'nai B'rith was rejuvenated locally with the founding of the Menorah Lodge by a cross-section of leaders, including old standby William Levy and up-and-coming Lithuanian-born attorney (and future judge) Philip Sykes. Hortense Moses and Sadie Crockin achieved a major breakthrough in 1916 when they founded the Federation of Jewish Women's Organizations, the first umbrella group to unite uptown and downtown organizations. The European relief drives of World War I greatly accelerated cooperation between the two communities: in a 1918 speech, Sykes, the president of the downtown United Hebrew Charities, noted "a sense of oneness" between his group and the uptown Federated Jewish Charities. The 1919 relief drive, chaired by William Levy's brother Julius, was especially effective in forging collective action from a disparate mix of labor unions and manufacturers, uptown temples and downtown shuls, landsman groups and the patrician Phoenix Club.[78]

The time seemed right to unite the two Jewish charity associations, but thorny turf issues continued to get in the way. The unifiers found their organizing genius in Louis H. Levin, professional head of the Federated Jewish Charities and former editor of the *Jewish Comment*. Levin was ideally suited to the task: an American-born son of Lithuanian immigrants, he was a mainstay of the uptown community. Influenced by his sister-in-law Henrietta Szold (he had worked in her Russian Night School), he had become a prominent advocate for immigrant culture. As a leader in the social work movement, he was also determined to modernize Baltimore's Jewish charities. Winning the confidence of the community's factions, in 1920 Levin brought about the merger of the uptown and downtown charity groups. "We have at last dropped all barriers and have become one people," declared William Levy after the founding meeting of the Associated Jewish Charities on January 16, 1921.[79]

The biggest challenge facing the new organization was not to maintain peace between factions; it was the need to restructure Jewish charities amid a fast-changing scene. As Jews relocated to Northwest Baltimore, they left communal institutions behind. Also, with immigration at a standstill since the war years, it was becoming

The creation of the Associated Jewish Charities was so momentous that Louis Levin wrote a play, *The Passing Years*, about it. *Left to right*, the performers are Mrs. Elkan Myers, Mrs. Harry Goldberg, Mrs. Adolf (Laura) Guttmacher, Mrs. Walter Hollander, and Edith Lauer. *Jewish Museum of Maryland.*

clear that the needs of a new generation of American-raised youth differed markedly from the past. Meanwhile, the field of social work was evolving, and the Associated's staffers were eager to apply new theories. "It was in this atmosphere of change—both internal and external—that the Associated embarked on a planned program of consolidation and innovation," wrote Louis Cahn.[80]

Actually, the transition to a post-immigrant community had already begun. The Baltimore Hebrew College and Teachers Training School opened in 1919 partly because "the flow of Hebrew teachers from Russia had stopped due to the First World War," stated Hymen Saye, an early graduate of the college. But its founders also believed that modern young people were ill served by old-style Hebrew schools. "Few . . . know anything about Judaism," its first president, Julius Levy, lamented. The dean, Israel Efros, aimed to produce educators who combined the intellectual rigor and knowledge of the immigrant Hebrew teacher with the "college student type" familiar to Americanized temples: "fluent in English and polished in manners."[81] The college opened in the vestry rooms of Chizuk Amuno, whose leaders shared Efros's philosophy of synthesizing old and new, immigrant and American. In 1921 Efros and Levy spearheaded the creation of the Board of Jewish Education, which was charged with modernizing the entire Hebrew school system. The founding boards of both organizations included Reform and Orthodox leaders who agreed on the need to overhaul an educational system that was failing to capture disaffected youth.[82]

Meanwhile, the Associated began modernizing the constituent agencies inherited from the Federated and United Hebrew Charities. It merged the community's two orphanages and moved the children into a new state-of-the-art facility in Northwest Baltimore named in honor of Louis Levin, who died in 1923 at age fifty-seven. But Levindale would soon take on a different purpose: faced with the deterioration of the homes serving the ill and elderly in East Baltimore and the insistence of social workers that the modern trend toward foster care would soon make the orphanage obsolete, the board turned Levindale into the site of the newly merged homes for the aged and infirm.[83]

Women social workers were at the forefront of change. Although the Associated's executive director post was held by men, women headed many constituent agencies, including Ada Rosenthal (Sinai Hospital), Gertrude Glick (Jewish Social Service Bureau), Edith Lauer and Laura Guttmacher (Jewish Children's Society), and Dorothy Kahn (Hebrew Benevolent Society). These women moved the reorganized agencies from the volunteer relief society model to the casework model, which applied scientific methods to address the "personal and environmental factors" that led to family crisis. Along with this scientific approach, wrote Lauer, social workers relied on a sense of humor to achieve "the art of case work in its highest sense."[84]

Amid all the reorganizing, relocating, and rebuilding of the Associated's first two decades, its agencies seized the opportunity to modernize (and Americanize) their names. Hebrew Hospital became Sinai Hospital during its expansion in 1926, signaling that Jewish leaders envisioned the hospital serving a broad clientele and taking its place among Baltimore's prominent institutions. As Rabbi William Rosenau noted, "Catholics do not call their hospital Catholic Hospital." In a 1938 reorganization, the venerable Hebrew Benevolent Society disappeared into the Jewish Family and Children's Bureau.[85]

The emergence of Sinai, Levindale, Baltimore Hebrew College, and the Board of Jewish Education reflected a national trend to move Jewish charity beyond service to the poor to focus more on special populations: the ill, the elderly, and, especially, the young. The Jewish Big Brother League addressed "juvenile delinquency" while other programs aimed to bolster youngsters' Jewish identity. Camp Louise, founded as a sylvan respite for immigrant working girls, transformed into a summer camp offering Jewish recreation and was joined by a boys' counterpart, Camp Airy. The JEA's popularity among children of immigrants enabled it to stay vital into the 1940s, even as Jews moved away from its East Baltimore locale. But capturing the allegiance of youths from upwardly mobile and more assimilated families was another matter:

The Young Men's and Young Women's Hebrew Association (the Y) strove to provide young people with American-style activities in a Jewish context. *Jewish Museum of Maryland.*

the settlement house model did not resonate with confident young Americans, who would rather "join in enterprises that are distinctly of their own making."[86]

These youths would find what they needed in a new type of organization. Around twenty young women led the way, gathering in December 1918 to organize the Young Women's Hebrew Association, thus "launching the Jewish community center movement in Baltimore," as the founding chair, Rose Esterson, later wrote.[87] Young men organized a YMHA in 1920, and the two groups merged in 1926. They were right on track: nationally, the post–World War I period saw the rise of the Jewish community center. Whereas the settlement house "taught immigrant Jews to live as Americans," historian David Kaufman wrote, "the Jewish center would teach their children to live as Jews in America." Along with athletics, Baltimore's Y offered recreational and social activities that conformed to "the highest standards of Jewish social and communal life."[88]

The drive to create a new, state-of-the-art Y building reflected the challenges of an era in transition. Convincing the Jewish community to pay for a recreational facility—a novel idea at the time—took some doing. Supporters portrayed the Y as an antidote to unsavory influences, a bulwark against assimilation, and a point of Jewish pride. Appeals called attention to the "260 licensed pool rooms" that attracted teenagers and the 400 young Jews who belonged to the YMCA for lack of a Jewish alternative. "Baltimore Jewry MUST take care of its own," one leaflet proclaimed, applying a venerable principle about caring for the Jewish poor to a decidedly middle-class enterprise. To care for their own, advocates implied, now meant addressing social and cultural needs rather than strictly economic needs. Meanwhile, selecting a site proved controversial. Northwest Baltimore was the obvious choice, but the "settlement of Negroes in increasing numbers" around North Avenue made the area unstable: it was difficult to predict which parts would remain Jewish. Instead, planners chose a site near downtown, home to few Jews but accessible to all. The Monument Street Y finally opened with fanfare in October 1930.[89]

The effort to modernize, expand, and create new institutions in the 1920s took place amid much optimism and strong community financial support. Annual Associated campaigns typically kicked off with Jacob Epstein's offer to match 10 percent of the amount raised, with his admonition, "I hope you will make it expensive for me!" Campaigns were organized "almost on military lines," recalled Louis Cahn, as teams with "lieutenants" and "captains" competed to raise the most money. But the Depression brought a swift drop in contributions that imperiled institutions new and old. Every week, it seemed, the *Jewish Times* announced another crisis. The Y nearly closed its doors in 1932, two years after opening. Sinai Hospital saw a steep decline in paying patients. It fell behind on its mortgage and closed off two floors of its new building, while its free clinic became inundated with the "new poor."[90]

As communal institutions fought for survival, the Associated struggled with the imperative to aid Jewish families newly plunged into poverty. There was no public welfare system when the Depression began; the growing numbers of poor and unemployed people turned to private charities when they became desperate. Like other major Baltimore charities, the Associated received emergency funds from the city, but not nearly enough. "Unless [more] public aid is secured the situation will be exceedingly critical," the charity reported in April 1932. Epstein quietly supplemented his annual gift with direct contributions to the relief budget; the local branch of the National Council of Jewish Women organized hundreds of women to distribute food and clothing. But such stopgap measures could not address the scale of the crisis.[91]

With the renewed focus on poor Jews, Jewish federations across the country faced the dilemma of how to address competing needs with dwindling resources. Harry Greenstein, named the Associated's executive director in 1928 after a successful tenure as the Y's first president, emerged as a national advocate for continuing the course set in the 1920s. "Pressure is being brought to bear on federations to eliminate, curtail, or drastically reduce" cultural activities, he noted in 1932. But these activities fill a "basic need" by contributing to "the preservation of Jewish community life."[92] His stance hinged on a firm conviction that only government could address the welfare needs of the population—and government needed to do much more. In 1933 he urged Baltimore's Jewish community to support New Deal legislation, saying, "We have prided ourselves on being able to take care of our own. Now we must realize that we no longer are sufficient unto ourselves."[93]

Greenstein's support for government aid to the poor and his insistence on community support for cultural institutions put him in the vanguard of leaders who guided Jewish charities to "reinvent themselves under the new conditions of the New Deal and the welfare state," as historian Beth Wenger put it. The magnitude of the Depression forced federations to give up the "cherished Jewish ideal" of community self-sufficiency. Some leaders worried that turning to public welfare to aid indigent Jews might "erode communal solidarity" or even call into question the very need for communal agencies. Others, like Greenstein, seized on the opportunity to create "a new ideological foundation for Jewish charity . . . devoted to ethnic persistence."[94] With the New Deal forging a national welfare system, federations could focus on programs designed to strengthen Jewish identity. The crisis of the Depression and the rise of the welfare state therefore confirmed the path federations like the Associated had embarked on during the previous decade and completed the process of enshrining Jewish survival as a prime goal of Jewish giving.

Through the growing pains of the 1920s and the financial crises of the 1930s, the Associated managed to maintain unity in addressing the communal needs of Baltimore Jewry. But the divide between uptown and downtown Jews did not disappear. Nor did it lessen as Jews of Eastern European origin Americanized and joined their longer-established coreligionists in Northwest Baltimore. Though the terms "uptown" and "downtown" lost geographic relevance, they remained in use—along with the equally inaccurate terms "German" and "Russian"—as shorthand to describe the very real cultural and social differences between Jews from the two different immigration waves. In some ways, the breach became even more noticeable. Though many Eastern Europeans acquired the means to join elite uptown organizations, they were not accepted. In fact, they knew better than to even apply. "You sort of knew where you belonged," one man recalled. "It was a strict line that you couldn't cross over."[95]

The 1920s, therefore, saw the rise of a parallel social scene for upwardly mobile Jews of Eastern European background. The in-town Amity Club, for example, offered an alternative to the Phoenix Club, and in 1927 well-off Eastern European Jews opened the lavishly appointed Woodholme Country Club as an alternative to the Suburban Club. More than mere snobbery separated the two clubs: Woodholme members tended to be Zionist and at least nominally Orthodox, Suburban members were generally neither, and so on. Their differing worldviews gave each group a feeling of superiority over the other. Woodholme's state-of-the-art golf course reflected the pride and confidence of self-made second-generation Eastern Europeans. They may not have been welcome at the Suburban Club, but they knew they were poised to surpass its members in wealth and influence.[96]

Because Jews of the great wave far outnumbered the earlier Jewish cohort, theirs became the dominant Baltimore Jewish culture during this period. Their organiza-

The mutual aid groups of the immigrant era remained a mainstay of Jewish social life between the world wars. *Jewish Museum of Maryland.*

tions reflected their own internal diversity: while Woodholme represented the most financially successful, the Workmen's Circle remained popular as an expression of its members' working-class, Yiddish-speaking roots. Four new Workmen's Circle branches formed from 1926 to 1933, for a total of eight branches and some 1,400 members. After moving its headquarters into the spacious former Talmud Torah building on East Baltimore Street in 1930, the organization provided free space to unions and housed the Baltimore office of the *Jewish Daily Forward*. As Jews left the garment industry (and the working class), cultural and social activities became the focal point for the rank and file: picnicking at the Workmen's Circle shore property, sending children to Yiddish school, debating the events of the day at branch gatherings.[97]

Landsmanshaften and fraternal orders also evolved as members' circumstances improved and the dearth of overseas arrivals removed the need to help new immigrants. Their focus turned from mutual aid to socializing, taking care of cemeteries they had founded, and raising funds for suffering Jews in Eastern Europe. New hometown associations, such as the Mlynover Verein and the Lutzker Relief Society, formed with the sole purpose of sending money abroad.[98]

When the Depression hit, the groups attempted to help members cope; the Brith Sholom Relief Committee, for example, held relief balls to aid "unfortunate members of our Order."[99] But the need was well beyond their capacity: the Associated and the New Deal were far better equipped to respond. Yet if mutual aid groups no longer played as critical a role as they had during the era of immigration, they remained woven into the fabric of the Jewish community. In 1925 Brith Sholom had twenty lodges with more than 2,200 members, while B'rith Abraham's seven lodges had 2,100 members. These extensive networks provided troops for the campaigns of the interwar period, including European relief, supporting Zionism, and protesting Nazism.[100]

Perhaps because it was the one thing all could agree on, Baltimore Jews continued to enact conspicuous displays of unity during campaigns for the relief of European Jewry. Professing to find it a "great pleasure to work with Reform Jews," Orthodox rabbi Reuben Rivkin continued to lead citywide mass meetings alongside the likes of Eli Frank, Albert Hutzler, and Mrs. Sydney Cone. Rivkin's stirring Yiddish speeches provoked "sobbing and wailing" from the crowd followed by scenes of "tumultuous giving that can hardly be described."[101]

Rivkin also was a key speaker at rallies on behalf of a Jewish homeland in Palestine. Zionism was hardly a unifying force: not only did many members of the Jewish elite remain opposed, but the factionalism that plagued the movement internationally had local repercussions. In 1921, for example, Harry Friedenwald and others resigned from the Baltimore branch of the Zionist Organization of America during the power struggle between Chaim Weizmann and Louis Brandeis over control of the movement.[102]

Such high-level controversies did not prevent Zionism from maintaining broad grassroots popularity, however, and the city's numerous and diverse Zionist groups managed to cooperate on a variety of projects. Local Poale (labor) and Mizrachi (religious) Zionists worked with Baltimore's branch of the Zionist Organization of America even though nationally the three organizations were at odds. Much local activity was organized by Labor Zionist Herman Seidel, who coordinated a series of large rallies. In August 1922 a "monster Palestine Mandate demonstration" featuring a parade of 800 automobiles "decorated with American and Jewish flags" wound its way from East Baltimore to Carlin's Park, where the city's largest Jewish crowd to date—some 30,000—gathered for speeches and entertainment.[103] A mass meeting to raise money for victims of the 1929 Arab riots featured Senator Millard Tydings and Governor Albert Ritchie among the speakers. The event was chaired by Sigmund Sonneborn, clothing manufacturer and unlikely patron of Seidel's Labor Zionist group. (Sonneborn even hosted the Gordonia labor youth camp on his Severn River property from 1935 to 1942.) The local Hadassah chapter coordinated many of the movement's spirited fundraising drives.[104]

- - - - - - - - - - - - - -

The Zionist religious youth group Hashomer Hadati on an outing at Druid Hill Park, c. 1930.
Jewish Museum of Maryland.

The coalition showed signs of fraying in the 1930s, however. In July 1933 Shaarei Zion's rabbi, Israel Tabak, a Mizrachi Party delegate to the World Zionist Congress, told the *Sun* that Jews fleeing Nazism would be welcome in Palestine, but not their Reform Judaism. His "bigoted" comment drew complaints, but local Mizrachi leaders grew increasingly vocal in criticizing their fellow Zionists. Like Tabak, Shaarei Tfiloh's rabbi, Nathan Drazin, represented a new breed of young, American-bred, and politically assertive Orthodox leaders. In March 1936 he touched off a firestorm in the *Jewish Times* when he called the socialist Zionist group Hashomer Hatzair "an enemy of Israel." Interestingly, the previous year, Herman Seidel had tangled with William Rosenau over the Reform rabbi's remark that "Palestine Labor is known to be anti-religious." It is likely that an antipathy to Labor Zionism was the only point of agreement between the Reform rabbi and his Orthodox colleagues.[105]

Aside from occasional grumblings by Rabbi Rosenau, Reform critics of Zionism were quiet through the interwar era. The tight-knit nature of the uptown community may have inhibited anti-Zionists from speaking out against their friends in the movement. Local socialist and Yiddishist resistance to Zionism was also more muted than elsewhere. Workmen's Circle leadership in other cities tended to be anti-Zionist; in Baltimore, its lodges participated in Labor Zionist activities. This relative lack of opposition to Zionism compared to other cities speaks to the intertwined networks that connected Baltimore Jews and to the broad popularity Zionism always enjoyed in the city.[106]

In its response to Nazism, Baltimore Jewry again worked to forge local unity in the face of a divided national leadership. A rancorous battle over strategy pitted the patrician American Jewish Committee against the ethnically assertive American Jewish Congress. The committee accused the congress and its president, New York rabbi Stephen Wise, of risking German Jewish lives by organizing a boycott of German goods and loudly protesting the Nazi regime. In turn, the congress called the committee's preference for behind-the-scenes action weak and cowardly. The conflict spilled over to Baltimore: after Rabbi Rosenau stated that "Dr. Wise will kill the Jews of Germany," Wise vowed in a letter to "nevermore have any word with you nor see you again." He and his "two dearest friends in Baltimore," Harry Friedenwald and Simon Sobeloff, agonized over the dispute in letters between Baltimore and New York.[107]

Nevertheless, Friedenwald and Sobeloff, leaders of the Baltimore branch of the American Jewish Congress, made herculean efforts to unite both factions locally around a course of action to combat Nazism. "We have been working assiduously trying to stimulate our more prominent but passive Jews," Sobeloff wrote to Wise in April 1933. "Some are beyond hope but we are meeting with encouragement among others."[108] In May the Baltimore branch drew an overflow audience to a protest meeting at the Southern Hotel. The most stirring address came from Judge Joseph Ulman, the prominent and thoroughly assimilated civic leader whom Friedenwald and Sobeloff saw as their most prized "convert" to the cause of Jewish defense. "Throughout my life I should have said that I was a Jewish American," Ulman told the crowd. "This is the first time I have done anything simply because I am a Jew." Stunned by the events in Germany, a nation he had "loved and admired," Ulman called on American Jews to unite to urge the US government to censure Germany and to reopen America's doors "to fugitives from religious and racial persecution."[109]

Baltimore's congress branch went on to lead a campaign that included rallies, a boycott of German goods, and a successful effort to improve newspaper coverage of the Nazi persecution of Jews. Its leaders reached out to everyone from the president of Johns Hopkins University to landsmanshaft members. Claiming the support of seventy-five affiliated groups, the branch overcame divisions that leaders on the national level could not.[110] But ultimately it had little to show for its efforts. Better newspaper coverage did not rouse the public to action; intense lobbying could not overcome powerful entrenched interests. In 1934 Baltimore leaders helped encourage Maryland's US senator, Millard Tydings, to introduce a resolution expressing the American people's "profound feelings of surprise and pain" over Germany's treatment of its Jewish citizens and urging the Nazi regime to "speedily alter its policy." If passed, it would have been the first official US condemnation of Nazism. But while Baltimore leaders and others worked to mount a nationwide lobbying effort, the bill remained bottled up in the Senate Foreign Relations Committee with key senators and the US State Department firmly opposed. Historians have faulted American Jewry for not doing enough to save Europe's Jews, citing the lack of unity as a grave flaw. The Baltimore experience suggests that even rigorous efforts to unite and pursue strategies on many fronts stood little chance of influencing US government policy or affecting the Nazis' war on the Jews.[111]

A different kind of grassroots campaign would help save thousands of Jewish individuals and families. Though the US government refused to alter its immigration policies, many American Jews worked within existing laws to bring German Jewish refugees to the United States in the years before the country entered World War II. In Baltimore, this effort was organized largely by the local branch of the National Council of Jewish Women (NCJW) with Harry Friedenwald's daughter, Julia Friedenwald Strauss, in the lead role. To obtain scarce US visas, refugees needed affidavits of financial support from American sponsors and assistance in overcoming obstacles imposed by an uncooperative US bureaucracy. Strauss and her husband issued affidavits to many refugees, and she recruited other sponsors from among the city's Jewish elite, including her niece Eleanor Kohn Levy, who sponsored numerous families, including distant cousins and total strangers. Aunt and niece spent long hours wading through the US bureaucracy on behalf of their German contacts.[112]

Once in the United States, the refugees had to find work in the midst of the Depression and adjust to new surroundings while recovering from their traumatizing encounter with Nazism. Strauss's NCJW branch joined with the local Hebrew Immigrant Aid Society and the Associated's newly formed Refugee Adjustment Committee to help them settle into Baltimore and find jobs. The local branch of German Jewish Children's Aid resettled some fifty children who came to Baltimore unaccompanied by parents. While some of the children's parents managed to follow them across the ocean, others perished in the Holocaust. Julia and Myer Strauss ended up adopting two refugee boys; Eleanor Levy and her husband, Lester, adopted a girl.[113]

At least 3,000 refugees settled in Baltimore between 1933 and 1941. They arrived not only through the assistance of Baltimore's Jewish elite but through other networks as well. The eminent child psychiatrist Leo Kanner had emigrated from Germany in 1924. From his post at Johns Hopkins Hospital (where he pioneered in the study of autism), he helped some 200 former colleagues escape Nazi territory and settle in the United States. Kanner contacted universities and hospitals across the nation to secure jobs, which enabled the medical professionals to obtain visas. Around twenty found places at Hopkins and settled in Baltimore.[114]

The Orthodox community also strove to bring Jews from Nazi-occupied Europe. Working with the National Refugee Service, the recently formed Ner Israel Rabbinical College sponsored some eighteen refugee rabbinical students per year in the late 1930s. By offering scholarships, room and board, and travel support, the college enabled these young men to qualify for student visas. In 1936, Congregation Shearith Israel—a longtime bastion of German Orthodoxy—hired Rabbi Simon

Two generations of Baltimore Jewish leadership: Julia Friedenwald Strauss and her father, Harry Friedenwald, 1938. *Jewish Museum of Maryland.*

Schwab, enabling the future Orthodox luminary to leave Ichenhausen, Germany, where a yeshiva he had attempted to open had been attacked by the Nazis.[115]

Meanwhile, the refugees themselves worked to bring over relatives and friends left behind, relinquishing their efforts only when the United States entered the war in 1941 and the door to Nazi Europe slammed shut. Not content to be passive recipients of charity, they also created their own self-help group, the Chevra Ahavas Chesed, which offered burial assistance and other mutual aid. A close-knit refugee community formed in the Druid Hill Park neighborhood. Rabbi Schwab, a beloved figure among religious and secular refugees alike, was its unofficial leader, serving as the Chevra's spiritual adviser and offering his home as a gathering place.[116]

- - - - - - - - - - - - -

From the Chevra to the Y, Baltimore Jews in the interwar era created organizations that reflected their diverse backgrounds and interests, but also embodied their shared Jewish identity. The bonds drawn by formal affiliations were reinforced by the vibrant neighborhood social scene on view at the delis, family circles, and myriad other places where Jews gathered. If both formal and informal associations helped to establish commonality among Baltimore Jews, religious issues were more divisive—but would nevertheless prove critical in shaping the future of Baltimore Jewry.

Keeping the Faith:
Religious Survival and the Roots of Revival

When Rabbi Schwab arrived at Shearith Israel, he found a "very traditional shul governed by dedicated officers," where the Shulchan Aruch (Code of Jewish Law) reigned as the "final arbiter in all questions," his son later wrote. But "all of this was only a beautiful veneer" that covered a seething controversy. Traditionally, full membership had been limited to strict Sabbath observers—and as a result, there were only 10 voting members in a congregation of 150. A sizable faction wanted to relax the rule but faced stiff opposition. After consulting rabbis and lay leaders in Baltimore and beyond, Schwab ruled that the Sabbath requirement would remain in place. The dissenters promptly seceded, forming Beth Jacob Congregation one block away.[117]

This story, typical throughout American Jewish history, was especially common in the interwar years, "a time of crisis and decline" for American Judaism, according to historian Jeffrey Gurock. With the end of mass migration the ranks of the devout were no longer automatically replenished, while religion played a negligible role for many acculturated Jews. To attract them, many congregations seized on a new model: the synagogue center, a multipurpose institution that offered culture and recreation along with worship and study. But even as such centers sprang up in second-generation neighborhoods, synagogue attendance and membership lagged—and plummeted further with the Depression. Congregations, many now saddled with heavy mortgages, faced financial disaster and a "spiritual depression" to match.[118]

Baltimore's Chizuk Amuno provides a textbook example. The congregation had begun to attract Eastern European Jews and confidently opened a new synagogue near Druid Hill Park in 1922, not realizing that its membership had peaked at 250 families in 1921. Not enough young adults were joining to replace members who passed away. Also, as men focused on economic advancement, they stopped attending, and soon most worshippers were women. The congregation tried holding shorter services and using more English, to no avail. Struggling with new building debt, Chizuk Amuno slid further during the Depression, hitting a low of 160 member families in 1937 amid an atmosphere of "general apathy" and

As religiosity declined, life cycle events became critical expressions of Jewish identity and community. Joseph Eisenberg at his bar mitzvah celebration, c. 1936. Flanking him are his parents, Mollie and Abraham; his grandmother Rachel Belilove; and his brother, Melvin. *Jewish Museum of Maryland.*

financial disarray. The sisterhood kept things together until recovery began in the late 1930s.[119]

Yet there was more going on in Baltimore Jewish religious life than crisis and decline. Certainly there were signs that religion was losing ground; as elsewhere, most people derived their Jewish identity more from their all-Jewish environment than from actual religious practice. But other signs pointed in the opposite direction. In a community that numbered roughly 67,500, some 10,400 families belonged to congregations in the mid-1920s.[120] This was a notably high affiliation rate compared to other large Jewish communities, possibly reflecting Baltimore's status as a less cosmopolitan city where religion had long been a focal point of local culture. In many congregations, heated battles over change reflected engagement rather than apathy. Orthodoxy in particular belied the seemingly downward trajectory that many observers discerned nationwide. As a cadre of assertive young rabbis at modern Orthodox synagogues won over the second generation by upholding halachic

standards in American form, more traditionally Orthodox leaders quietly built institutions that would thrive in the post–World War II era.

Old-style Orthodoxy continued to hold sway in East Baltimore—anachronistically,
many thought. Hasidic rabbi Zvi Hertzberg arrived in the late '20s and took over a
small shul, Anshe Sphard. His son Arthur, future Jewish scholar and activist, attended
the Yeshiva Torah Ve-Emunah (Hebrew Parochial School) on East Baltimore Street,
which he later recalled as "a very close approximation of an East European *heder*."
One of around 200 students, Hertzberg was acutely aware of being part of "a very
small minority among the thousands of Jewish children in Baltimore." He sensed that
the Orthodox world he inhabited was dying out. But not quite: the school, founded by
Rabbi Abraham Schwartz in 1917 as the first Jewish day school outside of New York,
started with only 5 students when it opened in the basement of Shomrei Mishmeres,
so it had grown considerably by the time Hertzberg arrived.[121]

The era saw some dedicated young East Baltimoreans attack the "lapsed Orthodoxy" of their immigrant parents. Around 1918, they formed Adath B'nei Israel to
promote Sabbath observance and to counter the lure of Christian missionaries. The
group held mass meetings "to preach about the holiness of Shabbos, and *Yiddishkeit*
in general," and sponsored youth groups "to draw children away from the homes of
their parents, violators of the Shabbos, to come to Shul."[122] Organized by Rae Mechanic, a saleswoman in her mid-twenties and the daughter of a shochet, the group
opened a synagogue on East Baltimore Street and ran an employment bureau for
Sabbath observers. By 1925 Adath B'nei Israel had 350 Sabbath-observant members
aged seventeen to thirty-five.[123]

The Jewish future lay in Northwest Baltimore, however, where several positive
developments were under way. Adath B'nei Israel joined forces with northwest
counterparts Shearith Israel and Chizuk Amuno to form the Society for the Promotion of Sabbath Observance in 1919 and later opened a northwest branch. The
Hebrew Parochial School built a substantial edifice in Lower Park Heights in 1938
under its new name, the Talmudical Academy.[124] Transplanted from the fertile soil
of East Baltimore, both would go on to play a strong role in the development of local
Orthodoxy.

But the most important new institution for the city's Orthodox future had its
roots in a less likely place: the middle-class northwest neighborhood of Forest Park,
where Tifereth Israel Congregation invited the young Talmudic scholar Jacob Ruderman to become its rabbi. The Lithuanian immigrant agreed on condition that the
congregation allow him to open a yeshiva. Despite some opposition from the shul's
Jewish neighbors, who perhaps feared that a yeshiva would not present a properly
Americanized appearance, in 1933 Ner Israel Rabbinical College opened with 14 students on two upper floors of the synagogue. Beyond a core of about thirty families,
Rabbi Ruderman found little support at first. His wife, Faiga, made the rounds of
Jewish businesses to solicit food, linens, and other necessities. The yeshiva survived

on donations such as "three fowls weekly" from a poultry company; the minutes of the ladies' auxiliary included a note thanking one woman for her gift of six herrings. In the late 1930s, support from the newly arrived Rabbi Simon Schwab, along with the college's role as a haven for refugee rabbinical students, helped it gain international recognition in the Orthodox world. By 1942 it had grown to 220 students and built a new, eleven-acre facility. In the post–World War II years, the impact of Ner Israel on Orthodoxy in Baltimore would be profound.[125]

While the Talmudical Academy and Ner Israel would emerge into prominence in a later period, it was Northwest Baltimore's burgeoning congregational scene that had the most immediate impact on religious life in the interwar years. Eastern European Jews established twenty congregations in the district by 1930 and ten more by 1940.[126] Some were small immigrant shuls tucked into converted row houses, where members squabbled and "lapsed" Orthodoxy ruled. At Petach Tikvah, members enjoyed European habits, like the taking of snuff, and Yiddish remained the language of conversation even as the congregation's youngsters came to view it as "a taunting symbol of their status as children of immigrants," recalled Harry London, the son of one founder. There were "many layers of observance from strict to almost none," he stated. Yet such shuls instilled a personal form of Judaism in impressionable children. As he put it, "Petach Tikvah was where I went as naturally and comfortably as breathing."[127]

On the other hand, the founders of the most influential northwest synagogues tended to be well-off, Americanized immigrants: merchants, small clothing manufacturers, wholesalers, lawyers, and realtors, who had arrived in the United States mostly as children. Shaarei Tfiloh, Shaarei Zion, and Beth Tfiloh all erected imposing buildings that reflected the aspirations of their members.[128] Though lacking the Old World atmosphere of smaller shuls whose founders remained closer to their roots, these synagogues too ensured that Judaism infused neighborhood life. During the high holidays, congregants promenaded through the area, starting in Druid Hill Park, stopping at Shaarei Tfiloh, then heading to Beth Tfiloh in Forest Park and from there toward Shaarei Zion in Park Heights. The ritual was "almost like the Easter Parade—everybody in their finery," a former resident recalled. To Sylvia Mandy, "the joy, the spirituality of the holidays, seemed to me to vibrate through the sidewalks" around Shaarei Tfiloh. On Yom Kippur, even those who did not attend services sat on their porches and listened to the sounds of the Kol Nidre emanating from the synagogue's open windows.[129]

These congregations blended Orthodox practice and modern style in a way that appealed to immigrants and their children as well. Indeed, the fastest-growing synagogues in Baltimore embraced what soon became known as "modern Orthodoxy." Beth Tfiloh's innovative approach made it the city's most popular new congregation. Its founders set the tone when they chose to build a community center (complete with gymnasium) before building a synagogue. The center proved an immediate hit, and Beth Tfiloh—still worshipping in a converted cottage, without a full-time

The Shaarei Tfiloh synagogue, located on the edge of Druid Hill Park, remains an imposing presence. *Photo by Frederic C. Chalfant, 2011.*

rabbi—became Baltimore's third-largest Jewish congregation, with more than 600 members, a mere four years after its founding.[130]

Enthusiasm over the community center did not prevent controversy, however. At a standing-room-only meeting in 1926 about women's seating in its new synagogue, Beth Tfiloh members voted to follow Chizuk Amuno's example and allow women to sit on platforms on either side of the men's section with no partitions separating them, if permitted by a beth din of three Orthodox rabbis. When the beth din gave a favorable ruling, some members broke off to form the more stringent Tifereth Israel. Their departure improved the position of the modernists for the next battle: hiring a rabbi. Trying out candidates from the Jewish Theological Seminary (JTS) (Conservative) and the Rabbi Isaac Elchanan Theological Seminary (Orthodox), members tussled over which man best combined the "forensic ability and culture of the newer type of rabbi" with "the piety and learning of the older type." They settled on JTS graduate Samuel Rosenblatt. It probably did not hurt that his father was the famed cantor Josef Rosenblatt, who performed at his son's installation in 1927.[131]

Rosenblatt showed his own penchant for innovation in the difficult 1930s, when "girls were leaving us in order to be confirmed in the Reform temple, and we were losing the families," he later said. "That is when I introduced the practice of bat mitzvah." Though the influential American rabbi Mordecai Kaplan had arranged the first bat mitzvah in 1922 for his daughter, the practice had not caught on. Rosenblatt's

Rabbi Israel Tabak was among a new generation of young, assertive modern Orthodox rabbis. *Jewish Museum of Maryland.*

version attempted to conform to Orthodox standards: girls remained seated while the rabbi presented them with certificates and their fathers were called to the Torah. In the assembly hall after the services, each girl gave a "short recitation" on a Jewish subject. Rosenblatt performed Beth Tfiloh's first bat mitzvah ceremony in 1936. "I think it saved the congregation," he later stated. By the late 1930s Beth Tfiloh flourished, soon billing itself as "the leading Orthodox synagogue south of New York."[132]

With its JTS-trained rabbi, Chizuk Amuno–style seating, and flexible approach, it is fair to ask whether Beth Tfiloh was actually Orthodox. Indeed, practices in Orthodox and Conservative synagogues were converging nationwide even as the movements developed separate institutional structures. Still, Beth Tfiloh's charter (forbidding any deviation from Orthodox custom without the entire congregation's consent) and its members' self-conception placed the congregation within the Orthodox fold. Rosenblatt later declared that Beth Tfiloh "was founded as an Orthodox congregation and I decided to keep it as such."[133]

Baltimore's other modern Orthodox rabbis shared Rosenblatt's youth, secular higher education, and modern appearance. As a newspaper article noted, Israel Tabak of Shaarei Zion "has been serving with elan the cause of traditional Judaism."[134] But they were less flexible than Rosenblatt and more likely to engage in polemics. In addition to tangling with Labor Zionists, in 1936 Nathan Drazin of Shaarei Tfiloh charged that Reform and Conservative Judaism used "pseudo-science" and called their adherents "sheep who have been led astray."[135] Such public statements fore-

Hymen Saye teaching at the Talmud Torah in East Baltimore, 1928. Saye trained at the Baltimore Hebrew College, which strove to combine rigorous Orthodoxy with modern pedagogy. *Jewish Museum of Maryland.*

shadowed Orthodoxy's move from a defensive posture to a more aggressive stance in advocating for traditional Judaism.

In contrast, Conservative Judaism—the era's fastest-growing movement nationally—claimed no new congregations locally, underscoring Baltimore's stance as more tradition-bound than other cities.[136] Its sole local affiliate, Chizuk Amuno, occupied the most traditional end of the Conservative spectrum, eschewing movement hallmarks such as mixed seating. Reform congregations, however, held their own. While Rabbi Edward Israel moved Har Sinai in the direction of Zionism and social justice, Baltimore Hebrew Congregation and the city's largest and most prestigious congregation, Oheb Shalom (the Eutaw Place Temple), focused on capturing the allegiance of youth. Baltimore congregations of all sorts embraced the synagogue center movement, with two—Baltimore Hebrew in addition to Beth Tfiloh—developing popular community youth centers.

Worried about losing the younger generation to assimilation, the entire Jewish establishment came together to address "the crying need for immediate action" over "the great number of Jewish children who are not securing any Hebrew education." Leaders across the religious spectrum participated in the new Board of Jewish Education, from Orthodox stalwart Tanchum Silberman to city public school super-

- - - - - - - - - - - - -

intendent David Weglein, a longtime member of Oheb Shalom.[137] The Board of
Jewish Education oversaw six freestanding Hebrew schools in East, Northwest, and
Southwest Baltimore. It also served synagogue-based Hebrew schools from the
classically Reform Har Sinai to the immigrant Orthodox Har Zion. It standardized
the Hebrew school curriculum, established uniform grades, and installed "modern
business methods," with little apparent controversy. What it could not do was force
children to attend. In 1925 some 4,100 children received Hebrew and religious instruction, around 32 percent of Jewish children in Baltimore under age thirteen. Ten
years later the situation was worse: fewer than 3,000 were enrolled.[138]

But many factors converged to reverse the decline in religious participation toward the end of the interwar era, including a turn to religious solidarity in the face
of Nazism; the arrival of refugees (many of whom joined synagogues) after years of
stagnant immigration; and the end of the Depression and the coming of war, which
gave people both the means and the motivation to return to their religious roots.
Several signs pointed to the coming new era. Chizuk Amuno, after reaching its na-
dir of membership in 1937, began to see small increases, which would get bigger
through the war. In 1938, Har Sinai purchased property in Upper Park Heights—a
harbinger of the suburbanization to come.[139] Though World War II would pose new
challenges for Baltimore's religious life, the developments of the interwar period laid
the groundwork for the religious scene that would emerge in the postwar period.

Insiders and Outsiders in a Border City

During the 1919 fundraising campaign for European Jewry, Baltimore Jews confidently appealed to their non-Jewish neighbors for help. The *Sun* offered glowing
coverage of gentiles' participation in the campaign. On one Saturday, "Gentile and
non-Orthodox Jewish workers were at their 'bucket' posts downtown and collected
large sums," the newspaper noted. The confirmation class of Oheb Shalom "gave
$8 after a little girl from St. Joseph's School of Industry brought in $5 from her
classmates."[140]

Over the following years, however, the Jewish community became less certain
of the support of their fellow Baltimoreans. Their doubts were confirmed in April
1936, when the Nazi warship *Emden* docked in Baltimore on a goodwill tour seven
months after Germany's Nuremberg laws stripped Jews of their citizenship. Thousands of curious citizens flocked to Recreation Pier to tour the ship during its ten-
day visit. The captain exchanged courtesy calls with Mayor Howard Jackson; city and
state officials drank a toast to Hitler at an officers' reception sponsored by local German societies. Some 450 Marylanders enjoyed a shipboard luncheon that showed off
"sea life's gay side." When the *Emden* steamed away, 2,000 onlookers bade it farewell
as its swastika flag fluttered and its band serenaded them with "Deutschland über
Alles" and "Anchors Aweigh."[141]

The *Sun* applauded the city for its gracious hospitality—while praising Baltimore

Jews for their "dignity and restraint" during what must have been "a trying period." The reaction of the organized Jewish community was indeed muted. The *Jewish Times* editorialized before the ship arrived that for Baltimore to "officially offer a friendly gesture of welcome" would be "unthinkable," but the newspaper reported no trace of an organized communal response to the city's embrace of the *Emden*. When the activist rabbi Edward Israel led an interfaith delegation to Mayor Jackson challenging the city's welcoming plans, he was "roundly criticized by cautious fellow-citizens, both Jew and Christian."[142]

The *Emden*'s visit revealed that efforts to create a climate of opinion against Nazism had not penetrated very deeply into the local culture. In fact, societal attitudes had been moving in entirely the wrong direction as rising xenophobia and antisemitism altered the landscape nationwide. The post–World War I debate over immigration restrictions had brought virulent anti-Jewish rhetoric to the fore; Henry Ford began distributing his influential antisemitic *Dearborn Independent* newspaper in 1920.[143] By the time the anti-Jewish radio broadcasts of Father Charles Coughlin gained national popularity in the mid-1930s, it had become clear that Jews could not count on the goodwill of mainstream society.[144]

But while the *Emden* affair illuminated the tenuous position of Baltimore Jewry, it also revealed the growing involvement of Jews in the diverse institutions of modern society, from politics to voluntary associations. Jews who did protest the *Emden* did so as members of labor unions, radical organizations, and progressive groups rather than Jewish organizations. (Thurgood Marshall of the NAACP spoke at one large anti-*Emden* demonstration.) The American Legion bowed to pressure from Jewish members, canceling its participation in the welcoming activities. Jewish politicians also rose to the occasion: City Councilman Sidney Traub criticized the reception plans, and five state legislators, including House Speaker Emanuel Gorfine, asked the State Department to cancel the ship's permit to dock. Though they were unsuccessful, the city did mute its more lavish plans in response to criticism.[145]

Historians use the phrase "insiders and outsiders" to refer to the position of Jews in American life, especially during the interwar period. That is because it accurately describes a world in which, for example, a Jew could be Maryland's Speaker of the House while Baltimore's mayor welcomes a Nazi ship to his city. Even as antisemitism reached its peak, Jews were more engaged than ever in Baltimore's civic and cultural life. As the city's largest new immigrant group and the one making the greatest economic strides, Baltimore Jewry was in a position to achieve influence in political, civic, and cultural affairs. At the same time, Jews' prominence presented a conspicuous target for resentment over the Depression and the rapid pace of change. While these dynamics were found in other cities, Baltimore's border culture and its particular racial and ethnic mix gave the position of Jews its own distinct character.

Interactions between Jews and non-Jews became more frequent and more intense during the interwar period as the city's racial and ethnic groups competed for housing, resources, and influence. Members of the younger generation experienced

The activist rabbi Edward Israel emerged as one of the Jewish community's
most high-profile civic leaders in the 1920s. *Jewish Museum of Maryland*.

serious clashes with non-Jewish youths. In Southwest Baltimore, a working-class,
predominantly Irish and German district, "we had to use our fists because of such
words as kike, sheenie, and Christ-killer," recalled David "Dutch" Baer. In East Baltimore, Jewish and Italian boys engaged in turf battles, though the two groups mostly
got along. The Polish area to the east was another story. "As soon as we crossed
over to the 1700 block of Gough Street, we'd hear 'sheeny Jews, dirty Jew,'" recalled
Minnie Schneider. Young Jews also faced hostility in Northwest Baltimore; Maurice
Paper recalled having to protect younger Jewish children when walking past some
local churches. Such experiences shaped a generation of tough kids. When Dutch
Baer was nine years old, five bigger boys attacked him in an alley. "They shouted
'Jew, kike, we are going to play church-on-fire.' They had my hands bound to a pole
and they urinated on me. I was the church and they were putting the fire out." After
that, Baer learned to fight, eventually graduating to "blackjacks and brass knuckles"
and becoming a self-described juvenile delinquent. As for Paper, "Nobody would
mess with me. . . . I would fight for anybody for anything. Parents wanted to put me
in reform school!"[146]

Searing encounters with antisemitism helped shape the worldview of many young people, but other kinds of interactions also occurred. Jews could be the aggressors as well, recalled Isadore Livov: "We used to pick battles with the *shvartzes*. . . . We would hide behind the wall and we would have teasers to get the *shvartzes* to run by, so we could waylay them." But friendships occasionally arose across racial and ethnic lines, especially in East Baltimore, where blacks, Jews, and Italians lived close together. Aaron Smelkinson roamed the waterfront with a black friend who lived in a nearby alley street, though he never set foot in his friend's house or vice versa. The oral histories of Jews and Italians reveal many positive interactions. One Italian woman recalled enjoyable visits to the JEA with her Jewish friends. Italian men had fond memories of serving as "Shabbos goyim," turning on lights and performing other chores forbidden to observant Jews on the Sabbath. Prominent political figure Thomas D'Alesandro Jr., who later developed close alliances with Jews, was one of them.[147]

If the outside world occasionally impinged on daily life—for good or ill—young people found security in their Jewish surroundings. Indeed, for most Jews who came of age during the interwar period, the gentile world was neither aggressively hostile nor a place to seek out friendship: it was a vaguely threatening fact of life that could be fairly easily ignored by staying on their own turf. Gil Sandler and his buddies, for example, enjoyed exploring the woods that bordered Park Heights on the east, but would not venture beyond the forest into Woodberry, "a neighborhood as dangerously off-limits to us boys as if it were peopled by hostile aliens from another planet."[148]

Many youths received an eye-opening introduction to life beyond the Jewish world when they went to high school. Attending the all-girls Eastern High School in the late 1930s "was quite an experience for me, 'cause I more or less lived in a ghetto," Norma Livov Wolod recalled. "I was exposed to a lot of gentile young women, and some of them became my best friends."[149] One school came to take on special importance for the Jewish community. For decades, Baltimore City College high school had provided an excellent public education for (white) boys of many backgrounds. During the interwar years, the sons of immigrant tailors and shopkeepers flocked to City College to receive the education their parents hoped would launch them into the middle class. By 1925, around 600 Jews attended City, 40 percent of the student body.[150] It was Jewish enough to be comfortable, but it also provided many boys with their first opportunity to interact with non-Jewish peers. Since City College served as a training ground for Baltimore's future leaders, these connections would prove valuable later in life.

High school instilled confidence in many young Jews. Not only did they excel in academics, they joined wholeheartedly in activities from debate societies to athletics. City College shone in a variety of sports. When the 1923 basketball squad won the league title, four of its five starters were Jewish, including acting captain Dan Kolker.[151] Yet, while they were accepted by non-Jews at their own school, they were

A page from the City College high school yearbook, *The Green Bag*, 1925.
Jewish Museum of Maryland.

marked as the "other" at schools where Jews were largely unknown. When City teams traveled to rival high schools to play, they were sometimes greeted with the chant "City once, City twice, City is a bunch of lice, / City College, the home of the Jews."[152]

Second-generation Jews became accustomed to this double standard. As they grew older, they continued to live in Jewish neighborhoods and socialize almost entirely with fellow Jews, but unlike their immigrant parents, most had neither the option nor the inclination to inhabit a completely Jewish world. Indeed, some of the people most deeply entrenched in the Jewish community also moved easily outside it—and this applied to both uptown and downtown Jews. Sadie Crockin was the president of Baltimore's League of Women Voters and of its Hadassah chapter, and she counted fellow suffragist Madeleine Ellicott as one of her best friends. Three of Rabbi Rivkin's sons worked at the *Baltimore Post*, two as editors and one in advertising. Along with such participation came an understanding of the limits of social interaction. Crockin belonged to a Jewish country club, and elite Jewish families continued to send their children to Park School, the only private school without quotas for Jews.[153]

As Jews moved deeper into the public sphere, they employed a range of strategies to deal with the prejudice they encountered: ignore, retreat, educate/enlighten, or fight. Ignoring bigotry or retreating into their own institutions generally seemed the judicious choice given the climate of the times. Jewish leaders may have hesitated to protest against the *Emden* partly because Jewish-owned businesses were being eyed suspiciously for hiring refugees from Nazism instead of non-Jewish Baltimoreans. Rumors circulated that Hochschild, Kohn had fired Christians in order to give jobs to Jews recently arrived from Germany; Isaac Potts was accused of "discharging American Bohemian help and replacing them with refugees" at his furniture store.[154] "This got to be a major problem in this country, and it happened in Baltimore very severely," recalled former Hochschild, Kohn executive Walter Sondheim Jr. Ignoring the rumors seemed the only way to keep them from spreading. Refugee aid groups took pains to keep a low profile; being out front on issues such as the *Emden* risked drawing attention to their work.[155]

On the other hand, initiatives to promote interfaith understanding and cooperation took off during the era. Jews were not the only targets of xenophobia; anti-Catholic sentiment was rampant, reaching a peak during the 1928 presidential campaign of the Catholic Democratic nominee, Al Smith. To combat the climate of intolerance, the National Conference of Christians and Jews was formed in 1927, and local groups followed. Baltimore Jews helped found the Religious Good Will League in 1928. The Federation of Church and Synagogue Youth held its initial meeting at Baltimore Hebrew Congregation in 1931. Rabbi Morris Lazaron took a special interest in interfaith work, becoming part of the National Conference of Christians and Jews' famous "tolerance trio" (a priest, a minister, and a rabbi), who drew large crowds and garnered wide publicity during barnstorming tours across the nation in the 1930s.[156]

In the late 1930s, Jewish communities around the nation formed organizations to combat antisemitism and promote better relations with the surrounding society.[157] The Baltimore Jewish Council was launched in 1939 with Simon Sobeloff as its first president. Although it was the first communal institution to engage in the "fight" strategy, the BJC went about its business quietly. Focusing at first on job discrimination, its usual method was to investigate fully and then meet privately with the offending employers, often calling on highly placed Jewish business or governmental leaders to reason with them. Such methods enabled the BJC to end discriminatory hiring at some companies, but as executive director Leon Sachs later observed, the group was only "scratching the surface of a major problem." More systemic solutions—and a more forceful approach—would wait until the 1940s.[158]

Around the same time that the BJC started up, an incident demonstrated that Jewish youths were ready for a more aggressive "fight" strategy than their elders were. In June 1939 Melvin Bridge, a Jewish student at Gwynns Falls Junior High School, was attacked one Friday by a group of boys, many sporting inked swastikas on their arms. In the melee, they reportedly cut an *H* (for Hebrew) on the back of his neck. Bridge's friend Morton Rosen, a nineteen-year-old former seaman, went to the school on the following Monday to protect him, got into a fight with two students, and was arrested for assault. Jewish students from City College also showed up to "get even" with Bridge's attackers, and police chased some thirty City boys through the woods near the school. Jewish school superintendent David Weglein suspended four City students and eighteen Gwynns Falls boys implicated in the attack on Bridge.[159]

The *Jewish Times* devoted significant coverage to the episode as reports circulated of a "secret bund organization" operating in the schools. School authorities downplayed the incident, describing it as a "boyish prank." Weglein ordered an investigation, which found no evidence of organized antisemitism at Gwynns Falls or any other school. Instead, the report deplored the "great amount of publicity," which had created an "exaggerated impression of what occurred." But *Jewish Times* columnist Maurice Shochatt proudly hailed Rosen's "solid punches in the defense of Melvin Bridge." He was not the only adult to approve the teen's actions: Rosen received pro bono representation from a prominent Jewish attorney (the charges against him were dropped) and was given a job by a Jewish businessman. Taking heart from the younger generation, the Jewish community, it seemed, was now in a more fighting mood.[160]

Meanwhile, despite the climate of antisemitism, the interwar period saw Baltimore's Jewish community become a political force to be reckoned with. If Jews had embraced the electoral process during the immigrant era, their growing level of political sophistication and organization now allowed them to claim a share of real power. They were aided by Baltimore's border city political culture, which had long combined the kind of ethnic-based machine politics common to northern industrial cities with the penchant for disenfranchising black voters characteristic of the South. These dynamics provided opportunity to a Jewish community that was not only significant in size, but ever more concentrated into a single section of the city. It only remained for someone to come along with the insight and ruthlessness to forge the Jewish population into a powerful voting bloc.[161]

That someone was James H. "Jack" Pollack. Pollack had grown up on the streets of East Baltimore and enjoyed a brief career as a boxer before becoming an enforcer in the bootlegging trade. Arrested for assault and liquor violations in his twenties, in 1921 he and three accomplices were indicted for killing a night watchman during a robbery. The case never came to trial, and Pollack soon embarked on a political career: in 1926, in the employ of Irish Democratic boss William Curran, he assaulted an election judge who questioned the qualifications of a man whom Pollack had brought in to register to vote. Curran himself represented Pollack at his hearing (Pollack was fined $26). Pollack rose in Curran's organization and became

David "Dutch" Baer (*left*) and Jack Pollack (*right*). *Jewish Museum of Maryland.*

his co-leader in the legislative Fourth District. The two were close; Pollack even named his son Morton Curran Pollack. Before long, however, he bucked his mentor and took over the district.[162]

Through his Trenton Democratic Club, Pollack "wielded nearly absolute control over the Jewish vote." The lopsided vote totals in his district could turn elections around. His personality traits aided his rise: astuteness, charisma and charm, and a vindictiveness that struck fear into potential adversaries. When opposed, "he would take measures to destroy you," a close acquaintance said.[163] Forging alliances with highly placed officials—after Curran, the most notable was Thomas D'Alesandro Jr., congressman, mayor, and former "Shabbos goy"—Pollack emerged by the early 1940s as the city's unchallenged political boss, a position he would hold for two decades as he "made" mayors, governors, city council members, state legislators, judges, housing inspectors, and liquor license holders.[164]

While on his way to amassing personal wealth and power, Pollack gave his fellow Jews access to the political spoils of a burgeoning welfare state: government jobs and contracts, city services, and favorable treatment from zoning boards and other public bodies. "He did for everybody," stated neighbor Louis Bluefeld, who recalled

Pollack dispensing favors to families who called him at home daily. In return, "everybody on the block" helped Pollack at election time.[165] Many Jewish public officials owed their elections to Pollack, who expected to be rewarded in turn. Yet he was uninterested in public policy. He often backed candidates who, "in keeping with the Jewish tradition, could be counted on to take the lead in the enactment of progressive legislation in the areas of education, health, welfare of the poor" without his interference, noted a politically connected observer. These politicians included the labor champion and New Dealer Jacob Edelman, elected to the Baltimore City Council in 1939, and state legislator E. Milton Altfeld, who sponsored anti–Jim Crow bills and other civil rights measures.[166]

It would be wrong, however, to credit Pollack with advancing black interests. He and Philip Perlman, another Jewish Democratic Party insider, played major roles during the interwar era in advancing the Baltimore power structure's ongoing project of keeping African Americans politically powerless and residentially confined. Perlman, as the city's solicitor in the 1920s, headed a governmental committee charged with promoting the de facto segregation of black people.[167] In the early 1930s, with black neighborhoods making up a large portion of Pollack's Fourth District, electoral boundaries were redrawn to split the black vote, shutting African Americans out of the city council and the state legislature. As with earlier Jewish Democratic politicians who had advanced disenfranchisement, their motivation was as much partisan as racist, since most African Americans voted Republican. But Pollack also played on the racial fears of his Jewish constituency. Indeed, excluding blacks was one of the "strongest cohesive forces" of his organization, stated political scientist Harvey Wheeler. Jews advanced politically, at least in part, at the expense of blacks.[168]

Jewish Republicans may have been the only Jewish officeholders to escape the taint of the machine. Popular Jewish reformer Daniel Ellison served as the "social conscience" of the city council and its lone Republican, despite running from the heart of Pollack territory; among other things, he lobbied "long, hard, and successfully" for the 1937 creation of the Baltimore Housing Authority.[169] The *Afro-American* saw Harry Levin, the city's sole Republican state legislator in the late 1920s, as a staunch ally; he later became the newspaper's attorney. Simon Sobeloff, once a protégé of Republican mayor William Broening, was responsible for enforcing Prohibition laws as the US attorney for Maryland in the early 1930s and somehow "emerged with the respect of both wets and drys." He would go on to serve as US solicitor general in the Eisenhower administration.[170]

But the days when Jews split their vote between the two parties were drawing to an end. The interwar years saw American Jews move solidly into the Democratic camp, and Baltimoreans were no exception.[171] The rise of Pollack's machine no doubt helped, but ultimately it was the Depression that transformed the Jewish electorate into a solidly Democratic constituency. From machine hacks to progressive reformers, from the labor movement to small businesspeople, Baltimore Jews embraced the New Deal.

- - - - - - - - - - - - -

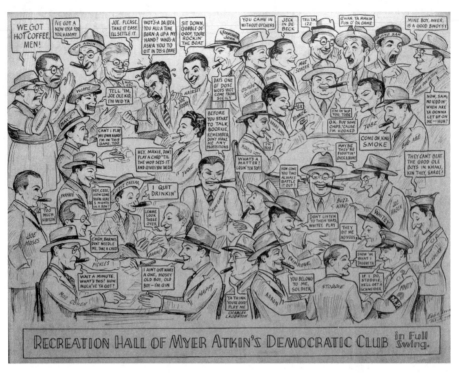

This 1944 depiction of "Myer Atkin's Democratic Club" by artist Eddie Levin captures Baltimore's semi-underworld of politics, gambling, and shady characters. *Jewish Museum of Maryland*.

Beyond the electoral process, Jews influenced local politics through their participation in the social movements that spanned the interwar era. It was a time of broad-based alliances: suffrage leader Sadie Crockin worked with union women in the campaign for women's right to vote; the upper-class friend of labor Jacob Moses advocated for a women's equal rights amendment; and the socialist Samuel Neistadt and Rabbi Edward Israel helped found the Maryland branch of the American Civil Liberties Union. The Jewish-led Amalgamated Clothing Workers of America became an important part of the city's political culture, sponsoring a popular lecture series that served as a gathering place for a wide spectrum of progressives. Though reformers and radicals made little headway in the politically conservative 1920s, once the Depression hit, the networks they had created helped revive the labor movement and forge the citizens' movements that pushed for solutions to the economic crisis.[172]

Given the anti–New Deal stance of public officials (including the mayor and governor), the ACWA and other progressive groups played a critical role in getting the New Deal to work in Maryland. As historian Beth Wenger observed, the Depression served as "a vehicle for Jewish integration" by pulling Jews into the public sphere as partners, advocates, and critics of the nation's evolving welfare system.[173] In the early years of the crisis, Baltimore officials, who wanted as little to do with welfare as possible, turned over much of the city's meager relief budget to four private agencies: the Associated Jewish Charities, Catholic Charities, the Salvation Army, and the Baltimore Family Welfare Association. After citizen agitation and federal pressure forced both city and state to create a welfare structure to channel New Deal funds, Baltimore's new relief agency worked closely with the Associated, and the agency's East Baltimore office was staffed by former Associated social workers.[174]

Jews played a critical role in the contentious process of forging the New Deal in Maryland, and none more so than Harry Greenstein. From 1933 to 1936 he served as the state's emergency relief administrator, "on loan" from the Associated.[175] To create a public works program, the governor turned to Abel Wolman, the Baltimore-born son of Russian Jewish immigrants and the chief engineer of Maryland's Health Department. Known for his pioneering work in developing water filtration systems, Wolman did not relish the political aspects of the job, but during his four-year tenure the Public Works Administration built highways, bridges, schools, hospitals, airports, and modern sewage systems around the state.[176] Former Levindale president Lee Dopkin, the chair of Maryland's old age pension commission, was a driving force behind the 1935 passage of a state pension law, and he lobbied tirelessly for social security.[177]

Some Jewish leaders joined with their non-Jewish counterparts to push reform from the outside. In January 1936, for example, clergy across Baltimore spoke out from their pulpits in a coordinated effort to push lawmakers to fix problems that had halted the flow of federal relief dollars. The most pointed remarks came from Har Sinai rabbi Edward Israel, who railed against the "miserable mess" caused by an "inconceivably inept" state legislature and a governor and mayor who were "proud anti–New Dealers." With people "at the point of starvation," the situation "would be laughable if it were not tragic," he fumed. More measured remarks from Presbyterian, Episcopal, and Methodist ministers made roughly the same point.[178]

Meanwhile, embracing the Popular Front strategy of building alliances with liberals, Maryland's Communist Party—with several Jewish members—gained influence in the 1930s and early 1940s. Jewish Communists worked as union organizers and attorneys, particularly in the maritime, shipyard, and steel industries. Johns Hopkins University professor Albert Blumberg was the Communist candidate for mayor in 1938 and for senator in 1940. Baltimore attorney Bernard Ades achieved fame defending Euel Lee, an African American accused of killing a white family of four on the Eastern Shore, in a case that drew comparisons to the Scottsboro Boys. Before the trial, Ades and a colleague were beaten by a mob that had gathered outside the courthouse in hopes of lynching Lee. Ades succeeded in having Lee's conviction overturned based on the exclusion of blacks from the jury; the *Afro* praised what "two Jewish lawyers, backed by the Communist Party," had accomplished. (Lee was convicted in a second trial, however, and executed.) Ades later joined twelve other Baltimore Jews who fought in the Spanish Civil War in the Abraham Lincoln Brigade.[179]

According to author Lillian Potter, "No other community in Baltimore aided the Black struggle as the Jewish community did."[180] Jack Pollack's racist ploys notwithstanding, Jewish elected officials were among the few white politicians to ally with African Americans and support black attempts to repeal Jim Crow laws (though the *Afro-American* suspected that some did so solely to woo black voters). Civic leaders such as Edward Israel and Urban League founder Sidney Hollander pressed city agencies and other public bodies to treat blacks more fairly. Rabbi Israel also angered Jewish department store owners—including the Hutzlers, who were members of his own congregation—by calling on them to desegregate.[181]

Yet, aside from Rabbi Israel, Jewish leaders were unwilling to confront Jewish-owned businesses that discriminated against or exploited black people. Indeed, while Jewish political and civic leaders may have supported civil rights, economic and social relations between blacks and Jews were fraught with tension. African Americans' frustrations at the oppression they faced often found expression against Jews, who were highly visible in the black community as landlords, store owners, and competitors for the same real estate. Articles in the *Afro-American* in the years after World War I pulled no punches: "Jews Making Barrels of Money from Colored Folk" is how an August 22, 1919, article described the role of Jewish real estate speculators in Northwest Baltimore's changing neighborhoods.[182] A June 3, 1921, article depicted a woman's attempt "to save her home from the clutches of Simon Needle, a Jewish real estate dealer." Perhaps because of the *Afro*'s developing relationship with Jewish political allies, however, such crude stereotypes disappeared from the headlines by the end of the decade.

The most concentrated Jewish retail presence in black West Baltimore was along Pennsylvania Avenue. Lined with shops, movie theaters, clubs, and concert halls that showcased America's top black entertainers, "the Avenue" was the thriving "hub of Negro life and activity in Baltimore." As one woman recalled, "downtown you couldn't try on a dress or stop and have a snack with a friend, but the Avenue was ours and, I'll tell you, it was a mighty fine place to go."[183] That most of the stores and many entertainment venues were owned by Jews had broad implications for Jewish-black relations. The reluctance of avenue merchants to hire black employees led many African Americans to blame Jews as a group. In the 1930s, activists led a "Buy Where You Can Work" boycott of the Avenue's stores. The campaign had mixed success, but one clear result was an increase in tension between blacks and Jews.[184]

Nevertheless, relationships between customers and merchants, employees and store owners, and black and Jewish neighbors could be positive as well. Mickey Steinberg's family lived above their store in an African American block of West Lanvale Street. "All my friends were 'colored,'" he recalled. "We played ball on the street." He rarely ventured into the white gentile area across Fulton Avenue where, as a Jewish kid, he was more likely to encounter hostility.[185] While some African Americans complained of high prices and exploitative credit practices, others believed that Jewish merchants provided a valuable service and that the Jews' experience of oppression made them sympathetic to the plight of black people. "In the Jews' stores, they would give you credit," Ruth Stewart explained in an oral history. "You couldn't go into the white [gentile-owned] stores and say my children need a loaf of bread or a chicken or whatever, and have them give it to you. But in a Jew's store, you could get that. It's interesting because the Jews also have a history of being oppressed. . . . And I think that's why they did for us."[186]

To many African Americans, that history of oppression made discrimination by Jewish-owned businesses all the more infuriating. As Baltimore NAACP leader Lillie Mae Jackson put it, "the Negroes naturally expect better treatment from the Jewish group." And nothing aroused the anger of Jackson and other black leaders as much as the racist policies of the downtown department stores, most of which were Jewish-owned.[187] Black customers "were not welcomed in any Baltimore department store," Hochschild, Kohn chief Martin Kohn later admitted. "They were not extended credit regardless of their worth. They could not try on clothes and they had no return privileges." They also were not served at the stores' lunch counters. Kohn claimed the stores had little choice: "Baltimore was a border city, and all prejudices were a little stronger here than other places." His use of the word "all" hints at the vulnerability felt by Jewish merchants. But more important, the owners believed that changing their policy involved too great a financial risk. Confronted by the NAACP in the 1930s and 1940s, Kohn related, "I am ashamed to say that we put them off by saying that it was not us, but our customers, who determined our policy. . . . We had customers who would get off an elevator if a black got on, and who would leave a counter if a black stood next to them."[188] Ironically, his rationale echoed that of real estate developer Edward Bouton for keeping Jews out of Roland Park.

Similar alliances and tensions between Jews and blacks could be found in other cities, but in Baltimore, the only city where "large Jewish and Black communities were juxtaposed in a southern-like Jim Crow environment," their interactions were likely more charged than they were elsewhere.[189] Local tensions burst onto the national scene in a 1936 exchange between Rabbi Israel and Lillie Mae Jackson in the NAACP magazine, *Crisis*. When Israel expressed dismay about the anti-Jewish sentiment he encountered at a civil rights forum, Jackson angrily responded with a barrage of charges against Jews, with special mention of the department stores.[190]

It is not surprising that civil rights leaders—drawn primarily from the black middle and upper classes—found exclusion from the downtown emporiums particularly galling. As "prominent sites of civic culture and modernity," in historian Paul Kramer's words, the department stores symbolized Baltimore's very identity during an age of rising consumerism. Hutzler's "was so 'Baltimore-ish' and very classy," one former customer said. "It was one of the big Baltimore traditions."

Hochschild, Kohn's Thanksgiving parade was "one of Baltimore's biggest and best-loved spectaculars."[191]

Their role in fashioning the downtown experience was not the only way Jews shaped Baltimore as it grew into a thriving modern city. From their circumscribed turf in Northwest Baltimore, their contributions to civic and cultural life were city-wide—and major: from the foods Baltimoreans identified as their own to the places they spent their leisure hours to the art that hung on the walls of that newly built monument to civic pride, the Baltimore Museum of Art. Despite antisemitism and the limits imposed by a segregated social life, the Jewish community became an integral part of the cultural fabric during the interwar era. And not just through the contributions of old elite families like the Hutzlers, Hochschilds, and Hechts, but even more so through the ambitions and preoccupations of the Eastern Europeans—acculturated immigrants and their children—who made up the bulk of the Jewish population.

The new generation of Jewish-owned businesses began to rival the department stores in cultural influence. Car dealerships, movie theater chains, advertising agencies, and radio stations represented the cutting edge of consumerism. Delis such as Nates and Leons became hangouts where (white) Baltimoreans from a variety of backgrounds could congregate. Isadore Rappaport's Hippodrome Theatre offered the latest in live entertainment, from big bands to comedy acts like Bob Hope and the Three Stooges. Hendler's Ice Cream ("The Velvet Kind") entered the peak of its popularity, while German Jewish refugee Gustav Brunn created the spice blend that he named Old Bay. Even the traditional Baltimore game of duckpin bowling received an update when the Shecter family opened the Charles Bowling Center in 1937, its 100 lanes making it the largest of its kind.[192]

As the Eastern Europeans' elder statesman and Baltimore's biggest booster, Jacob Epstein exerted a major influence on his adopted city. In the early 1920s he served as one of five members of the powerful Public Improvement Commission, charged with overseeing the development of the land the city had annexed in 1918. This role gave him a hand in the expansion of the city's water supply and school system, among other public projects. He joined the board of the Baltimore Museum of Art in 1923, and his personal art collection became one of its founding collections when it opened in Wyman Park in 1929.

Other Jewish Baltimoreans also played key roles in creating the institutions of the modern era. Dr. Bessie Moses, the first female obstetrical intern at Johns Hopkins, opened Baltimore's first birth control clinic in 1927. In 1938 she established the Northwest Maternal Health Center, the first in the nation staffed by black physicians. Jacob Moses led the drive to convert the former Hebrew Orphan Asylum into the West Baltimore General Hospital, an institution desperately needed in a rapidly growing part of the city.[193]

Jews contributed to Baltimore's cultural life from high to low. Etta and Claribel Cone amassed a good part of their renowned modern art collection during the

Hochschild, Kohn started its Thanksgiving parade to cheer Baltimoreans during the Depression. It quickly became a major civic event. Photo, 1940s. *Jewish Museum of Maryland.*

interwar period; the sisters' close relationship with Henri Matisse brought him to Baltimore for a visit in 1930. Their cousin Saidie Adler May, an equally adventurous collector, made her first substantial gift to the Baltimore Museum of Art in the 1930s. The May and Cone donations gave the museum one of the nation's finest collections of modern European art. At the other extreme was Max Cohen, whose marketing genius helped make The Block into a cultural site that may have exceeded the art museum in popularity, if not in taste. Traveling businessmen, soldiers, and sailors flocked to the district, while some husbands even brought their wives for an evening of unusual entertainment. For Baltimore males, it was a veritable rite of passage.[194]

Some cultural figures bridged the gap between high and low. The immigrant violinist Benjamin Klasmer founded the Jewish Educational Alliance youth orchestra in 1919. Under his baton it became a respected ensemble, and he recruited some of its musicians to join him in the fledgling Baltimore Symphony Orchestra. At the same time, he served as the city's leading director of pit orchestras, arranging and conducting the live music that accompanied silent movies and vaudeville. After sound movies replaced silent films, Klasmer settled into a permanent gig at the Hippodrome, where he led the orchestra and performed as part of a two-person musical comedy act. His most significant contribution to Baltimore's civic life may have come in 1947 when he co-wrote the Baltimore Colts theme song with Jo Lombardi.[195]

Klasmer's career exemplifies the boundary crossing that characterized Jewish life and culture during the interwar era. In close-knit Northwest Baltimore, people who took widely different paths in life attended the same synagogues, met at the same delis, cooperated in building communal organizations, and often remained friends for life. Milton Bates and Sid Weinberg, for example, hung out at Easterwood Park as teens. Bates grew up to become a radical activist, blacklisted during the McCarthy era. Weinberg became an accountant for gangster Ike Sapperstein's Club Charles before founding his own accounting firm. Both would help organize the Easterwood Park Boys alumni group, where they socialized with fellow alums: doctors, lawyers, judges, teachers, and business owners.[196]

Meanwhile, though Jews resided within well-defined geographic boundaries, the borders of their interactions with the larger society were porous, from their political alliances to their economic relationships to their civic and cultural activities. Inevitably, they absorbed influences from their surroundings. For many families, the steamed crab feast became a valued tradition, although often this rite was confined to the basement and tables were scrupulously covered with newspaper to avoid contact with otherwise kosher surroundings. (This behavior perhaps helped justify the large ads touting the "best seasoned steamed crabs" placed in the *Jewish Times* by Gordon Sea Food on West North Avenue.)

Having embraced local influences, Jews became adept at reflecting them back out. As a boy in the late 1930s, Jerry Leiber delivered goods to the black families who lived around his mother's West Baltimore grocery store. "Inside those households, radios were always playing," he later wrote. "Music was everywhere, running through my head and coursing through my veins." He grew up to become half of the Leiber-Stoller songwriting team, which gave the world such seminal rock-and-roll hits as "Jailhouse Rock," "Hound Dog," and "Kansas City."[197]

American Jewish historians have termed the Jews who came of age during the interwar period as a "lost generation." Henry Feingold, for example, wrote about them as "transitional, belonging fully to neither American nor Jewish culture," and noted a "rudderless quality in American Jewish communal life."[198] Without a doubt, Baltimore Jews were not aimed toward a common goal; they were branching off in many directions. But they were not "rudderless" in the sense of lacking leadership. And their leaders were not isolated from each other or from the larger society. Socialists like Samuel Neistadt worked with Republicans like Simon Sobeloff in founding the Baltimore Jewish Council—and both collaborated with non-Jews in civic and political pursuits. Orthodox rabbi Reuben Rivkin aligned with Reform Har Sinai congregant Jacob Moses in Zionist activities. Such collaborations, which would be unusual today, seemed natural at the time.

Moreover, although the community secularized, religion was not cast aside. Despite a drop in the number of observant Jews and intense conflicts over modernization, the crisis of faith detected by historians on the national level did not characterize Baltimore Jewry. Even for many on the Left, traditional religion remained important; the socialist labor leader David Schnaper, for example, was a founder of Agudas Achim Anshe Sphard, an Orthodox congregation in Lower Park Heights. Religious young people disturbed by their elders' lapsed ways joined together to form Adath B'nei Israel and helped create a network of Orthodox institutions that would emerge later in the century as a defining feature of the Jewish community.[199]

Despite the challenges posed by internal conflict, antisemitism, and the Depression, Baltimore Jews moved forward with purpose on all fronts: religious, political, economic, and cultural. The interwar period was indeed transitional, bridging the gap between the immigrant era and the post–World War II era, when a fully American Jewish community emerged. It was a time of tremendous energy and change — and a time during which the contours of the future were firmly established.

5

From Baltimore to Pikesville

Looking back in 1979 on a long career in retailing, Martin Kohn had some regrets. Hochschild, Kohn's downtown department store—no longer owned by his family— had recently shut down. "The closing makes me remember 1946, when we opened our first suburban store," he reminisced. Although business at the downtown store was good, fewer customers took the streetcar to the city center. "There was always a parking problem. A branch store could offer free, ample parking, longer hours and an informal atmosphere." Hochschild, Kohn became the first Baltimore department store to venture into the future with the opening of its Edmondson Village branch. It was the right move at the right time, but later Kohn wrote, "I wonder how much our suburban ventures contributed to the deterioration of downtown. Did we lead or follow the flight of middle-income families from the city?"[1]

There is no easy answer to his question. What is certain is that the post–World War II nationwide rush to suburbia transformed Baltimore as it did other American cities and that Jews were deeply involved in every aspect of the transformation as retailers and realtors, homeowners and developers, communal and civic leaders. Their role at the forefront of suburbanization signaled the postwar emergence of Jews as an integral part of the Baltimore scene, vital participants in the trends that would shape the metro area.

There were other signs as well. The younger generation completed their parents' march into the middle and upper middle classes, aided by a booming postwar economy, government policies that benefited a broad swath of Americans, and a marked decline in antisemitism. No longer tethered to family businesses, young adults capitalized on increased opportunities to succeed in the city's professional and corporate arenas. Meanwhile, prominent Jewish individuals became deeply ensconced in Baltimore's political, civic, philanthropic, and cultural leadership.

But even as Jews became more integrated into the Baltimore mainstream economically and socially, they became more segregated residentially. When they decamped for suburbia, they moved in a single direction: farther northwest, with suburbs such as Randallstown and Pikesville exerting a magnetic pull. In 1960, the *Jewish Times* bemoaned that despite their impressive advances, Baltimore Jews had "succeeded in ghettoizing ourselves even more."[2] The creation of a Jewish suburbia reflected the national Jewish phenomenon of the "gilded ghetto." But residential concentration remained more pronounced in Baltimore than in most places: by 1968, more than 90 percent of Baltimore Jews lived in the metro area's northwest corridor.[3] This relative isolation from non-Jews, along with the ability of their historically strong Orthodox institutions to adapt to the suburban environment, would enable them to maintain a greater degree of traditionalism compared to Jews in other suburbias.

As during the interwar era, the intensification of Jewish residential concentration reflected choices made by Jews within the limits set by the city's distinctive racial and ethnic dynamics. With a history that combined the South's Jim Crow and the North's ethnic group competition, Baltimore had more reason than most to be balkanized. Similarly, Baltimore's border city character would influence the Jewish response to the era's defining events, such as the civil rights movement—which found Baltimore Jews much more outspoken in support of blacks than were Jewish communities to the south, but more conflicted than northern Jewish communities about how far to go in their support.

Issues of race loomed large in the postwar era for Baltimore as a whole and for its Jewish community. "White flight" contributed significantly to the exodus from city to suburbs. The civil rights movement had a profound impact on the Jewish population, making already-tangled relations between Jews and blacks even more complex. Jewish activists and civic leaders continued to be the black community's closest white allies while Jewish retailers remained key targets of the movement. Some Jewish politicians championed civil rights while others saw blacks as a threat to their power and acted accordingly. Later in the period, the April 1968 riots shook Baltimore Jewry, with ramifications that lingered into the 1970s and beyond.

Many patterns of life in postwar Baltimore had roots in the interwar era. And yet, the landscape had utterly changed, figuratively and literally. Of course, the watershed event of World War II came between "interwar" and "postwar," accelerating some previous trends but altering others. The war ended the Great Depression, stimulating the growth of industrial cities such as Baltimore, whose role in steelmaking and shipbuilding made it particularly valuable to the war effort. Military service and homefront activities broadened the experiences of Baltimoreans and brought Jews and non-Jews into greater contact. The war also expanded the role of government in peoples' lives.

Newcomers who arrived to work in Baltimore's defense industry swelled the population and changed the city's demographic profile. The metro area's population grew more than 40 percent between 1940 and 1950 and increased another 40 percent over the next twenty years. As a result, the Jewish percentage of the region's population steadily dropped even though the number of Jews rose. After hovering around 9 percent through the interwar period, the proportion of Jews started shrinking after the war and fell to around 5 percent by 1968. Ironically, in that year the Jewish population reached a record height of 106,000; although the number subsequently dropped, the momentum coming out of the war years had permanently enlarged Baltimore Jewry.[4] If the Jewish community looked vastly different in 1979 than it had in 1939, World War II is the place to start tracing its transformation.

Life during Wartime

After failing as a pioneer in Palestine, Polish-born William Uris came to Baltimore where, according to his son Leon, he proceeded to fail as a paperhanger, shopkeeper, and husband. Leon Uris started down his father's path—flunking English repeatedly at City College high school—before World War II gave him the opportunity to change course. The seventeen-year-old enlisted in the marines shortly after Pearl Harbor and shipped out to the South Pacific. His 1953 novel, *Battle Cry*, based on his wartime experiences, set him on the road to literary fame.[5]

Thousands of sons and daughters left the confines of Jewish Baltimore to go off to war. Some, like Uris, found a whole new world opened up to them. Others wanted only to return safely to their families. On furlough to recover from wounds after fighting in North Africa, army private Melvin Baskin insisted to a Baltimore reporter that war had not changed him. "There's only one thing different about me— I love my home more." While serving on a hospital ship in the Mediterranean, US Navy Nurse Corps lieutenant Edna Jontiff found herself turning down an arranged marriage with the head of Gibraltar's Jewish community. "I had a mother waiting for me at home," she later explained.[6] But even as they longed for the comforts of home, few returned unchanged.

The war against Nazism enabled Jewish service members to bring together their priorities as Americans and as Jews. For some, fighting the enemy of the Jewish people alongside their fellow US citizens powerfully melded their two identities. In Germany with George Patton's Third Army in April 1945, Albert Goldstein served with the combat engineers who moved in ahead of US troops in order to prepare the infrastructure. When seizing property needed by the occupiers, he relied on the smattering of Yiddish he possessed to communicate with the Germans. "I've thrown hundreds of people out of their homes, being especially rough on those I thought were Nazis," the Baltimore private wrote in his diary. If they complained, "I would tell them I was a Jew and they got out quick." He especially relished declaring his Jewish identity at a house that contained SS uniforms and ammunition.[7] Moreover, military service brought Americans from all walks of life into contact, enlarging the experience of Jews and non-Jews alike. Although antisemitism in the US military was certainly not unknown, many Jews came out of the war feeling more firmly included in the national polity and more secure in their American Jewish identity.[8]

Of course, many who went off to war never came home. As the weekly obituary pages of the *Jewish Times* revealed, Baltimore Jews of all classes and backgrounds

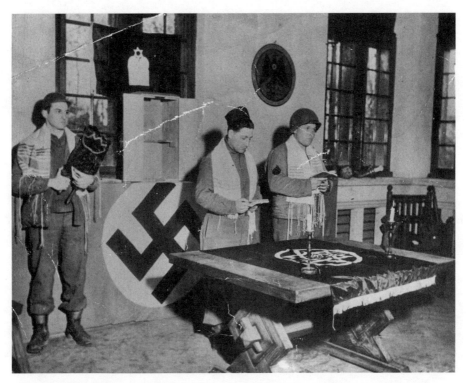

Rabbi Manuel Poliakoff, an army captain, conducts services at a former castle owned by Joseph Goebbels, 1945. Corporal Martin Willen, a fellow Baltimorean, serves as cantor. Holding the Torah is Private First Class Abraham Mirmelstein. *Jewish Museum of Maryland.*

died in combat, from Guadalcanal and Iwo Jima to the beaches of Normandy and the Ardennes forest. Among them was Sergeant Isadore Jachman, a paratrooper and Talmudical Academy graduate, who was killed during the Battle of the Bulge after he dashed across open ground through a hail of fire, seized a bazooka, and fired on two enemy tanks, causing them to withdraw. He was posthumously awarded the nation's highest military award, the Congressional Medal of Honor.[9]

While the war changed the lives of those who served in the military, it also profoundly shaped those who remained in Baltimore. They, too, found that the war strengthened the link between their Jewish and American identities. Not only had the United States finally joined the fight against Hitler, but the shared sacrifices of World War II—from the loss of loved ones to wartime measures that impinged on everyday life—both connected Jews to the larger society and brought the Jewish community closer together.

Involvement in homefront activities contributed to this sense of togetherness. Congregations and clubs participated in scrap metal drives and raised funds for the Red Cross. Synagogues provided kosher meals to Jewish servicemen passing through town, and Har Sinai ran a weekend hostel for Jewish soldiers at its Bolton

As part of the war effort, Har Sinai congregation participated in civil defense activities, such as this 1942 first aid class. *Jewish Museum of Maryland.*

Street Temple. The YMHA became the Jewish USO (there was also a Catholic USO and two black USOs, among others). The Y's Monument Street building teemed with activity; attendance in 1943 exceeded 750,000. The Y also sent "100 girls each month" to serve as dancing partners at nearby military bases. The young women were carefully selected and chaperoned, the Y assured the community.[10]

The city's religious leaders worked to forge unity and bring order to a fast-growing and diversifying population as the rapid rise of the defense industry threatened to turn Baltimore into a chaotic boomtown. At the request of the YWCA, the Jewish Y welcomed non-Jews, holding dances for swing-shift defense workers on Fridays from 1:00 a.m. to 4:30 a.m. The Jewish Y also held interfaith programs for children, black and white. Meanwhile, prominent Jewish-owned businesses fostered a spirit of patriotism. Department stores created military-themed displays and erected massive signs urging pedestrians to buy war bonds.[11] They also responded to wartime demands with innovations that would carry into the postwar era. Hochschild, Kohn became the first downtown store to open in the evenings to serve the large numbers of women who worked full time in defense jobs. "We decided to stay open one night a week and were surprised by the swarm of customers," recalled Martin Kohn.[12] The hordes of shoppers exemplified one side effect of the war: the Depression was well and truly over.

But even as the war brought improved fortunes and promoted togetherness, the

With the wartime rationing of rubber causing a shoe shortage, shoe repair shops did a booming business. *Courtesy of the Library of Congress, FSA-OWI Collection.*

conversion to a war economy highlighted old tensions and created new ones. The nascent Baltimore Jewish Council (BJC) received numerous complaints from Jews denied jobs in local defense plants, and it worked to persuade employers to change their ways. A landmark federal order banning war industry discrimination gave minorities some leverage, but enforcement was uneven.[13] Meanwhile, migrants— mostly southern whites and blacks—poured into the city to work in the shipyards and steel mills, causing social turmoil, workplace antagonisms, and a severe housing shortage. Competition for jobs and housing played out along racial lines, with Jews often squarely in the middle.

At Bethlehem Steel's Fairfield shipyard, where Liberty ships essential to the war effort were built, whites staged violent protests in November 1942 when management attempted to promote blacks in order to comply with the federal nondiscrimination order. With the shipbuilders' union, Local 43 of the Congress of Industrial Organizations, firmly in support of the black workers, white protest leaders charged that "Jewish Communists are running the Union" and hinted darkly about "the large number of Jews from New York in the yards." Indeed, most of the 400 or so Jewish shipyard workers were from out of town, like the vast majority of the 40,000-strong workforce (and some union leaders *were* Jewish Communists). Local 43 fought back, calling the protest leaders "Hitler supporters" who were being "used by outside forces to disrupt the production of this shipyard." The union managed to retain the support of the majority of the workforce until the end of the war.[14]

Some Jewish defense workers endured discrimination by management and harassment by other workers (especially Poles and Germans), but their experiences were not all bad. Milt Seif, a welder and union steward at Bethlehem Steel's Key Highway shipyard, recalled good relations with fellow workers, who appreciated his skill at his job and his advocacy on their behalf. And antagonism toward Jews lessened over time. In 1941 laborer Rubin Rubinstein described the Fairfield yard as "filled with anti-Semitism," with company officials "somewhat to blame." Three years later the BJC reported cooperation from the company in stemming "anti-religious and anti-racial" activities that might "cause disunity in the yard and harm the war effort."[15]

Appeals to wartime unity did not help much when it came to another flash point in race relations: living space. The housing shortage afflicting Baltimore was especially critical for African Americans, who already lived in overcrowded conditions. Some 34,000 black people came to the city between 1940 and 1943, putting a tremendous strain on black districts. In 1944, blacks starting moving across Fulton Avenue into a predominantly white, Catholic, working-class neighborhood. They had help from real estate investors, mostly Jewish, who bought up modest row houses from easily panicked white residents and quickly sold them at inflated prices to black home buyers. It was an early example of blockbusting, a practice that would become infamous in the postwar years.[16]

White residents responded with fury to what was commonly referred to (by whites, including the press) as a "Negro invasion." Reluctant to blame their fleeing neighbors, they searched for a culprit in what seemed to be a concerted attempt to destroy their close-knit community. They soon identified the guilty party. "All we want the colored people to do is stay in their place, and we'll stay in ours," a protest leader stated. This would happen "if you'd keep these things out of the hands of g— d— Jew real estate owners." An attendee at a community meeting at St. Martin's Church reported to the BJC that the mood was "more of an anti-Semitic nature than a Negro problem," with some in the crowd urging that "something be done regarding the Jewish situation."[17]

Pulled into the fray, the BJC stepped carefully. The council opposed the enforced segregation of blacks and respected their right to move across Fulton Avenue, but it also deplored the unscrupulous behavior of some Jewish realtors—both on principle and because their actions provoked antisemitism, its leaders believed. The BJC executive director, Leon Sachs, embarked on a surprisingly cordial correspondence with the leader of the white Fulton Improvement Association, who seemed eager to "stem the tide" of blacks into his community without resorting to racism or antisemitism. Sachs worked behind the scenes to persuade Jewish realtors not to enter certain blocks, while the community leader made concessions of his own. At one point he thanked Sachs for helping a particular block to stay "on the white side" for a year and reported that the association's leaders were now "conceding" the block, though "we would not want any of the residents to know." The Fulton Avenue controversy would spill over into the postwar period, and similar conflicts would spread to neighborhoods across the city.[18]

Wartime conditions heightened tensions between Jews and blacks as well. The tight housing market led to skyrocketing rents, with tenants "gouged daily by unscrupulous landlords," as Leon Sachs put it. Because Jews owned much of the housing in black districts, black protests "soon revealed overtones of antisemitism." Sachs again engaged in a "quiet campaign" to educate Jewish landlords about the consequences of their actions.[19] In 1943, with their contributions to the war effort and improved economic situation making African Americans increasingly impatient with their second-class status, civil rights leaders renewed their drive to desegregate the downtown department stores. The campaign stalled but set the stage for the postwar years, when department stores and other Jewish-owned businesses would find themselves the target of sustained protest.[20]

But Jews also joined with black people in wartime attempts to advance civil rights, helping to push against Jim Crow practices that seemed increasingly out of date. State senator E. Milton Altfeld introduced anti–Jim Crow legislation in 1945— as he had done in previous years, to no avail—but supporters hoped that this time, shared wartime sacrifice would convince legislators that segregation was a "relic of a previous age," in Sidney Hollander's words. Eastern Shore legislators managed to defeat the bill once again, but this time the measure drew support across a wide spectrum, from Catholic and Protestant churches to the local branch of the Orthodox Rabbinical Council of America.[21]

On a broad cultural level, the fight against fascism fostered wider public acceptance of ethnic and religious minorities. Not only did Americans unite to face a common foe, but concepts of pluralism and diversity became positively patriotic in contrast to the Nazis' glorification of racial purity. The attempt of national leaders to forge a multicultural consensus on behalf of the war effort had surprising results: along with Catholicism and Protestantism, Judaism became one of the three "fighting faiths of democracy," attaining "a legitimacy unanticipated at the start of the war," writes historian Deborah Dash Moore. After peaking in the early 1940s, antisemitism became discredited within a few short years. Of course, bigotry and prejudice did not disappear, but no longer would figures such as Father Coughlin have free rein to promote their views in the mainstream media.[22]

- - - - - - - - - - - - - -

B'nai Abraham and Yehuda Laib Family Circle meeting, 1944. Founded before the war to help relatives in the old country, the society could do little for those trapped in Nazi-occupied Europe. *Jewish Museum of Maryland.*

Meanwhile, the Jewish population was moving further away from its immigrant roots: in 1940, for the first time, the number of native-born American Jews exceeded the number of foreign-born Jews. After the war, this profound demographic shift, along with the more outward-looking orientation of returning Jewish veterans, would combine with the nation's more tolerant cultural atmosphere to cause Jews to experience "a lowering of economic and social barriers unprecedented in American history," in the words of historian Edward Shapiro.[23] In Baltimore and elsewhere, these developments would give impetus to modernizing trends in Jewish communal affairs among Reform, Conservative, and Orthodox alike.

Simultaneously, grief over the annihilation of Jewish communities in Europe reinforced Jews' feelings of separation from other Americans. Communal groups that had worked for decades to aid European Jewry could do little more than stand helplessly by during the war. A notice in Yiddish and English from the Baltimore Committee of the American Federation for Lithuanian Jews urged readers to come to a November 1943 mass meeting to "learn of the fate of your relatives and friends in the lands of horrors." Chizuk Amuno hosted a joint service that brought "orthodox and reformed" rabbis together to emphasize "Jewish unity resulting from Nazi persecutions abroad." Army sergeant Sol Goldstein was among the liberators of Buchenwald concentration camp. He never forgot the reply of the first survivor he spoke to, after telling the man, in Yiddish, that he was an American Jew: "What took you so long?" The encounter would motivate the Baltimorean to become an activist for Soviet Jewry decades later.[24]

Army sergeant Sol Goldstein (*left*) in Belgium.
Jewish Museum of Maryland. Courtesy of Sol Goldstein.

In the decade following the end of the war, the appearance on these shores of Holocaust survivors—including leading figures of ultra-Orthodox Judaism and their followers—would have a significant impact in countering trends toward assimilation. Baltimore's religious scene, with its strong traditionalist tendencies, proved particularly welcoming to Orthodox adherents. As American Jews learned the full extent of the Holocaust, its shadow became a defining feature of Jewish life. But as the nation entered the postwar era triumphant after two turbulent decades of depression and war, most Jews, like other Americans, chose to keep the tragic undercurrents of the past well below the surface of their daily lives. In Baltimore as elsewhere, domesticity and material comfort became the focus.

Suburbia: A Community Transplanted

Nineteen-year-old Irene Fishman met Bernie Siegel during the traditional high holiday promenade through Druid Hill Park in 1948. She was struck by the twenty-six-year-old "man of the world," who had spent the war years as a chemical engineer at the army's Edgewood Arsenal. They married in 1951, and Irene soon became pregnant. She had to quit her teaching job at her alma mater, Forest Park High School (school policy barred pregnant teachers), so she prepared for her new life as a housewife, taking cooking lessons from her mother and learning to drive a car. After her son was born she spent her days with him in the couple's Park Heights apartment, off busy Reisterstown Road. Soon, she was pregnant again, and the pair searched for a home more suitable for a growing family.[25]

The Siegels were about to embark on a journey that was both commonplace and momentous: without crossing an ocean, they were moving to a whole new way of life, along with so many others of their generation. They discovered Ranchleigh, "a new, innovative development" in Baltimore County, "way out in the country," and moved into a ranch-style house in early 1954. "When we moved in, telephone lines were still being installed, our street was unpaved, our spacious backyard had mounds of fertilizer and no grass, and our back porch had no rails," Irene Siegel recalled. Nevertheless, "I felt as if I had moved into a mansion." Most of her neighbors were young couples, and the suburban pioneers soon bonded.[26]

Powerful forces came together to cause a national rush to suburbia among Jews and (white) gentiles alike in the three decades after the war. The GI Bill helped create a generation of homeowners by subsidizing the mortgages of millions of veterans. Real estate developers constructed homes to capture this new consumer market, with crucial support from government investments in roads, schools, and other infrastructure. Soon, farms and woodlands turned into modern suburbs that promised more space, greater privacy, and a better environment to raise children—lots of them, as the end of the war marked the start of the baby boom. Meanwhile, city neighborhoods, which had deteriorated from wartime overcrowding and deferred maintenance, continued to decay as the nation lavished resources on suburbia. Add-

Irene Siegel and her children Marc, Joan, and Paul cool off
in their Ranchleigh pool in the summer of 1959. *Jewish Museum of Maryland.
Courtesy of Bernard and Irene Siegel.*

ing to urban woes, the mortgage industry (with federal encouragement) refused to
make loans in older districts, a practice known as "redlining."[27]

Many young couples lived in cramped city homes, often with relatives—out of
step with society's new emphasis on the nuclear family. Baltimorean Morty Weiner met his future wife while stationed in Missouri during the war, and the couple
moved in with his parents after their marriage. By 1951, "we had to leave my in-laws'
house," recalled Esther Weiner. "We had a baby and I felt it was time to go." She and
her husband, a newly minted pharmacist, purchased their new home with the help
of a GI loan.[28]

Given the advantages of buying new and the disadvantages of staying put, young
couples were inevitably drawn to the suburban frontier. As yet another powerful
incentive, suburban living came to be seen as the embodiment of the American
Dream, idealized in popular media and countless ads for real estate and consumer
goods. Barbara Sachs's family moved from Druid Hill Park to Cheswolde in 1954.
"My parents wanted to get away from the row houses," she recalled. "They wanted
a place they could say was their dream home."[29] American Jews, seemingly at odds
with their reputation as an urban people, showed a particular enthusiasm for suburbia. This was partly because Jews were in a good economic position to move; their
incomes tended to be higher on average than those of other urban residents. Nationally, at least one-third of Jewish city dwellers decamped for the suburbs between 1945
and 1965, a percentage higher than that of other Americans.[30]

But in Baltimore and some other cities, additional factors pushed the rate of

Teenager Leslie Polt mows the lawn with help from his little brother Gilbert in the Cross Country section of Upper Park Heights. *Jewish Museum of Maryland. Courtesy of Leslie and Audrey Polt.*

Jewish suburbanization much higher than that. Most important, the shadow of race hovered over the process. Despite the plethora of forces driving the suburban stampede, to many Baltimore Jews one dominant cause stood out. In the mid-1960s, "Forest Park became deserted overnight," recalled former resident Rose Cohen. "The neighborhood changed completely, it became all black. And all the neighbors just fled out of there."[31] Across the nation, fears of crime, declining schools, and decreasing property values swept through white urban neighborhoods when black people attempted to purchase homes. Blockbusting real estate companies encouraged such fears by spreading rumors as they canvassed door-to-door, blanketed blocks with For Sale signs, and found other ways to induce panic and solicit cheap sales.[32]

White flight was undoubtedly behind the dramatic and rapid turnover of some Jewish neighborhoods in Baltimore. For example, Lower Park Heights was 92 percent white in 1960—and 95 percent black by 1970. The transformation occurred after highway construction destroyed a nearby black district and caused an influx of "hundreds of families who were not prepared to move financially and were forced to run simply to find shelter," according to Rev. Theodore Jackson, an African American community leader. Their arrival hastened the departure not only of Jews, but of "middle class black families who had moved to the area a few years earlier." Minnie Conn lived on Shirley Avenue. "My husband didn't want our children to play with the black children," she recalled. "We wanted to get out of the neighborhood real fast. We paid like $11,000 for the house and we only got $6,000."[33]

But if the suddenness of the turnover led observers and participants to ascribe the entire cause to white flight, it would be more accurate to see race as one factor— if often the most immediate one—among the many trends promoting suburbanization. Rabbi Israel Tabak of Shaarei Zion Congregation would later recall that his congregation "had been a victim of blockbusting tactics" in the 1960s. Yet Jews had been planning their exit from Lower Park Heights well before the threat of racial change. His own congregation had purchased land for a new synagogue in Upper Park Heights in 1954 and had operated at both locations before finally quitting its original home in 1967.[34]

One final factor contributed to the decline of interwar Jewish neighborhoods: American Jews after World War II were moving not only to nearby greener pastures, but also much farther afield, showing a propensity to relocate to other cities. Many young Jewish Baltimoreans, especially those whose horizons had been broadened by their wartime experiences, departed their childhood homes for Florida, California, and other burgeoning centers. Although not a popular destination like Los Angeles or Miami, Baltimore too saw an influx of Jews from elsewhere in the United States, especially the spouses of natives who returned after the war. These new arrivals almost all chose the suburbs.[35]

By 1968, the suburban exodus of Baltimore Jewry was nearly complete. The northwestern city neighborhoods that had nurtured the generation that went to war—Lower Park Heights, West North Avenue, Druid Hill Park, Forest Park—had been largely abandoned by Jewish families; though around 10 percent of Baltimore's Jews still lived there, they tended to be older people or families who would depart over the next few years. Four out of five Jews now lived in greater Northwest Baltimore, from Upper Park Heights deep into Baltimore County.[36]

If the creation of Northwest Baltimore's interwar Jewish neighborhoods resulted from a mix of internal and external factors, the reasons for the community's resegregation in postwar suburbia were equally complex. This time, however, discrimination played a less prominent role. Anti-Jewish restrictions did continue to limit where Jewish families could reside during the early postwar years, but these started to recede with the general postwar lessening of antisemitism, a 1948 Supreme Court decision making deed restrictions unenforceable, and more aggressive Jewish efforts to fight back in the 1950s. Nevertheless, the psychological effects lingered: as one observer noted, "a persistent fear that they were unwanted in gentile areas" contributed to Jews continuing to choose the friendly confines of greater Northwest Baltimore well after discrimination became illegal with the passage of the Fair Housing Act in 1968.[37]

However, the tight-knit nature of Baltimore Jewry created its own special momentum, which was much more significant than wariness about the receptivity of non-Jews. Everyone seemed to be in on the suburban act, including developers, retailers, neighbors, synagogues, and other communal institutions. Jewish homebuilders filled the rolling hills between Park Heights Avenue, Reisterstown Road, and Liberty Road with enticingly named subdivisions aimed at drawing their coreligionists into Baltimore County. With these familiar corridors extending in a northwesterly direction, Baltimore's very geography seemed to conspire with the developers to facilitate the movement northwest.

Jewish builders not only supplied the product, they also helped create the demand. By saturating the *Jewish Times* with advertisements, they added their local voices to a national media heavily invested in selling the suburban ideal. By targeting their audience, they contributed to the creation of solidly Jewish subdivisions. Jewish developers and realtors understood their community and marketed accordingly. Ads touted proximity to popular synagogues and assured buyers that there were homes for every pocketbook, with "no money down for vets." From $12,000 ranchers to $35,000 "custom contemporaries," families across a wide income spectrum could find their "dream home." As during the interwar period, the new geography of Jewish Baltimore was stratified by income, with the just-starting-out settling in and around affordable Randallstown while the more affluent gravitated toward Pikesville. When incomes rose, many families made the move from Randallstown to Pikesville.[38]

Almost immediately, synagogues followed their congregants to the suburbs. Unlike Catholic churches, which were tied to territorially based parishes and governed by a hierarchy that prevented local decision-making, Jewish congregations had the

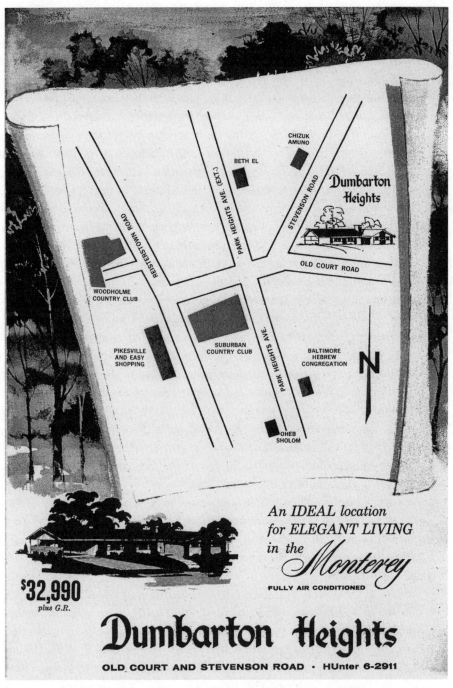

In the *Jewish Times*, Jewish real estate developers heavily marketed greater Northwest Baltimore to their coreligionists. This typical advertisement points out several synagogues and two Jewish country clubs. *Jewish Museum of Maryland*.

flexibility to relocate. In turn, lagging congregants followed the synagogues that left them behind. This communal dynamic accelerated the pace of suburbanization. As early as May 1948, Beth Jacob (Orthodox) broke ground for a suburban-style edifice in Upper Park Heights while Baltimore Hebrew Congregation (Reform) announced plans for a new temple even farther north on Park Heights Avenue, on the border between city and county.[39] Even small shuls lacking the financial means found a way to move: they merged with each other and used their combined resources to happily (or contentiously) plot their way out. Synagogues that stayed behind found themselves in trouble. Beth Tfiloh, the most popular shul of the interwar era, hit the doldrums in the late 1950s. It finally departed its beloved Forest Park synagogue center and moved to Pikesville in 1966. "Now that the congregation has followed its membership it is beginning to thrive again," noted Rabbi Samuel Rosenblatt.[40]

Early suburbanites also created brand-new congregations that enticed other Jewish families to their locations. Beth Israel, the first congregation in the Liberty Road corridor, opened in a farmhouse in 1956 and moved into a modern new building in 1959. A rare Conservative alternative for Baltimore, its popularity helped fuel the rapid growth of Randallstown's Jewish community. Temple Emanuel, Baltimore's first significant new Reform entity since the nineteenth century, also opened along Liberty Road in the mid-1950s. The first brand-new Orthodox congregation in Baltimore County opened in 1956. Fittingly, it came to be known simply as Suburban Orthodox.[41]

Officials of the Associated Jewish Charities made a commitment to suburbia early on. Back in the 1920s, hesitation over moving to Northwest Baltimore had caused the agency to build the Y on Monument Street in a sort of no-man's land on the edge of downtown, a decision that was later criticized. After the war, communal leaders made sure this would not happen again. A 1947 community study detected an incipient trend toward Upper Park Heights while confirming that few Jews remained in East Baltimore. Accordingly, in 1951 the Associated merged the JEA and the Y into the new Jewish Community Center, and though most Jews still lived in densely settled, closer-in northwest districts, it commenced to build a home for the JCC above Northern Parkway, the long-planned crosstown boulevard that would soon separate Upper and Lower Park Heights. An enlarged home for Baltimore Hebrew College would be built alongside it. The campus opened in 1960 after a $2 million campaign chaired by Joseph Meyerhoff.[42]

Adding to the suburban momentum, other institutions joined what Associated historian Louis Cahn called "the great building boom" of the 1950s. Indeed, the *Jewish Times* in 1957 referred to Upper Park Heights as "little more than a series of excavations." Park Heights Avenue became known as "Rue de la Shul" for the many synagogues along its course. Sinai Hospital moved from East Baltimore to a plot of land across from the Levindale nursing home, creating a Jewish medical complex. Baltimore's most prominent Orthodox institutions, Ner Israel and the Talmudical Academy, completed the relocation of the Jewish community in the 1960s by building substantial suburban campuses.[43]

The opening of the Jewish Community Center on Park Heights Avenue in 1960 symbolized the Jewish community's move to Upper Park Heights and the suburban lands beyond. *Jewish Museum of Maryland.*

Developers who catered to the Jewish consumer, institutions that promptly relocated, homeowners who found comfort living in Jewish surroundings, concerns about being unwelcome in non-Jewish areas, and even Baltimore's geography—all these factors combined to make the northwest exodus seem natural, even inevitable. As one woman said about her family's move to Pikesville, "That's just where Jewish people lived. I don't think my parents seriously considered any other area."[44] The *Jewish Times* was right in suggesting that Jews were becoming more segregated than ever. An Associated study estimated that Upper Park Heights was 83 percent Jewish in 1968, while a demographer put it at more than 90 percent two years later. In 1979 a student at Pikesville High School (91 percent Jewish) told a reporter, "Pikesville is like Israel—Judaism is not your religion, it's your life."[45]

Abetted by the economic opportunities afforded by suburbanization, the shift in Jewish occupational pursuits that had started in the interwar period culminated in a new economic profile by the 1960s. With rising affluence, reliance on the small family business waned, and the Jewish working class virtually disappeared. The suburban-based economy yielded both winners and losers: in the late 1950s, a bitter fight over the creation of the Reisterstown Road Plaza pitted Jewish developers

Mark Helman, president of Carpet Fair surveys site of new location, 8011 Liberty Road

The growth of suburbia offered opportunities to home-furnishing businesses,
as this 1966 *Jewish Times* ad attests. *Jewish Museum of Maryland.*

and politicians against Jewish family businesses along Pimlico's thriving shopping strip. The new mall won out, and the shopping strip went into decline.[46] The postwar era was very good to businesses that fed off the suburban boom, from real estate firms and contractors to appliance stores and car dealerships. Meanwhile, affordable education for veterans through the GI Bill and a lessening of discrimination in white-collar employment enabled the postwar generation to leave the world of small business far behind.

By 1968 only 10 percent of Baltimore Jewish men and 3 percent of Jewish women owned small businesses; 28 percent of men were professionals, 22 percent were executives, and 32 percent held sales positions or other lower-level white-collar jobs. One-third of women were in the workforce: around half of them had clerical jobs and 21 percent were professionals, overwhelmingly teachers. Some 35 percent of Jewish household incomes qualified as upper middle class or affluent, and half were considered middle class. In 1970 Pikesville had the highest average family income and home value in Baltimore County.[47]

Some businesses thrived not only by embracing the suburban market but by helping to forge a new kind of Jewish community. As Gilbert Sandler wrote, "shopping centers and malls became Jewish community centers." Nathan Ballow, whose North Avenue deli had catered to an older, Yiddish-speaking crowd, went

Suburban delis became community gathering places, serving up a perfect blend of corned beef, Yiddishkeit, and free parking. *Courtesy of the Baltimore Museum of Industry, BGE Collection.*

into partnership with his son-in-law Joe Mandell in 1956, and the pair opened the Mandell-Ballow deli in the Hilltop shopping center on Reisterstown Road. The Suburban House restaurant, opened in 1965, became a favored Pikesville gathering place. Such kosher-style establishments were wildly popular, selling a hefty dose of nostalgia along with the bagels and blintzes.[48] While ethnic-oriented delis served a multigenerational crowd, purely American-style eateries, such as the Hilltop Diner (the model for Barry Levinson's *Diner*), offered a place for postwar youth culture to flourish. Jewish social life continued to have its own local character: to many, steamed crabs qualified as kosher and—as journalist Michael Olesker put it—"the football Colts were the great secular religion."[49]

Many descriptions of American Jewish suburbanization depict "scattered and isolated" families who found themselves in a "new and largely alien suburban world," cut adrift from "the protective womb of the urban Jewish subculture." To regain a sense of community, they created new suburban-style synagogues that became the locus of Jewish identity. Affiliation rates soared—but without old-style ethnicity, Jewishness became "weaker and narrower," causing commentators to claim that suburban Jewish life lacked authenticity. Key to this narrative was the assertion that unlike the urban milieu, suburbia "was not populated primarily by Jews."[50] Clearly Baltimore Jewry provides a strong counterexample. Its families did not make the move to suburbia in isolation. Jews were not in the minority in their new locales, and most did not join new synagogues since their old ones moved along with them. Rather than being dependent on the synagogue, Baltimoreans' Jewish identity was more place-based than ever: "Pikesville" came to be practically synonymous with "Jewish"—and remains so to this day.

At the same time, suburbia could indeed be isolating, even with Jewish neighbors. The greater distances, the reliance on cars, and the lack of street-level Yiddishkeit all presented a sharp break with the past. In Baltimore, at least, it was not a lack of Jews that posed a challenge to an authentic Jewish way of life, it was the suburban lifestyle itself. Perhaps no one captured the dangers that suburbia posed to Jewish culture and identity better than Barry Levinson in his 1990 film, *Avalon*, which traces the breakup of a Baltimore immigrant family over three generations. The Krichinsky brothers start out as a close-knit clan after arriving from Eastern Europe, but their relationship ultimately cracks under the pressures of upward mobility and, especially, the flight to the suburbs. At the film's climax, the family suffers an irreparable breach when conflict erupts over that most American of holidays, Thanksgiving. The eldest brother and family patriarch, who still lives in the city, arrives late to his nephew's suburban home and finds that the others have started the meal without him. "It took us hours to get here," he yells. "It's too far, for God's sake. Too far for relatives!"[51]

Even without explicit reference to Jewish religion or identity, *Avalon* dramatizes the loss of ritual and dilution of ethnic culture inherent in the decline of the extended family and the multigenerational household. Indeed, suburbia's emphasis on the nuclear family distanced young couples from their parents, and grandchildren from grandparents. It separated individual families from the larger family groupings that, before the war, had often served as the basis of social life and allowed young people to experience the chain of Jewish tradition.

This distance was especially isolating for women, many of whom spent their days caring for children, cleaning house, preparing meals, and doing countless loads of laundry. Like Irene Siegel, women who had jobs tended to quit upon marriage. The suburban ideal emphasized strict gender roles: husbands commuted to their jobs while wives stayed home and kept the modern household running. "I was busy from early morning until late night, folding dozens of diapers and preparing the baby's bottles," Siegel recalled. "My husband was up at 6 a.m. and returned at 6 p.m. I was strictly on my own while he was away." The era of the family store—when wives might keep one eye on the business and the other on the kids—had all but disappeared; the separation of work and home life was virtually complete.[52]

Despite the pressure on women to conform to their idealized role in the all-important nuclear family, some managed to break the mold. Rosalie Silber Abrams grew up with the example of her mother, Dora Silber, who enjoyed a fulfilling career in the family business. Rosalie worked in her parents' bakery as a teen and wanted to go to college, but her family would not pay the tuition—her brothers' education took priority. As her father put it, "What do you need to go to college for to wash diapers?" After a stint as a navy nurse during the war, she married and became a homemaker while earning degrees from Johns Hopkins University and volunteering in political campaigns. In 1966, at age fifty, it occurred to her that instead of helping others get elected, she could run for office herself. For the next three decades, as a state legislator and then as head of the state Office on Aging, she focused on women's issues, health, and welfare, winning better treatment for rape victims, rewriting the state's mental health code, and passing a landmark health reform law.[53] When gender norms began to break down in the late 1960s with the feminist movement, Abrams served as a model for those who followed.

Suburban youth, almost entirely disconnected from the immigrant past, created a social scene that drew more than ever on American popular culture. To some elders, the emergent youth culture seemed at best rootless and possibly even dangerous. In the late 1950s the Associated convened the Special Committee on Youth Problems to address concerns about vandalism, joy-riding, drunkenness, and gambling. While interwar leaders had bemoaned the divide between immigrants and their children, attention now focused on the decreasing role of religion in daily life, the car culture that gave young people the freedom to roam far from home, and a loss of family unity as parents and children spent less time around each other.[54] Soon parents had even more to worry about as the 1960s brought rebellion, drugs, and a newly identified "generation gap." As members of the World War II generation settled into a suburban lifestyle characterized—many young people thought—by conformity and materialism, their children began to experiment with new ways of relating to the world around them: the poolrooms of the 1950s gave way to the pot parties of the 1960s.[55]

Nevertheless, suburbanites found ways to rebuild community and family togetherness. Living among other Jewish families in the same stage of life enabled them to form strong bonds with their neighbors. Kitchen coffee klatches and backyard cookouts, country clubs and summer camps, school events and shopping centers brought people together. Though striving to maintain a suburban lifestyle preoccupied breadwinners and homemakers alike, some people also found time to devote to communal pursuits, especially women, who found respite from their domestic duties in volunteering. If Baltimore Jews did not need to rely on religious affiliation to maintain a strong Jewish identity, the suburban synagogue would nevertheless form the basis of formal Jewish engagement and community.

Religious and Communal Life in the Suburban Age

The postwar years saw a religious revival in the United States. Religious affiliation not only offered stability and community in response to cataclysmic events abroad and vast changes at home, but also became a key part of the American consensus in the face of "godless Communism" as the United States plunged into the Cold War.

The wartime enshrinement of religious pluralism as an important American value enabled Jews to participate enthusiastically in this revival. In suburbs where Jews were in the minority, belonging to a synagogue enabled them to gather together and express their Jewishness in ways that conformed to societal norms, unlike ethnic expressions of Jewishness, which set them apart at a time when conformity was the rule of the day. Meanwhile, the need to build anew in suburbia offered the chance to update their synagogues and make adaptations that reflected their new status as mainstream Americans.[56]

Unlike Jews in many other suburbanizing areas, Baltimore Jews did not need to belong to a religious institution in order to experience Jewish community, nor did they feel compelled to downplay their ethnicity in places where they constituted a majority. Yet with religion now serving as a force for integrating their American and Jewish identities, they too felt the attraction of defining themselves primarily as a religious group. Moreover, the spread-out nature of suburbia made ethnic Jewish social life less accessible than before, while the community's tendency toward higher affiliation rates than other Jewish centers predisposed Baltimore Jewry to join the national trend of synagogue expansion. Chizuk Amuno, which had reached a low of 160 member families in 1937, saw its membership climb to 260 families during the war, leap another 100 between 1945 and 1946 alone, and continue to rise. Even before moving to suburbia, the Reform temples Oheb Shalom and Har Sinai saw membership increases of around one-third in the early 1950s, to 1,100 and 800 families, respectively, by 1955. Baltimore Hebrew Congregation, the first to suburbanize, surpassed them all. In the four years after its 1951 move to Slade Avenue, its membership nearly doubled from 750 to 1,450 families.[57]

Among the postwar American synagogue's adaptations to modern life, the changing role of women stood out. Women had taken on increased congregational responsibilities during the war and pressed for a more equal role in decision-making afterward. Chizuk Amuno took steps toward opening board membership to women in 1946 after the sisterhood urged the board to "accede to the modern trend" of recognizing women's leadership abilities. Modern Orthodox congregations were not immune; Bess Fishman served on the board of Beth Tfiloh. Baltimore Hebrew Congregation became a national leader in gender equality: when Helen Dalsheimer was elected president in 1956, she became the first woman to lead a major American congregation.[58]

That emblem of the interwar era, the synagogue center, reached new heights in the suburban age as American Jewry embarked on another building boom. Congregations eagerly incorporated the aesthetics of suburbia into their new synagogues. They built expansive campuses with spacious parking lots and even attempted to reflect the suburban emphasis on the single family home, according to Chizuk Amuno rabbi Israel Goldman. "The new generation of American-born Jews wants a new type of home," he proclaimed in 1955. "It is no wonder that there has evolved a new concept of Synagogue Architecture which brings into the modern edifice and

With its large scale and modernist design, Baltimore Hebrew Congregation's new home on Slade Avenue reflected trends in postwar synagogue architecture. *Jewish Museum of Maryland.*

its auxiliary buildings the same pleasures and conveniences." Some congregations, though, acknowledged that suburbia had its drawbacks. Temple Emanuel aimed to serve those who might find in its "small, friendly congregation an answer to the rootlessness and alienation that trouble some of today's mobile young families."[59]

A major reason for the upsurge in congregational membership was an expanded emphasis on children. In the suburban environment, religion increasingly became seen as the most important way to pass down Jewish heritage. Synagogues became more child-centered than ever and strove to offer programming attractive to the young. In perhaps a bit of wishful thinking, one Baltimore Reform leader exclaimed that "the children today are bringing their parents to Temple!"[60] Synagogue campuses sprouted impressive educational facilities as congregations of all sorts participated in a national resurgence of Jewish education. Oheb Shalom's religious school, for example, grew from 300 students in 1947 to more than 1,000 in 1955. Beth Tfiloh continued to be in the vanguard in its emphasis on youth. In the late 1940s it started the first congregational day school in the country.[61]

Baltimore's system of Jewish education was modernized under the guidance of Louis L. Kaplan, who headed the Board of Jewish Education and Baltimore Hebrew College for forty years. Kaplan oversaw the transition from freestanding Hebrew schools to a congregationally based religious school system. He transformed the college from a training school for Hebrew teachers to an institution of higher Jewish learning, attracting to the faculty scholars from every branch of Judaism. A charismatic and highly respected leader, Kaplan managed to keep Orthodox, Reform,

By involving children at their groundbreaking events, suburban-style congregations explicitly linked their new buildings to the future: the baby boom generation. Temple Oheb Shalom, 1959. *Jewish Museum of Maryland.*

and Conservative representatives working together to improve and standardize all aspects of Jewish education.[62]

But cooperating in Jewish education did not prevent the widening rifts apparent in religious life. The temptation to modernize ritual in the postwar environment was a key source of conflict. The major fault line in the early postwar years could be found on the boundary between Orthodox and Conservative Judaism. In 1947, eight prominent members of Beth Tfiloh, "disillusioned by the repeated failure to introduce liberal practices" such as the mixed seating of men and women, broke off to found Congregation Beth El. Billing itself as Baltimore's first truly Conservative congregation, the upstart group found immediate success and pushed confidently into the suburban future with plans to construct Baltimore's "first temple built on strictly modernistic lines."[63]

At Chizuk Amuno, which had long hesitated to define itself as Conservative despite being a founding member of the movement nationally, leaders worried about losing members to Beth El. In 1947 they embarked on a campaign to bring mixed seating to their synagogue. Though a majority of members desired it, any ritual change required 90 percent approval, and a determined minority stood in the way. After a bruising debate carried out over many meetings, the innovators won, and in January 1948 Chizuk Amuno held its first service featuring mixed seating. It was a defining moment for a prominent synagogue finally forced to choose between Conservative and Orthodox Judaism, and the aftershock in the Jewish community was notable. Orthodox leaders, provoked by the "apostasy" of the very congregation founded to defend tradition during a previous era of change, launched a vigorous attack on Conservative Judaism in the pages of the *Jewish Times* over the following months.[64]

Clearly, Conservative Judaism made inroads in postwar Baltimore with the founding of two popular congregations, Beth El and Randallstown's Beth Israel, and Chizuk Amuno's decision to commit to Conservative practice. Yet the movement found nowhere near the success locally that it achieved nationally. Conservative Judaism was the big winner in American Jewish suburbanization, "capturing the allegiance of a clear plurality of America's Jews and becoming the largest of the Jewish religious movements," writes Jonathan Sarna.[65] Orthodox Judaism tended to be left behind, associated with the immigrant ghettos of the past. Yet Baltimore Jewry remained more loyal to Orthodoxy than other Jewish communities did, at the expense of Conservative growth. In 1963, roughly 30 percent of Baltimore Jews identified as Orthodox and 30 percent as Conservative (36 percent identified as Reform). Affiliation rates were even more favorable to Orthodoxy: 45 percent of Jewish households belonged to Orthodox shuls and only 17 percent to Conservative ones. Apparently, many self-identified Conservatives attended Orthodox shuls.[66]

It is not surprising that Orthodoxy held its own in Baltimore compared to other American Jewish communities given the more traditional nature of the Jewish population historically. Moreover, the high degree of residential segregation put Jews under less pressure to assimilate than elsewhere. A third reason was the alacrity with which Baltimore's modern Orthodox synagogues moved to suburban areas, where they retained the allegiance of enough members to inhibit the growth of Conservative alternatives. After all, attending an Orthodox synagogue had never meant—and still did not mean—rigorously following Orthodox practice. During the Chizuk Amuno controversy, one *Jewish Times* letter writer wryly noted that the difference between an Orthodox shul and a Reform temple was "two blocks," referring to where Orthodox Jews parked their cars so that they could appear to be walking to shul. Indeed, in the 1950s, Shearith Israel and Adath B'nei Israel were "the only shuls with all shomer Shabbos [Sabbath-observant] members," states local historian Eli Schlossberg.[67]

Many Orthodox synagogues seemed more concerned with joining the suburban rush than with maintaining religious standards. In the late 1950s, Baltimore's Council of Orthodox Congregations twice tried to stop member shuls from moving too close to already-established suburban Orthodox outposts, in one case suggesting a merger and in the other telling the upstart shul to back off and find a new location. The council also fought to uphold the ritual integrity of member congregations. In addition to the "lax Orthodoxy" evident since the immigrant era, shuls faced pressure to modernize their rituals to match their new locales. Urging its congregations to strengthen their constitutions to prevent the introduction of "non-permissible innovations" such as mixed seating, the council worked to defeat "attempts, from within and without, to change the orthodox character and rites of our Houses of Worship."[68]

But while Orthodox congregations struggled to maintain standards, the city's ultra-Orthodox institutions, led by Ner Israel Rabbinical College, were preparing to emerge as a major force within the Jewish community and beyond. Ner Israel's founder, Jacob Ruderman, and executive director, Rabbi Herman Neuberger, embarked on an ambitious program of growth after the war. They brought over scores of rabbinical students from Europe's displaced persons camps and received federal approval to educate veterans for the rabbinate under the GI Bill. They also became certified by the Maryland State Board of Education and developed the nation's first doctorate in Talmudic law. By 1970 Ner Israel had 480 students from around the world learning on its sixty-six-acre campus in Pikesville. Its reputation for scholarship and institutional strength made it a magnet for observant Jews from around the country and greatly fortified the local Orthodox scene. "Almost every Orthodox endeavor in the Baltimore community is headed by one of our former students," Neuberger later asserted.[69]

Ner Israel headed a growing network of institutions that made Baltimore a major center for American Orthodoxy. But the seminary's success was not solely due to its leaders' skillful stewardship: Ruderman and Neuberger built on a solid base of Baltimore Orthodoxy that stretched back to the unusually robust contingent of German Jews who upheld tradition at Chizuk Amuno and, especially, Shearith Israel. It was Shearith Israel that recruited leading Orthodox rabbi Simon Schwab from Germany in the 1930s; a strong ally of Ner Israel, in 1942 he founded Bais Yaakov, the first girls' day school outside of New York. Another friend of Ner Israel, the noted Talmudic scholar Michael Forshlager, lent his prestige to Baltimore Orthodoxy while teaching at Chizuk Amuno (though he regretfully resigned after mixed seating came along). Meanwhile the Talmudical Academy, founded during the Eastern European immigrant era by Rabbi Abraham N. Schwartz, expanded through the postwar period and by 1968 billed itself as "the largest Hebrew day school on this continent."[70]

Holocaust survivors who arrived in the late 1940s and 1950s increased the ranks of strictly observant Jews. And though Baltimore Orthodoxy was rooted in the yeshiva-oriented Lithuanian tradition of Schwartz and Ruderman rather than in Hasidism, the small Hasidic community that developed after the war added its influence to the burgeoning ultra-Orthodox scene. After arriving in 1952, Rabbi Yitzchok Sternhell opened a day school for sons of Holocaust survivors where the language of instruction was Yiddish; it grew into the Torah Institute of Baltimore. Soon Upper Park Heights and Pikesville acquired the kinds of services that a strictly observant community needs. By 1961 a freestanding mikvah opened (in addition to one that already existed at Shearith Israel), and in the late 1970s the first eruv was established.[71]

Orthodox Jewry's increasingly strong organizational voice made it a force to be

Rabbi Simon Schwab speaks at the dedication of the Holocaust memorial at the Chevra Ahavas Chesed cemetery, 1951. *Jewish Museum of Maryland.*

reckoned with in community affairs, reinforcing the traditional character of Baltimore Jewish life. Associated Jewish Charities leaders placed a priority on maintaining unity, and as a result, communal decision-making proceeded with caution. Clashes between Orthodox and non-Orthodox figures occurred from the 1940s to the 1960s and generated heat in the *Jewish Times*. In 1957, for example, Rabbi Morris Lieberman charged that "organized orthodox rabbinical pressure" had been applied to keep certain Jewish companies from doing business with a Reform congregation, generating weeks of lengthy back-and-forth articles. Nevertheless, significant cooperation also could be found. Leaders from all camps made efforts to get along; Rabbis Neuberger and Sternhell, for example, had a "friendly and respectful relationship" with the Board of Jewish Education head, Louis Kaplan, despite his reputation for iconoclasm.[72]

The 1970s were a time of transition for communal life. In 1973, a *Sun* article noted that compared to other American cities, "the Baltimore Jewish community is unique in at least its outward appearance of unity." Although there seemed to be "more tensions today between religious groupings," as one rabbi put it, three factors helped bind the community: residential concentration, strong institutions, and "outstanding leadership." The article concluded, "When the chips are down Baltimore Jews are in there fighting for what they want—together."[73]

By the end of the decade, that unity seemed less certain. In 1977, a second Jewish Community Center opened in Owings Mills. From the start it was a source of controversy, as the Associated's decision-makers seemed to have gotten too far ahead of the suburban curve this time around. They placed the facility so far northwest that few Jews lived nearby, causing complaints about its location and poor access roads. (Rumors abounded that Jewish developers with an interest in Owings Mills had been instrumental in the site's selection.) But that was nothing compared to the uproar that arose when, to entice patrons to the underused facility, the JCC board voted to open on Saturdays. The Orthodox community mounted a campaign against the decision that included letter writing, bumper stickers, a full-page ad in the *Jewish Times*, a protest march at the new JCC, and a rally that drew an impressive 1,400 people. Billed as "A Plea for Shabbos," the rally focused on the importance of the Sabbath rather than the perfidy of the JCC—but the point was made. The Associated overruled the JCC board and imposed a compromise: the grounds could be open but the buildings would remain closed. It was a harbinger of things to come.[74]

For the time being, however, one overriding concern did much to promote harmony. For American Jewry, Israel emerged as a central pillar of Jewish identity in the aftermath of the 1967 Six-Day War, when the threat of a "second Holocaust" followed by Israel's swift victory galvanized Jews and intensified their commitment to the Jewish state. In Baltimore, 8,000 people rallied at the Pikesville Armory, and activities on behalf of Israel surged. The 1973 Yom Kippur War provoked further community-wide shows of support. "Israel today is a cause behind which the Jewish community can unite almost without exception," observed a *Sun* article that appeared shortly after the war.[75]

With its strong Zionist history, Baltimore Jewry had been deeply involved in supporting Israel throughout the postwar era. Indeed, some Baltimoreans played a dramatic part in the state's founding. Rudolf Sonneborn, son of Sigmund and a past protégé of Harry Friedenwald, was a major Zionist fundraiser. At a secret 1945 meeting in his New York apartment with David Ben-Gurion, donors pledged to supply Israel's pre-state military, the Haganah, with the ships, matériel, and funds that, Ben-Gurion later wrote, "enabled us to create our military industry." The group also provided ships to transport Holocaust survivors to Palestine in defiance of the British blockade.[76]

One of those ships made history. The *President Warfield*, a former Chesapeake Bay steamer, was covertly acquired, rebuilt, and outfitted in Baltimore's harbor by local Zionists led by retired liquor distributor Mose Speert, who had attended Sonneborn's meeting. The longtime Baltimore Zionist leader Dr. Herman Seidel amassed medical supplies for the ship's voyage and conducted physicals of the crew. From Baltimore the *President Warfield* sailed to Europe, picked up some 4,500 refugees, and went on to Palestine where, in the waters outside Tel Aviv, it unfurled

After Israel declared its independence in 1948, Baltimore Jews mobilized
to help the new state. *Jewish Museum of Maryland.*

The Talmudical Academy enthusiastically joined the Youth Salute to Israel parade, 1969.
Support for Israel was a unifying force for the Jewish community in the late twentieth century.
Jewish Museum of Maryland.

its new name, *Exodus 1947*. Famously, the ship was turned back in a battle with the British, but it became a cause célèbre that generated international support for the Jewish cause, "the ship that launched a nation."[77]

Seidel also participated in a network that aided Baltimore Jews (including many veterans) who wanted to fight for the Haganah. Ralph Finkel was one local former marine who joined the Mahal, the cadre of overseas troops who fought in the 1948 Arab-Israeli War. He later recalled being sent to Seidel for a physical and a psychological exam, and then being passed along to others, who arranged his clandestine trip to Palestine. Finkel, who changed his name to Raphael Ben-Yosef, was among the first of many Baltimoreans who would go as volunteers to Israel and end up staying permanently. Meanwhile, the creation of the state on May 14, 1948, was celebrated by Zionist and non-Zionist Jews alike. An overflow crowd gathered at Beth Tfiloh, and hundreds milled outside listening to the speeches and music over four loudspeakers. Afterward, young people sang Hebrew songs and danced along Fairview Avenue late into the night.[78]

But there were also anti-Zionists in the city, most notably Baltimore Hebrew Congregation's longtime rabbi, Morris Lazaron. Though many Reform Jews supported Zionism and served in the movement's top leadership, classical Reform Judaism's belief in universalism and its emphasis on Jews as members of a religious group rather than a nationality had long fostered reservations about Zionism that ranged from discomfort to outright opposition. Lazaron, once a Zionist himself, had become disillusioned by the movement's rhetoric and publicly broke with it in the 1930s. He supported Palestine as a haven and a spiritual center for Jews, but insisted that "Judaism cannot accept as the instrument of its salvation the very philosophy of nationalism which is leading the world to destruction." In 1942 he and other Reform rabbis founded the anti-Zionist American Council for Judaism (ACJ). Convinced that "to found a State based on race or creed is fundamentally wrong," he became a principal ACJ spokesman. He also organized a Baltimore branch shortly before Israel declared statehood; 300 people attended its founding meeting.[79]

Not surprisingly, Lazaron's activities angered local Zionists. After he criticized the movement in his 1947 high holiday sermon, Rabbi Israel Tabak charged him with "committing treason against his own people." The Baltimore Jewish Council "eventually decided that Lazaron was getting out of hand," Leon Sachs recalled, and the council challenged the rabbi in a letter to the *Jewish Times*. "It was very respectful, but it gave him hell." Support for the ACJ plummeted after Israel became a state, but Lazaron went on to decry Israeli policy regarding its Arab citizens. In 1949 his congregation asked him to desist. Instead, he resigned as rabbi emeritus and moved away.[80]

One ACJ criticism of Zionism was that it delegitimized the diaspora. Indeed, Israeli leaders began to call on all Jews to move to the new state, asserting that Israel was the only place where they could live authentic Jewish lives. Anti-Zionists fretted that Jews would be accused of dual loyalty: how could they be true Americans

David Ben-Gurion, Jacob Blaustein, and Golda Meir (*left to right*) announce the
Blaustein–Ben-Gurion Agreement, 1950. *Reprinted with permission. American Jewish Committee.*

if, as Israelis claimed, they owed allegiance to another state? Other Jewish leaders
shared these concerns, clouding the early relationship between Israel and American
Jewry.[81] In 1950 the two sides met to resolve their differences, with Israel represented by Prime Minister David Ben-Gurion and American Jewry represented by the
prominent Baltimorean Jacob Blaustein, who was the first Jew of Eastern European
origin to lead the American Jewish Committee.

The resulting document, known as the Blaustein–Ben-Gurion Agreement, chart-
ed a course for relations between Israel and American Jewry. Ben-Gurion acknowledged that American Jews owed no political allegiance to Israel and confirmed the
"right and integrity" of diaspora communities "to develop their own mode of life."
Blaustein repudiated the notion that Jews in the United States were in exile and
affirmed that "to American Jews, America is home." He promised that American
Jews would help Israel develop a "flourishing democracy" without interfering in its
affairs. While the agreement would not be strictly followed by either side, it laid the
groundwork for future cooperation.[82]

However, an obscure Baltimorean with no ties to the organized Jewish community had an even greater impact on US-Israel relations. Novelist Leon Uris had

spent his childhood as an outsider, a "sad little Jewish boy" who bounced between Baltimore, Norfolk, and Philadelphia after his parents separated. His epic saga of Israel's founding, *Exodus*, became a worldwide publishing sensation in 1958, and the 1960 movie version was a box office smash. Its hero, Ari Ben Canaan, a tough and resourceful sabra who fought for his people, was the opposite of Uris's father, whom he described as an ineffectual "shtetl Jew."[83] But Uris was not just rewriting his own family history. To the generation of Jews who had come up in the antisemitic America of the 1930s and then witnessed the destruction of European Jewry from afar, *Exodus* forcefully rebutted the stereotype of Jewish weakness.

By portraying Israel's founding as redemption from the Holocaust, *Exodus* helped create the powerful identification that American Jews began to have with the new state. Meanwhile, its impact on the general public helped cement the US-Israel alliance. Together the book and movie fixed in the public mind the view of Israel as a heroic underdog fighting for Jewish dignity and freedom, a view that defined Israel in American popular culture for years to come. Though critics disparaged its historical inaccuracies and simplistic portrayal of Arabs, "it persuasively associated Israel's founding with forces of democratic freedom," writes M. M. Silver.[84]

For Baltimore Jewry, support for Israel offered a communal focus at a time when Jewish organizational life was otherwise diminishing as a force to bring people together. Associated Jewish Charities fundraising campaigns continued to garner widespread support, but as communal agencies grew into larger institutions run by professional staff, they shed their grassroots character. Though some immigrant-based societies devoted themselves to aiding Holocaust survivors, many passed from the scene as their members died off. The personal networks that had mitigated the diversity of interwar Jewish life weakened under the forces of suburbanization and generational change. The commute from suburbia left men even less time than before to pursue communal activities, leaving the field largely to women.[85]

Women's groups offered a bright spot on the communal scene. The local Federation of Jewish Women's Organizations continued to strive for Jewish unity, making special efforts to bring Orthodox, Reform, and Conservative sisterhoods together to work on common interests. The Baltimore branch of the National Council of Jewish Women worked effectively on a range of issues; in 1960, for example, it brought the national Meals on Wheels program to Baltimore, using the Levindale kitchen to cook meals that its volunteers delivered to elderly Baltimoreans across the city. In the 1970s, the growing feminist movement influenced both groups as equal pay for women, domestic violence, and reproductive rights became key advocacy issues.[86]

The women also expanded their interfaith efforts. In the early 1960s, the National Council of Jewish Women helped Presbyterian and Lutheran women organize their own Meals on Wheels programs, and the Federation of Jewish Women's Organizations became recognized as "a power in the [larger] community" for its efforts to "meet unmet needs for human welfare."[87] As the generational torch passed, leadership was assumed by women who had come into adulthood at a time when antisem-

Holocaust survivors arriving in Baltimore, early 1950s. As with earlier migrations, communal agencies mobilized to help the newcomers adjust. *Jewish Museum of Maryland.*

itism had lost much of its power and Judaism had become an all-American faith. Indeed, for the Jewish community as a whole, relations with non-Jews took on a new cast in the postwar era as their newfound status as part of the American mainstream encouraged Jews to more confidently assert themselves in many arenas. As before, however, their interactions with others would be profoundly shaped by the distinct social environment that characterized the border city of Baltimore.

On the Border and in the Middle:
Ethnicity, Race, and Jewish-Gentile Relations

As Jews moved from immigrant-era East Baltimore to interwar Northwest Baltimore to postwar suburbia, each generation had to discover for itself how to define its place in the social order. Despite the vast changes wrought by World War II, some conditions seemed to outlast the war years. Most obviously, Jewish residential segregation still limited intergroup contact and caused many Jews to look on gentiles as the unknown "other." Also, although antisemitism in America would dwindle "to the point of insignificance" by the 1970s, it was still a factor from the 1940s to the 1960s even if in decline.[88]

- - - - - - - - - - - - - -

Jewish Baltimoreans wrestled with the lingering manifestations of bigotry, from clear-cut instances of exclusion to vague feelings of nonacceptance. By 1960 the Baltimore Jewish Council's Leon Sachs could report that "there is very little anti-Semitic activity and there are few defamation incidents. . . . Restricted housing is on its way out." However, the BJC leader noted that "ghettoization in the Jewish community" was growing nevertheless, and he worried that the lack of contact between Jews and non-Jews engendered "dangerous prejudicial attitudes."[89]

The idea that residential separation fostered bigotry against Jews was axiomatic for American Jewish leaders; studies showed that gentiles who had the least contact with Jews had the most prejudices. In Baltimore, the fact that many Jews had little experience with non-Jews contributed to feelings of unease. In a 1963 Associated survey, fewer than 20 percent of Baltimore Jews reported direct experience with antisemitism, but more than 50 percent said that relations with gentiles were "somewhat strained" (6 percent thought they were "very strained"). And while almost 40 percent said relations were "not at all strained," many respondents explained that this was "because there were no relationships at all."[90]

The survey must be seen in the context of overall Baltimore social relations, long marked by a peculiar mix of small-town parochialism, big-city ethnic diversity, and a social elite intent on policing racial boundaries. As Elsbeth Levy Bothe later put it, "Baltimore is such a polarized city. . . . You could tell from an address what the religion, the income, even the social outlook of people was." Bothe grew up in the 1930s and 1940s in the "German" Jewish community, which she depicted as extremely insulated; when she attended Park School, she was related to around 10 percent of the student body. She also asserted that her parents would rather she marry a gentile than a "Russian" Jew, a reminder that prejudice was not simply a matter of non-Jew versus Jew. (She obliged them by marrying Bert Bothe in 1964 after living with him for many years. Ever the maverick, she broke with her Park School friends, whom she found parochial, and became a well-known civil rights activist, defense attorney, and judge.)[91]

If by 1960 the BJC was cautiously optimistic, in the early 1950s it had been frustrated. As upwardly mobile Jews tested barriers in housing, education, and employment, the persistence of discrimination caused some leaders to lose patience with the behind-the-scenes approach. In 1950 the council threatened to sue the University of Maryland over its medical school quota. It succeeded in getting the quota raised but not abolished; it did not really disappear until a state legislative committee pursued the matter a few years later. The BJC was more circumspect with Johns Hopkins University. Discrimination was difficult to prove because Hopkins did not have a strict numerical target that could be pointed to. Also, the university's ties to the Jewish community—including its role in providing a haven for refugee scholars—made criticism difficult. Sachs himself was a graduate and had also taught there.[92]

Hopkins had not fully committed to quotas until the 1940s, when its relatively

The restricted Meadowbrook Swimming Club, located in heavily Jewish
Mount Washington, was a potent symbol of the continued exclusion of Jews from mainstream
society. *Jewish Museum of Maryland.*

high number of Jewish students caused President Isaiah Bowman to fear his school
would become "practically Jewish" unless action was taken.[93] In keeping with Bowman's personal brand of antisemitism (as well as the financial needs of the university, which counted on Jewish donors), restrictions were applied only to lower-income
Jews of Eastern European descent: Park School students had no trouble getting in,
but City College students were shut out. This scheme aligned with internal Jewish
divisions, but whether that contributed to the BJC's less-than-aggressive response
is unclear. Sachs claimed it was a lack of proof that made the council tread lightly.
"We had some conversations with them, not accusatory, but showing our concern,"
he recalled. In 1951 the university agreed to stop asking about religion on its application form, thus eliminating a key device used to screen out Jews. When Sachs
discovered a few years later that the religion question had crept back in, he wrote to
the admissions director (whom he knew well) that he was "pretty damned sore."[94]
Clearly some of the frustration of Jewish leaders was because they expected better:
if seeming allies continued to discriminate, how could the problem ever be solved?
(This feeling, by the way, was shared by black leaders vexed by Jewish-owned department store policies.)

The anti-Jewish restrictions of Jewish real estate owners also provoked anger. In
1948 the BJC decided the time had come to "clean our own house," and it launched

a campaign against Jews who discriminated against Jews.[95] But developers insisted they were bound by prior agreements or claimed that removing restrictions would hurt their business. The most prominent, Joseph Meyerhoff, warned that if Jewish companies lifted restrictions while non-Jewish companies did not, Jews would be seen as "leading the parade in upsetting the protected neighborhoods." Indeed, to appease neighborhood groups that feared an influx of Jews into a restricted enclave near Hopkins, in 1951 developer Victor Frenkil turned the management of his up-scale new Marylander Apartments over to a subsidiary of the Roland Park Company, long skilled at screening out Jews. The BJC confronted Frenkil after the Marylander rejected the nephew of broadcasting titan David Sarnoff, helpfully informing the Hopkins student that its Jewish quota was already filled. Sachs intervened to get him accepted, but his embarrassment was palpable. Negotiations with Frenkil and the Roland Park Company resulted in a promise to adjust the policy.[96]

The unwillingness of Jewish firms to buck long-established norms spurred the BJC to change tactics and target non-Jewish companies. After being held back for years by its more hesitant board members, in 1953 it launched its first aggressive public campaign against gentile developer George Morris, "one of the principal architects of anti-Jewish discrimination," who was up for reappointment to the city's Redevelopment Commission. In city council hearings, Jewish leaders condemned Morris's restrictive housing policies as well as his operation of the Meadowbrook Swimming Club in Mount Washington, where a prominent sign limiting entry "only to approved gentiles" had for years been a slap in the face to the neighborhood's many Jewish residents. With two Italian American members leading the way, the Baltimore City Council voted nineteen to one to reject Morris's reappointment.[97]

The BJC followed up this resounding success with letters to non-Jewish realtors and meetings with the real estate board. As Sachs later noted, the episode "undoubtedly had some impact in the local real estate fraternity."[98] It was a turning point in the battle against housing restrictions and a turning point as well for the BJC, which became more assertive in taking on public campaigns. In the mid-1950s, the council allied with the NAACP and the Urban League to push for a city fair employment law that would aid both blacks and Jews, though caution remained part of its modus operandi: "there was a hesitancy to initiate such legislation with only Jewish and Negro support." Only after behind-the-scenes lobbying to get white labor and church groups on board did the BJC take an overt leadership role. When the law—drafted in the BJC office—passed in 1956, it was the first fair employment law below the Mason-Dixon Line. The council would push for other civil rights legislation in the coming years.[99]

In Barry Levinson's film *Liberty Heights* (1999), a swimming club based on Meadowbrook symbolizes the exclusion of Jews from the gentile social scene of 1950s Baltimore. The film offers a revealing portrayal of the changing relations between Jews and non-Jews. Main character Ben Kurtzman, a sheltered Forest Park High School student, starts out believing "the whole world is Jewish" but then discovers "the other kind," namely, blacks who start to integrate his predominantly Jewish public school and white gentiles who inhabit the land "across Falls Road." Both groups are objects of fascination as Ben and his friends test their Jewish identity in a postwar terrain of shifting geographic and social barriers. Through forays into the black and white gentile worlds, they gain a complex understanding of social relations, learning that it is not simply a case of "us" versus "them." The non-Jewish world continues to attract, yet they decide there are times when it is important to stand up for their Jewishness, which they do in the film's final scene—at the restricted swimming pool.[100]

For postwar Jewish youths, cultural change led to a "headlong rush to explore the new territory that had opened to us," as native Baltimorean Leonard Fein put it.[101] Many young people ventured out of Northwest Baltimore and into the different subcultures that thrived even in socially conservative Baltimore. Three young women went further than most. Ellen Naomi Cohen often rose before dawn to work in her parents' food truck, serving construction workers building the Mondawmin Mall, before heading to Forest Park High School, where she suffered socially from being nonconformist and overweight. But she had a powerful singing voice and soon began performing in clubs in the Baltimore-DC area under a new name, Cass Elliot. She would later become perhaps Jewish Baltimore's most famous cultural export as part of the legendary pop group the Mamas and the Papas.[102]

Less well known was Alyse Taubman, a budding social worker and part-time fiddler who rejected her parents' wealthy lifestyle and joined the local bohemian community. The jam sessions she hosted at her city apartment became "one of the popular forums in the city where country and urban people met," including musicians from the city's large Appalachian community.[103] Shirley "Deborah" Chessler had a talent for songwriting and an interest in black music. The Forest Park High graduate "worked in a shoe store by day and visited black and white theaters at night," soaking up influences and trying to sell her songs. In 1948, a black vocal group had a smash hit with her song "It's Too Soon to Know," now considered a landmark rhythm-and-blues recording. The newly renamed Orioles became R&B pioneers, with Chessler as their manager and songwriter.[104]

Chessler was not the only young Baltimorean drawn to black culture, as films such as *Liberty Heights* and John Waters's *Hairspray* (1988) attest. Jews especially showed an openness to African Americans. City College high school integrated easily, and friendships developed there between African American and Jewish boys, who would later work together as civic leaders.[105] Carolyn Holland Cole was the first black student at Pimlico Junior High in the 1950s. "Jewish people had a whole different way of thinking," she recalled, "and we were warmly embraced." Penny McCrimmon formed lifelong friendships with Jewish girls at Western High, though another student who integrated Western recalled that "no one spoke to me for two years." Yet she was grateful that she faced no overt hostility at the heavily Jewish school, as African Americans did at other city high schools.[106]

- - - - - - - - - - - - - -

Relations between Jews and African Americans underwent continual adjustment through the postwar era as the ground shifted beneath them.[107] This evolution took on particular nuances in Baltimore, where the two communities were more intertwined than elsewhere. Blacks may have felt more comfortable moving into Jewish areas than other neighborhoods, but this did not prevent Jews from packing up and leaving. Jews were more prone to racism than they wanted to admit: use of the term *shvartze* instead of other pejoratives was one way to distance themselves from the outwardly hate-filled behavior of other whites. Yet Jewish "white flight" was not simply a matter of racism. As the city's economy declined, as poor black people continued to arrive from the South in search of ever-shrinking opportunity, and as urban renewal destroyed older black districts, poverty and crime began to spread, black frustrations grew, and race relations became more fraught. "There was a lot of unpleasant interaction between the white and black kids at my junior high school," one Jewish man recalled. Eventually his family moved away.[108]

Relations were similarly complex in black neighborhoods where Jews owned stores. Thanks to pressure from local activists, most store owners now hired black workers; in 1967, 85 percent of the employees on Pennsylvania Avenue were African American. Close ties often developed between employers and workers. Isidor Cooper "was like one of the family," journalist DeWayne Wickham said about the man who employed Wickham's mother and aunt. Customers continued to appreciate the credit that was denied them elsewhere; local pastor Harold Knight referred to it as "economical benevolence." Said Penny McCrimmon, "During times of financial difficulty or lay-off, many families would have gone hungry without this assistance." Storeowners also were active in community affairs; Herman Katkow, for example, was a leader of the multiracial Pennsylvania Avenue merchant association, which sponsored a popular Easter parade, voter registration drives, and other events.[109]

But some Jewish businesses provoked animosity rather than good feeling. "People complained that their prices were high and their attitudes toward black folks ranged from condescension to outright hostility," noted Wickham.[110] The exploitative behavior of some landlords was a major source of bitterness toward Jews as a group. Herbert Kaufman, perhaps the largest owner of inner-city real estate in Baltimore, was notorious for neglecting his buildings. At one point 200 of his 1,000 properties were in housing court.[111] The city's most active blockbusters were Jewish realtors such as Manny Bernstein and Morris Goldseker. After encouraging white flight, blockbusters raised home prices and steered black buyers into dubious "rent to own" arrangements that promoted frequent turnover. Shut out of suburbia and refused service by conventional mortgage lenders, African Americans who wanted to join the postwar homeownership boom had little choice but to turn to these companies. The financial strain on black families—forced to overpay for often substandard housing while suburban-bound whites shed the burden of maintaining an aging urban housing stock—hastened the deterioration of the inner city.[112]

Yet the very realtors blamed for busting city blocks also helped African Amer-

Pennsylvania Avenue, c. 1948. When the Jewish owner of Herbert's Men's Wear died in 1952, the *Afro-American* newspaper praised his policy of hiring African American high school and college students. *Courtesy of the Maryland Historical Society, HEN.00.B1-111.*

icans break out of overcrowded ghettos. Blockbusters "violated the real estate industry's code of ethics," observes legal historian Garrett Power, but the primary "ethical precept" they violated was the strict segregation of African Americans.[113] Blockbusters expanded the range of housing available to black people and, like local shopkeepers, offered credit not otherwise obtainable. They provided a convenient scapegoat for problems rooted in the racism of white homeowners, the lending industry, and a real estate fraternity intent on racial apartheid. In fact, blockbusting realtors who were not Jewish were, for the most part, black. One of the largest advertisers in the *Afro-American* newspaper was Manning-Shaw Realty, a partnership between Manny Bernstein and black realtor Warren Shaw. The company touted its role in helping black people buy homes in areas formerly barred to them. As one 1962 ad noted, "You can't buy Brotherhood, but you can buy Neighborhood." Bernstein was friendly with NAACP leader Lillie Jackson. Her grandson, the future political leader Clarence Mitchell III, once worked as a Manning-Shaw salesman.[114]

Shaping Jewish-black relations was the fact that Baltimore was "of the South" but did not share "the worst excesses of the region," historian Lee Sartain notes. In a racial system tempered by northern influences and by an ethnic diversity that blurred the black-white divide, Jews were under less pressure to conform to rigid racial norms than were their coreligionists farther south. On the other hand, as Leon Sachs succinctly put it, "You had a black leadership that was typically northern, and a white attitude that was typically southern." This was potentially dangerous to people caught in the middle, whether as business owners or community leaders — one reason Sachs rejected an "all-out alliance between Blacks and Jews" in favor of building broad coalitions.[115]

Yet when civil rights groups campaigned to integrate stores and restaurants, some of their early successes involved Jewish-owned businesses. The Read's Drug Store chain desegregated lunch counters at its thirty-seven Baltimore area stores shortly after the Congress of Racial Equality and Morgan State College students launched sit-ins at two of its stores in 1955, five years before the famous Greensboro, North Carolina, sit-ins. "Our sympathy has been with the cause," said company president Arthur Nattans Sr., and the speed with which Read's capitulated gave credence to his statement.[116] After enduring two months of picket lines in 1960, Nathan Herr announced that his popular North Avenue deli, Nates and Leons — where the surrounding blocks had become increasingly black — would open to African Americans, acknowledging that the times "require a change in the old way of thinking."[117]

As for the department stores, they ran out of excuses in 1960, six years after Hochschild, Kohn executive Walter Sondheim Jr., as president of the Baltimore School Board, led fellow board members in a unanimous vote to desegregate the school system promptly after the *Brown v. Board of Education* decision — the only school board south of the Mason-Dixon Line to do so. After decades of NAACP and Urban League pressure, a renewed push by Morgan State students did the trick. Well-organized, polite, and dressed in their Sunday best, some sat down in store restaurants and waited to be served while others walked picket lines. Hochschild, Kohn broke first. According to Martin Kohn, upon hearing that a busload of students was on the way, "We had a quick meeting and decided that we and the others had been wrong. The girls and boys from Morgan were shocked and surprised when we seated them and asked for their orders."[118]

The other department stores held out for a few more weeks but soon fell into line. Hutzler's vice president E. L. Leavey insisted that the stores had always wanted to integrate. "It was never a question of principle. It was a matter of time. And we think this is the time." But store executives' fears that integration would dampen white patronage proved not unfounded: the stores received a flood of letters from angry white shoppers vowing never to return. Some were suburbanites who warned that the integration of downtown provided one more reason for whites to withdraw from the city. Since many of the stores by that time operated suburban branches, the store owners had given them the means to do so.[119]

Indeed, under an implicit understanding among whites that the suburbs were to remain theirs alone, suburban businesses resisted integrating much longer than downtown did — though Jews again showed some ambivalence. When an interracial group of clergy (including three rabbis) attempted to integrate two suburban restaurants in 1962, they were refused service at the non-Jewish establishment. Mandell-Ballow served the men, though only as a one-time courtesy. The restaurant would remain segregated, stated the manager, until legislation passed "that would require all restaurants to serve Negroes."[120] It was the common refrain of Jewish business owners: they had no objection to desegregating if the law required their competitors to do so as well. After open-housing activists targeted his suburban properties in 1967, Joseph Meyerhoff insisted, "It is not within my power to alter a deep rooted pattern. No developer could possibly continue in business if he attempted to ignore the desires of the public." Expressing support for open-housing laws, he added that the matter is "one that the total community must decide through their elected representatives." Given the scope of Meyerhoff's holdings, civil rights groups rejected the developer's protestations of powerlessness, but Meyerhoff refused to budge until fair housing became the law of the land in 1968.[121]

Although Jewish business owners were reluctant to challenge the views of the pro-segregation white majority upon whom they relied to make their living, Jewish leaders and institutions seemed less concerned about hewing to racial norms than during previous eras. In 1961, for example, Sinai was the only Baltimore hospital that accepted African American interns and residents aside from the traditionally black Provident Hospital. And though the BJC often took a cautious approach in its civil rights work, it was more out front than Jewish organizations elsewhere in the South, where Jews saw public support for civil rights as too risky.[122]

Baltimore Jews contributed to the postwar civil rights movement in many ways. Young Jewish leftists played a significant role in the protest that launched the movement locally. In 1948, the interracial Young Progressives of Maryland joined with the all-black Baltimore Tennis Club to hold an interracial tennis tournament at segregated Druid Hill Park. After they refused to stop playing when ordered to by police, thirteen blacks and ten whites were arrested in an early example of the nonviolent civil disobedience that would come to characterize the movement. At least eight of the whites were Jewish, including eighteen-year-old Mitzi Freishtat, who had grown up across the street from the park and had imbibed activism from her parents, who were Workmen's Circle members. Jews continued to provide ground troops for civil rights actions; one black leader estimated that up to two-thirds of the local movement's white participants were Jewish.[123]

As attorneys, elected officials, and activists, Jews were involved in notable civil rights victories. In 1952 future judge Marshall Levin (for the Urban League) joined future Supreme Court justice Thurgood Marshall (for the NAACP) at a hearing before the Baltimore School Board that led to the integration of Baltimore Polytechnic Institute, the city's elite technical high school for boys, two years before the *Brown* decision. They successfully argued that since the city lacked an equal alternative for black students, the "separate but equal" doctrine required their admission to Poly. Jewish public officials were instrumental in passing city and state antidiscrimination

GWYNN OAK PROTEST HELD

About 100 Arrested In 2d Civil Rights Demonstration

(Continued from Page 34)

rael Goldman, who is vice chairman of the Maryland Interracial Commission, several protestant ministers, among them, the Rev. David Andrews, the white assistant chaplain at Morgan State College, who donned a red, white and blue Uncle Sam suit for the occasion, and the entire families of two Johns Hopkins faculty members were among those hauled off in school buses or patrol cars to the armory.

Yesterday's arrests brought to almost 400 the number taken into custody since July 4, when more than 280 were arrested on charges of violating the Maryland trespass law in another — and much calmer — demonstration at the amusement park.

Missing yesterday was much of the courtesy and calm which was evident at Gwynn Oak on the Fourth of July.

The demonstrators, themselves, were, for the most part, completely nonviolent. But the crowd of onlookers was much larger, much noisier and much meaner than the one which showed up to watch the goings-on last Thursday.

Complicating the situation yesterday was the appearance of a picket line of about twelve members of the Fighting American Nationalists—an offshoot of the American Nazi party—who got into the act.

Several of the civil rights demonstrators were ordered by their leaders — ministers, priests and officials of the Congress for Racial Equality—to leave the picket line when they started to bandy insults with the neo-Nazis.

Group Meets At Church

telling another group at the sloping entranceway:

"This is a harassing tactic. I don't blame you for what you're trying to do, but for the way you're going about it."

As the separate arguments were going on, the onlookers were building up their roars and shouts to the point where one observer lik-

UNDER ARREST—Rabbi Israel M. Goldman, of Chizuk Amuno Congregation, a member of the Maryland Commission on Interracial

chaplain, resplendent in his Uncle Sam costume, was taken into custody.

At just about that time, several boys—spectators—started running toward the falls. First a few, then hundreds of other spectators took after them at a gallop. Policemen joined in the chase. And soon it looked like a stampede. As the

Problems and Relations, submits to fingerprinting at Pikesville Armory after being arrested at Gwynn Oak Park yesterday.

NEW CAMBRIDGE SIT-INS PLANNED

Will Follow National Guard Removal At Noon

Chizuk Amuno rabbi Israel Goldman is fingerprinted after his arrest at the Gwynn Oak Park demonstration. When this photo appeared in the *Sun*, his congregants had decidedly mixed feelings. *Permission granted from the* Baltimore Sun. *All rights reserved.*

bills in the early 1960s; among them was Levin's father-in-law, Jacob Edelman, the garment union lawyer who became a city councilman. In two upper-middle-class city neighborhoods, Ashburton and Windsor Hills, Jewish residents spearheaded a movement to resist white flight and promote integration. In 1959 their efforts led to the creation of Baltimore Neighborhoods, Inc., the first local group to tackle issues of blockbusting and open housing.[124]

Rabbis played a conspicuous role in civil rights, though not always with the approval of their flocks. As vice chair of the Maryland Interracial Commission in the

1960s, Chizuk Amuno's rabbi, Israel Goldman, was frequently in the newspapers. In 1963 the *Sun* printed a large photo of him being fingerprinted after his arrest during a mass demonstration to integrate the Gwynn Oak Amusement Park. At first, "I got the silent treatment from the Board," he recalled—until the congregation received a flood of approving letters from around the nation. Morris Lieberman's sermons often challenged his Baltimore Hebrew congregants to support civil rights. When Lieberman, too, was arrested during the Gwynn Oak protest, some congregants criticized him, but others were inspired. All of the city's Reform rabbis participated in civil rights activities in the early 1960s, and even modern Orthodox rabbis played a role. As the president of the Synagogue Council of America, Beth Jacob's rabbi, Uri Miller, delivered a prayer at the March on Washington in August 1963; he considered it the most memorable moment of his life.[125]

But the black-Jewish civil rights partnership had its strains. Jewish leaders never got along with NAACP leader Lillie Jackson, who since the 1930s seemed to go out of her way to call out Jews when protesting unfair treatment by department stores and other businesses. There were differences over tactics too; in 1961, for example, Leon Sachs publicly accused CORE demonstrators of jeopardizing legislation to desegregate Baltimore County restaurants.[126] Also, it became clear that apparent victories did not necessarily lead to real change. Though the Sondheim-led school board readily accepted integration after the *Brown* decision, its desegregation plan, based on offering free choice to all, proved ineffective. The fair employment law suffered from weak enforcement, and the city's 1964 civil rights law got watered down.[127]

As historian Cheryl Greenberg points out, American Jews—who had thrived under national ideals of religious tolerance and liberty—tended to see racial justice as simply a matter of extending equal rights to all; they did not recognize how deeply racism was embedded in the economic and social structures of society. To black people in the 1960s, however, this was becoming all too clear. As urban conditions deteriorated, African Americans became more militant. Speaking for a great many Jews, Leon Sachs later stated, "When whites were pushed out of the civil rights movement, this was a terrible blow for people like myself." Meanwhile, anger over stalled economic progress caused charges of "Jewish exploitation" to reverberate more loudly than ever through the black community.[128]

Increased crime took a toll on Jewish-owned businesses. Nates and Leons shut its doors in August 1967 because "things had gotten too rough," said Nathan Herr. Newspapers treated the deli's closing like the end of an era. After Auschwitz survivor Henry Last was gunned down during a robbery in January 1968, a group of fellow merchants, also Holocaust survivors, petitioned the mayor to do something about the violence.[129] In black neighborhoods, even Jewish store owners who maintained good customer relations had shops that began to look like armed fortresses. Then came the April 1968 riots, which started on East Baltimore's Gay Street commercial strip two days after Dr. Martin Luther King Jr.'s assassination. As the turmoil spread to other shopping districts, Jewish-owned businesses suffered much damage. By all accounts, stores were not targeted because Jews owned them, but because they were in the path of destruction. However, the chaotic nature of the uprising, as well as its complex origins, made other conclusions difficult to draw.[130]

In fact, many assertions about the event's impact—especially that it caused the wholesale withdrawal of Jews and other whites from the city—are simplistic at best, as shown by the varied experiences of Jewish merchants. Though many stores were destroyed, others saw little or no damage. Some merchants packed up, but a surprising number stayed and rebuilt. For merchants already worn down by years of declining business, the riots served not as the impetus to leave, but as the final straw. Hilda Goodwin's father owned a Gay Street store that suffered no damage, yet he decided to close. The decade-long deterioration of the street and his own business problems (which he ascribed to competition from mall-based discount stores) gave him "no more heart for this place where he had spent almost half a century." His customers were sorry to see him go.[131]

Ultimately, the psychological damage was worse than the physical damage. Attitudes between blacks and whites hardened; communication became more difficult. High school student Sharon Pats viewed the ruins of her family's North Avenue store shortly after the riots. But the real blow came on her first day back at Western High, when a black girl whom she considered a friend announced that store owners "got exactly what they deserved." As Pats recalled, "That cut me like nothing else could. I thought, 'What is happening in this world? These are not the people that I thought I knew.'" As personal relationships deteriorated and as the circumstances of black urban life grew more desperate through the 1970s, fewer and fewer Jewish merchants were willing to remain.[132]

But the departure of Jewish residents and businesses from the city did not mark the end of Jewish involvement in urban affairs. Nor did it mark the end of black-Jewish cooperation: members of the two groups continued to come together in the civic and professional arenas, while in politics they both clashed and coalesced. Even as Jews shifted much of their political activity from the city to the suburbs, they continued to play a prominent role in the political and civic life of Baltimore City and the surrounding region.

Impact on the City and Region:
Politics and Civic Life

In 1970, Parren Mitchell became the state's first African American to serve in the US Congress. His landmark victory came at the expense of incumbent Sam Friedel, who had served his Northwest Baltimore district for eighteen years. Warring Jewish factions tried to unite on Friedel's behalf, but their effort fell short—by a mere thirty-eight votes, one of the closest elections in memory. Friedel, a pro–civil rights, War on Poverty liberal, was baffled and hurt by the rejection. But black people now

RE-ELECT
Sam Friedel
FOR CONGRESS
7th CONGRESSIONAL DISTRICT
Your full-time—full service—
open-door-policy Congressman
DEMOCRATIC PRIMARY
SEPTEMBER 15, 1970
(SEE REVERSE SIDE)

VOTE FOR A RECORD OF EXPERIENCE—ACTION—RESULTS

Longtime congressman Samuel Friedel's reelection loss in 1970 signaled a shift in black-Jewish political relations. *Jewish Museum of Maryland.*

made up a majority of his district, and it was time for them to flex their newly won political muscle.[133]

Friedel never recovered from the shock, but other Jewish political leaders did. When they learned the next year that Governor Marvin Mandel's redistricting plan would split the Jewish vote over three congressional districts in order to carve out a safe seat for Mitchell, they mobilized to get the boundaries redrawn. Asserting that Jews constituted an ethnic group with political rights and that the plan "disenfranchised" them in order to aid blacks, state senator Rosalie Abrams publicly accused Mandel of "selling out his own Jewish constituency."[134]

Behind the scenes, Abrams and other Jewish politicians met with Associated officials to decide an important question: in proposing new boundaries that would encompass the bulk of their community, should they adjust the current city-based district to include county Jews, or place city Jews (who mostly lived in Upper Park Heights, the suburban-style area adjoining Pikesville) into a new county-based district? Agreeing that "it would be more helpful and healthy for the Jewish community not to be in competition with the blacks," as Abrams later put it, they decided to push for the creation of a county-based district that would include the remaining Jewish portion of the city. They were successful: the legislature, with Mandel's approval, adjusted the redistricting plan to gather the Jewish population into a single district based in Baltimore County.[135]

As historians have noted, the black civil rights movement spurred other ethnic minorities to consider their own group rights—and the rhetoric in the redistricting battle offers a textbook example.[136] But the episode had other implications as well. By seeking guidance from communal leaders regarding the boundaries of their ethnic group's district, Jewish politicians opened a discussion over the very identity of their community. The creation of a county-based district therefore confirmed Jewish suburbanization not only as a political reality, but as a defining feature of Baltimore Jewry. And by successfully asserting its group rights, the Jewish community emerged more self-assured as it adapted to its suburban status.

Suburbanization, the rise of African Americans, and the replacement of machine politics with modern methods combined to shape the postwar political scene. It was an eventful era. Jack Pollack reached the pinnacle of his power and then declined, and a new Jewish political boss emerged whose style was more suited to the times. Maryland elected its first Jewish governor, and Baltimore briefly had its first Jewish mayor. Some things did not change, however: the geographically concentrated Jewish community continued to serve as a strong political base, while the ability to form alliances with non-Jews remained key to achieving real power.

The election of Tommy D'Alesandro Jr. as mayor in 1947 confirmed Jack Pollack as Baltimore's reigning political boss. During D'Alesandro's twelve years in office, "every aspect of city government was under Pollack's influence," a prominent lawyer later recalled.[137] Yet Pollack's behavior mortified Jewish communal leaders: a 1958 BJC memo lambasted his reputation for promoting Jewish candidates at the expense of black candidates, the wars he conducted against some Jewish factions, and above all his habit of hurling "false charges of antisemitism" at critics. Leaders of the BJC were particularly incensed whenever Pollack declared that an attack on him was an attack on the entire Jewish community. Through letters to the editor and other means, they publicly denied that Pollack represented or spoke for his fellow Jews. Indeed, on the "one and only occasion" they had asked him for support (in abolishing quotas at the University of Maryland), Pollack promised to help but did nothing.[138]

The BJC's disdain did nothing to loosen Pollack's grip on power, but other forces would do just that. Not surprisingly, changing demographics undermined his base of support. At first he simply continued his usual tricks: in the 1950 election, "poison pen letters aimed at stirring up racial prejudice" were traced to his office. By 1954 he was putting token black candidates on his ticket, but that year saw two other black candidates defeat him in his own district. In response, he moved his entire organization northwest to the adjoining district.[139] But the rise of television was reducing the value of such organizations: politicians could now reach voters directly, without the aid of a machine. In the 1959 mayoral election, D'Alesandro's opponent, Harold Grady (an Irish American former FBI agent), used television commercials on an unprecedented scale to position himself as a fresh alternative to the "bossism" and corruption of the past. Railing against "the tremendous power Mr. Pollack has had over the Mayor for the last twelve years," Grady won handily.[140]

Supporting Grady were two key Jewish operatives: Irvin Kovens, a wealthy discount furniture dealer with gambling connections, and Philip Goodman, who became the Baltimore City Council president running on Grady's ticket. When Grady resigned to take a judgeship in 1962, Goodman served out the rest of his term, becoming Baltimore's first (and, so far, only) Jewish mayor. He lost the 1963 mayoral election to the popular former mayor and governor Theodore Roosevelt McKeldin, a Republican who was backed by none other than Jack Pollack. Even with reduced influence, the canny Pollack remained relevant into the 1970s.[141]

But Irv Kovens, a master fundraiser, campaign strategist, and media expert (with the help of his friend, the ad man Lou Rosenbush), emerged as the new kingmaker of Maryland politics. "From his office 'the furniture man' ran a fundraising juggernaut that launched governors, mayors, and county executives, reaping plenty of spoils after they won," writes Antero Pietila.[142] Kovens allied with a wide range of political figures. One of his closest associates was the African American businessman (and former numbers runner) Willie Adams; in fact, the pair had helped the black candidates who defeated Pollack's machine in 1954. Kovens guided the careers of two men who came to dominate Maryland politics, Marvin Mandel and William Donald Schaefer. Schaefer, who presided over Baltimore's late twentieth-century renaissance, started his political life as "Irv Kovens's designated gentile," in commentator Fraser Smith's words. Kovens's mentorship was so important to Schaefer that Smith called their first meeting one of the "twelve events that shaped Baltimore" over the previous century.[143]

Like so many other Jews of his generation, Marvin Mandel was born in East Baltimore and then made the move northwest. The attorney and World War II veteran entered the state legislature as a Pollack man in 1952. He later broke with Pollack, allied with the Kovens-Goodman faction, and became Speaker of the state House. When Governor Spiro Agnew resigned in order to become the US vice president in 1969, the Maryland General Assembly chose Mandel to complete his term. Unlike Philip Goodman, Mandel then won two elections in his own right and served as governor through the 1970s. Personally popular, he pushed through a variety of governmental reforms, launched a public school construction program, and won a tough state gun control law (it helped that he was an avid hunter).[144]

But then it all blew up. First came the revelation of an adulterous affair, leading to a divorce from his wife, who kicked him out of the governor's mansion. More damaging were charges that emerged from a federal investigation of Maryland political corruption—the same probe that brought down Vice President Agnew. Mandel was accused of accepting bribes from friends, including Irv Kovens, in return for pushing legislation to benefit a racetrack they secretly owned. In Mandel's second term, he, Kovens, and four others were convicted of mail fraud and racketeering. Mandel did not resign as governor, but turned his duties over to his lieutenant governor while the case was appealed. He later served nineteen months in federal prison before his sentence was commuted by President Ronald Reagan. Kovens served six months, released early due to ill health. Mandel insisted he had committed no crime, and in 1987 a federal judge overturned the conviction, enabling him to resume his

Rosalie Silber Abrams (*top left*) and Governor Marvin Mandel (*bottom left*) at a signing ceremony for legislation Abrams sponsored. *Jewish Museum of Maryland*.

law practice and reenter the political scene, though he never again ran for office. In later years, the cloudiness of the case and Mandel's achievements as governor caused his legacy to be reassessed positively.[145]

A younger generation of Jewish public officials also rose to prominence in the postwar era. Benjamin Cardin ran for the state House at age twenty-three in 1966 on an anti-Pollack ticket with another political neophyte, fifty-year-old Rosalie Abrams. Their campaign manager was William Donald Schaefer. Along with their liberal bent, the two shared impeccable Baltimore Jewish pedigrees, Abrams as a daughter of the bakery Silbers and Cardin as a son of the Cardin political family (he won his uncle's old seat; his father was a legislator and judge).[146] Abrams became the first woman to serve as Senate majority leader and to chair Maryland's Democratic Party, while Cardin went on to become a US senator in 2006. Leon Sachs's son Stephen became Maryland's attorney general in 1978 and forged a reputation as an anti-machine politician. Hyman Pressman served almost thirty years as city comptroller; invariably described as "colorful," he was known for his effusive style and his bad poetry.[147]

By the 1970s, Jews were an integral part of the state's political scene at all levels. Despite their determination to carve out a Jewish congressional district and though they tended to share a liberal outlook, they rarely acted as a bloc, engaging in a diversity of alliances and often opposing each other. In 1986, for example, Stephen Sachs ran for governor with the African American leader Parren Mitchell as his running mate; he lost the Democratic primary to Mayor Schaefer, whose running mate was Mickey Steinberg. Schaefer and Steinberg went on to win the general election with a whopping 82 percent of the vote. Meanwhile, liberal Republican Theodore McKeldin found much support among Democratic Jewish politicians and voters; as governor he carried around his own yarmulke, embroidered with the state seal of Maryland, to wear when occasion arose. (Ready for any situation, he also reportedly carried rosary beads.)[148]

Jewish political activity extended to the radical movements of the 1960s and beyond. In the early postwar era, however, activists faced persecution that decimated the Jewish left locally and nationally. Baltimore's shipyard unions expelled radicals from their ranks in late 1945. In 1946, five employees at nearby Aberdeen Proving Ground were publicly fired "in the interest of national security." All were union activists and all were Jews.[149] Leftists were prosecuted under the state's antisubversive Ober Law. The Maryland Communist Party leader Albert Blumberg went into hiding, but his wife, Dorothy (a local clothing manufacturer's daughter), served two years in jail for subversion. From 1944 to 1957 the House Un-American Activities Committee (HUAC) held a series of hearings to rid Maryland of radical influences, leaving jail sentences and destroyed careers in its wake. Stanley Askin, a leader of the Druid Hill Park interracial tennis protest, was blacklisted from his radio career, and fellow tennis player Mitzi Freishtat was also targeted. The large number of Jewish names mentioned during the highly charged, well-publicized hearings may have caused pangs of distress in the local Jewish community; nationally, mainstream Jewish groups in the postwar era tried hard to distance themselves from anything that smacked of Communism.[150]

Some victims of McCarthyism reemerged during the 1960s, however. The former Progressive Party leader Harold Buchman, a mentor to the Druid Hill Park tennis protesters, tangled with HUAC for years and saw his law career decline. He later became a noted activist attorney who served on the defense team of the famed Catonsville Nine in 1968. Interestingly, the prosecutor on that high-profile case was a scion of Baltimore Jewish liberalism, state's attorney Stephen Sachs.[151] Howard Silverberg, a former merchant marine, labor organizer, and Communist Party member, lost his job at Sparrows Point in the purges of the 1950s (he was also kicked out of his bowling league) but found new purpose in the 1970s as head of the Southeast Community Organization. The local antiwar movement and other 1960s movements drew in a new generation of Jewish activists, including "red diaper babies" such as Leonard Helfgott, whose mother had been a stalwart in Baltimore's Communist Party.[152]

Like Silverberg, some Jewish Baltimoreans remained dedicated urbanites who worked to revitalize the city through grassroots activism. Ruth Rehfeld was a mainstay of the Citizens Planning and Housing Association, the leading nonprofit trying to stem neighborhood decline. Her impact was felt especially in the downtown Mount Vernon district, where she lived, and Park Heights, where she directed a community group in the 1970s. Several neighborhood activists came from prominent families with deep roots in the Jewish community, such as Stanley Panitz, Melvin Sykes, and Sidney Hollander Jr., leaders of the open-housing group Baltimore Neighborhoods, Inc.[153]

Clearly, suburbanization did not lead to withdrawal from urban affairs. Jewish business leaders maintained a strong economic interest in the city's well-being, and none more so than the downtown department store owners. Even as they pursued suburbanizing customers with shiny new branch stores in the early 1950s, they could not help but notice that the area surrounding their flagship stores was starting to crumble. Baltimore's Inner Harbor had become derelict as a modernizing shipping industry abandoned its shallow waters and outmoded wharves. The worn skyline had added only one new building since the 1920s. Cars choked the city streets, usually on their way to somewhere else. In 1954, O'Neill's Department Store became the first large downtown retailer to shut its doors. For J. Jefferson Miller, Hecht's vice president, it was a wake-up call. Shortly after presiding at the grand opening of his firm's Northwood branch, he brought his fellow retailers together. They formed the Committee for Downtown and raised seed money to improve the central business district because of "its vital role as the heart of metropolitan Baltimore."[154]

Miller's call to action launched the civic effort that would become known as the Baltimore renaissance. Within months, another group of businesspeople, led by the non-Jewish attorney Clarence Miles, organized the Greater Baltimore Committee,

J. Jefferson Miller (*at podium*) convenes a 1959 gathering of the Committee for Downtown, one of two key organizations behind the redevelopment of downtown Baltimore. *Jewish Museum of Maryland.*

with Miller's fellow Hecht executive Robert Levi as a key member. Together, the GBC and the Committee for Downtown initiated the two projects that would re-shape central Baltimore in the coming decades: the Charles Center redevelopment (the most ambitious downtown renewal plan of its time) and the pioneering Inner Harbor project, which became an international model for cities looking to trans-form obsolete industrial waterfronts into shopping and tourist meccas.[155]

Though Mayor Schaefer and developer James Rouse became the two people most closely identified with the Baltimore renaissance, it made sense that Jewish department store executives provided a major impetus; they had as large a stake in downtown as anyone. Jeff Miller became the general manager of the Charles Center project (at an annual salary of one dollar). He also chaired Charles Center–Inner Harbor Management Inc., which did the early Inner Harbor planning. He was suc-ceeded by Walter Sondheim Jr., "Baltimore businessman/public servant extraordi-naire," who had helped advance both projects through his chairmanship of the city's urban renewal agency.[156]

It would be an understatement to say that Jews in the postwar era had a signifi-cant impact on the Baltimore region. As reporter Laura Scism put it in 1979 in the *Baltimore News-American*'s five-part series on the Jewish community, "Jews have a major role in defining the character of Baltimore—from the baseball team it roots for to the paintings that hang in its museums to the vitality of its downtown."[157] Indeed, the city's wealthiest family was Jewish—and despite Jacob Blaustein's oil-based fortune and his role in international politics, the Blausteins maintained substantial business, real estate, and philanthropic interests in Baltimore.

The 1962 founding of the Center Club, the first business club to admit Jews, belatedly ratified the expanding Jewish role in civic affairs. Organized by GBC chair Clarence Miles, Joseph Meyerhoff, and a few others, the club, based in the sparkling new Charles Center, became the gathering place for the city's most dynamic and progressive business leaders. African American men were invited to join in 1963, another first for the city's elite club scene. Women were admitted by the early 1970s (though for years they were barred from the main dining room, provoking a lawsuit by one affronted Jewish member, boutique owner Ruth Shaw).[158]

Jewish real estate developers did much to shape the postwar built environment, from downtown to the suburbs and back. Meyerhoff built the first suburban-style shopping center, Edmondson Village, in 1947. Willard Hackerman, who had once worried that his boss, G. W. Whiting, would fire him if he found out he was Jewish, presided over the Whiting-Turner Company as it built two key pieces of the Inner Harbor, Harborplace and the National Aquarium, and became Maryland's premier contracting firm. The politically connected Victor Frenkil constructed public buildings that served as the backdrop for daily life in Baltimore. As the *Sun* put it, "If you were born in city hospitals, you were born in a Frenkil building. If you went to school at Poly-Western, you went to school in a Frenkil building. If your graduation was held at the civic center, you graduated in a Frenkil building." Stanley Panitz, "a real estate developer with a social conscience," promoted city neighborhoods through his projects as well as his civic activism. In 1967 he moved into his own landmark Bolton Square row house development in transitional Bolton Hill; during the riots, he saw the city burn from his rooftop. Bolton Square would help stabilize the neighborhood by attracting a diverse, middle-class clientele.[159]

There were also Jews whose actions contributed to urban decline. Harry Weinberg built a real estate empire that spanned many states. As an absentee landlord in his native Baltimore, he let his properties decay, frustrating renewal efforts. "Mayor Schaefer and other city officials have had little success in convincing Mr. Weinberg to develop his numerous Baltimore holdings," the *Sun* noted in 1984. Fellow real estate owner Herbert Kaufman became known as the city's chief housing "abandoner."[160] The Block, whose establishments were still largely owned by Jews, offered a major example of urban distress as the burlesque houses, nightclubs, and relatively upscale strip shows of the interwar period gave way in the 1960s to tawdry bars and strip joints, with prostitution and drug dealing ever present.

Meanwhile, in 1951 the US Senate's Kefauver hearings on organized crime revealed how integral Jews remained to Baltimore's underworld scene: Ike Sapperstein, George Goldberg, and other Jewish members of the gambling fraternity figured prominently. Though the city's rackets were reportedly controlled by out-of-town syndicates, many local players were Jewish.[161] In one of the most famous episodes in the annals of Baltimore organized crime, Julius "the Lord" Salsbury, the "king of Block rackets," vanished mysteriously in 1970, "leaving behind an $80,000 bail bond and a fifteen-year sentence for running a gambling racket from the back room of the Oasis." He was never heard from again; one theory had him "embalmed in the cement of the fast lane" under the Jones Falls Expressway while another had him escaping to Israel.[162]

But problems such as crime and abandoned housing were as much symptoms as causes of the city's decline. National and global economic trends spelled trouble for older industrial cities like Baltimore. Incentives for businesses and residents to move to suburbia, the flight of manufacturing overseas, and a declining property base were just some of the factors working against urban well-being. In addition, the postwar growth of Washington, DC, and Atlanta eroded Baltimore's significance as a regional commercial center. The city lost 10,000 residents in the 1950s, starting a downward slide that continued into the twenty-first century. The worst loss occurred in the 1970s, when the population dropped by 120,000.[163] The revitalization of downtown offered one bright spot in the urban gloom. Meanwhile, the suburbs of Baltimore County continued to thrive, though unchecked sprawl became an increasing concern.

These trends helped complete the transformation of traditional Jewish businesses. Wholesalers left downtown, displaced by Charles Center. Some retailers suburbanized while others succumbed to urban renewal, competition from chain stores and malls, or a lack of interest from the younger generation (all more devastating than the riots). A trend toward upscale clothing boutiques drew new entrepreneurs, including women such as Ruth Shaw, Ada Becker ("Ada Bernard"), and Frances Berman. Some old-style retailers did find ways to thrive: Joseph A. Bank and Eddie Jacobs built on their niche in classic men's clothing. Israel Myers kept the tradition of clothing manufacturing alive, scoring a hit with his London Fog brand. But though his company was headquartered in Baltimore, by the 1970s his factories were located elsewhere.[164]

As the downtown shopping district continued to deteriorate, it became clear that the department stores would not participate in the revitalization their executives had done so much to promote. The shopping district lay outside the boundaries of Charles Center and the Inner Harbor: it was close, but not close enough. In the end, the loss of strong local leadership completed the stores' downfall. Hochschild, Kohn led the way as it had with suburbanization and integration. The family sold out to investor Warren Buffett in 1966, hoping he would provide long-term stability, but he later sold it, and the store closed in 1977. Harry Weinberg gained control of Brager-Gutman's and neglected it as he did his other properties. The management of Hecht's was taken over by its Washington operation. Hutzler's stayed in the family almost to the end, but the younger generation became mired in dissension and confusion over how to meet the challenges the business faced. Hutzler's, Hecht's, and Brager-Gutman's all closed their downtown stores in the 1980s.[165]

The demise of the department stores was a blow to the civic identity of Baltimore. For decades, the downtown district and its homegrown emporiums had symbolized the city's unique character and provided a space for Baltimoreans to come together. Around the nation, the homogenization of commerce and the decline of downtown districts had the same effect. But increasingly, other institutions were assuming this role: sports teams, museums, symphony orchestras, and the like. Professional sports in particular became a locus of civic pride, and the fact that Baltimore lacked major league football and baseball teams in the early 1950s was seen as a clear sign that the city had "lost some of its big-league stature."[166]

Jewish business leaders played a critical role in rectifying this situation. Jerrold Hoffberger and Zanvyl Krieger shared a similar profile: fortunes rooted in rival family-owned breweries and extensive business and philanthropic interests. As major investors and behind-the-scenes players, they backed the successful effort of Clarence Miles and Mayor D'Alesandro to bring Major League Baseball back to Baltimore in 1953. Hoffberger became president of the Orioles during the team's glory years in the 1960s and 1970s when his National Brewing Company became majority owner.[167] Meanwhile, the National Football League promised to grant Baltimore a team if fans would buy 15,000 season tickets by the end of January 1953. As the deadline approached and sales looked to be almost 2,000 shy, the Blaustein family's American Oil Company stepped in to guarantee the balance. The NFL awarded the Colts franchise to a group led by businessman Carroll Rosenbloom that also included Krieger. Rosenbloom, son of a local clothing manufacturer, presided over the Colts when the team won the NFL championship in 1958, beating the New York Giants in "the greatest game ever played," a nationally televised thriller that caused pro football's popularity to surge nationwide. The Colts became a source of pride that united city and suburbs.[168]

The horse-racing industry also received a boost from Jewish entrepreneurs. When scrap industry titan Morris Schapiro acquired Laurel Park racetrack in 1951, his "junk-man background . . . stirred tremors among the older racing gentry," the *Sun* noted. But he and his son John made substantial improvements to the track's operation, and by the time Queen Elizabeth II ran a horse at Laurel Park in 1954, Schapiro was being heralded as "the man who has given new life to Maryland and American racing."[169] Meanwhile, the Schapiros sold their interest in Pimlico Race Course to businessmen brothers Herman and Ben Cohen. Pimlico thrived under the Cohens' stewardship from the 1950s until they sold it in the 1980s. They turned the venerable Preakness Stakes into a week-long festive event that became a cherished part of the city's social scene.[170]

Jewish support also helped other institutions become important markers of the city's stature. When Joseph Meyerhoff became president of the Baltimore Symphony Orchestra in 1965, the orchestra shared inadequate quarters in the Lyric Opera

House. To secure public funding for a new home, in 1978 he pledged $5 million toward the cost—"the largest private donation I have ever known," enthused Mayor Schaefer (who was not known for understatement). In the end, the state-of-the-art facility cost Meyerhoff twice that amount. When Joseph Meyerhoff Symphony Hall opened to great acclaim in 1982, he became "the millionaire philanthropist who is mentioned in the same breath as Hopkins, Pratt, and Walters," the *Sun*'s John Kelly wrote. To Meyerhoff, the symphony hall symbolized "the resurgence of Baltimore as a thriving metropolitan community."[171]

Jews continued to play prominent roles in all aspects of entertainment, culture, and the arts. A group of young, socially conscious Jewish artists who had started out during the Depression emerged as leaders of the city's art scene in the postwar era, including Jacob Glushakow, Herman Maril, Aaron Sopher, Edward Rosenfeld, Perna Krick, Amalie Rothschild, and Reuben Kramer. Kramer, a sculptor, opened the first racially integrated art school in Baltimore in 1944. Rothschild founded an annual art festival in Druid Hill Park that enlivened the cultural scene in the 1950s and 1960s. Donald Rothman and Ed Golden founded the leading repertory theater company Center Stage in 1963, while actress Vivienne Shub became a legendary figure on the Baltimore stage. Theater owner Morris Mechanic built the brutalist-style venue that served as the cultural heart of Charles Center after it opened in 1967. The Mechanic Theatre "succeeded in doing what it was meant to do: bringing Broadway shows to Baltimore and bringing people back downtown to see them," noted the *Sun*'s architecture critic, Ed Gunts, though the theater faltered in later years and was torn down in 2014.[172]

As elsewhere in postwar America, the rise of television struck at the vibrancy of cultural institutions, from The Block to the Mechanic Theatre. Jews were key to the development of a local TV industry, both on the air and off. With Sam Carliner, Ben and Herman Cohen founded the city's third TV station, WAAM (later called WJZ) in 1948, years before the brothers purchased Pimlico. Royal Parker (born Royal Pollokoff) was known as Baltimore's "Mr. Television" for his various on-air roles, and performer Rhea Feikin became the face of Maryland public TV. Such local personalities helped Baltimoreans retain a sense of shared identity in the face of the homogenizing impact of national television on American culture.[173]

Looking at Baltimore during the postwar era can be a glass half-empty or half-full proposition. While the city experienced population loss, riots, and elevated levels of poverty and crime, thousands of families embraced a suburban lifestyle and achieved their American Dream. Through the civil rights movement, African Americans became full-fledged members of the urban polity, prominent in politics, business, and cultural affairs—though inequities deeply rooted in the structures of US social and economic life stood in the way of full equality. Downtown fell and then rose again. Neighborhoods declined, but some began to revitalize. New sports teams brought disparate segments of the population together. Thriving cultural institutions in central Baltimore withstood competition from TV and showed that even with the rise of suburbia, the city remained the vital center of the metropolitan area.

Jews participated in all of it. Unlike elsewhere in the United States, suburbanization did not disperse them—it actually served to strengthen their already close-knit community, providing a shared place for them to enact their Jewish identity. But even as Baltimore Jewry became synonymous with "Pikesville," it did not lose its identity as "Baltimore." Jews were more involved than ever in all facets of the city's development. In her study of Detroit Jewry, Lila Corwin Berman notes that postwar Jews "created a new politics of urban investment that was intensified, not diminished, by urban flight and upheaval." To Jewish activists and leaders, "suburbanization" did not signify "abandonment."[174] In diverse ways, Jewish Baltimoreans demonstrated the same commitment. Heading into the twenty-first century, they remained, distinctly, Baltimore Jews.

Epilogue

THE CHALLENGES OF A NEW CENTURY

"Is there a Jewish future in Randallstown?" asked a bold headline in the *Jewish Times* in January 1986. We now know the answer was no, but at the time the topic seemed open for debate. In the early 1970s Randallstown, at the far end of Liberty Road, was an up-and-coming suburb especially popular with young, growing Jewish families. The Liberty Road corridor rivaled Pikesville as a Jewish population center while Upper Park Heights, with an aging population, stood on the verge of decline. But by the mid-1980s Liberty Road had lost half its Jewish residents, and Pikesville had emerged as the uncontested heart of Baltimore Jewry. Upper Park Heights, meanwhile, seemed poised for a dramatic recovery.[1]

As the *Jewish Times* and its readers debated Randallstown's fate in articles and letters, the discussion revealed the trends that shaped Jewish life at the end of the twentieth century. An obvious cause of Randallstown's Jewish population loss was, once again, white flight, as middle-class African Americans followed Jews to the suburbs in the years after discrimination became illegal. But many Randallstown supporters insisted that integration had occurred smoothly and successfully. Some Jewish residents even appreciated the fact that Randallstown was more diverse and less densely Jewish than Pikesville was.[2] Reporter Phil Jacobs drew attention to other possible causes: the growing affluence of families who could now afford to live in Pikesville, where houses were larger and pricier; competition from newer and trendier Owings Mills, home of the new JCC; and the lack of a Jewish infrastructure (aside from synagogues) in the Liberty Road corridor. Above all, he astutely surmised, "perhaps the greatest loss facing Randallstown is that of a once thriving Orthodoxy community." As one former resident told him, her family had recently moved to Upper Park Heights because "we wanted to be in an area of Orthodox Jewish growth. This is where the action is, not Randallstown."[3]

She was right—and the action was about to explode as Baltimore became an epicenter of the national resurgence of Orthodoxy that took place in the late twentieth century. Today, almost one-third of the metro area's Jews identify as Orthodox, a far

Orthodox Jews walk past the Chanukah House on Park Heights Avenue on their way to synagogue, 2006. Photo by Sarah Nix. *Permission granted from the* Baltimore Sun. *All rights reserved.*

higher share than in any American city except New York.[4] Not only has the percentage returned to where it was in the early 1960s, but today's Orthodox adherents are,
on the whole, much more observant than in the past. The impact of Orthodoxy's
rise has been profound not only on Jewish geography, but on the size of Baltimore's
Jewish population, the vibrancy of religious and cultural life, the development of
communal institutions, and the cohesiveness of the community. Nevertheless, the
Orthodox are far from a majority, and Baltimore's other Jewish movements have
undergone transformations of their own.

Meanwhile, Jews have become ever more integrated into the local social, political,
and cultural scene. Economic trends have continued to shape geographic patterns,
community life, and interactions with non-Jews. This chapter examines how the
events of recent decades have built on the previous 250 years to bring Baltimore
Jewry to where it is today.

Where, What, When

Of the nation's top twenty Jewish communities, only West and South Palm Beach,
Florida, are as segregated as Baltimore: in 2010, around 77 percent of Jews lived in
the metro area's northwest section, with 30 percent in Pikesville alone.[5] But this
fact obscures a great deal of movement over the previous forty years, both within
Northwest Baltimore and beyond it. As the case of Randallstown shows, a look at

the wanderings of Baltimore Jews can lead to a deeper understanding of both community dynamics and relations between Jews and non-Jews.

Despite their current high level of concentration compared to Jews elsewhere, Baltimore Jews actually began to spread out slowly but steadily after 1968, when a whopping 90 percent lived within the friendly confines of Northwest Baltimore. In 1975 Roland Park appeared for the first time in an Associated population study. Its Jewish cohort was small (around 1,200 people) but symbolic: seven years after the Fair Housing Act of 1968, the most famously restricted neighborhood in Baltimore was seen as a viable residential choice for Jews. "Crossing Falls Road" became commonplace for Jewish suburbanites, who found homes in northern Baltimore County locales such as Towson and Lutherville. Jews also participated in the rejuvenation of central Baltimore; by 1999, a growing number once again lived in neighborhoods near downtown.[6]

Meanwhile, big changes were taking place within Northwest Baltimore. The 1980s and 1990s saw the dramatic rise of Owings Mills, where a bustling suburb appeared out of recent farmland. The northwest frontier continued to advance as Jewish homeowners crossed into Carroll County. Upper Park Heights showed the stirrings of revival: its Jewish population was becoming younger, and its share of Jewish newcomers to Baltimore surpassed that of other areas. In the late 1990s the neighborhood entered a period of growth that has not stopped. New arrivals included both US residents and immigrants: for the first time in decades, Baltimore Jewry's foreign-born population was on the rise. While Upper Park Heights benefited most, in-migration had community-wide implications, helping to halt the decline in Jewish population that occurred from the late 1960s to the mid-1980s, when few newcomers arrived to counter attrition caused by death, a dropping birth rate, and out-migration. After topping 100,000 in the late 1960s, the Jewish population dropped to around 91,700 by the mid-1980s and then slowly began inching back up; the Associated's 2010 study counted 93,400 Jews (though other estimates were higher).[7]

Communal institutions played an important role in these developments. Not only did they work to attract and resettle immigrants, but they were deeply implicated in the rise and fall of Jewish neighborhoods. By placing its second JCC in Owings Mills instead of Randallstown in 1977, the Associated's planners chose to invest not in an area with a large existing Jewish population, but in an area of predicted growth.[8] Whether they made an accurate prediction or whether their decision caused Owings Mills to grow at Randallstown's expense was a question raised by many. Meanwhile, as a *Jewish Times* writer noted in 1992, areas with a strong Jewish infrastructure continued to receive the lion's share of Associated resources because of the federation's need to "protect its institutional investment." His observation reflected how internal and external forces combined to influence community life: protecting its investment meant, above all, trying to ensure that Jews remained put and did not engage in white flight.[9]

In the post-1968 era, memories of the rapid turnover in Lower Park Heights and Forest Park were fresh in people's minds. As upwardly mobile African Americans sought better housing in the 1970s, many looked to Upper Park Heights and the Liberty Road corridor. Both offered nice homes at affordable prices, and both adjoined black city neighborhoods. Plus, as an African American realtor observed, "I don't know of any acts of violence perpetrated on the homes of blacks by Jewish people."[10] Though some Jewish residents welcomed their new neighbors, others noted their arrival with unease—especially when a black family's appearance was followed by a visit (or call or letter, or all three) from a friendly realtor, hinting that it might be time to sell. The Liberty Road corridor in particular became known for yet another dubious real estate practice: steering, a subtle form of blockbusting. By steering black home buyers toward racially changing neighborhoods, realtors helped to quickly resegregate blacks while benefiting from the rapid departure of whites. If racial change was not the major cause of the exodus of Jews from the Randallstown–Liberty Road area, it was surely part of the mix.[11]

While the changes taking place along Liberty Road were worrisome, Associated officials became truly alarmed when Upper Park Heights began to lose Jewish residents. Ranged along Park Heights Avenue stood the original JCC, Baltimore Hebrew University, social service agencies, and a plethora of synagogues, with Levindale and Sinai Hospital nearby. As former board chair Jonathan Kolker later acknowledged, "There was a major Jewish infrastructure there. We had to take some action."[12] As usual, reasons for the area's Jewish population loss were many, including the allure of more spacious Pikesville to upwardly mobile families. But to the Associated, the prospect of white flight was the most immediate problem because of its panic-driven nature.

As a result, when the Northwest Baltimore Corporation, a coalition of community groups, brought together blacks and Jews in Upper Park Heights to address local issues in the mid-1970s, the Associated's planning director, Carmi Schwartz, played a leadership role.[13] In 1983 the Associated became more directly involved in stabilizing the area when it created Comprehensive Housing Assistance, Inc. (CHAI), which sponsored neighborhood improvement projects, marketed the area to Jewish home buyers, and offered homeowner assistance programs that proved popular with African American and Jewish residents alike. By serving as a bridge between blacks and Jews, CHAI joined with grassroots groups to ensure that the racial mix in Upper Park Heights signified a stable and integrated community, not one that was transitioning from white to black. "Many African Americans were pleased that the organized Jewish community was standing up for these neighborhoods," CHAI director Ken Gelula later noted.[14]

In post-riot Baltimore, where contacts between blacks and Jews were less and less frequent, this network of community support stood out as a model of ongoing black-Jewish cooperation. Northwest Baltimore Corporation's director, Ruth Rehfeld, would go on to head BLEWS, the Black-Jewish Forum of Baltimore. Links

CHAI Senior Home Repair Day, c. 2010. The organization is an example of how communal agencies have evolved to serve the Jewish community's changing needs. *Jewish Museum of Maryland. Courtesy of CHAI and the Associated: Jewish Community Federation of Baltimore.*

forged between community leaders did not necessarily extend to black and Jewish residents, whose relations could more accurately be described as wary coexistence rather than neighborliness. Also, parts of the area did resegregate. Nevertheless, as the years passed and the Jewish presence strengthened, many observers came to see Upper Park Heights as a rare example of successful integration in Baltimore.[15]

Many of CHAI's Jewish clients were moderate-income, newly arrived Orthodox families who benefited from its home loan programs. The agency built on the amenities that already made Upper Park Heights attractive to observant Jews—its JCC, synagogues, affordable home prices, and relative walkability compared to other Jewish areas. Together, these resources positioned the neighborhood to become the natural place for the Orthodox community to grow. Jewish institutions and services also helped Upper Park Heights attract Russian, Iranian, and Israeli immigrants, who formed their own mini-communities within its environs.

The Liberty Road corridor lacked the Jewish resources to compete. From the outside looking in, white flight might have seemed to be the cause of the Randallstown Jewish community's decline, but Upper Park Heights and Owings Mills also had significant black populations. Rather, as in previous decades, racial turnover played a highly visible role in a larger reality. In this case, Jewish life along the Liberty Road corridor had come to seem less viable to many of the Jews who resided there. By the time CHAI opened an office in the neighborhood around 1990, it was too little, too late.

A Community Divided?

In May 2009, the *Jewish Times* once again marked a defining moment for the Jewish community with a question: "Are We One?" The context was the recent decision to open the Owings Mills JCC on the Sabbath. Twice before, in 1977 and in 1997, the JCC's bid to open on Saturdays had been quashed by the Associated after vigorous Orthodox opposition. This time the opposition was just as vigorous, but the Associated board approved the JCC's request by a 97–33 secret ballot vote.[16]

In a way, the decision was surprising. Baltimore's Orthodox community, long known for its strong institutions, had boomed during the national rise of ultra-Orthodox Judaism in the late twentieth century. In the twelve years since the JCC had last broached the Saturday issue, the Orthodox share of the Jewish population had surged from 21 to 32 percent—almost three times the national average—thanks to a flood of *frum* (pious) families from New York and elsewhere, attracted by the city's affordability, convenient location, and religious vitality.[17] Not only was local Orthodoxy larger, stronger, and more self-confident than ever, it was noted for its influence in the broader Jewish community. As the *Forward* observed in 2007, "In contrast to other cities," Baltimore's Orthodox leaders, "even those furthest to the right religiously," had a history of engaging with non-Orthodox leaders and working closely with the local federation.[18]

Indeed, Baltimore Jewry's ongoing traditionalist orientation derived both from the city's historically conservative religious scene and from the willingness of Orthodox leaders to interact with, rather than shun, the broader Jewish community. The most influential, Ner Israel's Rabbi Herman Neuberger, cultivated relations beyond the Orthodox sphere locally, nationally, and internationally. It was the politically masterful Neuberger, many thought, who was behind the Associated's 1997 veto of JCC Saturday openings. In the 1980s and 1990s, as the *frum* community grew, its representatives maintained close ties to the Associated. *Jewish Times* editor Neil Rubin recalled "ongoing talk about Jewish unity" and "a vibrant Orthodox/non-Orthodox dialogue."[19]

But community dynamics began to shift at the turn of the new century. Changes in leadership on both sides, including the death of Rabbi Neuberger in 2005, caused the dialogue to falter. Though some ultra-Orthodox leaders remained committed to Neuberger's approach, the most prominent, Rabbi Moses Heinemann, seemed to care little for diplomacy. Among other things, he termed Reform Judaism "a different religion" and called for a boycott of the *Jewish Times*.[20] Meanwhile, the Orthodox community's expansion and growing self-sufficiency promoted isolationism. In the *frum* neighborhood that stretched from Upper Park Heights into Pikesville, observed Rubin in 2009, "one can live a robust Jewish life and rarely interact meaningfully with non-Orthodox Jews."[21]

The creation of a self-contained Orthodox neighborhood can be traced to the late 1970s, when a committee formed to construct an eruv. While the immediate purpose of an eruv is to enable observant Jews to carry items on the Sabbath, the committee's president, Bert Miller, pointed out its deeper function when he announced its completion in 1981: "to unite a community and bring its inhabitants closer together." Or, as Rabbi Heinemann put it during the construction phase, "What we are trying to do is wall in northwest Baltimore."[22]

Soon Miller began publishing an annual directory of residents and businesses located within the eruv, which expanded into a hefty book listing a vast array of businesses, professional services, and community resources catering to Orthodox residents. Kosher stores and restaurants proliferated, from pizza places to gourmet Chinese to Israeli falafel joints. Seven Mile Market opened in 1989 and grew into the largest kosher supermarket in the United States. A network of Orthodox-based charities and services developed, ranging from traditional Jewish *chesed* to the Northwest Citizens' Patrol, a neighborhood watch program with hundreds of members.[23]

Baltimore's day schools and yeshivas remained the Orthodox community's most noted asset, with Ner Israel College reigning over all. In addition to providing rabbinic leadership, the seminary proved to be a significant draw: families moved to Baltimore after their sons were admitted, and graduates often stayed in the area. Other religious institutions also gained national renown. By the late 1980s local Orthodox realtors were advertising in Brooklyn Jewish newspapers, often touting their properties as being near well-known shuls. Under Rabbi Heinemann's supervision, the local Va'ad Ha-Kashrus developed the internationally respected Star-K kosher certification label. Known for its stringent kosher standards, it too added to the city's Orthodox élan.[24]

Meanwhile, the rest of the Jewish community was moving in the opposite direction demographically and ideologically. Although Baltimore Jewry remained among the most close-knit in the nation, a low birth rate, a rise in intermarriage, and a decreased involvement of Jews in communal life caused "a sense of contraction," in Rubin's words. According to the 2010 community study, young adults especially figured into a "growing minority" of Jews who were not engaged in Jewish life. Perhaps most disturbing to communal leaders, 42 percent of non-Orthodox married young adults were intermarried, though this was lower than the national norm, which a 2013 Pew Center study put at more than 55 percent. In general, fewer intermarried couples were raising Jewish children than were doing so ten years earlier.[25]

These trends were nothing new: they had accelerated through each decade of postwar American Jewish life. The communal response in Baltimore mirrored the response of Jewish communities in other cities. Resources flowed to new day schools, which were seen as prime territory for instilling Jewish identity among the young. The Conservative movement launched the Krieger Schechter Day School in

Beth Tfiloh High School classroom, 2016. The school continues to attract a cross-section of students despite divisions in the Jewish community. Photo by Rina Goloskov. *Jewish Museum of Maryland. Courtesy of Beth Tfiloh Dahan Community School.*

1980. Beth Tfiloh expanded its day school offerings in 1986 when it opened a high school, which, like its decades-old lower school, catered to students of all levels of religious observance. In 1991 the modern Orthodox Yeshivat Rambam high school opened, and Baltimore Hebrew Congregation launched the area's first Reform day school. The Shoshana S. Cardin Jewish Community High School was created in 2001 to serve Jewish students from all religious streams.[26]

As elsewhere, Reform and Conservative congregations embraced new attitudes about gender, sexual orientation, and inclusivity. Baltimore got its first woman rabbi in 1979 when Baltimore Hebrew Congregation hired Sheila Russian, one of the first women ordained by Hebrew Union College. In 2004 it hired the openly gay rabbi Elissa Sachs-Kohen; she soon became a strong local advocate of the national movement toward "big tent Judaism," which welcomes nontraditional families of all sorts as a way to engage the unaffiliated. Reconstructionist congregations and *havurot* (fellowship groups) joined the religious scene. A greater emphasis on traditional ritual and spiritual practice accompanied these liberalizing trends, a phenomenon that historian Jack Wertheimer describes as "change in both directions." Given Baltimore Jewry's reputation for small-*c* conservatism, its moves toward inclusivity occasionally brought national attention. When Beth El rabbi Mark Loeb performed a commitment ceremony for a same-sex couple in 2003, before the Conservative movement officially sanctioned such ceremonies, the *Forward* saw it as evidence that support for same-sex unions had spread be-yond the West Coast.[27]

The communal establishment had also not forgotten a time-honored way to en-gage nonpracticing Jews: through the Jewish Community Center. Owings Mills JCC leaders had long argued that being closed on Saturdays undermined the Associ-ated's primary vehicle for capturing the unaffiliated and exposing them to Jewish programming. On a more practical level, it hampered the JCC's ability to attract the memberships needed to sustain itself financially. In the midst of a severe re-cession, the financial imperative loomed large in the Associated's 2009 delibera-tions—though JCC leaders emphasized the benefit that opening on Saturdays would bring to the cause of Jewish engagement. "This will enable us to connect with more families and individuals," said JCC president Buddy Sapolsky after the Associated board voted in the JCC's favor. "We have some plans to make Shabbat at the JCC a very exciting day."[28]

Afterward, Sapolsky reflected on the long-sought victory. "There are no winners or losers," he stated. "We look forward to working with the Orthodox community going forward to try to build bridges together." Orthodox rabbi Moshe Hauer con-demned the decision, but said he remained committed to "trying to work together to develop the kind of real, real understanding and appreciation we obviously do not have enough of." The involvement of Hauer and some other Orthodox leaders in the deliberations encouraged Associated officials to hope that the battle did not signify a communal breach. "I'm disappointed, but this is a great Jewish community," Or-thodox board member Ronnie Rosenbluth stated. "It has to stay united." But board chair Jimmy Berg came close to acknowledging the bifurcation of Baltimore Jewry when he said, "We're making a huge statement to the Jewish world that Baltimore has two JCCs. One of them is closed [on Saturdays], because we respect our Ortho-dox community. But we're also willing to take risks and be open to the unaffiliated."[29]

To *Jewish Times* publisher Andy Buerger, the JCC vote was one more sign that "Orthodox and non-Orthodox groups are continuing to move farther apart physi-cally and spiritually." His answer to the question "are we one?" was an unequivocal no, and his own newspaper served as his prime example. Ever since his family had founded the *Jewish Times* in 1919, it had attempted to serve Baltimore Jews in all their diversity, with an emphasis on promoting unity that went back to the very first issue. But recently, after every column by a woman rabbi, cover photo with a woman in a sleeveless dress, or ad for a non-kosher restaurant, "the cancellations came in." Indeed, Orthodox Jews now had their own monthly newsmagazine, *Where What When*. "We have two great, but basically separate, villages," Buerger concluded. "Just as the *Jewish Times* cannot be the uniter, neither can the JCCs, Beth Tfiloh Commu-nity School, or even the Associated."[30]

As Orthodox synagogues adopted a more rigorous style of observance, some old-timers began to feel out of place. One native Baltimorean recalled that his el-derly mother stopped attending her longtime shul after a new rabbi took over and "all the black hats" started coming in. "She couldn't go there anymore. She felt un-welcome." Older Park Heights residents felt besieged by the influx of newcomers, who mostly seemed to come from New York. A 1992 *Jewish Times* article captured the early stages of this phenomenon, quoting one resident as saying, "I hear it all the time, 'the *frummies* are coming, the *frummies* are coming.'"[31] Orthodox natives complained that the newcomers were responsible for Orthodoxy's growing insular-ity; recent arrivals lacked the sense of history and intertwining relations that had characterized the close-knit Jewish community for decades.

Indeed, many people attributed the growing divide between the ultra-Orthodox and other Jews less to religious factors than to the fact that many "*frummies*" were not native Baltimoreans. The community's closeness had long benefited from its stability: as late as 1968, 70 percent of Jewish Baltimoreans had been born in Balti-more. By 1999 the ratio had dropped to 50 percent. This trend was not limited to the Orthodox. The percentage of native-born Jews from other religious streams had also fallen, and new arrivals generally showed less community attachment.[32]

Such changing dynamics contributed to a climate of community disarray. Even Orthodox institutions with deep roots in Baltimore started to distance themselves from the rest of the Jewish community: as early as 1989, the Talmudical Academy refused to participate in a basketball tournament for Jewish day schools at Beth Tfiloh (it preferred to play against Christian schools). Modern Orthodox leaders fumed at the slight but remained anonymous when commenting on the incident in the *Jewish Times*, showing their growing diffidence as Orthodoxy moved to the right.[33] Not surprisingly, new institutions that aimed for the middle ground faced an uphill battle. In 2011 and 2013, two of the recently founded Jewish high schools folded, and observers saw polarization at work. Yeshivat Rambam and the Shoshana S. Cardin High School had both sought to combine a rigorous Jewish education with a modern outlook; both failed to attract enough support to offset financial prob-lems exacerbated by the recession. The *Jewish Times* itself went into bankruptcy and changed ownership, mostly because of its costly legal battle with its printer, though some believed that the loss of Orthodox readers played a contributing role. Clearly religious differences had reshaped the Baltimore community as they had Jewish communities nationally, as signaled by a stream of books and articles that began appearing in the 1990s, such as *Jew vs. Jew* and *A People Divided*.[34]

Nevertheless, local communal leaders sought with some success to prevent Bal-timore Jewry from fracturing—if not by promoting unity, a goal that seemed in-creasingly unrealistic, then at least by managing diversity. The Associated, for one, appreciated the demographic boost the Orthodox had given Baltimore Jewry and worked hard to bring leaders of all stripes together. And despite appearances to the contrary, the ultra-Orthodox community needed the federation: though its day schools were crowded with students, most families could not pay the full price, and Associated-related allocations kept them solvent.[35] Meanwhile, efforts to em-brace a more open, less insular brand of Orthodoxy began to gain traction, from "breakaway" shuls such as Netivot Shalom (whose founders adhered to the national "open Orthodoxy" movement) to B'nai Israel, the sole surviving synagogue in East Baltimore, which strove to attract the growing number of Jewish families moving into the central city.[36]

The most significant attempt to absorb and integrate the trends shaking the Orthodox world occurred at Beth Tfiloh, the pillar of modern Orthodoxy in Baltimore. Its struggles—like the mixed-seating controversy at Chizuk Amuno in the early postwar era—demonstrated the challenges of trying to occupy the middle ground in the evolving relationship between tradition and modernity. In 1974 the self-described "largest Modern Orthodox synagogue in America" nearly left the Orthodox fold when the Beth Tfiloh board voted to affiliate with the Conservative movement's United Synagogue of America, only to be rebuffed by the membership.[37] As Orthodoxy moved rightward, Beth Tfiloh did too—at the urging of some members but to the dismay of others. Because its sanctuary lacked a *mechitza* (a barrier between the men's and women's sections), in 2003 Rabbi Mitchell Wohlberg announced plans to construct one "to permit us to continue to define ourselves as Orthodox."[38] While this step pleased a new generation of more observant members, Wohlberg also moved to increase women's religious participation (in halachic ways) in order to keep the allegiance of more moderate members, especially women who thought the *mechitza* was sexist.

To Wohlberg, the congregation's strength was in its "unique" ability to maintain religious diversity amid polarizing trends, and he worked assiduously to keep his congregation from going too far in either direction. Somehow, it worked. "Never before have we had as many families affiliated with Beth Tfiloh," he noted in 2014. "We are able to reach out to so many . . . because we have been able to remain faithful to our tradition, but never 'stuck' in our ways."[39] Key to Beth Tfiloh's success was its popular day school, a thriving example of cooperation among seemingly intractable opposites: the student body was religiously diverse, and the teachers ranged from secular to strictly observant.

In many ways the communal scene remained a jumbled mix of countervailing forces. Even the ultra-Orthodox community was not as monolithically rigid as it appeared to outsiders. Chana Weinberg, the wife of Ner Israel religious leader Yaakov Weinberg (and the daughter of founder Jacob Ruderman), established safe houses for battered women and became an outspoken advocate for victims of domestic violence in the Orthodox world; the Associated consulted with her in starting CHANA, the Counseling, Helpline and Aid Network for Abused Women. She also dispensed commonsense wisdom on balancing Orthodox practice and modern life in "Shalom Bayis," her advice column in *Where What When*. Her fellow *Where What When* contributor Eli Schlossberg celebrated the vibrancy of local Orthodoxy but also cited the example of previous generations of Orthodox leaders in urging his readers to "grant greater respect and understanding to those who are not exactly like us."[40]

As communal institutions navigated this complex scene, they also responded to

Volunteers at Kayam Farm in Baltimore County, 2016. The farm offers a Jewish take on sustainability and the environment. *Jewish Museum of Maryland. Courtesy of Greg Strella, Pearlstone Center, and the Associated: Jewish Community Federation of Baltimore.*

evolving economic and societal trends. CHANA, the Northwest Citizens' Patrol, and CHAI are just a few examples of entities formed to meet newly recognized or growing needs. SHEMESH was founded to assist Jewish children with learning disabilities. The Jewish Cemetery Association was created because the mutual aid groups that had operated their own cemeteries were aging and disappearing, leading to cemetery neglect and deterioration. In 2007, interest in environmentalism and sustainability coalesced in three initiatives: the formation of the Baltimore Jewish Environmental Network, the launch of a sustainability project to enact a "green strategy" for Associated facilities, and the founding of Kayam Farm, a five-acre plot at the Associated-supported Pearlstone Center that is dedicated to community-supported agriculture and environmental education.[41]

At the dawn of the new century, the community still supported the old standbys but often with a new rationale. Sinai Hospital remained a communally backed institution despite some critics' belief that such support was no longer justified, since Jewish medical personnel and patients were now well integrated into other area hospitals. Supporters pointed to the services it provided to a growing Orthodox population as well as the goodwill it generated by serving a broader urban (largely African American) constituency. Israel was still a major focus of philanthropy; the 2010 community study reported that Baltimoreans showed a "much higher" attachment to the Jewish state than did American Jewry as a whole. Services for the elderly remained a top priority, expanding along with the rising number of Jewish senior citizens. The recession of 2008 brought an increase in Jews needing financial support: not only recent immigrants, the elderly, and large Orthodox families, but now members of the mainstream middle class.[42]

Jewish education received more financial resources than any other single item, but the record was decidedly mixed. The closings of Yeshivat Rambam, Cardin High School, and the Baltimore Hebrew Congregation day school (in 2013) revealed the limits of the day school strategy as a tool for bolstering Jewish identity. Despite initial enthusiasm, Baltimore Hebrew's school could not compete with secular public and private schools, on the one hand, or more rigorously Jewish day schools, on the other. Its failure to attract students caused one disappointed parent to conclude, "it is obvious there is not a need for this school." A much older institution also fell out of step with the times: Baltimore Hebrew University shut its doors in 2009 after ninety years of service to the community, its declining enrollment part of a national trend of closings of stand-alone Jewish colleges—in large part because of the rise of Jewish studies programs in American universities. Indeed, Baltimore Hebrew University did not so much close as transform: its faculty, students, library, and degree programs became absorbed into the newly created Baltimore Hebrew Institute at Towson University.[43]

In the 1970s, a new rallying point for communal activity emerged as the migration of Jews from the Soviet Union put Jewish agencies back in the resettlement business for the first time in a generation. The Hebrew Immigrant Aid Society (HIAS) helped resettle some 1,800 Soviet Jews during that decade, and far greater numbers came in the 1990s with the breakup of the Soviet Union. By 2000, HIAS and other local agencies had assisted more than 10,000 Russians. Jewish Family Services provided financial assistance, furnished apartments, and other aid to new arrivals; the Park Heights JCC hired Russian-speaking staff and offered programs that ran the gamut from English classes to Jewish education to how to shop at an American supermarket. Job services revved up, and a new army of volunteers was recruited to help families acculturate. As with earlier migrations, the resettlement process was not always smooth, with cultural differences causing frustration for both the Russians and their helpers. Also as with earlier migrations, the newcomers fashioned their own vibrant subculture to ease the transition between the Old World and the New.[44]

Russians were not the only new arrivals from overseas: a significant cohort of Ira-

----

Naturalization ceremony at the Lloyd Street Synagogue, 1993. *Jewish Museum of Maryland.*

nian Jews came to Baltimore in the late twentieth century. Their presence can be traced to Rabbi Neuberger, who established a link between Ner Israel and Iran's Jewish community in the 1970s. After the 1979 Islamic revolution, "large numbers of Iranian men arrived at Ner Israel as a way for their parents to send their children to safe haven," the *Jewish Times* later reported. As it had done for German refugees in the 1930s, the yeshiva provided crucial student visas and scholarships. Neuberger used his diplomatic and political connections to help his Iranian students bring their families (and many others) to the United States, thus becoming a major figure in facilitating the exodus of Iran's Jews to America. Most settled in New York and Los Angeles, but the more religious gravitated to Baltimore, where Ner Israel was training a new generation of Iranian Jewish religious leaders. Encouraged by Neuberger to maintain their Sephardic rituals so they could "teach their own community," as he put it, they went on to lead Iranian congregations in other cities. A local Iranian community gathered around the Ohr Hamizrach synagogue on Park Heights Avenue, whose Middle Eastern–inspired architecture offered a colorful contrast to the street's other shuls.[45]

Neuberger's assistance to the Jews of Iran put him in the company of other Jewish leaders whose activities transcended the local arena. The Free Soviet Jewry movement had a strong and active Baltimore contingent. One of the most effective activists for the cause was Fabian Kolker, whom the *Jewish Times* described in 1984 as "almost a one-man State Department with a single portfolio: liberating Soviet Jews."

Shoshana Cardin speaks at a Washington, DC, rally for Soviet Jewry, 1987. Photo © Robert A. Cumins. *Jewish Museum of Maryland. Courtesy of Shoshana Cardin.*

Kolker made numerous trips to Russia and personally helped hundreds of families emigrate.[46]

The most influential Baltimorean on the world stage was Shoshana Cardin, who made her mark in areas as diverse as women's rights, Jewish education, Soviet Jewry, and US-Israel relations. Locally she chaired the Maryland Commission for Women and in 1983 became president of the Associated, the first woman in the United States to lead a major Jewish federation. She went on to break ground as the first woman to head three national Jewish groups: the Council of Jewish Federations in 1984, the National Council for Soviet Jewry in 1988, and the Conference of Presidents of Major American Jewish Organizations in 1991. Cardin's organizational savvy, diplomatic skills, and firm advocacy enabled her to influence US policy on Soviet Jewry and Israel. Following in the footsteps of Jacob Blaustein, she also played a major role in resolving tensions between Israel and the American Jewish community: in her case, over the contentious "who is a Jew?" issue.[47]

Twenty-First-Century Baltimoreans

As Shoshana Cardin rose from local activism to a larger arena, so did her cousin by marriage Ben Cardin, who was elected US senator in 2006. With ethnicity becoming a less conspicuous factor in political life, Cardin was one of several Jewish public officials to serve a broad constituency. Three of the metro area's five suburban counties had Jewish chief executives in 2010: Democrats Kevin Kamenetz of Baltimore County and Ken Ulman of Howard County and Republican John Leopold of Anne Arundel County. The path to political success no longer had to run through Northwest Baltimore's Jewish community. Leopold (who was later found guilty of misconduct and removed from office) hailed from Philadelphia, and Ulman was born and raised in Columbia, Howard County's sole metropolis (though his parents were native Baltimoreans). Kamenetz had deep Northwest Baltimore ties but had to move well beyond his base to gain the support of Baltimore County residents, a diverse lot in just about every way: ethnic, racial, cultural, economic, and geographic.[48]

Though their political activity by now was largely suburbia-based, Jews continued to play an active if reduced role in city politics. Baltimore's first elected black mayor, Kurt Schmoke, had close contacts in the Jewish community thanks to his years at City College and his membership in the Lancers, a predominantly Jewish youth club founded by Judge Robert Hammerman to mentor future leaders. Jewish advisers served in Schmoke's historic 1987 campaign and in his administration. Rochelle "Rikki" Spector joined the Baltimore City Council in 1977 serving Upper Park Heights; when she retired in 2016 she was considered the "dean of the City Council" as its longest-serving member.[49]

Jewish business leaders became less prominent in Baltimore's civic life as the twenty-first century approached—though not because they lived in the suburbs. The globalization of the economy meant that large local businesses with a stake in the city's well-being were becoming a thing of the past. This was evident in the passing of downtown department stores from the scene, but was certainly not a phenomenon confined to Jewish-owned firms. As one Center Club member pointed out, "We used to have eight local banks, four to five brokerage firms, a utility company, insurance companies, our own railroad and our phone company. Now, all those companies are gone."[50] The *Sun* recognized the implications when Willard Hackerman died in 2014. While acknowledging that the prominent builder's actions "sometimes blurred the lines of public service and private gain," an editorial commented, "his combination of civic-mindedness and financial largesse is a rarity that Baltimore might never see again. The city simply doesn't have that many large corporate headquarters and CEOs from which such a person might spring forth."[51]

Indeed, longtime Jewish civic and philanthropic leaders came to be recognized as exemplars of a dying breed. A 1990 *Baltimore Magazine* article lamented that the city's charities and cultural institutions relied on the same families for support, while "the donor pool has been ravaged by corporate takeovers." Four of the five "most generous" stalwarts cited in the article were Jewish: the Blausteins, the Meyerhoffs, Hackerman, and Robert and Ryda Hecht Levi. (The fifth was the Knott family.) The article also profiled a new player on the scene: the recent death of developer Harry Weinberg had resulted in the creation of the nation's twelfth-largest charitable foundation. Soon, thanks to the proviso that "any project receiving upwards of $200,000 must bear the name 'Harry and Jeanette Weinberg,'" the posthumous couple became associated with virtually every type of social service in the city. In death, the developer revamped his legacy from an absentee landlord known for deteriorated properties to a funder of modern new buildings that housed the elderly, served the poor and sick, and offered recreation to the young.[52]

Perhaps nostalgia for the civic leaders of the past was behind the extraordinary attention paid to the death of Walter Sondheim in 2007, at age ninety-eight. An extensive front-page *Sun* article was followed by several days' worth of stories, letters to the editor, and editorials. Governor Martin O'Malley ordered state flags to be flown at half-staff, and Sondheim's accomplishments, from the desegregation of the school system to the building of the Inner Harbor, were recounted in detail (with some exaggeration, as he would no doubt have complained). In part, the impetus for all this attention could be found in the fact that, as his obituary stated, "His life was intimately entwined with the history of Baltimore." This was something that could be said about many Jewish members of his generation, though few were in a position to contribute to the city to such an extent.[53]

Recent generations of Jewish Baltimoreans have been more likely to leave the area to make their mark and especially to find economic success beyond the opportunities now offered locally. Nevertheless, a significant share of Baltimore Jewry has demonstrated a desire to remain in the region. Four- and five-generation families are not hard to find in Northwest Baltimore. Only 5 percent of respondents in the Associated's 2010 community study planned to move outside the area in the coming five years. Interestingly, young adults (ages eighteen to thirty-four) expressed less desire to move away than did older respondents.[54] While Baltimore may have declined as a business center, its areas of strength — health, education, and the arts — still provide an economic base to sustain the Jewish community, if not to the extent that the garment industry did a century ago. Hospitals, universities, research centers, and cultural institutions offer twenty-first-century opportunities to Jews from Upper Park Heights, Pikesville, and Owings Mills to the revitalized city neighborhoods of Canton and Bolton Hill.

Jews have been critically involved in the growth of this new economy; Zanvyl Krieger's $50 million gift to the Johns Hopkins University School of Arts and Sciences in 1992 offers just one notable example.[55] They have provided leadership as well as money. For example, Fred Lazarus, scion of an Ohio-based department store family, arrived in 1978 to head the Maryland Institute College of Art and oversaw its growth from a "sleepy, second-tier art and design college" to a "world-class institution" that attracts students from around the globe. On his retirement in 2013 he was lauded for his broader contribution to the city: according to the *Sun*, he "helped pioneer the idea of institutions of higher learning as neighborhood anchors" that could lead the way in revitalizing their communities.[56]

If Baltimore Jewry is not producing as many civic-minded business leaders as it once did, Jews at the grassroots level continue to participate in efforts to build a

In the 1990s, Marc Steiner launched his first radio show to air "ideas that are never talked about and people who never talk to each other." Photo by Mary C. Gardella. *Baltimore Jewish Times Collection, Jewish Museum of Maryland.*

better Baltimore. As individuals they can be found in the ranks of activists working to alleviate homelessness, promote neighborhood development, and address other critical issues, while several Jewish institutions continue to engage in social action. For example, Beth Am synagogue—formed by a small group of committed urbanites who remained at Chizuk Amuno's Eutaw Place synagogue after Chizuk moved to the suburbs—has placed neighborhood outreach at the core of its identity. Native Baltimorean Marc Steiner and transplant David Simon have been prominent voices in the ongoing conversation about urban problems and social justice in Baltimore, Steiner through twenty-five years as host of an influential public affairs radio show and Simon through his groundbreaking TV series *The Wire*.[57] Their work has helped define the city, for good or ill.

Steiner and Simon, native and transplant, exhibit a fierce, if critical, love for their city and its eccentricities. In fact, Jewish writers, journalists, and other media figures have been among the most dedicated commentators and observers of life in Baltimore over the past half century. Two in particular—Michael Olesker and Gilbert Sandler—have chronicled the broad sweep of city life and what makes Baltimore special while also reserving a portion of their work to explore the Jewish community. Their different perspectives (Olesker is a baby boomer and a journalist; Sandler, a born storyteller, grew up in Depression era Lower Park Heights) offer complementary evocations of Baltimore's past and present: while Olesker writes of the tangled relations between blacks and Jews, Sandler reminds readers what it was like to ride the streetcars with his fellow Baltimoreans and recalls the antipathy that once existed between Jews of German and Russian descent. Both are popularizers of the notion that Baltimore is "a big city with the heart of a small town," a trope that is at the core of Baltimore's identity.[58]

The success of Sandler's book *Jewish Baltimore* (2000) showed that many Jews at the dawn of the twenty-first century were eager to explore their shared past. Indeed, ever since a group of Jewish Baltimoreans came together in 1960 to save the endangered Lloyd Street Synagogue from the wrecking ball, the Baltimore Jewish community has offered significant support to efforts to preserve and examine its own history. The Jewish Museum of Maryland, which has its roots in that successful preservation effort, grew into the nation's largest Jewish regional museum with a campus that includes not just the Lloyd Street Synagogue but its neighbor B'nai Israel and, in between, a museum building that houses an extensive archival collection of local Jewish history: in effect, the community's memory.[59] Anchored in the old immigrant neighborhood of East Baltimore, the museum remains a locus of Baltimore Jewish identity and offers a portal to the world where that identity took root.

Yet the existence of a distinct "Baltimore Jewish" identity has been tested in recent years. Divisions within the Jewish community call into question the very idea of a shared culture through which such an identity can be sustained. Meanwhile, twenty-first-century mobility and global connectedness undermine attachment to a particular city. Communities are less defined by geography than they used to be: "virtual communities" of people with shared interests have become common, and far-flung networks (always a Jewish specialty) are easier to maintain than ever, enabling people to transcend their immediate surroundings and associate with like-minded others across great distances.

But division has always characterized Baltimore Jewry and American Jewry more generally: over religion (as during the battles over reform in the late nineteenth century) or culture (Eastern Europeans versus Germans) or class (garment industry workers versus employers). In Baltimore, Jews continue to stubbornly cling together despite their differences. In the early postwar era they chose the northwest suburbs as their home, and there they remain more than a half century later—a show of stability unprecedented in their 200-plus years of history. The synagogues ranged along Park Heights Avenue tell a coherent story, from the fiercely Orthodox Shearith Israel to the south to the proudly Reform Baltimore Hebrew Congregation to the north, both founded in the nineteenth century. And in between, the modernist (in architecture and in outlook) Temple Oheb Shalom, the ultra-Orthodox Agudath Israel, the Iranian Ohr Hamizrach, and many others. Baltimore may have diverse Jewish communities, but they are nevertheless connected.[60]

Members of those various congregations have different ideas about how to interact with the surrounding society. Some try to limit their interaction as much as possible while others follow a tradition of participation in the life of their city that extends back to the days of Elkin Solomon, Jacob I. Cohen Jr., and Solomon Etting. The activities of Jewish individuals and families, businesses and philanthropies, civic and political leaders, activists and cultural figures continue to demonstrate how deeply Jews remain woven into the fabric of the region. For now, both the Baltimorean and the Jewish aspects of Baltimore Jewish identity seem secure.

Notes

Abbreviations

AA   *Afro-American* (Baltimore)

AI   *American Israelite* (Cincinnati)

AJA   American Jewish Archives (Cincinnati)

AJH   *American Jewish History*

AJHQ   *American Jewish Historical Quarterly*

AJHS   American Jewish Historical Society (New York)

ATFH   Edward S. Shapiro, *A Time for Healing: American Jewry since World War II* (Baltimore: Johns Hopkins University Press, 1995)

ATFS   Henry Feingold, *A Time for Searching: Entering the Mainstream, 1920–1945* (Baltimore: Johns Hopkins University Press, 1992)

AZJ   *Allgemeine Zeitung des Judethums*

BA   *Baltimore American*

BCD   *Baltimore city directory*

BDA   *Baltimore Daily Advertiser*

BGDA   *Baltimore Gazette and Daily Advertiser*

BJC   Baltimore Jewish Council

BNHP   Baltimore Neighborhood Heritage Project, Langsdale Library Special Collections, University of Baltimore

BP   *Baltimore Patriot*

BPEA   *Baltimore Patriot and Evening Advertiser*

BPMA   *Baltimore Patriot and Mercantile Advertiser*

COB   John Thomas Scharf, *The Chronicles of Baltimore* (Baltimore: Turnbull, 1874)

FG   *Federal Gazette*

FGBDA   *Federal Gazette and Baltimore Daily Advertiser*

JC   *Jewish Comment* (Baltimore)

JE   *Jewish Exponent* (Philadelphia)

JMM   Jewish Museum of Maryland (Baltimore)

JOB   Isidor Blum, *The Jews of Baltimore: An Historical Summary of Their Progress and Status* (Baltimore: Historical Review Publishing Company, 1910)

JT   *Jewish Times* (Baltimore)

MAJC   Isaac M. Fein, *The Making of an American Jewish Community: The History of Baltimore Jewry from 1773 to 1920* (Philadelphia: Jewish Publication Society of America, 1971)

MHM   *Maryland Historical Magazine*

MHS   Maryland Historical Society (Baltimore)

MJ   *Maryland Journal*

MJBA   *Maryland Journal and Baltimore Advertiser*

MS   manuscript

MSA   Maryland State Archives (Annapolis)

321

NIMN Antero Pietila, *Not in My
Neighborhood: How Bigotry Shaped a
Great American City* (Chicago: Ivan R.
Dee, 2010)

OH Oral history interview

PAJHS *Publications of the American
Jewish Historical Society*

SJH *Southern Jewish History*

STCM Earl Pruce, *Synagogues, Temples,
and Congregations of Maryland, 1830–
1990* (Baltimore: Jewish Historical Society
of Maryland, 1993)

TCAP Jacob Rader Marcus, *To Count a
People: American Jewish Population Data,
1585–1984* (Lanham, MD: University
Press of America, 1990)

VF vertical file

Introduction

1. Ralph Brunn memoir, 65, Memoir Collection, JMM.

2. Ibid., 67; Linda Lowe Morris, "The World of Seasoning, Baltimore Style," *Baltimore Sun*, August 1, 1982, H1; Kim Clark, "McCormick Buys Locally Invented Old Bay Crab Spice," *Baltimore Sun*, November 1, 1990, 1E.

3. Gilbert Sandler, *Small Town Baltimore: An Album of Memories* (Baltimore: Johns Hopkins University Press, 2002). Our book draws on several works on Baltimore's development: Joseph Arnold, "Thinking Big about a Big City: Baltimore, 1729–1999," in *From Mobtown to Charm City: New Perspectives on Baltimore's Past*, ed. Jessica Elfenbein, John R. Breihan, and Thomas L. Hollowak (Baltimore: Maryland Historical Society, 2002), 3–13; Robert J. Brugger, *Maryland: A Middle Temperament, 1634–1980* (Baltimore: Johns Hopkins University Press, 1996); Elizabeth Fee, Linda Shopes, and Linda Zeidman, eds., *The Baltimore Book: New Views of Local History* (Philadelphia: Temple University Press, 1993); Barbara Jeanne Fields, *Slavery and Freedom on the Middle Ground: Maryland during the Nineteenth Century* (New Haven, CT: Yale University Press, 1987); and Sherry H. Olson, *Baltimore: The Building of an American City* (Baltimore: Johns Hopkins University Press, 1980).

4. The standard work on Baltimore Jewish history is Isaac M. Fein, *The Making of an American Jewish Community: The History of Baltimore Jewry from 1773 to 1920* (Philadelphia: Jewish Publication Society of America, 1971) (hereafter *MAJC*). Though groundbreaking for its time, Fein's study ends in 1920 and was written before the development of the field of new social history. Other works include Isidor Blum, *The Jews of Baltimore* (Baltimore: Historical Review Publishing Company, 1910) (hereafter *JOB*); Philip Kahn Jr., *Uncommon Threads: Threads That Wove the Fabric of Baltimore Jewish Life* (Baltimore: PECAN Publications, 1998); and Gilbert Sandler, *Jewish Baltimore: A Family Album* (Baltimore: Johns Hopkins University Press, 2000).

The only comprehensive narrative history of a major Jewish community outside New York written in recent decades is Fred Rosenbaum, *Cosmopolitans: A Social and Cultural History of the Jews of the San Francisco Bay Area* (Berkeley: University of California Press, 2009). Most other works have been anthologies or histories that focus on a discrete time period. Among the most valuable are Jonathan D. Sarna, Ellen Smith, and Scott-Martin Kosofsky, eds., *The Jews of Boston* (New Haven, CT: Yale University Press, 2005); Deborah Dash Moore, *To the Golden Cities: Pursuing the American Jewish Dream in Miami and L.A.* (New York: Free Press, 1994); and Murray Friedman, ed., *Philadelphia Jewish Life, 1940–2000* (Philadelphia: Temple University Press, 2003).

5. Few full-length studies of Baltimore's ethnic groups exist, although works on Catholics and on the white working class have covered some of this ground. See Thomas W. Spalding, *The Premier See: A History of the Archdiocese of Baltimore* (Baltimore: Johns Hopkins Uni-

versity Press, 1989); Gilbert Sandler, *The Neighborhood: The Story of Baltimore's Little Italy* (Baltimore: Bodine, 1974); Dieter Cunz, *The Maryland Germans: A History* (Princeton, NJ: Princeton University Press, 1948); Kenneth D. Durr, *Behind the Backlash: White Working-Class Politics in Baltimore, 1940–1980* (Chapel Hill: University of North Carolina Press, 2003); Fee et al., *The Baltimore Book*.

6. Joseph L. Arnold, uncompleted manuscript on the history of Baltimore, 62, Joseph L. Arnold Papers, Special Collections, University of Maryland, Baltimore County.

7. Statistics on the Jewish population are from *TCAP*. Baltimore had the seventh-largest Jewish population in the United States around 1930 and the tenth-largest in the late twentieth century.

8. On the Eastern European Jewish immigrant community in Baltimore, see, for example, Deborah R. Weiner, Anita Kassof, and Avi Decter, eds., *Voices of Lombard Street: A Century of Change in East Baltimore* (Baltimore: Jewish Museum of Maryland, 2007).

9. *Jewish Community Study of Greater Baltimore, 1999* (Associated: Jewish Community Federation of Baltimore, 2001), vi, Baltimore Jewish Population Studies VF, JMM. In 1999, Baltimore actually had a higher percentage of Orthodox Jewish households than New York had.

10. Antero Pietila, *Not in My Neighborhood: How Bigotry Shaped a Great American City* (Chicago: Ivan R. Dee, 2010) (hereafter *NIMN*).

11. Campbell Gibson and Kay Jung, *Historical Census Statistics on Population Totals by Race, 1790 to 1990* (Washington, DC: US Census Bureau, 2005).

12. Levinson's Baltimore movies span the twentieth century and include *Diner* (1982), *Tin Men* (1987), *Avalon* (1990), and *Liberty Heights* (1999). Although all are rooted in the Baltimore Jewish experience, only the last film deals explicitly with Jewish themes.

13. In a 2010 survey of Baltimore Jews, 82 percent of respondents thought it was "very" (48 percent) or "somewhat" (34 percent) important to belong to the Jewish community. Almost 60 percent of Jewish households participated in a Jewish organization. See "2010 Greater Baltimore Jewish Community Study," Associated: Jewish Community Federation of Baltimore, 72, 83, jewishdatabank.org.

Chapter 1.
Baltimore's First Jews

1. *Massachusetts Centinel* (Boston), Sept. 16, 1786, 4; S. Broches, *Jews in New England: Six Monographs* (New York: Bloch, 1942), 61–65; Lee Max Friedman, "Miscellanea," *PAJHS* 40 (1950–1951): 76–80.

2. Chancery Court, Chancery Papers, Aug. 29, 1799, 428, MSA.

3. Ibid.; Robert E. Wright, *The Wealth of Nations Reconsidered: Integration and Expansion in American Financial Markets, 1780–1850* (Cambridge: Cambridge University Press, 2002), 123–30; Robert A. East, *Business Enterprise in the American Revolutionary Era* (New York: Columbia University Press, 1938), 269–73.

4. *MJBA*, Oct. 24, 1786, 4.

5. *Federal Intelligencer*, May 26, 1795, 3; *FG*, Jan. 25, 1798, 4; *American and Commercial Daily Advertiser*, May 30, 1809, 3.

6. *MAJC*, 13–25; Aaron Baroway, "Solomon Etting, 1764–1847," *MHM* 15 (Mar. 1920): 1–20; Aaron Baroway, "The Cohens of Maryland," *MHM* 18 (Dec. 1923): 355–75; 19 (Mar. 1924): 54–71; and W. Ray Luce, "The Cohen Brothers of Baltimore: From Lotteries to Banking," *MHM* 68 (Fall 1973): 288–308. Ira Rosenwaike provides the most comprehensive account of

early Baltimore Jewry in his three-article series: "The Jews of Baltimore to 1810," *AJHQ* 64 (June 1975): 291–320; "The Jews of Baltimore: 1810 to 1820," *AJHQ* 67 (Dec. 1977): 101–24; and "The Jews of Baltimore: 1820 to 1830," *AJHQ* 67 (Mar. 1978): 246–59.

7. This finding is based on a survey of all the marriages mentioned in Rosenwaike's articles (see previous note) and those listed in Bill Reamy and Martha Reamy, *Records of St. Paul's Parish: The Anglican Church Records of Baltimore City and Lower Baltimore County*, 2 vols. (Westminster, MD: Family Line Publications, 1988); and Henry C. Peden Jr., *Methodist Records of Baltimore City, Maryland*, vol. 1 (Westminster, MD: Family Line Publications, 1994).

8. Rosenwaike, "Jews of Baltimore: 1810 to 1820," 101; Lance J. Sussman, *Isaac Leeser and the Making of American Judaism* (Detroit, MI: Wayne State University Press, 1995), 33; *TCAP*.

9. Ira Rosenwaike, *On the Edge of Greatness: A Portrait of American Jewry in the Early National Period* (Cincinnati, OH: American Jewish Archives, 1985), 31.

10. Eric L. Goldstein, *Traders and Transports: The Jews of Colonial Maryland* (Baltimore: Jewish Historical Society of Maryland, 1993), 2, 19.

11. Ibid., 2, 6–14. For the argument that Maryland was religiously forbidding to Jews, see Benjamin H. Hartogensis, "Ye Jew Doctor and Maryland," in his *Studies in the History of Maryland*, ed. Simon Cohen (Baltimore: N.p., 1939), 76–85; Jacob H. Hollander, "Some Unpublished Material Relating to Dr. Jacob Lumbrozo of Maryland," *PAJHS* 1 (1893): 25–39; and Hollander, "The Civil Status of the Jews in Maryland, 1634–1776," *PAJHS* 2 (1894): 33–44. More recent scholarship on the politics of religion in seventeenth-century Maryland includes John D. Krugler, *English and Catholic: The Lords Baltimore in the Seventeenth Century* (Baltimore: Johns Hopkins University Press, 2004); and Maura Jane Farrelly, *Papist Patriots: The Making of an American Catholic Identity* (Oxford: Oxford University Press, 2012).

12. Goldstein, *Traders and Transports*, 14–26, 38–47; Jacob Rader Marcus, *The Colonial American Jew, 1492–1776* (Detroit, MI: Wayne State University Press, 1970), 239, 336–39; Paul Gordon and Rita Gordon, *The Jews beneath the Clustered Spires* (Hagerstown, MD: Hagerstown Bookbinding and Printing, 1971), chap. 1.

13. Goldstein, *Traders and Transports*, 27–36.

14. Proceedings of the Old Bailey, oldbaileyonline.org, case no. t17631019-38; *Maryland Gazette*, July 12, 1764, 3.

15. *Pennsylvania Gazette*, Dec. 25, 1766, 2 (Levy Barnett), and Jan. 10, 1771, 4 (Abraham Peters); Baltimore County Convict Record, 1770–1783, 331–33, 335, 383–89, MSA (Charles Barew, Henry Hart, Samuel Jacobs, Hart Levy, Benjamin Phillips); Account of Servants for Stevenson, Randolph and Cheston, 1774–1775, Cheston-Galloway Papers, box 6, MHS (Benjamin Solomon aka Solomon Wolfe; Emanuel Miers). On the phenomenon of convict servants more generally, see E. Robert Ekirch, *Bound for America: The Transportation of British Convicts to the American Colonies, 1718–1775* (Oxford: Clarendon, 1987).

16. Clarence P. Gould, "The Economic Causes of the Rise of Baltimore," in *Essays in Colonial History Presented to Charles McLean Andrews* (New Haven, CT: Books for Libraries Press, 1931), 238; Rosenwaike, "Jews of Baltimore to 1810," 292–93.

17. Rosenwaike, "Jews of Baltimore to 1810," 292–93.

18. Ibid., 295–98, 299–300; Goldstein, *Traders and Transports*, 49.

19. Michael Gratz to Barnard Gratz, July 6, 1770, in William Vincent Byars, ed., *B. and M. Gratz: Merchants in Philadelphia, 1754–1798* (Jefferson City, MO: Hugh Stephens, 1916), 111.

20. Worthington C. Ford et al., eds., *Journals of the Continental Congress, 1774–1789* (Washington, DC: US Government Printing Office, 1904–1937), 6:1046.

21. Miriam Gratz to Michael Gratz, June 2, 1777; and Thomas Burling to Michael Gratz, June 26, 1777, both in Byars, *B. and M. Gratz*, 164–66.

22. Rosenwaike, "Jews of Baltimore to 1810," 299–300, 304; *MJ*, Jan. 14, 1785, 2; *MJBA*, Apr. 18, 1786, 3.

23. Rosenwaike, "Jews of Baltimore to 1810," 304–5.

24. *Decennial Register of the Pennsylvania Society of Sons of the American Revolution, 1888–1898* (Philadelphia: Lippincott, 1898), 299; John Wolf Jordan, *Colonial and Revolutionary Families of Pennsylvania: Genealogical and Personal Memoirs* (New York: Lewis Publishing, 1911), 3:1243.

25. Rosenwaike, "Jews of Baltimore to 1810," 300.

26. Ibid., 301-2n32. On Isaac Solomon's residence in St. Eustatius, see *JOB*, 4.

27. Rosenwaike, "Jews of Baltimore: 1810 to 1820," 106–7; Malcolm H. Stern, "Moses Myers and the Early Jewish Community of Norfolk," *Journal of the Southern Jewish Historical Society* 1 (1958): 5–13; "The Myers Family," chrysler.org/about-the-museum/historic-houses/the-moses-myers-house/the-myers-family.

28. Gary Lawson Browne, *Baltimore in the Nation, 1789–1861* (Chapel Hill: University of North Carolina Press, 1980), 64.

29. *Baltimore Price Courant*, May 3, 1817, 3; *BP*, May 12, 1817, 2; *BPMA*, May 26, 1817, 3; Mar. 31, 1818, 1; Apr. 2, 1818, 3; May 7, 1818, 1; Aug. 15, 1818, 3; Sept. 15, 1818, 3; Mar. 6, 1819, 3; Mar. 10, 1819, 3; Mar. 16, 1819, 1.

30. Quoted in Rosenwaike, "Jews of Baltimore: 1810 to 1820," 107.

31. Ibid.; "The Myers Family."

32. Browne, *Baltimore in the Nation*, 26–27, 51–54, 70–76.

33. Ira Rosenwaike, "An Estimate and Analysis of the Jewish Population of the United States in 1790," *PAJHS* 50 (Sept. 1960): 23–67; Malcolm H. Stern, "The 1820s: American Jewry Comes of Age," in *Bicentennial Festschrift for Jacob Rader Marcus*, ed. Bertram Wallace Korn (New York: KTAV Publishing, 1976), 539–49.

34. Herbert Ezekiel, "The Jews of Richmond," *PAJHS* 4 (1896): 21; *American and Commercial Daily Advertiser*, Jan. 1, 1807, 1.

35. Rosenwaike, "Jews of Baltimore to 1810," 314; Baroway, "The Cohens of Maryland," 357–75; Luce, "Cohen Brothers."

36. Rosenwaike, "Jews of Baltimore to 1810," 292–93, 300–308; David Brener, "Lancaster's First Jewish Community, 1715–1804: The Era of Joseph Simon," *Journal of the Lancaster County Historical Society* 80 (1976): 265–319; *Washington Spy* (Hagerstown, MD), Apr. 21, 1795; June 23, 1795; Jan. 16, 1797.

37. *Columbian Mirror and Alexandria* (VA) *Gazette*, Apr. 24, 1800, 1; Guido Kisch, "German Jews in White Labor Servitude in America," *PAJHS* 34 (1937): 11–49; Rosenwaike, "Jews of Baltimore to 1810," 315–19; J. Hall Pleasants and Howard Sill, *Maryland Silversmiths, 1715–1830* (Baltimore: Lord Baltimore Press, 1930), 99, 114, 164, 284, 286.

38. Rosenwaike, "Jews of Baltimore to 1810," 315–19; Rosenwaike, "Jews of Baltimore: 1810 to 1820."

39. Rutter and Etting Account Book (1796–1802), MS 2193, MHS; *MJ*, Jan. 3, 1794, 4; *FG*, Nov. 22, 1796, 1; Nov. 9, 1797, 4; Jan. 25, 1799, 4; *American and Commercial Daily Advertiser*, Apr. 4, 1809, 1; Joseph L. Blau and Salo W. Baron, eds., *Jews of the United States, 1790–1840: A Documentary History* (New York: Columbia University Press, 1963), 1:141.

40. *FG*, Apr. 27, 1796, 2; *MJ*, Oct. 24, 1783; Mar. 5, 1784; June 15, 1784; *BDA*, Jan. 26, 1798, 4.

41. *BCD*, 1807.

42. Luce, "Cohen Brothers"; Rosenwaike, "Jews of Baltimore to 1810," 300; *Democratic Republican and Commercial Daily Advertiser*, June 16, 1802, 1.

43. *MJ*, Aug. 15, 1786, 3; Chancery Papers, 1799, case 3249 (Insolvent Estate of Jacob F. Levy), MSA; *Federal Intelligencer and Baltimore Daily Gazette*, Nov., 25, 1794, 1; *Democratic Republican and Commercial Daily Advertiser*, Aug. 13, 1802, 2; *MJBA*, Oct. 24, 1786, 4; *Federal Intelligencer*, May 26, 1795, 3; *FG*, Jan. 25, 1798, 4; *American and Commercial Daily Advertiser*, May 30, 1809, 3; Rosenwaike, "Jews of Baltimore to 1810," 298, 300.

44. *BP*, Feb. 17, 1813, 1; June 17, 1816, 4; Rosenwaike, "Jews of Baltimore to 1810," 306–8.

45. Rosenwaike, "Jews of Baltimore to 1810," 294–95; Rosenwaike, "Jews of Baltimore: 1810 to 1820," 103.

46. Ezekiel, "Jews of Richmond"; Robert Harry McIntire, "Pryse, Thomas," in his *Annapolis, Maryland, Families* (Baltimore: Gateway, 1979); Reamy and Reamy, *Records of St. Paul's Parish*, 2:28, 49, 66, 107, 119.

47. Edwin Wolf 2nd and Maxwell Whiteman, *The History of the Jews of Philadelphia from Colonial Times to the Age of Jackson* (Philadelphia: Jewish Publication Society of America, 1957), chap. 1; Reamy and Reamy, *Records of St. Paul's Parish*, 2:32.

48. Reamy and Reamy, *Records of St. Paul's Parish*, 2:22, 56.

49. Rosenwaike, "Jews of Baltimore to 1810," 303.

50. Ibid., 316; Pleasants and Sill, *Maryland Silversmiths*, 99.

51. Rosenwaike, "Jews of Baltimore to 1810," 317–18.

52. Ibid., 303, 307–8, 316–17; Rosenwaike, "The Jews of Baltimore: 1810 to 1820," 104, 108, 111–12, 119, 122; Rosenwaike, "Jews of Baltimore: 1820 to 1830," 252 ; Reamy and Reamy, *Records of St. Paul's Parish*, 1:68, 110, 122; 2:22, 32, 40, 56, 66; Peden, *Methodist Records of Baltimore City*, 1:22, 31, 34, 67, 68.

53. Three of the Etting sisters—Kitty, Hetty, and Sally—remained single, as did Jacob I. Cohen Jr., his brothers Mendes and Joshua, and their sister Maria. See Malcolm H. Stern, *First American Jewish Families: 600 Genealogies, 1654–1988*, 3rd ed. (Baltimore: Ottenheimer, 1991), 32, 67.

54. Malcolm H. Stern, "Two Jewish Functionaries in Colonial Pennsylvania," *AJHQ* 57 (Sept. 1967): 35–48; Wolf and Whiteman, *History of the Jews of Philadelphia*, 125; Charlotte Louise Sturm, "A Consuming Heritage: Baltimore's Eastern European Jewish Immigrant Community and Their Evolving Foodways, 1880–1939," MA thesis, University of Maryland, College Park, 2013, 32–36.

55. Rosenwaike, "Jews of Baltimore to 1810," 313.

56. *MAJC*, 25.

57. Rosenwaike, "Jews of Baltimore to 1810," 315–17; Rosenwaike, "Jews of Baltimore: 1810–1820," 111–14, 115–17.

58. Peden, *Methodist Records of Baltimore City*, 1:68. The marriage of Levi Benjamin and Rachel Herron in 1817 seems to be another example of this trend. See ibid., 1:67; and Rosenwaike, "Jews of Baltimore: 1810 to 1820," 110.

59. Rosenwaike, "Jews of Baltimore to 1810," 296; Reamy and Reamy, *Records of St. Paul's Parish*, 1:84; 2:11, 33, 52, 74, 85.

60. *MAJC*, 19–20; *Memoirs of the Dead and Tomb's Remembrancer* (Baltimore: Printed for the Editors, 1806), 100, 111; Jane B. Wilson, *The Very Quiet Baltimoreans* (Shippensburg, PA: White Mane, 1991), 70–75; Robert L. Weinberg, *The Murder of a Graveyard* (Baltimore: Jewish Historical Society of Maryland, 1990).

61. Rosenwaike, "Jews of Baltimore: 1810 to 1820," 112, 118.

62. Ibid., 112–13.

63. *BPMA*, Apr. 27, 1820, 3; Dec. 1, 1820, 3; Feb. 13, 1822, 3; Luce, "Cohen Brothers," 291–92.

64. *BPEA*, June 21, 1814, 1.

65. Edward Eitches, "Maryland's 'Jew Bill,'" *AJHQ* 60 (Mar. 1971): 258–78; E. Milton Altfeld, *The Jews' Struggle for Civil and Religious Freedom in Maryland* (Baltimore: M. Curlander, 1924); Blau and Baron, *Jews of the United States*, 1:33–55.

66. Baroway, "The Cohens of Maryland," 369; *BGDA*, Feb. 25, 1832, 1.

67. *BGDA*, Feb. 25, 1832, 1.

68. Charles G. Steffen, *From Gentlemen to Townsmen: The Gentry of Baltimore County, Maryland, 1660–1776* (Lexington: University Press of Kentucky, 1993), 163; Robert Brugger, *Maryland: A Middle Temperament* (Baltimore: Johns Hopkins University Press, 1996), 102, 144; Suzanne Ellery Greene, *Baltimore: An Illustrated History* (Woodland Hills, CA: Windsor Hill, 1980), 18, 20, 28.

69. Terry Bilhartz, *Urban Religion and the Second Great Awakening: Church and Society in Early National Baltimore* (Rutherford, NJ: Fairleigh Dickinson University Press, 1986), 123; Louis P. Hennighausen, comp., *History of the German Society of Maryland* (Baltimore: Sun Job Printing, 1909), 174–76.

70. Christopher Phillips, *Freedom's Port: The African American Community of Baltimore, 1790–1860* (Urbana: University of Illinois Press, 1997), 32–34; Rosenwaike, "Jews of Baltimore to 1810," 319; Rosenwaike, "Jews of Baltimore: 1810–1820," 123; and Rosenwaike, "Jews of Baltimore: 1820–1830," 258 (corrections have been made for Jews known to be missing in Rosenwaike's accounting).

71. *BGDA*, Jan. 30, 1828, 2; J. H. B. Latrobe, *Maryland in Liberia* (Baltimore: Maryland Historical Society, 1885), 29n1. For other histories of the society, see Penelope Campbell, *Maryland in Africa: The Maryland State Colonization Society, 1831–1857* (Urbana: University of Illinois Press, 1971); and Richard L. Hall, *On Afric's Shore: A History of Maryland in Liberia, 1834–1857* (Baltimore: Maryland Historical Society, 2003).

72. Frank A. Cassell, "The Structure of Baltimore's Politics in the Age of Jefferson, 1795–1812," in *Law, Society, and Politics in Early Maryland*, ed. Aubrey C. Land, Lois Green Carr, and Edward C. Papenfuse (Baltimore: Johns Hopkins University Press, 1977), 279.

73. Ibid., 281; Rosenwaike, "Jews of Baltimore to 1810," 302; "Letters and Documents: Postscript to Sterett-Hadfield Duel," *MHM* 6 (Sept. 1911): 274–75; *MJ*, Oct. 1, 1790, 3; Oct. 5, 1790, 1; May 8, 1792, 3; May 15, 1792, 3; Aug. 28, 1792, 4; June 18, 1793, 4; *Edward's BDA*, Dec. 24, 1793, 1; *FG*, Dec. 26, 1798, 2; Dec. 31, 1798, 3.

74. Samuel Smith to James Madison, May 26, 1801, in *The Papers of James Madison: Secretary of State Series*, ed. Robert J. Brugger et al. (Charlottesville: University of Virginia Press, 1986), 1:230–31; *FG*, May 29, 1801, 3.

75. *COB*, 262.

76. *Baltimore Daily Intelligencer*, June 9, 1794, 3; *FGBDA*, Dec. 23, 1796, 3; Apr. 26, 1796, 3.

77. *FGBDA*, Jan. 19, 1796, 4; Apr. 5, 1796, 3; *North American and Mercantile Daily Advertiser*, Feb. 3, 1808, 3; *BPEA*, Feb. 9, 1814, 3.

78. *FGBDA*, Feb. 10, 1796, 1; Aug. 23, 1796, 3.

79. *Maryland Herald and Hagerstown Weekly Advertiser*, Mar. 28, 1804, 1; *BP*, July 7, 1813, 3; Nov. 12, 1822, 2.

80. *Republican Star; or, Eastern Shore General Advertiser* (Easton, MD), Sept. 3, 1805, 4; *BP*, May 7, 1813, 3; Apr. 3, 1822, 2.

81. *Republican Star* (Easton, MD), Mar. 29, 1803, 3.

----

82. See *BPMA*, Sept. 2, 1818, 2; Sept. 24, 1821, 3.

83. Baroway, "The Cohens of Maryland," 369. On the early history of the Mechanical Company of Baltimore, see Charles G. Steffen, *The Mechanics of Baltimore: Workers and Politics in the Age of Revolution, 1763-1812* (Urbana: University of Illinois Press, 1984).

84. *MJ*, Nov. 4, 1793, 1; *Edward's BDA*, Dec. 24, 1793, 1; July 16, 1794, 3; *FG*, Apr. 30, 1796, 3; Aug. 14, 1798, 4; *COB*, 248; *Republican; or Anti-Democrat*, May 6, 1803, 3.

85. Ira Rosenwaike, "Simon Magruder Levy: West Point Graduate," *AJHQ* 61 (1971-1972): 69-73; Brener, "Lancaster's First Jewish Community," 256.

86. William M. Marine, *The British Invasion of Maryland, 1812-1815* (Baltimore: Society of the War of 1812 in Maryland, 1913), 133-34, 139-41.

87. Robert Fulton to Solomon Etting, Nov. 26, 1814, in Blau and Baron, *Jews of the United States*, 1:118.

88. Leon Huhner, "Jews in the War of 1812," *PAJHS* 26 (1918): 186-88, gives a list of Jewish participants in the war, but most of the names are suspect. We have included here only the names of those whom other sources make clear were Jews.

89. Baroway, "The Cohens of Maryland," 371-73.

90. Ibid. On Etting's injury, see Marine, *British Invasion*, 172-73.

91. Marine, *British Invasion*, 249, 356, 386; *Matchett's BCD*, 1814; Pleasants and Sill, *Maryland Silversmiths*, 99; Rosenwaike, "Jews of Baltimore to 1810," 318.

92. *BP*, Apr. 17, 1815, 3.

93. Brugger, *Maryland: A Middle Temperament*, 228-29; Eitches, "Maryland's 'Jew Bill,'" 258, 262-64.

94. Eitches, "Maryland's 'Jew Bill,'" 264.

95. Cohen to Ebenezer S. Thomas, Dec. 16, 1818, in Blau and Baron, *Jews of the United States*, 1:36.

96. Jacob I. Cohen Jr. to Mordecai M. Noah, Feb. 2, 1819, in Blau and Baron, *Jews of the United States*, 1:45.

97. Eitches, "Maryland's 'Jew Bill,'" 266-67; *Niles' Weekly Register*, Dec. 28, 1822, 262.

98. *BPMA*, Sept. 27, 1823, 2.

99. *Speeches on the Jew Bill in the House of Delegates of Maryland* (Philadelphia: J. Dobson, 1829), 101-56; John McMahon, *Remarks of John McMahon, in House of Delegates of Maryland, on 28th January, 1824* (Hagerstown, MD: W. D. Bell, 1824); Eitches, "Maryland's 'Jew Bill,'" 267-68, 270, 277. Already after the 1819 defeat of the bill, Cohen had expressed his feeling that it was more strategic for its advocates to address the lack of Jewish civil rights only and not to aim for the "universal toleration" of minority groups. See Cohen to Noah, Feb. 2, 1819.

100. Blau and Baron, *Jews of the United States*, 1:53. For charges during the course of the bill's progress that it would give license to "infidels" and "blasphemers," see *BPMA*, Sept. 3, 1823, 2; Sept. 15, 1823, 2.

101. Eitches, "Maryland's 'Jew Bill,'" 268.

102. *Speeches on the Jew Bill*, 69, 114; *BPMA*, July 2, 1819, 2; June 4, 1822, 2.

103. *Speeches on the Jew Bill*, 114.

104. When Worthington told this story to the General Assembly in 1824, he claimed that Cohen was unable to accept the commission "in consequence of the existence of the test law." *Speeches on the Jew Bill*, 114; Baroway, "The Cohens of Maryland," 55-56; *BPMA*, Mar. 7, 1823, 3.

105. *Speeches on the Jew Bill*, 129.

106. *BGDA*, Nov. 5, 1829, 2

- - - - - - - - - - - - -

107. Brugger, *Maryland: A Middle Temperament*, 187–88, 198–206.

108. Ibid., Feb. 25, 1832, 1; Luce, "Cohen Brothers."

109. Rosenwaike, "Jews of Baltimore: 1820 to 1830," 247–55.

110. See Wendy A. Woloson, *In Hock: Pawning in America from Independence through the Great Depression* (Chicago: University of Chicago Press, 2009).

111. *BPMA*, Dec. 14, 1821, 3.

112. The letter is reproduced in *PAJHS* 27 (1920): 233–35.

113. Rosenwaike, "Jews of Baltimore: 1820 to 1830," 257.

Chapter 2.
A "City and Mother in Israel"

1. *Sun*, Dec. 16, 1880, 1.

2. Ibid.

3. For estimates of the Jewish population in these cities, see I. J. Benjamin, *Three Years in America, 1859–1862*, trans. Charles Reznikoff (Philadelphia: Jewish Publication Society of America, 1956), 1:304–5.

4. Avraham Barkai, *Branching Out: German-Jewish Immigration to the United States, 1820–1914* (New York: Holmes and Meier, 1994), 55, 69–70, 136; Fred Rosenbaum, *Cosmopolitans: A Social and Cultural History of the Jews of the San Francisco Bay Area* (Berkeley: University of California Press, 2009), 25; *Statistics of Jews of the United States* (Philadelphia: Union of American Hebrew Congregations, 1880), 9, 11, 15, 19, 35, 48.

5. This Hebrew moniker (*ir ve-em be-Yisrael*) for great centers of Jewish learning and piety is derived from the Bible: 2 Samuel 20:19. Jacob Rader Marcus, the late "dean" of American Jewish historians, used this phrase to describe Baltimore during the subsequent period of Eastern European Jewish immigration, but given the city's more significant national profile during the mid-nineteenth century, it is even more appropriately applied to these years. See Marcus, *United States Jewry, 1776–1985* (Detroit, MI: Wayne State University Press, 1993), 3:101.

6. Finding aid for the Breidenbach Jewish Community Collection, Leo Baeck Institute, Center for Jewish History, New York; Paul Arnsberg, *Die Jüdischen Gemeinden in Hessen* (Frankfurt am Main: Societäts, 1971), 1:90–92.

7. *JOB*, 165.

8. *AZJ*, May 15, 1848.

9. Charles Behrend Sonneborn, *Sonneborn: The Next Generations* (N.p.: Privately published, 1993), 4–6.

10. Michael Meyer, ed., *German-Jewish History in Modern Times* (New York: Columbia University Press, 1997), vol. 2, chaps. 1–3; Barkai, *Branching Out*, chap. 1; Hasia Diner, *A Time for Gathering: The Second Migration, 1820–1880* (Baltimore: Johns Hopkins University Press, 1992), chaps. 1–2.

11. Meyer, *German-Jewish History*, vol. 2, chaps. 1, 8 (esp. 24, 29, 47, 297, 293); James F. Harris, *The People Speak! Anti-Semitism and Emancipation in Nineteenth-Century Bavaria* (Ann Arbor: University of Michigan Press, 1994).

12. Alexandra Lee Levin, *Vision: A Biography of Harry Friedenwald* (Philadelphia: Jewish Publication Society of America, 1964), 5–7.

13. Barkai, *Branching Out*, chap. 1; Diner, *Time for Gathering*, chap. 2.

14. Figures were calculated from a survey of Jewish names in Robert Andrew Oszakiewski, comp., *Maryland Naturalization Abstracts*, vol. 1: *Baltimore County and Baltimore City, 1784–1851* (Berwyn Heights, MD: Heritage, 2009).

---

15. Rudolf Glanz, "The 'Bayer' and the 'Pollack' in America," *Jewish Social Studies* 17 (Jan. 1955): 27–42.

16. Oszakiewski, *Maryland Naturalization Abstracts*.

17. *STCM*, 47, 48, 99.

18. Steven M. Lowenstein, *The Mechanics of Change: Essays in the Social History of German Jewry* (Atlanta, GA: Scholars Press, 1992), chap. 1.

19. The "German" identity of Jewish immigrants from the German states and from Central Europe more broadly has been a topic of heated debate. See Michael A. Meyer, "German Jewish Identity in Nineteenth Century America," in *Toward Modernity: The European Jewish Model*, ed. Jacob Katz (New York: Transaction, 1987), 247–67; and Tobias Brinkmann, "Jews, Germans, or Americans? German-Jewish Immigrants in the Nineteenth-Century United States," in *The Heimat Abroad: The Boundaries of Germanness*, ed. Krista O'Donnell, Renate Bridenthal, and Nancy Reagin (Ann Arbor: University of Michigan Press, 2005).

20. Dean R. Esslinger, "Immigration through the Port of Baltimore," in *Forgotten Doors: The Other Ports of Entry to the United States*, ed. M. Mark Stolarik (Cranbury, NJ: Associated University Presses, 1988), 61–74; Sherry H. Olson, *Baltimore: The Building of an American City* (Baltimore: Johns Hopkins University Press, 1980), 91; Moses Aberbach, "The Early German Jews of Baltimore," *Report of the Society for the History of the Germans in Maryland* 35 (1972): 29–30.

21. Campbell Gibson, *Population of the 100 Largest Cities and Other Urban Places in the United States: 1790 to 1990* (Washington, DC: US Bureau of the Census, 1998), tables 6, 7, and 8, census.gov/population/www/documentation/twps0027/twps0027.html.

22. Robert J. Brugger, *Maryland: A Middle Temperament, 1634–1980* (Baltimore: Johns Hopkins University Press, 1996), 196, 203, 251–52; Leonard Rogoff, *Down Home: Jewish Life in North Carolina* (Chapel Hill: University of North Carolina Press, 2010), 53, 61, 87–88. An excellent illustration of Baltimore's role as a hub for Jews in these regions is provided by two circumcision record books of the period: Elizabeth Kessin Berman, "M. S. Polack's Circumcision Record Book: A Record of 911 Jewish Families from 1836–1862," *Generations* (Fall 1989): 10–16; Eric L. Goldstein, "Daniel Herman's Circumcision Record Book, 1852–1870," *Generations* (Summer 1991): 11–15.

23. Simeon Hecht memoir (as told by Meyer Hecht), 1–10, Memoir Collection, JMM.

24. For an excellent study of a Jewish ethnic economy in a different American setting during this period, see William Toll, *The Making of an Ethnic Middle Class: Portland Jewry over Four Generations* (Albany: State University of New York Press, 1982), chap. 1.

25. Dean Krimmel, "Merchant Princes and Their Palaces: The Emergence of Department Stores in Baltimore," in *Enterprising Emporiums: The Jewish Department Stores of Downtown Baltimore*, ed. Avi Y. Decter and Melissa Martens (Baltimore: Jewish Museum of Maryland, 2001), 16–18; Eric L. Goldstein, "Beyond Lombard Street: Jewish Life in Maryland's Small Towns," in *We Call This Place Home: Jewish Life in Maryland's Small Towns*, ed. Karen Falk and Avi Decter (Baltimore: Jewish Museum of Maryland, 2002), 29.

26. All statistics in this paragraph are based on our analysis of the 1845 *BCD*.

27. Eric L. Goldstein, "A Different Kind of Neighborhood: Central European Jews and the Origins of Jewish East Baltimore," in *Voices of Lombard Street: A Century of Change in East Baltimore*, ed. Deborah R. Weiner, Anita Kassof, and Avi Decter (Baltimore: Jewish Museum of Maryland, 2007), 26–29.

28. Ibid.; Alfred Pairpoint, *Uncle Sam and His Country; or, Sketches of America in 1854-55-56* (London: Simpkin, Marshall, 1857), 220.

29. Philip Kahn Jr., *A Stitch in Time: The Four Seasons of Baltimore's Needle Trades* (Baltimore: Maryland Historical Society, 1989), 25–28.

30. *JOB*, 7–8. The United Hebrew Benevolent Society should not be confused with the Hebrew Benevolent Society, mentioned at the beginning of this chapter. The latter organization had its roots in the Hebrew Assistance Society, founded in 1846, which was reorganized as the Hebrew Benevolent Society in 1856. By that time the United Hebrew Benevolent Society had passed out of existence.

31. The founding of the Hebrew Assistance Society is often incorrectly dated to 1843, as in *MAJC*, 74. The date of 1846 provided in *JOB*, 9, is correct, as evidenced by the society's announcement of its "second anniversary ball" in the *Sun*, Dec. 16, 1848, 3. For the founding of B'nai B'rith in Baltimore, see *MAJC*, 130.

32. *JOB*, 133, 137; Krimmel, "Merchant Princes," 17.

33. *Sun*, May 4, 1848, 1.

34. Ibid., Dec. 29, 1851, 1.

35. Carla L. Reyes, "Naturalization Law, Immigration Flow, and Policy," in *Transforming America: Perspectives on U.S. Immigration*, ed. Michael C. LeMay (Santa Barbara, CA: Praeger, 2013), 152.

36. *BGDA*, July 29, 1834, 2; Sept. 17, 1834, 2; Oct. 13, 1834, 3; Jan. 20, 1835, 2; *Sun*, Oct. 24, 1837, 2; Jan. 3, 1838, 3; Feb. 16, 1839, 1; Apr. 17, 1839, 2; June 18, 1839, 3; Aug. 5, 1839, 2. On the rise of the Whigs in Baltimore, see W. Wayne Smith, *Anti-Jacksonian Politics along the Chesapeake* (New York: Garland, 1989), chap. 4.

37. *BGDA*, Sept. 8, 1834, 2; June 25, 1835, 2.

38. Robert E. Shalhope, *The Baltimore Bank Riot: Political Upheaval in Antebellum Maryland* (Urbana: University of Illinois Press, 2009), 62–63, 72, 81, 85; David Grimstead, "Rioting in Its Jacksonian Setting," *American Historical Review* 77 (Apr. 1972): 387–89; Frank Otto Gatell, ed., "Roger B. Taney, the Bank of Maryland, and a Whiff of Grapeshot," *MHM* 59 (Sept. 1964): 266. Roger Brooke Taney, writing to Vice President Martin Van Buren, claimed that John Dyer was the "Captain of the Mob, and directed all of its operations." It is obvious that he meant Leon Dyer, since he described his subject as having "fled from the State" and having been "first Vice President of the Young Men's Whig Committee." Bernard Steiner, "Taney's Correspondence with Van Buren," *MHM* 8 (Dec. 1913): 313.

39. Rose Greenberg, *The Chronicle of Baltimore Hebrew Congregation, 1830–1975* (Baltimore: Baltimore Hebrew Congregation, 1976), 10; Ira Rosenwaike, "Leon Dyer: Baltimore and San Francisco Jewish Leader," *Western States Jewish Historical Quarterly* 9 (1977): 135–43.

40. Aberbach, "Early German Jews," 181–82; Jean H. Baker, *Ambivalent Americans: The Know-Nothing Party in Maryland* (Baltimore: Johns Hopkins University Press, 1977); Benjamin Tuska, *Know-Nothingism in Baltimore, 1854–1860* (N.p.: Privately published, c. 1930). For the national context, see Bertram W. Korn, "The Know-Nothing Movement and the Jews," in his *Eventful Years and Experiences: Studies in Nineteenth Century American Jewish History* (Cincinnati, OH: American Jewish Archives, 1954), 58–78. In Baltimore, as the evidence presented here demonstrates, the Know Nothings were not as benign toward Jews as Korn suggests.

41. *Sun*, Sept. 10, 1850, 1.

42. Harry Friedenwald, ed., *Life, Letters, and Addresses of Aaron Friedenwald, M.D.* (Baltimore: Lord Baltimore Press, 1906), 29–30.

43. Hecht memoir, 22; *The Miscellaneous Documents Printed by Order of the House of Representatives* (Washington, DC: James B. Steedman, 1858), 163–64, 322–31, 366–88, 400–418, 429–32, 438–45, 834; House of Delegates of the State of Maryland, *Papers in the Contested*

Election Case from Baltimore City (Annapolis: B. H. Richardson, 1860), 118–19. See also *Sun,* Oct. 9, 1856, 1, for the case of Simon Frank, whose son was shot during an Election Day riot when walking home from synagogue on Yom Kippur.

44. Neander later worked as a Presbyterian missionary. Pamela Douglas Webster, "John Neander: The Presbyterian Board of Foreign Missions and Proselytizing the Jews, 1848–1876," *Journal of Presbyterian History* 75 (Spring 1997): 1–12.

45. Max Eichhorn, *Evangelizing the American Jew* (New York: Jonathan David Publishers, 1978), 82–83, 85, 92. See also the ASMCJ's journal, *Jewish Chronicle* 1 (Apr. 1845): 272–75; 2 (Dec. 1845): 191–92.

46. Eichhorn, *Evangelizing the American Jew,* 92; *Nineteenth Annual Report of the Board of Foreign Missions of the Presbyterian Church in the United States of America* (New York: Board of Foreign Missions, 1856), 103.

47. Twelve years later, Fuld renounced Christianity and returned to Judaism. *Jewish Messenger,* July 20, 1860, 21. For other Jews who converted, see *Jewish Herald* 1 (Sept. 1846): 225; (Nov. 1846): 282; *Twenty-Fourth Report of the American Society for the Melioration of the Condition of the Jews* (New York: American Society for the Melioration of the Condition of the Jews, 1847), 31.

48. Louis Hennighausen, "Reminiscences of the Political Life of German-Americans in Baltimore during 1850–1860," *Report of the Society for the History of the Germans in Maryland* 7 (1892–1893): 53–59; 11–12 (1897–1898): 3–18.

49. *Sun,* June 9, 1843, 2. Biographical information is from the Simpson Papers, JMM.

50. Felix Reichmann, "German Printing in Maryland: A Checklist, 1768–1950," *Report of the Society for the History of the Germans in Maryland* 27 (1950): 24; Dieter Cunz, *The Maryland Germans: A History* (Princeton, NJ: Princeton University Press, 1948), 255–56; Salomon Ephraim Blogg, *Erzählungen Meiner Erlebnisse* (Hannover, Germany: Telgener, 1856), 15.

51. Gustav Adolf Zimmerman, *Deutsch in Amerika: Beiträge zur Geschichte der Deutsch-Amerikanischen Literatur* (Chicago: Ackermann and Eyler, 1892), 28; *Sun,* Oct. 12, 1905, 12.

52. *MAJC,* 93–94.

53. Joseph Simpson, *The Missionary Scape-Goat, Employed by Brutal Covert-Hunting Nimrods, Riding on a Beastly Crowing Rooster* (Baltimore: Hanzsche, 1853).

54. *MAJC,* 75; Max Kohler, "Incidents Illustrative of American Jewish Patriotism," *PAJHS* 4 (1896): 81–99.

55. *MAJC,* 105–6. These examples contradict the argument of some historians that Jewish immigrants of this period shied away from assertions of difference when operating in the civic sphere, where they favored a policy of "political neutrality." For this view, see Naomi W. Cohen, *Encounter with Emancipation: German Jews in the United States, 1830–1914* (Philadelphia: Jewish Publication Society of America, 1984), 129–58.

56. *Sun,* Sept. 10, 1850, 1.

57. Ibid., Jan. 26, 1859, 2.

58. Korn, "The Know-Nothing Movement," 74. For the text of the resolution, see *Congressional Globe,* Jan. 10, 1859, 290–91.

59. Christopher Phillips, *Freedom's Port: The African American Community of Baltimore, 1790–1860* (Urbana: University of Illinois Press, 1997), 196–97.

60. This analysis is based on a survey of local Jewish households in the 1850 and 1860 US Censuses, as well as the absence of Jewish names in the published list of Baltimore slaveholders in Ralph Clayton, *Slavery, Slaveholding, and the Free Black Population of Antebellum Baltimore* (Berwyn Heights, MD: Heritage, 1993).

- - - - - - - - - - - - - -

61. *Sun*, Jan. 29, 1830, 2; Jan. 30, 1839, 2; Feb. 12, 1839, 1; Jan. 28, 1843, 2; Feb. 4, 1846, 2; Feb. 7, 1846, 2; Seth Rockman, *Scraping By: Wage Labor, Slavery, and Survival in Early Baltimore* (Baltimore: Johns Hopkins University Press, 2009), 186–88.

62. *Sun*, Jan. 24, 1838, 3; Oct. 15, 1839, 3; Feb. 3, 1840, 2; June 4, 1840, 1; Apr. 17, 1847, 3; Jan. 31, 1850, 2; June 19, 1852, 4.

63. Aberbach, "Early German Jews," 33–34; Isaac M. Fein, "Baltimore Rabbis during the Civil War," in *Jews and the Civil War: A Reader*, ed. Jonathan D. Sarna and Adam Mendelsohn (New York: New York University Press, 2010), 181–82.

64. *Sun*, Sept. 4, 1839, 4.

65. Barkai, *Branching Out*, 17–23; Goldstein, "Different Kind of Neighborhood," 26–29.

66. *JOB*, 9.

67. *BA*, Feb. 21, 1856, quoted in *MAJC*, 75; see also Cohen, *Encounter with Emancipation*, 114–29.

68. Dianne Ashton, *Rebecca Gratz: Women and Judaism in Antebellum America* (Detroit, MI: Wayne State University Press, 1997), chap. 3; Kathleen D. McCarthy, *American Creed: Philanthropy and the Rise of Civil Society, 1700–1865* (Chicago: University of Chicago Press, 2003), 65–66.

69. *JOB*, 49; *Sun*, Apr. 12, 1856, 2; Sept. 12, 1862, 2; *AI*, Jan. 30, 1863, 234.

70. *Sun*, June 29, 1863, 2; Oct. 14, 1871, 1; *AI*, Jan. 16, 1864, 228; Feb. 19, 1864, 27; Jan. 27, 1871, 7; *JOB*,141.

71. Cornelia Wilhelm, *The Independent Orders of B'nai B'rith and True Sisters: Pioneers of a New Jewish Identity, 1843–1914* (Detroit, MI: Wayne State University Press, 2011), 117–25, esp. 124; *MAJC*, 131–32; *Sun*, Sept. 22, 1854, 3; Jan. 24, 1855, 2; Aug. 10, 1860, 2; Apr. 25, 1864, 3.

72. Wilhelm, *Independent Orders of B'nai B'rith*, 74–79; Lowenstein, *Mechanics of Change*, chap. 7.

73. On this trend nationally, see Barkai, *Branching Out*, 152–90.

74. Levin, *Vision*, 13; Hebrew Young Men's Literary Association meeting notes, reports, and clippings, JMM, 1988.235.

75. For example, Amicable Lodge No. 25 of the Masons had many Central European Jewish members. See *Sun*, Oct. 29, 1873, 1; Nov. 6, 1882, 4; Feb. 1, 1889, 4; Mar. 6, 1890, 6; Aug. 28, 1902, 7; Nov. 11, 1908, 9.

76. *Sun*, Sept. 17, 1861, 1; Aug. 9, 1865, 1; Mar. 27, 1868, 1; John C. French, "Otto Sutro and Music in Baltimore," *MHM* 47 (1952): 260–62; *MAJC*, 126.

77. *Sun*, Aug. 26, 1862, 2; *AI*, Aug. 30, 1861, 69; Alexandra Lee Levin, *The Szolds of Lombard Street: A Baltimore Family, 1859–1909* (Philadelphia: Jewish Publication Society of America, 1960), 72, 394.

78. *AI*, May 23, 1856, 393.

79. Eric L. Goldstein, *The Price of Whiteness: Jews, Race, and American Identity* (Princeton, NJ: Princeton University Press, 2006), 12–13.

80. French, "Otto Sutro," 262; Henry Shepherd, *History of Baltimore from Its Founding as a Town to the Current Year, 1729–1898* (Baltimore: S. B. Nelson, 1898), 902 (sketch of Dr. Abram B. Arnold). Jörg Echternkamp badly overstates the incidence of intermarriage between Baltimore Jews and non-Jews of German background during this period due to his misreading of some names as non-Jewish in the marriage register of Rabbi Henry Hochheimer. Hochheimer was a moderate reformer and would likely not have performed intermarriages. See Echternkamp, "Emerging Ethnicity: The German Experience in Antebellum Baltimore," *MHM* 86 (Spring 1991): 9. On Hochheimer, see Moshe Davis, *The Emergence of Conservative*

Judaism: The Historical School in Nineteenth Century America (Philadelphia: Jewish Publication Society of America, 1963), 339–40.

81. *MAJC*, 126–27. See also the description of a charity ball in 1857, to which "Christians were, in general, not invited." *AZJ*, Feb. 23, 1857, 119.

82. On Ahrens, see Ira Rosenwaike, "The Jews of Baltimore: 1820–1830," *AJHQ* 67 (Mar. 1978): 247–48. For the burial incident, see Greenberg, *Chronicle*, 13. On Rice, see I. Harold Scharfman, *The First Rabbi: Origins of Conflict between Orthodox and Reform* (Malibu, CA: Pangloss, 1988); Moshe Davis, "Abraham I. Rice: Pioneer of Orthodoxy in America," in his *America and the Holy Land: With Eyes toward Zion* (Westport, CT: Praeger, 1995), 4:97–105; and Israel Tabak, "Rabbi Abraham Rice of Baltimore," *Tradition* 7 (Summer 1965): 100–120.

83. Charles A. Rubenstein, *The History of Har Sinai Congregation of the City of Baltimore* (Baltimore: Kohn and Pollock, 1918); Abraham Shusterman, *The Legacy of a Liberal* (Baltimore: Har Sinai Congregation, 1967), 9.

84. See, for example, Michael Meyer, *Response to Modernity: A History of the Reform Movement in Judaism* (New York: Oxford University Press, 1988), 235–37; and Hasia Diner, *The Jews of the United States, 1654 to 2000* (Berkeley: University of California Press, 2004), 129.

85. On the difficulty of using denominational labels to understand American Judaism of this period, see Marc Lee Raphael, " 'Our Treasury Is Empty and Our Bank Account Is Overdrawn': Washington Hebrew Congregation, 1855–1872," *AJH* 84 (June 1996): 81–98.

86. Baltimore County Court, Chancery Papers, Sept. 6, 1830, no. C 295–1068, MSA.

87. *Sun*, Mar. 31, 1842, 2.

88. Greenberg, *Chronicle*, 17–21.

89. Marsha Rozenblit, "Choosing a Synagogue: The Social Composition of Two German Congregations in Nineteenth-Century Baltimore," in *The American Synagogue: A Sanctuary Transformed*, ed. Jack Wertheimer (Cambridge: Cambridge University Press, 1987), 330–32; Goldstein, "Different Kind of Neighborhood," 32–33.

90. Greenberg, *Chronicle*, 8, 20.

91. *JOB*, 133, 137; Levin, *Vision*, 11; Greenberg, *Chronicle*, 9–10.

92. *Sun*, Sept. 23, 1870, 4.

93. *Sun*, Sept. 27, 1845, 1; Sept. 16, 1848, 2; David Kaufman, *Cornerstones of Community: The Historic Synagogues of Maryland, 1845–1945* (Baltimore: Jewish Museum of Maryland, 1999), 17–20.

94. Goldstein, "Different Kind of Neighborhood," 32–33.

95. Tabak, "Rabbi Abraham Rice," 102–3; Adolph Guttmacher, *History of the Baltimore Hebrew Congregation* (Baltimore: Lord Baltimore Press, 1905), 27, 40; *AI*, Mar. 14, 1856, 291; Aug. 31, 1860, 68.

96. Shusterman, *Legacy*, 11.

97. Rubenstein, *History of Har Sinai*.

98. A. B. Arnold, "Circumcision," *New York Medical Journal* 9 (1869): 514–24.

99. *AI*, Aug. 31, 1860, 68.

100. Leon Jick, *The Americanization of the Synagogue, 1820–1870* (Hanover, NH: Brandeis University Press, 1976), 71, 185; Louis Cahn, *History of Oheb Shalom, 1853–1953* (Baltimore: Oheb Shalom Congregation, 1953), 29; Jeffrey S. Gurock, "The Orthodox Synagogue," in Wertheimer, *American Synagogue*, 39.

101. David Einhorn, "Der Schicksal der Oheb Schalom Gemeinde," *Sinai* 4 (1859): 321–39; Einhorn, "Abvertigung," *Sinai* 5 (suppl.) (1860): 1–28; Benjamin Szold, *Der Enthüllte Einhorn* (Baltimore: W. Polmyer, 1860).

102. Marc Lee Raphael, *Profiles in American Judaism* (New York: Harper and Row, 1988), 15, 65, 83.

103. *AI*, Aug. 10, 1855, 39; Sept. 7, 1855, 68; *Sun*, Aug. 15, 1855, 2; Har Sinai Congregation protest, Nov. 6, 1855, SC-13090, American Jewish Archives, Cincinnati. For a complete account of the Cleveland Conference, see Zev Eleff, *Who Rules the Synagogue? Religious Authority and the Formation of American Judaism* (New York: Oxford University Press, 2016), 107–14.

104. *AI*, Feb. 10, 1860, 260.

105. Har Sinai Congregation protest, Nov. 6, 1855; Solomon Lauer, "Personal Recollections of Dr. David Einhorn," in *Inaugural Sermon Delivered in the Temple of the Har Sinai Verein by Dr. David Einhorn* (Baltimore: Har Sinai Congregation, 1909), 19–22.

106. Guttmacher, *History of the Baltimore Hebrew Congregation*, 40–41; Jick, *Americanization of the Synagogue*, 72–73.

107. *Sun*, Oct. 18, 1864, 1.

108. Mark E. Neely Jr., *The Fate of Liberty: Abraham Lincoln and Civil Liberties* (New York: Oxford University Press, 1991), 99–103; *Proceedings and Speeches at a Public Meeting of the Friends of the Union* (Baltimore: John D. Toy, 1861), 3.

109. Haiman Philip Spitz, "An Autobiography," in *Memoirs of American Jews, 1775-1865*, ed. Jacob Rader Marcus (Philadelphia: Jewish Publication Society of America, 1955), 1:300.

110. Frank Towers, "Ruffians on the Urban Border: Labor, Politics, and Race in Baltimore, 1850–1861," PhD diss., University of California, Irvine, 1993, 695–96; and Towers, *The Urban South and the Coming of the Civil War* (Charlottesville: University of Virginia Press, 2004), 159–60, 174. At least two Jews—Mendes I. Cohen and Solomon Lewyt—served as vice presidents of Breckinridge's local campaign. *Sun*, Sept. 7, 1860, 1; Oct. 23, 1860, 1; Nov. 16, 1860, 1.

111. *Sun*, Nov. 2, 1860; *BA*, Mar. 24, 1912.

112. *MAJC*, 88–89, 97.

113. Benjamin [*sic*] Illowy, "The Wars of the Lord," *Occident*, Jan. 24, 1861, 267–68.

114. *Daily Exchange*, Feb. 9, 1861, 1; Feb. 18, 1861, 2; Feb. 19, 1861, 2.

115. For Einhorn's response to Raphall, see *Sinai* 6 (Feb. 1861): 2–22. On the "indignation meeting," see ibid., 32.

116. *Sinai* 6 (June 1861): 135–42. The quotation is from the English translation in *Generations* (2005–2006): 21.

117. Illowy, "Wars of the Lord," 268.

118. Benjamin Szold, "Peace and Union," *AI*, Jan. 11, 1861, 220.

119. Henry Hochheimer, "The Double Call," *AI*, Jan. 25, 1861, 236.

120. *Sun*, Feb. 1, 1861, 2.

121. *Proceedings and Speeches*, 3; *American and Commercial Advertiser*, Jan. 7, 1861; *Sun*, Jan. 7, 1861, 2; Jan. 11, 1861, 1; Towers, *Urban South*, 162. For the dangers faced by Jewish business owners during the secession crisis, see the statements regarding Wiesenfeld and Company in the *Daily Exchange*, Mar. 25, 1861, 1; Mar. 26, 1861, 2.

122. Towers, *Urban South*, 173; Levin, *Vision*, 19–20; Herbert Ezekiel and Gaston Lichtenstein, *History of the Jews of Richmond from 1769 to 1917* (Richmond, VA: Herbert T. Ezekiel, 1917), 202–3.

123. Isaac M. Fein, "Baltimore Rabbis during the Civil War," in *Jews and the Civil War: A Reader*, ed. Jonathan D. Sarna and Adam Mendelsohn (New York: New York University Press, 2010), 181–96.

124. Spitz, "An Autobiography," 300–301; William B. Catton, "The Baltimore Business

Community and the Secession Crisis, 1860–1861," MA thesis, University of Maryland, 1952, 96–102.

125. William E. Doster, *Lincoln and Episodes of the Civil War* (New York: Putnam's, 1915), 141–47 (quote, 141).

126. *Sun*, Apr. 15, 1863, 1; *Philadelphia Inquirer*, Feb. 21, 1863, 1; Mar. 12, 1863, 2; Feb. 15, 1864, 2.

127. Hecht memoir, 27; Olson, *Baltimore*, 145–46.

128. Towers, *Urban South*, 126–27; *Sun*, Oct. 29, 1863, 1. For other Jews involved in Unionist politics, see *Sun*, Apr. 6, 1864, 1.

129. See a reprint of the *Clipper*'s editorial in *AI*, Dec. 27, 1861, 206.

130. Bertram W. Korn, *American Jewry and the Civil War* (Philadelphia: Jewish Publication Society of America, 1951), 171.

131. Neely, *Fate of Liberty*, 101–3; copy of letter from Leopold Blumenberg to R[obert] Murray, US marshal, New York, Jan. 1865, in Wiesenfeld Papers, JMM, 1962.2.7.

132. Korn, *American Jewry*, chap. 7; Jonathan D. Sarna and Benjamin Shapell, *Lincoln and the Jews: A History* (New York: Thomas Dunne, 2015), 183–86; Olson, *Baltimore*, 147; Simon Wolf, *The American Jews as Patriot Soldier and Citizen* (Philadelphia: Levytype, 1895), 199–200. Wolf provides a short list of Maryland Jews who fought in the war, although many of the names are doubtfully Jewish. See also the Certificate of Exemption for Michael Rosenfeld, June 17, 1864, which records his hiring of an "alien substitute," JMM, 1968.22.11.

133. Gibson, *Population of the 100 Largest Cities*, tables 8, 9, and 10; Marcus Spiegel, *Your True Marcus: The Civil War Letters of a Jewish Colonel*, ed. Frank L. Byrne (Kent, OH: Kent State University Press, 1985), 188–89; Olson, *Baltimore*, 149–50.

134. Kahn, *Stitch in Time*, 32–34, 43–44; Brugger, *Maryland: A Middle Temperament*, 316; *JOB*, 137.

135. Kahn, *Stitch in Time*, 208; Edward K. Muller and Paul A. Groves, "The Changing Location of the Clothing Industry: A Link to the Social Geography of Baltimore in the Nineteenth Century," *MHM* 71 (1976): 404–10.

136. Krimmel, "Merchant Princes," 18, 24; Ira Rosenwaike, "Characteristics of Baltimore's Jewish Population in a Nineteenth-Century Census," *AJH* 82 (1994): 128–30; Jessica Elfenbein, "Baltimore's M. S. Levy and Sons: Straw Hat Makers to the World, 1870–1960," *Essays in Economic and Business History* 26 (Jan. 2008): 89–102.

137. *STCM*, 47; *Ha-magid* (Lyck, Prussia), Oct. 11, 1876, 344.

138. Evelyn Bodek Rosen, *The Philadelphia Fels, 1880-1920: A Social Portrait* (Madison, NJ: Fairleigh Dickinson University Press, 2000), 38–40, 53–54; *Sun*, Aug. 9, 1865, 2; Sept. 4, 1865, 1; Sept. 12, 1865, 4; Dec. 31, 1888, 4; *Jewish Messenger*, Aug. 25, 1899, 2–3; Theodore Rosengarten and Dale Rosengarten, eds., *A Portion of the People: Three Hundred Years of Southern Jewish Life* (Columbia: University of South Carolina Press, 2002), 129–30; Dale Rosengarten, "Mordecai, Moses Cohen," in *South Carolina Encyclopedia*, scencyclopedia.org/sce/entries/mordecai-moses-cohen; *In Memoriam: Isaac Strouse* (Baltimore, 1913), 7–8, 17–18; Kahn, *Stitch in Time*, 50.

139. Douglas Collins, *Photographed by Bachrach: 125 Years of American Portraiture* (New York: Rizzoli, 1992); *New International Encyclopedia*, 2nd ed. (New York: Dodd, Meade, 1915), 14:36; *JOB*, 130, 199.

140. John Russel Quinan, *Medical Annals of Baltimore from 1608 to 1880* (Baltimore: Press of Isaac Friedenwald, 1884), 99–101; Levin, *Vision*, chap. 5.

141. *Jewish Encyclopedia* (1906), s.v. "Hochheimer"; *Biographical Directory of the United States Congress, 1774-2005*, s.v. "Rayner, Isidor."

142. *Sun*, June 16, 1875; Aaron Baroway, "The Cohens of Maryland," *MHM* 18 (Dec. 1923): 376; *Biographical Directory of the United States Congress, 1774-2005*, s.v. "Rayner, Isidor." For Jewish officeholders, see *JOB*, 57–58; and *Jewish Encyclopedia* (1906), s.v. "Baltimore."

143. *AI*, June 26, 1857, 404; Jan. 24, 1868, 1; Jan. 31, 1868, 4.

144. *Sun*, July 28, 1868, 1; Aug. 6, 1868, 2; Aug. 17, 1868, 1; Feb. 12, 1872, 6; Dec. 16, 1875, 1.

145. *Laying of the Cornerstone of the Baltimore Asylum for Israelites, Beth Machase Umishtor, and the Addresses upon the Occasion* (Baltimore: W. Winkler and J. L. Leucht Jr., 1867), 6; George W. Howard, *The Monumental City: Its Past History and Present Resources* (Baltimore: J. D. Elders, 1873), 620–21.

146. *COB*, 696; Nurith Zmora, *Orphanages Reconsidered: Child Care Institutions in Progressive Era Baltimore* (Philadelphia: Temple University Press, 1994), 20–23; *Sun*, May 25, 1868, 1.

147. On Wiesenfeld and his philanthropic legacy, see *Memorial of the Late Moses Wiesenfeld, Containing the Service and Addresses at His Funeral* (Baltimore: Deutsch and Golderman, 1871). Program booklet of the twenty-fifth anniversary of the Harmony Circle held at Concordia Hall, Oct. 31, 1889, JMM, 1991.185.2.

148. *Purim Gazette Extra*, JMM, 1993.141.2. See also 1993.141.3.

149. *Sun*, July 27, 1865, 1.

150. *Sun*, Feb. 22, 1871, 1; Feb. 21, 1868, 3; Dec. 10, 1879, 1.

151. *An die Israeliten Baltimore's* (N.p.: n.d. [c. 1867]), JMM, 1993.141.1.

152. *MAJC*, 125–26. On the changes to public education during this period, see Charles Hirschfeld, *Baltimore: 1870-1900: Studies in Social History* (Baltimore: Johns Hopkins University Press, 1941), chap. 3.

153. Shepherd, *History of Baltimore*, 691–92; Kurt F. Stone, *The Jews of Capitol Hill: A Compendium of Jewish Congressional Members* (Lanham, MD: Scarecrow), 46.

154. Greenberg, *Chronicle*, 24.

155. Jan Bernhardt Schein, *On Three Pillars: The History of Chizuk Amuno Congregation, 1871-1996* (Baltimore: Chizuk Amuno, 2000).

156. *JT*, Aug. 28, 1964; Shearith Israel VF, JMM. See also Jessica Elfenbein, "Uptown and Traditional," *SJH* 9 (2006): 69–102.

157. *Sun*, Apr. 26, 1942, SM2; Raphael, *Profiles in American Judaism*, 11. On a national level, the crystallization of Reform Judaism as a distinct movement was signified by the issuance of the Pittsburgh Platform by the Central Conference of American Rabbis in 1885. For the full text, see Meyer, *Response to Modernity*, 387–88.

158. *STCM*, 47–49, 99; Marc Lee Raphael, *Judaism in America* (New York: Columbia University Press, 2010), 52. On the immigration of Jews from Bialystok more broadly, see Rebecca Kobrin, *Jewish Bialystok and Its Diaspora* (Bloomington: Indiana University Press, 2010).

159. Goldstein, "Different Kind of Neighborhood," 36.

Chapter 3.
The Great Wave Hits Baltimore

1. *Sun*, Aug. 20, 1891, 6.

2. Ibid., Aug. 27, 1891, 6; *AI*, Sep. 3, 1891, 5.

3. This discussion draws heavily on Eric L. Goldstein, "The Great Wave: Eastern European Jewish Immigration to the United States, 1880–1924," in *The Columbia History of Jews and Judaism in America*, ed. Marc Lee Raphael (New York: Columbia University Press, 2008), 71–72.

4. Ibid., 72. For an interesting case study of this psychological impact, see Natan Meir, "'A Sword Hanging over Their Heads': The Significance of Pogroms for Russian Jewish Everyday

Life and Self-Understanding (The Case of Kiev)," in *Anti-Jewish Violence: Rethinking the Pogrom in East European History*, ed. Jonathan Dekel-Chen et al. (Bloomington: Indiana University Press, 2010), 111–30.

5. Goldstein, "The Great Wave," 72–73.

6. *JE*, May 27, 1887, 9.

7. The term "great wave" was used often during this period to describe the mass migration of Eastern European Jews to the United States. See, for example, *Jewish Encyclopedia* (1906), s.v. "America"; and Charles Bernheimer, *The Russian Jew in the United States* (Philadelphia: John C. Winston, 1905), 64.

8. *TCAP*, 57, 87, 92, 150, 194.

9. Dean Essingler, "Immigration through the Port of Baltimore," in *Forgotten Doors: The Other Ports of Entry to the United States*, ed. M. Mark Stolarik (Cranbury, NJ: Associated University Presses, 1988), 69–70; Bureau of Immigration, *Annual Report of the Commissioner General of Immigration* (1914), 35, archive.org; *Report of the Bureau of Industrial Statistics of Maryland* (1900), 159; (1901), 193, archive.org; *Report of the Bureau of Statistics and Information of Maryland* (1903), 274–75; (1904), 186–89; (1905), 312–15; (1906), 194–96; (1907), 194–95; (1908), 400–403; (1909), 209–12; (1910), 209–12, archive.org.

10. Joel Perlmann, *The Local Geographic Origins of Russian-Jewish Immigrants, circa 1900* (Annandale-on-Hudson, NY: Levy Economics Institute of Bard College, 2006); and Simon Kuznets, "Immigration of Russian Jews to the United States: Background and Structure," *Perspectives in American History* 9 (1975): 35–124.

11. One study reveals that Lithuania was not as free from pogroms as previously thought, but nonetheless confirms that such violence was far less prevalent in this region than in the south of Russia. See Darius Staliūnas, *Enemies for a Day: Antisemitism and Anti-Jewish Violence in Lithuania under the Tsars* (New York: Central European University Press, 2015).

12. Lester S. Levy, *Jacob Epstein* (Baltimore: Maran, 1978), 1; *JOB*, 213, 305; Peggy Pearlstein, "Israel Fine: Baltimore Businessman and Hebrew Poet," *SJH* 9 (2006): 103–39; *STCM*, 9, 18, 42–43, 89.

13. *JE*, Apr. 5, 1907, 23.

14. Campbell Gibson, *Population of the 100 Largest Cities and Other Urban Places in the United States: 1790 to 1990* (Washington, DC: US Bureau of the Census, 1998), tables 11–15, census.gov/population/www/documentation/twps0027/twps0027.html.

15. Ibid.

16. Essingler, "Immigration," 69–70.

17. See statistics for the years 1910, 1920, and 1930 in US Department of Commerce, *Negroes in the United States, 1920-32* (Washington, DC: US Government Printing Office, 1935), 55.

18. US Department of Commerce, *Fourteenth Census of the United States Taken in the Year 1920* (Washington, DC: US Government Printing Office, 1922), 3:423.

19. These findings are based on the data regarding the "mother tongue of the foreign white stock" recorded in the US Census in 1910 and 1920. We have assumed that, in addition to those listing Yiddish or Hebrew as their "mother tongue," the majority of those reporting Russian as their native language were also Jews. On the recording of Jews as Russians in US Census records, see Elliott Barkan, *Immigrants in American History: Arrival, Adaptation, and Integration* (Santa Barbara, CA: ABC-Clio, 2013), 588.

20. *Sun*, Oct. 26, 1998, 3B; *Immigrants in Industries: The Clothing Manufacturing Industry* (Washington, DC: US Governent Printing Office, 1911), 269.

----

21. Andor Skotnes, *A New Deal for All? Race and Class Struggles in Depression-Era Baltimore* (Durham, NC: Duke University Press, 2013), 93; James Barrett, *Work and Community in the Jungle: Chicago's Packinghouse Workers, 1894–1922* (Urbana: University of Illinois Press, 1987), 44–47; William P. Marchione, *Boston Miscellany: An Essential History of the Hub* (Charleston, SC: History Press, 2008), 116–18; Mark Reutter, *Making Steel: Sparrows Point and the Rise and Ruin of American Industrial Might* (Urbana: University of Illinois Press, 1988); Department of Commerce and Labor, Bureau of the Census, *Industrial Statistics, 1905: Manufactures and Population* (Washington, DC: US Government Printing Office, 1909), 52.

22. An 1890 study does not mention garment work among the occupations of Baltimore's African Americans: Jeffrey R. Brackett, *Notes on the Progress of the Colored People of Maryland since the War* (Baltimore: Publications Agency of the Johns Hopkins University, 1890), 29–32. A few African Americans worked in Baltimore sweatshops by 1901, but they constituted less than 1 percent of the employees. *Sun*, Sept. 28, 1901, 12. Around World War I, black workers entered the industry in larger numbers, but a 1922 study of several factories found that African Americans still comprised less than 3 percent of workers in the men's clothing industry and only about 8 percent in the women's and children's clothing industry: US Department of Labor, *Women in Maryland Industries* (Washington, DC: US Government Printing Office, 1922), 9. See also Skotnes, *New Deal*, 24; and Hasia R. Diner, *In the Almost Promised Land: American Jews and Blacks, 1915–1935*, 2nd ed. (Baltimore: Johns Hopkins University Press, 1995), 213.

23. DeWayne Wickham, *Woodholme: A Black Man's Story of Growing Up Alone* (New York: Farrar, Straus and Giroux, 1995), 12; Skotnes, *New Deal*, 161.

24. For a description of Baltimore as the most religious city in the United States, see *Sun*, June 15, 1896, 10.

25. *Sun*, Sept, 18, 1888, 6; Oct. 15 1888, 2; Michael J. Lisicky, *Hutzler's: Where Baltimore Shops* (Charleston, SC: History Press, 2009), 17, 19.

26. Dean Krimmel, "*Merchant Princes* and Their Palaces: The Emergence of Department Stores in Baltimore," in *Enterprising Emporiums: The Jewish Department Stores of Downtown Baltimore*, ed. Avi Y. Decter and Melissa Martens (Baltimore: Jewish Museum of Maryland, 2001), 13–19; Philip Kahn Jr., *A Stitch in Time: The Four Seasons of Baltimore's Needle Trades* (Baltimore: Maryland Historical Society, 1989), 43–131; "Israelites at the Johns Hopkins University," *American Jews Annual for 5649* (1889): 48–50; Joseph Fels, "Jews at the Johns Hopkins University, 1876–1901," MS, JMM, 1989.180.1; Lewis Putzel, "The Jew in Political Life," in *JOB*, 57–58.

27. For the classic national study of this trend, see John Higham, "Social Discrimination against Jews in America, 1830–1930," *PAJHS* (Sept. 1957): 1–33.

28. Miss Remington, *Society Visiting List of 1889 and 1890, Baltimore, MD* (Baltimore: Thos. E. Lycett, 1889); Robert J. Brugger, *The Maryland Club: A History of Food and Friendship in Baltimore, 1857–1997* (Baltimore: Maryland Club, 1998).

29. *Sun*, May 4, 1889, 4.

30. Remington, *Society Visiting List*, 27, 115, 139; Brugger, *Maryland Club*, 245–46.

31. Brugger, *Maryland Club*, 177; Remington, *Society Visiting List*, 15, 45; Karen Hunger Parshall, *James Joseph Sylvester: Jewish Mathematician in a Victorian World* (Baltimore: Johns Hopkins University Press, 2006), 231, 233; "Israelites at the Johns Hopkins University"; and Fels, "Jews at the Johns Hopkins University."

32. For cases of intermarriage among these individuals and their families, see *Sun*, Jan. 12, 1893, 8 (Fabian Franklin); Oct. 24, 1895, 6; Aug. 21, 1917, 4 (Alfred J. Ulman's family); July 3, 1937, 8 (Isidor Rayner); Feb. 26, 1907, 6; Aug. 4, 1914, 7 (Mendes Cohen's family).

33. James B. Crooks, *Politics and Progress: The Rise of Urban Progressivism in Baltimore, 1895 to 1911* (Baton Rouge: Louisiana State University Press, 1968), 4, 7, 19, 27.

34. *Sun*, Aug. 24, 1895, 10; Dec. 16, 1893, 8. On the history of the Carroll Mansion, which was owned by Carroll's son-in-law Richard Caton and was the signer's final residence, see Helen Straw Whitmore, "The Carroll Mansion, 800 East Lombard Street, Baltimore, Maryland: A Historical and Architectural Study," MS thesis, University of Maryland, 1969.

35. *Sun*, Sept. 29, 1890, 6; Clayton Coleman Hall, *Baltimore: Its History and Its People* (New York: Lewis Historical Publishing, 1912), 1:678.

36. *Sun*, Aug. 30, 1898, 7; Dec. 7, 1903, 12; Mar. 6, 1909, 14; Mar. 29, 1909, 9.

37. Ibid., Sept. 29, 1890, 6; Nov. 24, 1905, 12; Nov. 26, 1906, 11.

38. Ibid., May 26, 1900, 4; Mar. 12, 1907, 4.

39. See, for example, *Sun*, Sept. 26, 1900, 12.

40. *Sun*, Jan. 3, 1889, 5.

41. Ibid., Apr. 23, 1911, LS7.

42. Ibid., Dec. 19, 1884, 2; Apr. 4, 1898, 12; Jan. 1, 1900, 10; Oct. 11, 1905, 4; Dec. 1, 1905, 1; July 2, 1916, 8. On government failure and corruption, see Crooks, *Politics and Progress*, 20.

43. *Sun*, Nov. 21, 1900, 4; Dec. 13, 1903, 4.

44. See, for example, *Children of Immigrants in Schools* (Washington, DC: US Government Printing Office, 1911), 7–9. For the national context, see Thomas Kessner, *The Golden Door: Italian and Jewish Immigrant Mobility in New York City, 1880–1915* (New York: Oxford University Press, 1977); Stephen Steinberg, *The Ethnic Myth: Race, Ethnicity, and Class in America* (Boston: Beacon, 1981), chaps. 3, 5, and 6.

45. Cyrus Adler, ed. *The Voice of America on Kishineff* (Philadelphia: Jewish Publication Society of America, 1904), 16–39; *Sun*, Feb. 27, 1902, 8; Mar. 4, 1902, 7; Feb. 4, 1903, 9; May 4, 1903, 7; Madison C. Peters, *Justice to the Jew* (New York: McClure, 1908).

46. William Rosenau, "Cardinal Gibbons and His Attitudes toward Jewish Problems," *PAJHS* 31 (1928): 219–28; Adler, *Voice of America*, 19–20.

47. Adler, *Voice of America*, 242–64; Till van Rahden, "Beyond Ambivalence: Variations of Catholic Anti-Semitism in Turn of the Century Baltimore," *AJH* 82 (1994): 7–43.

48. *MAJC*, 203–4; Rahden, "Beyond Ambivalence"; Gilbert Sandler, *Jewish Baltimore: A Family Album* (Baltimore: Johns Hopkins University Press, 2000), 161.

49. *AA*, June 4, 1898, 2; Jan. 14, 1899, 1; June 13, 1903, 1.

50. *Sun*, Nov. 17, 1891, 3; Nov. 18, 1891, 6; Apr. 8, 1902, 7.

51. Ibid., Nov. 28, 1900, 12; Jan. 17, 1901, 10; May 7, 1901, 6.

52. Marsha Rozenblit, "Choosing a Synagogue: The Social Composition of Two German Congregations in Nineteenth-Century Baltimore," in *The American Synagogue: A Sanctuary Transformed*, ed. Jack Wertheimer (Cambridge: Cambridge University Press, 1987), 333–35, 340–41.

53. Sunday services continued at Har Sinai until 1918. See Charles A. Rubenstein, *The History of Har Sinai Congregation of the City of Baltimore* (Baltimore: Kohn and Pollock, 1918), n.p.

54. See Jessica Elfenbein, "Uptown and Traditional," *SJH* 9 (2006): 69; *STCM*, 55; Nancy J. Ordway, "A History of Chizuk Amuno Congregation: An American Synagogue," PhD diss., Baltimore Hebrew University, 1997, 97, 169–70, 176, 179–81.

55. Israel M. Goldman, "Henry W. Schneeberger: His Role in American Judaism," *AJHQ* 57 (Dec. 1967): 153–90; *Sun*, Sept. 19, 1895, 8.

56. Rozenblit, "Choosing a Synagogue," 352; David Kaufman, *Cornerstones of Community: The Historic Synagogues of Maryland* (Baltimore: Jewish Museum of Maryland, 1999), 35–36.

- - - - - - - - - - - - -

57. *MAJC*, 144; *Sun*, July 8, 1882, 1; Aug. 14, 1882, 1; Apr. 9, 1883, 6; May 22, 1883, 1; Sept. 1, 1883, 4.

58. This portrait of Schlossberg is drawn from Jo Ann E. Argersinger, *Making the Amalgamated: Gender, Ethnicity, and Class in the Baltimore Clothing Industry, 1899-1939* (Baltimore: Johns Hopkins University Press, 1999), 37.

59. D. Randall Beirne, "The Impact of Black Labor on European Immigration into Baltimore's Oldtown, 1790-1910," *MHM* 83 (Winter 1988): 338-43.

60. *Sun*, Aug. 27, 1891, 6.

61. Sandler, *Jewish Baltimore*, 11-15; *STCM*, 92-93.

62. Ida S. Porges, *From the Shtetl to the States: Leaves from a Family Tree* (Chicago: Circle Press, n.d.), 40.

63. Joseph L. Arnold, "Baltimore Neighborhoods, 1800-1980," *Working Papers from the Regional Economic History Research Center* 4 (1981): 76-98.

64. Quoted in *MAJC*, 159.

65. Janet E. Kemp, *Housing Conditions in Baltimore: Report of a Special Committee of the Association for the Improvement of the Condition of the Poor and the Charity Organization Society* (Baltimore: Federated Charities, 1907), 14, 19-21, 79-80.

66. "Autobiography of Abe Gellman, Petersburg, VA," 12, Memoir Collection, JMM.

67. *Annual Report of the Bureau of Industrial Statistics of Maryland* (1894), 80-114, esp. 80-82, archive.org.

68. Ibid., 80, 103.

69. Ibid., 82.

70. Argersinger, *Making the Amalgamated*, 28-30.

71. Kessner, *The Golden Door*; Steinberg, *The Ethnic Myth*, chaps. 3, 5, and 6; Aaron Michael Glazer, "Entrepreneurship among Eastern European Jewish Immigrants in Baltimore, 1881-1914," MA thesis, Johns Hopkins University, 1992; and Lauraine Kartman Levy, "Jewish Occupational Roots in Baltimore at the Turn of the Century," *MHM* 74 (Mar. 1979): 52-61. For Jewish professionals among the immigrants, see *Sun*, July 17, 1902, 9; Feb. 4, 1905, 7 (attorney Israel Gomborov); Jan. 26, 1908, 20 (attorney William Weissager); and Apr. 12, 1908, 17 (physician Maurice Chideckel).

72. Levy, "Jewish Occupational Roots"; Glazer, "Entrepreneurship"; *JOB*, 269, 400; Sandler, *Jewish Baltimore*, 76-83, 87-89.

73. Kahn, *Stitch in Time*, 72-100, 106-8, 116-21; *JOB*, 213, 428.

74. *Sun*, Dec. 20, 1944, 17; Mar. 11, 1983, B1; *JOB*, 178, 229; Mary Ellen Hayward and Charles Belfoure, *The Baltimore Rowhouse* (New York: Princeton Architectural Press, 1999), 139-40, 150, 163; *NIMN*, 12.

75. Levy, *Jacob Epstein*, 15-34; *Evening Sun*, Oct. 5, 1910, 1; Deborah R. Weiner, "Filling the Peddler's Pack: Southern Jews and Jacob Epstein's Baltimore Bargain House," paper presented at the Southern Jewish Historical Society annual conference, Baltimore, 2005.

76. *Sun*, Nov. 14, 1889, 6; Mar. 12, 1894, 8; June 24, 1905, 9; Nov. 16, 1905, 12; Jan. 9, 1928, 4; Jan. 16, 1928, 3; Oct. 7, 1934, T4; Jan. 6, 1935, 3; Feb. 29, 1936, 8; Sept. 2, 1949, 18; *Prayers of Comfort*, 7th ed. (Baltimore: Levinson and Bros., n.d.), 57, 61.

77. Hymen Saye, "I Remember Papa," *Generations* 1 (Dec. 1980): 27; State of Maryland, *First Biennial Report of the State Tax Commission of Maryland* (Baltimore: Sun Book and Job Printing Office, 1916), 200, 204, 213-14.

78. *Sun*, Dec. 10, 1888, 4; Jan. 28, 1889, 4; June 3, 1899, 12; May 23, 1902, 12; June 30, 1902, 8; July 23, 1905, 16; July 25, 1905, 12; Mar. 14, 1906, 7; Jan. 11, 1909, 12; Aug. 4, 1910, 8. For an

overview of Jewish fraternal lodges of this period, see Daniel Soyer, *Jewish Immigrant Associations and American Identity in New York, 1880–1939* (Cambridge, MA: Harvard University Press, 1997), 38, 41–42, 61–66.

79. *Souvenir Album: Diamond Jubilee, 1888–1963* (Baltimore: Hebrew Young Men's Sick Relief Association, 1963), in Hebrew Young Men's Sick Relief Association VF, JMM.

80. *Sun*, Mar. 8, 1898, 7; Feb. 5, 1902, 6; June 3, 1906, 7; Nov. 9, 1907, 9; Dec. 2, 1908, 12.

81. Ibid., June 23, 1902, 12; June 13, 1904, 12.

82. Ibid., Feb. 23, 1905, 6; Mar. 13, 1905, 7.

83. Ibid., Dec. 16, 1892, 1; Jan. 16, 1896, 8; Jan. 30, 1902, 7; Nov. 5, 1902, 12; Mar. 10, 1912, 9.

84. Ibid., Jan. 24, 1903, 6; June 17, 1903, 7; Nov. 13, 1910, 5; May 8, 1911, 6; Sept. 29, 1911, 5; Apr. 4, 1915, society section, 10; *JOB*, 54; Abraham Glushakow, ed., *A Pictorial History of Maryland Jewry* (Baltimore: Jewish Voice Publishing, 1955), 125.

85. Louis Levine, *The Women's Garment Workers: A History of the International Ladies' Garment Workers' Union* (New York: Heubsch, 1924), 34. Levine gives the date as 1884, but *MAJC*, 167, shows that it was actually 1889.

86. *Arbayter tsaytung* (New York), Aug. 1, 1890; Dec. 13, 1895; Levine, *Women's Garment Workers*, 77–78.

87. Jewish immigrants returned to Europe in greater numbers than popular myth would suggest, but overall this trend was less common than among other groups. See Jonathan D. Sarna, "The Myth of No Return: Jewish Return Migration to Eastern Europe, 1881–1914," *AJH* 71 (Dec. 1981): 256–69. For return migration among other groups, see Mark Wyman, *Round Trip to America: The Immigrants Return to Europe, 1880–1930* (Ithaca, NY: Cornell University Press, 1996).

88. Argersinger, *Making the Amalgamated*, chap. 2.

89. *Children of Immigrants in Schools*, 7–9.

90. Barry Kessler, "Bedlam with Corned Beef on the Side: The Jewish Delicatessen in Baltimore," *Generations* (Fall 1993): 2–3. For the national context of immigrant Jews' embrace of commercial culture, see Andrew Heinze, *Adapting to Abundance: Jewish Immigrants, Mass Consumption, and the Search for American Identity* (New York: Columbia University Press, 1990).

91. Robert K. Headley, *Motion Picture Exhibition in Baltimore: An Illustrated History and Directory of Theaters, 1895–2004* (Jefferson, NC: McFarland, 2006), 7–53, 216, 247–48, 373–74; Porges, *From the Shtetl*, 27; Deborah R. Weiner, "A Smelkinson's Eye View of the World: Place, Memory, and Stories of an East Baltimore Childhood," *Generations* (2005–2006): 37; *Sun*, Jan. 6, 1912, 14; Sept. 28, 1912, 7; May 3, 1915, 12; Jason Rhodes, *Maryland's Amusement Parks* (Charleston, SC: Arcadia, 2005), 45–49, 53–54.

92. Boris Thomashefsky and Bessie Thomashefsky, "The Early Years of Yiddish Theater in America," Memoir Collection, JMM.

93. *JE*, Jan. 3, 1896, 4. For more on the fire and its aftermath, see *Sun*, Dec. 28, 1895, 2, 4, 8; Dec. 30, 1895, 10.

94. *Sun*, May 13, 1875, 4; Oct. 12, 1900, 7; Mar. 16, 1903, 12; July 13, 1915, 14; *JE*, July 3, 1908, 13.

95. *JC*, May 10, 1907, 74; July 19, 1907, 234; Dec. 29, 1911; *Sun*, Jan. 20, 1908, 12; Apr. 8, 1912, 9.

96. *Konstitushon fun khevre B'ney Yisroel* (Baltimore: Flom, 1913), 4, JMM.

97. "Pinkas me-khevre Shomrei Mishmeres Ha-Kodesh Anshei Volin," 1890, MS 29, box 7, folder 33, JMM.

98. Isador Terrell, OH 260, Aug. 9, 1991, JMM.

99. *Sun*, Dec. 22, 1905, 6; Dec. 25, 1905, 8; Dec. 2, 1907, 9; Apr. 26, 1909, 14. See also Naomi

Kellman, "Jewish Education in Baltimore," *JT*, June 10, 1983, 46–53. English was first mentioned by the *Sun* as the Talmud Torah's language of instruction on May 29, 1905 (p. 9), but the shift from Yiddish likely occurred a year or more earlier, as is suggested by the centrality of the language question in the founding of a competing school, Talmud Torah Ve-Emunah, in 1904.

100. For examples of immigrant "reverends," see *Sun*, Nov. 21, 1887, 4; Oct. 10, 1890, 4 (Joseph Eisner); Sept. 5, 1894, 8 (Moses Schreiber).

101. Simon Isaac Finkelstein, *Sefer En Shimon* (New York: N.p., 1935), 1:7; *Jewish Criterion* (Pittsburgh, PA), May 31, 1918, 100; *American Jewish Year Book* 5 (1904): 54, 100.

102. *Sun*, Mar. 19, 1891, 6. On Levinson's background, see *BA*, July 14, 1895; Abraham J. Karp, *Jewish Continuity in America: Creative Survival in a Free Society* (Tuscaloosa: University of Alabama Press, 1996), 52–55, 70–71; and biographical sketches in Rabbi Abraham Levinson VF, JMM.

103. *Brooklyn Daily Eagle*, Feb. 5, 1937, 35.

104. Abraham J. Karp, "New York Chooses a Chief Rabbi," *PAJHS* 44 (Mar. 1955): 129–99.

105. *Sun*, July 25, 1908, 6.

106. Porges, *From the Shtetl*, 11.

107. *Sun*, Apr. 13, 1904, 8; Feb. 22, 1907, 9; *American Jewish Year Book* 9 (1907–1908): 198.

108. *MAJC*, 192; *American Jewish Chronicle*, Dec. 15, 1916, 185; Apr. 13, 1917, 762.

109. *JT*, July 4, 1969.

110. Louis E. Shecter, "I Remember Shomrei Mishmeres," Memoir Collection, JMM.

111. *Sun*, Apr. 19, 1909, 9; June 14, 1909, 9; June 16, 1909, 7; June 18, 1909, 14; June 28, 1909, 14; Sept. 6, 1909, 12; Oct. 4, 1909, 11; Apr. 4, 1910, 14; June 4, 1911, 9.

112. Karp, "New York Chooses"; Elizabeth Kessin Berman, "Threads of Life: Overcoming the Conflicts between Jewish Employers and Jewish Workers in Baltimore's Garment Industry," in *Threads of Life: Jewish Involvement in Baltimore's Garment Industry* (Baltimore: Jewish Historical Society of Maryland, 1991), 16.

113. Avrum K. Rifman, "In My Mother's and Father's Court," Memoir Collection, JMM.

114. Lawrence B. Goldstein, interview by Eric L. Goldstein, 2002.

115. S. S. Garson, "A kampf tsvishn tsvey ideologyes," 27, American-Jewish Autobiographies Collection, record group 102, YIVO Institute for Jewish Research, New York; *Sun*, Jan. 3, 1889, 5. Garson was probably referring to the lecture given by Rabbi Henry W. Schneeberger on the Anglo-Jewish poet Grace Aguilar. See *Sun*, Nov. 18, 1889, 4.

116. Garson, "A kampf."

117. *Arbayter fraynd* (London), Jan. 31, 1890, 6; *Sun*, Jan. 6, 1890, 6; Jan. 13, 1890, 6; Feb. 24, 1890, 6; May 5, 1890, 6; Moses Aberbach, *Solomon Baroway: Farmer, Writer, Zionist, and Early Baltimore Social Worker* (Baltimore: Jewish Historical Society of Maryland, 1990), chap. 4.

118. *Sun*, Sept. 29, 1890, 6; Feb. 6, 1891, 6; Feb. 7, 1891, 6.

119. *JE*, June 13, 1890, 4; *Sun*, June 6, 1890, 3; *Yidishe gazetn* (New York), Apr. 20, 1894, 10; Dovid Katz, "Alexander Harkavy and His Trilingual Dictionary," in *Yiddish-English-Hebrew Dictionary*, ed. Alexander Harkavy (New York: Schocken, 1988), vii–xxiii.

120. Jacob Kabakoff, "The Role of Wolf Schur as Hebraist and Zionist," in *Essays in American Jewish History* (Cincinnati, OH: American Jewish Archives, 1958), 429; *JE*, Feb. 13, 1891, 4; Levine, *Women's Garment Workers*, 78; *Sun*, Dec. 29, 1907, 13; Nov. 13, 1908, 9. One complete issue of *Der vegvayzer* (May 8, 1902) is available on microfilm at YIVO. The paper seems to have started in 1895, but the exact date is unknown. The first mention of it in another source is *American Hebrew*, Oct. 11, 1895, 569.

- - - - - - - - - - - - - -

121. *Sun*, Apr. 12, 1908.

122. *Sun*, Nov. 8, 1904, 12; Nov. 12, 1908, 9. Hebrew Union College Library in Cincinnati holds the *Baltimor Amerikaner* (*Baltimore Jewish American*) on microfilm. A clipping from the Baltimore edition of the *Yidishes tageblat* is in the Rabbi Reuben Rivkin scrapbook, JMM.

123. *JE*, Sept. 23, 1887, 5; Bessie Thomashefsky, *My Life Story: The Sorrows and Joys of a Yiddish Star Actress* (New York: Wahrheit, 1916); Boris Thomashefsky, *My Life Story* (New York: Trio, 1937); *Der vegvayzer*, May 8, 1902; *Sun*, Mar. 29, 1902, 7; May 30, 1906, 7.

124. *Sun*, Nov. 11, 1917, B2.

125. *Ha-melitz* (St. Petersburg, Russia), Oct. 9, 1889, 6; Aberbach, *Solomon Baroway*, chap. 5; Kabakoff, "Wolf Schur," 441; *Sun*, Sept. 10, 1894, 8; Sept. 1, 1896, 8; Moshe Falk Mervis, "L'toldot ha-Tsiyonut ve-ha-tenuah ha-Ivrit be-Baltimore," *Ha-doar* 22 (1942); Pearlstein, "Israel Fine."

126. Avi Y. Decter, "The American Delegate(s) at the First Zionist Congress," *Generations* (2007–2008): 25–33.

127. *Sun*, Oct. 14, 1901, 6; Dec. 2, 1901, 10; Feb. 24, 1902, 7; Aug., 24, 1903, 12.

128. Ibid., Dec. 24, 1905, 6. A Poale Zion conference had been held in Philadelphia earlier in the year, but it was dominated by socialist territorialists who favored diaspora nationalism over the establishment of a Jewish homeland in Palestine. The Baltimore conference was organized by the pro-Palestine faction, which declared its independence from the territorialists and laid the groundwork for Labor Zionism in the United States. See C. Bezalel Sherman, "The Beginnings of Labor Zionism in the United States," in *Early History of Zionism in America*, ed. Isidore S. Meyer (New York: AJHS and Theodor Herzl Foundation, 1958), 279–80.

129. *Sun*, Nov. 7, 1915, 4.

130. Ibid., Nov. 27, 1899, 7; Sept. 20, 1901, 7; Feb. 24, 1902, 7; Sept. 14, 1903, 12; May 15, 1905, 12; July 3, 1905, 6.

131. Henrietta Szold, "Early Zionist Days in Baltimore," *Maccabaean* 30 (June–July 1917): 265; Eric L. Goldstein, "The Practical as Spiritual: Henrietta Szold's American Zionist Ideology, 1878–1920," in *Daughter of Zion: Henrietta Szold and American Jewish Womanhood*, ed. Barry Kessler (Baltimore: Jewish Historical Society of Maryland, 1995), 17–33; Alexandra Lee Levin, *Vision: A Biography of Harry Friedenwald* (Philadelphia: Jewish Publication Society of America, 1964), 147–48, 171–78, 222–24; *Sun*, Nov. 27, 1899, 7; Oct. 14, 1901, 6.

132. *MAJC*, 169.

133. *Sun*, Sept. 10, 1901, 9.

134. Ibid., Aug. 28, 1901, 7; Dec. 6, 1902, 12; Dec. 18, 1902, 7.

135. Rubin Livov, untitled [History of the Workmen's Circle in Baltimore], n.d., Workmen's Circle VF, JMM.

136. Ibid.; *Sun*, May 2, 1913, 3; Dec. 25, 1915, 6. The Progressive Labor Lyceum had been founded in 1906 by leaders of the Workmen's Circle. It maintained a more modest meeting place and library in at least one other location before the opening of the hall at Aisquith and Lexington. *Sun*, Mar. 23, 1906, 9; Feb. 5, 1908, 8.

137. Livov, [History of the Workmen's Circle]; *Sun*, Apr. 6, 1911, 9; May 1, 1911, 11; Apr. 26, 1915, 7.

138. *Sun*, Feb. 14, 1908, 12.

139. Ibid., Apr. 30, 1911, LS8.

140. Ibid., Apr. 24, 1905, 8; May 6, 1907, 12; Aug. 18, 1909, 7; Nov. 3, 1913, 7; Apr. 26, 1915, 5; *Baltimore Sun Almanac* (1906): 44, 46; (1908): 49–53, 107–9; (1910): 129; (1912): 138.

141. *Sun*, Aug. 31, 1905, 12; Nov. 30, 1914, 12; Dec. 3, 1914, 12; Apr. 9, 1915, 16; Argersinger, *Making the Amalgamated*, 39–43. Argersinger does not mention Levin in her narrative.

142. *Sun*, Feb. 22, 1915, 7; May 8, 1915, 9; June 2, 1915, 10.

143. Ibid., Nov. 15, 1892, 8; Nov. 27, 1894, 8; July 19, 1895, 8; July 8, 1896, 10; Oct. 2, 1896, 10; Aug. 6, 1897, 8; Sept. 25, 1897, 10; Oct. 15, 1898, 7.

144. *BA*, Mar. 1, 1903, 11; *Sun*, Apr. 1, 1903, 12; May 22, 1903, 12; Dec. 30, 1903, 10; Jan. 27, 1904, 2.

145. *Sun*, Sept. 8, 1894, 8; May 7, 1900, 12; Dec. 28, 1901, 6; May 2, 1902, 12; Apr. 17, 1909, 14; Aug. 27, 1910, 14; Apr. 8, 1912, 9.

146. Ibid., Nov. 30, 1903, 7; May 1, 1905, 12; Apr. 30, 1906, 6; David Paulson, "Historical Sketch of the Independent Order Brith Sholom of Baltimore," in *Independent Order Brith Sholom of Baltimore: Dedication of the Home and History, January 31st, 1915* (Baltimore: Romm, 1915), 1–15.

147. *JE*, Aug. 4, 1905, 8; Aug. 25, 1905, 9; *Sun*, June 5, 1908, 7.

148. *Sun*, May 17, 1914, 5.

149. Ibid., May 31, 1910, 5; May 28, 1911, 7; May 30, 1911, 5; May 18, 1913, 5.

150. *JC*, Mar. 27, 1896, 4.

151. *JE*, July 5, 1895, 7. On Benderly in Baltimore, see Jonathan B. Krasner, *The Benderly Boys and American Jewish Education* (Waltham, MA: Brandeis University Press, 2011), chap. 1.

152. *Sun*, Jan. 19, 1908, 7.

153. Ibid., Sept. 14, 1897, 6.

154. Ibid., Oct. 15, 1896, 6; Sept. 24, 1898, 12.

155. Ibid., Nov. 10, 1890, 6; Apr. 13, 1906, 6.

156. Ibid., Jan. 27, 1904, 2.

157. "Dos ervartete iz endlikh geshehn," Yiddish campaign leaflet for Joseph Seidenman, 1903, Politics VF, JMM.

158. *AA*, Dec. 7, 1907, 4; Dec. 14, 1907, 4. For an overview of the disenfranchisement movement in Maryland during this period, see Margaret Law Collcott, *The Negro in Maryland Politics, 1870–1912* (Baltimore: Johns Hopkins University Press, 1969), chap. 5.

159. *Sun*, Oct. 30, 1909, 9.

160. Ibid., Oct. 5, 1909, 14 (quote); Oct. 9, 1909, 16; Oct. 26, 1909, 13; *BA*, Jan. 15, 1909, 14; Oct. 6, 1909, 14; Oct. 12, 1909, 14; Nov. 1, 1909, 12; Collcott, *Negro in Maryland Politics*, 130.

161. Argersinger, *Making the Amalgamated*, 40–47, 50–59; Berman, "Threads of Life," 16.

162. *Sun*, Jan. 6, 1902, 7; Jan. 9, 1902, 6; Sept. 22, 1902, 12; Nov. 21, 1904, 12; Aug. 3, 1905, 10; Dec. 27, 1915, 3.

163. Ibid., June 5, 1906, 14.

164. *MAJC*, 213–15; Alexandra Lee Levin, *Dare to Be Different: A Biography of Louis H. Levin of Baltimore* (New York: Bloch, 1972), chap. 5; *JC*, May 11, 1906; *Sun*, Oct. 4, 1906, 12.

165. *Sun*, July 23, 1907, 9; Sept. 14, 1907, 6; Apr. 4, 1910, 5.

166. Ibid., Sept. 16, 1907, 14.

167. Ibid., Jan. 3, 1910, 14.

168. Ibid., June 12, 1908, 12.

169. Ibid., Sept. 14, 1907, 6; May 6, 1908, 9; Apr. 9, 1909, 9; *BA*, Apr. 9, 1909, 12.

170. Szold, "Early Zionist Days," 265–66; Baila Round Shargel, *Lost Love: The Untold Story of Henrietta Szold* (Philadelphia: Jewish Publication Society of America, 1997); Harry Friedenwald, "Solomon Schechter," *Students Annual of the Jewish Theological Seminary of America*

3 (1916); Levin, *Vision*; Joan Dash, *Summoned to Jerusalem: The Life of Henrietta Szold* (New York: HarperCollins, 1979), 22 (quote).

171. Goldstein, "Practical as Spiritual," 19–21; Benjamin Hartogensis, "The Russian Night School of Baltimore," *PAJHS* 31 (1928): 225–28; Alexandra Lee Levin, "Henrietta Szold and the Russian Immigrant School," *MHM* 57 (1962): 1–15.

172. Szold, "Early Zionist Days"; Yonathan Shapiro, *Leadership of the American Zionist Organization, 1897-1930* (Urbana: University of Illinois Press, 1971), 37, 91.

173. Crooks, *Politics and Progress*, 75–76, 204–5.

174. Argersinger, *Making the Amalgamated*, 43, 64–65; *Sun*, Oct. 1, 1900, 7; Oct. 14, 1901, 6; Feb. 8, 1909, 14; Jan. 3, 1910, 14; Nov. 11, 1915, 8.

175. Elfenbein, "Uptown and Traditional," 72–78; *Sun*, Jan. 4, 1909, 16; Jan. 3, 1910, 14; Jan. 28, 1910, 8; Mar. 28, 1910, 11; Dec. 5, 1910, 14.

176. Jennifer Vess, "A 'Children's Playground' and 'Centre for Adults': The Story of the Jewish Educational Alliance, 1909–1952," *Generations* (2009–2010): 32–43.

177. *Sun*, Feb. 12, 1912, 8.

178. Ibid., July 3, 1915, 5.

179. Ibid., Nov. 4, 1912, 14; Mar. 28, 1915, S3.

180. Jonathan D. Sarna, ed., *The American Jewish Experience*, 2nd ed. (New York: Holmes and Meier, 1997), 360; Bureau of Immigration, *Annual Report of the Commissioner General of Immigration* (1916), 73; (1917), 33; (1919), 114; (1920), 120; (1921), 64, catalog.hathitrust.org /Record/011159819.

181. *Sun*, Feb. 1, 1918, 1; Feb. 24, 1919, 7.

182. Ibid., June 23, 1918, 9; Aug. 7, 1918, 5; Apr. 23, 1967, magazine section, 2.

183. Ibid., July 25, 1921, 5; Oct. 31, 1921, 5.

184. Ibid., Dec. 13, 1917, 7.

185. For the national background, see Arthur Goren, *The Politics and Public Culture of American Jews* (Bloomington: Indiana University Press, 1999), 24–25, 129.

186. For articles, broadsides, and other ephemera documenting the activities of the American Jewish Relief Committee in Baltimore from the perspective of the immigrants, see the Reuben Rivkin scrapbook, JMM.

187. *Sun*, Dec. 30, 1918, 5; Nov. 16, 1920, 7.

188. Ibid., June 10, 1917, 7; June 11, 1917, 5; *American Jewish Chronicle*, June 8, 1917, 155; June 15, 1917, 186.

189. *American Jewish Chronicle*, Sept. 14, 1917, 499–500; July 5, 1918, 203–4; Abraham Shusterman, *The Legacy of a Liberal* (Baltimore: Har Sinai Congregation, 1967), 50; *JT*, Sept. 24, 1919.

Chapter 4.
Bawlmer Jews: The Interwar Years

1. *JT*, Jan. 28, 1921, 22.

2. The Immigration Restriction Act of 1921 reduced annual immigration from Southern and Eastern Europe from around 700,000 people to 160,000. In 1924, the Johnson-Reed Act went even further, limiting total European immigration to 150,000 people per year and cutting the Southern and Eastern European share to a small fraction of that amount.

3. Sherry H. Olson, *Baltimore: The Building of an American City* (Baltimore: Johns Hopkins University Press, 1980), 302.

4. US Census, 1910, 1920, 1930, 1940; Olson, *Baltimore*; Joseph L. Arnold, "Suburban

Growth and Municipal Annexation in Baltimore, 1745–1918," *MHM* 73 (Summer 1978): 120–21. The city's population rose from 558,485 in 1910 to 859,100 in 1940; through this period, Baltimore ranked as the nation's seventh- or eighth-largest city.

5. Olson, *Baltimore*, 325.

6. *American Jewish Year Book* 22 (1920–1921), 373–74, 46 (1944–1945), 496–97; "Study of the Recreational, Social and Cultural Resources of the Jewish Community of Baltimore," 1925, 13–14, Associated Collection, MS 170, folder 297, JMM. This study was commissioned by the Baltimore YMHA (hereafter 1925 YMHA study). Despite its growth, Baltimore's Jewish community dropped from America's sixth-largest to eighth-largest from 1918 to 1937, being surpassed by the Los Angeles and Detroit Jewish communities. However, Baltimore Jewry far outpaced the Jewish populations of St. Louis and Pittsburgh, which in 1918 had roughly the same number of Jews that Baltimore had.

7. Deborah Dash Moore, *At Home in America: Second Generation New York Jews* (New York: Columbia University Press, 1981), 61.

8. *Evening Sun*, Dec. 19, 1972, C1; Leon Sachs, "Review of Baltimore Jewish Council Program," c. 1958, 8, BJC VF, JMM.

9. *Evening Sun*, Dec. 19, 1972, C1; Robert M. Fogelson, *Bourgeois Nightmares: Suburbia, 1870–1930* (New Haven, CT: Yale University Press, 2007), 65.

10. Olson, *Baltimore*, 325; Garrett Power, "The Residential Segregation of Baltimore's Jews," *Generations* (Fall 1996): 5–7; *NIMN*, 56, 74; Roland Park Company marketing brochure, 1930, Roland Park VF, JMM.

11. BJC memos, Jan. 31, 1941, and Mar. 4, 1942, Baltimore Jewish Council Records (hereafter BJC Records), MS 107, folders 352, 331, JMM.

12. Joseph Meyerhoff, OH 63, June 3, 1977, 19, JMM; *NIMN*.

13. Garrett Power, "Apartheid Baltimore Style: The Residential Segregation Ordinances of 1910–1913," *Maryland Law Review* (1983): 289–328; *NIMN*, xi.

14. In 1920 African Americans in New York, Chicago, Detroit, and Cleveland made up around 3–4 percent of the population; in Philadelphia, around 7 percent. In 1930, Baltimore still had the largest percentage of black people of the nation's ten largest cities: almost 18 percent. Southern cities had large black populations but small numbers of Jews. Campbell Gibson and Kay Jung, *Historical Census Statistics on Population Totals by Race, 1790 to 1990* (Washington, DC: US Census Bureau, 2005).

15. Phyllis Orrick, "Northwest Exodus: The Migration of Baltimore's Jews," *City Paper*, June 5, 1987, 11–17 (Sachs quote); *NIMN*, 56.

16. Alexandra Lee Levin, *Vision: A Biography of Harry Friedenwald* (Philadelphia: Jewish Publication Society of America, 1964), 338–39. See *NIMN* on Marbury as a segregationist leader.

17. The seven new congregations joined five that had been established earlier by Central European Jews. See *STCM*.

18. 1925 YMHA study; Gilbert Sandler, *Jewish Baltimore: A Family Album* (Baltimore: Johns Hopkins University Press, 2000).

19. On Mount Washington, see Sandler, *Jewish Baltimore*, 60. On Windsor Hills, see Sarah Hartman, ed., *Windsor Hills: A Century of History* (Baltimore: Windsor Hill Neighbors, 1995), 14; Sandler, "Aristocratic Touch," *JT*, July 3, 1998. On Dumbarton, see *NIMN*, 71–72.

20. 1925 YMHA study, 16, 135; *Sun*, Apr. 13, 1924, F1; Deborah Weiner, Anita Kassof, and Avi Decter, eds., *Voices of Lombard Street: A Century of Change in East Baltimore* (Baltimore: Jewish Museum of Maryland, 2007), 152–59.

----

21. Barnett Berman, "Baltimore's Little Jerusalem," *Generations* (Fall 1999): 10–13; Gedaliah Cohen, "Notes from a Hebrew Teacher's Notebook," *Generations* (Dec. 1983): 32; "Recreational Study of the Park Heights Area," 1935, conducted for the Jewish Educational Alliance (hereafter 1935 Park Heights study), JMM, 1995.98.57.

22. *JT*, Oct. 15, 1982, 46–47 (Keiser); Sandler, *Jewish Baltimore*, 114; Sandler, "On the Avenue," Gilbert Sandler Manuscript Collection, JMM.

23. 1925 YMHA study, 18, 28; Gilbert Sandler, "Landmark Occasion," *JT*, Aug. 24, 2007; Gilbert Sandler, "A Front-Row Seat on Cottage Avenue," *Generations* (2003): 25.

24. Sandler, *Jewish Baltimore*, 133; Barry Kessler, "Bedlam with Corned Beef on the Side," *Generations* (Fall 1993): 2–6 (quote, 5).

25. Barry Kessler, *Druid Hill Park: Jewish Baltimore's Green Oasis, 1920-1960* (Baltimore: Baltimore Jewish Environmental Network, 2009); Gilbert Sandler, "Halcyon Days," *JT*, Aug. 26, 2005 (Easterwood Park and Sherman quote); Sandler, "Front-Row Seat."

26. 1935 Park Heights study, 15–17; Harry London, "Shul Mentsch, Shul Kid: Becoming an American Jew in Pimlico's 'Doorway to Hope,'" *Generations* (Fall 1998): 20–25.

27. Sandler, "On the Avenue."

28. Kenneth D. Durr, *Behind the Backlash: White Working-Class Politics in Baltimore, 1940-1980* (Chapel Hill: University of North Carolina Press, 2003), 13; Olson, *Baltimore*, 292–93, 304.

29. Sachs, "Review," 5–6. Many oral histories in the JMM collection discuss encounters with job discrimination. On McCormick, see Ralph Brunn memoir, Memoir Collection, JMM.

30. Philip Kahn Jr., *A Stitch in Time: The Four Seasons of Baltimore's Needle Trades* (Baltimore: Maryland Historical Society, 1989), 130, 138; Jo Ann E. Argersinger, *Making the Amalgamated: Gender, Ethnicity, and Class in the Baltimore Clothing Industry, 1899-1939* (Baltimore: Johns Hopkins University Press, 1999), 64, 108, 121–22, 155.

31. Kahn, *Stitch in Time*, 148; Argersinger, *Making the Amalgamated*, 108, 123.

32. Argersinger, *Making the Amalgamated*, 108, 123–30, 139; Kahn, *Stitch in Time*, 137–38.

33. Argersinger, *Making the Amalgamated*, 146, 140, 145; Jacob Edelman, OH 29, Nov. 2, 1975, JMM. See also Andor Skotnes, *A New Deal for All? Race and Class Struggles in Depression-Era Baltimore* (Durham, NC: Duke University Press, 2013).

34. Philip Kahn Jr., *Uncommon Threads: Threads That Wove the Fabric of Baltimore Jewish Life* (Baltimore: PECAN Publications, 1998), 190; Israel Myers obituary, *Sun*, Dec. 29, 1999; US Census, 1930. On the entrance of black workers into the garment industry nationally, see Eric L. Goldstein, *The Price of Whiteness: Jews, Race, and American Identity* (Princeton, NJ: Princeton University Press, 2006), 150–51.

35. Kahn, *Stitch in Time*, 148; Polan Katz VF, JMM; George B. Hess Sr., "Footloose and Fancy: A Personal History of Hess Shoes," c. 1972, Hess Shoes VF, JMM.

36. *Sun*, July 6, 2008, E1; "The Hoffbergers," *Baltimore Magazine*, Sept. 1994, clipping in Hoffberger Family VF, JMM.

37. *Sun*, July 12, 1936, SM6; Oct. 28, 1951, SM9; Morris Schapiro obituary, *Sun*, May 4, 1969; Sandler, *Jewish Baltimore*, 76–83.

38. Kahn, *Stitch in Time*, 143. Epstein sold out to the Butler Brothers of Chicago in 1929.

39. Sandler, *Jewish Baltimore*, 84; Kahn, *Uncommon Threads*, 169; Louis F. Cahn, *Man's Concern for Man: The First Fifty Years of the Associated Jewish Charities and Welfare Fund of Baltimore* (Baltimore: Associated Jewish Charities and Welfare Fund, 1970), 13.

40. *Tips and Taps*, Nov. 1925, 1; Steve Norwitz, "Brager-Gutman's Centennial Recalls Great Moments of Past," *Baltimore News-American*, June 13, 1976; Hutzler Brothers Business Papers,

MS 153, JMM. For more, see Avi Y. Decter and Melissa Martens, eds., *Enterprising Emporiums: The Jewish Department Stores of Downtown Baltimore* (Baltimore: Jewish Museum of Maryland, 2001).

41. Jayne Guberman and Shelly Hettleman, "All in the Family: Jewish Women in Baltimore Family Businesses," *Generations* (2002): 2–15; Dora Silber obituary, *Sun*, Mar. 12, 1989.

42. Bess Fishman, OH 633, Mar. 30, 2001, JMM; Sandler, "They Lived over the Store" (Albin, Yousem), Gilbert Sandler Manuscript Collection, JMM.

43. Sandler, *Jewish Baltimore*, 73–76.

44. A January 1931 survey of black West Baltimore by the *Afro-American* newspaper found that black professionals outnumbered white professionals 73 to 41. Of the district's retail stores, 30 were owned by blacks, 308 by whites. Though the survey did not indicate the ethnicity of the white merchants, city directories and other sources show that a substantial majority were Jews. On the national scene, see, for example, Cheryl Greenberg, *Troubling the Waters: Black-Jewish Relations in the American Century* (Princeton, NJ: Princeton University Press, 2006), chapter 2.

45. Eric Holcomb, *The City as Suburb: A History of Northeast Baltimore since 1660* (Chicago: Center for American Places, 2010); M. Hirsh Goldberg, *Joseph Meyerhoff: A Portrait* (Baltimore: N.p., 1987), 32–33; Maurice R. Shochatt, "Victor Frenkil," *JT*, July 14, 1950; Olson, *Baltimore*, 338.

46. Jo Ann E. Argersinger, *Toward a New Deal: Citizen Participation, Government Policy, and the Great Depression in Baltimore* (Chapel Hill: University of North Carolina Press, 1988), 2 (first quote); *Sun*, Oct. 29, 1985 (Legum); Louis J. Fox VF, JMM.

47. Blaine J. Yarrington, "American Oil: How a Father and Son Knocked Out the Knock," *Nation's Business*, Feb. 1972, 66.

48. Philip Glass, *Words without Music* (New York: Norton, 2015), 4–6. On Zamoiski, *Sun*, Feb. 19, 1950, MA2.

49. Avi Y. Decter, ed., "Chronology: Entertaining Maryland," *Generations* (2003): 74–81; *Sun*, Apr. 20, 1993, 7C, on Blaustein; Dean Krimmel and Steve Liebowitz, "Now Playing at the Hippodrome," *Generations* (2003): 28–39; "West Baltimore Squares: Remembering the Celestial Ceiling of the Harlem Theatre," baltimoreheritage.org; *AA*, Oct. 15, 1932, 10.

50. Jack Portney VF, Izzy Rainess VF, both JMM. Other Baltimore Jewish boxers included Leon Luckman (aka Izzy Caplan), Benny Goldstein, Abraham Sobel, Sylvan Bass, Benny Schwartz, Benjamin Lipsitz (aka Frankie Rice), Nate Carp, Herman Weiner, Sid Lampe, and Eddie Leonard. Thomas Scharf, *Baltimore's Boxing Legacy, 1893-2003* (Charleston, SC: Arcadia, 2003).

51. Deborah R. Weiner, "Always Have Kind Words for the Place That Feeds You: Jews on 'The Block,' " *Generations* (2003): 6–17.

52. Joseph L. Arnold, "The Last of the Good Old Days: Politics in Baltimore, 1920-1950," *MHM* 71 (Fall, 1976): 443–48; Olson, *Baltimore*; *Sun*, Jan. 6, 1930, 24; Marni Davis, *Jews and Booze: Becoming American in the Age of Prohibition* (New York: New York University Press, 2012).

53. *Sun*, Jan. 14, 1922, 16; Apr. 5, 1922, 26.

54. Kahn, *Uncommon Threads*, 161; *Sun*, Jan. 15, 1923, 18.

55. See, for example, *Sun*, Apr. 9, 1929, 20; Feb. 4, 1936, 22; Nov. 13, 1937, 18; "1730 Ruxton Avenue: The Story of Mike and Ida Glaser and Their Children," Memoir Collection, JMM, 18.

56. Antero Pietila, "Sid Weinberg Took His Secrets to Grave," *Baltimore Examiner*, July 18, 2007. On Sapperstein, *Sun*, Feb. 4, 1936, 22; Sept. 9, 1939, 22; Dec. 2, 1953, 42. On Goldberg, *Sun*, Jan. 25, 1936, 20; "Sunlight on Sports," *Sun*, Feb. 21, 23, and Mar. 2, 1936.

----

57. Sidney Offit, *Memoir of the Bookie's Son* (New York: St. Martin's Griffin, 1995). Barry Levinson's 1999 film, *Liberty Heights*, offers a revealing glimpse of how attitudes toward such shady enterprises changed in the post–World War II era.

58. US Census, 1930; 1930 *BCD.*

59. Gilbert Sandler, "Hard Times, Shattered Dreams," Gilbert Sandler Manuscript Collection, JMM (first quote); Sydney Cohen, OH 709, Feb. 26, 2007, JMM; Argersinger, *Toward a New Deal*, 8–9, 18–19.

60. Quoted in Sandler, "Hard Times."

61. *JT*, Jan. 2, 1931; Jan. 24, 1932; Feb. 17, 1933; board minutes, 1931–1932, Associated Collection, JMM.

62. Aaron Sopher obituary, *Sun*, Apr. 28, 1972, C24; *JT*, Oct. 14, 1932, 27; "A New Year's Resolution," *JT*, Sept. 9, 1932, 19.

63. Kahn, *Uncommon Threads*, 189–90; Kahn, *Stitch in Time*, 169; Sandler, "Hard Times"; Martin Kohn, "Hochschild, Kohn and Company: A Personal Account," 1979, Hochschild, Kohn VF, JMM; Norwitz, "Brager-Gutman's."

64. K. Meghan Gross, ed., "Chronology: Baltimore's Downtown Department Stores," *Generations* (2001): 56; Francis F. Beirne, *Hutzler's: A Picture History, 1858–1968* (Baltimore: Hutzler Brothers, 1968); Norwitz, "Brager-Gutman's"; Sandler, "H-K Days," n.d., Hochschild, Kohn VF, JMM.

65. "Rose Shanis Loans—Fifty Years Old," Rose Shanis Loans Collection, MS 159, folder 11, JMM; " 'Santa' Shanis: A Labor of Lending," unidentified newspaper article, c. 1982, Rose Shanis VF, JMM; Rosalee Davison, OH 565, May 30, 2003, JMM.

66. "Interview with Dr. Herbert Goldstone," *Generations* (June 1983): 26–30.

67. US Census, 1910; Gilbert Sandler, "Blazing Trails," Gilbert Sandler Manuscript Collection, JMM (quote); Rose Zetzer Collection, MS 86, JMM.

68. *Sun*, Nov. 27, 1923, 14; "Jews in America," *Fortune* (Feb. 1936): 141.

69. Marcia Graham Synott, "Anti-Semitism and American Universities: Did Quotas Follow the Jews?" in *Anti-Semitism in American History*, ed. David A. Gerber (Urbana: University of Illinois Press, 1986), 233–71; Leon Sachs, OH 257, Feb. 6, 1991, JMM; *NIMN*, 133–34.

70. Willard Hackerman, OH 477, May 4, 2001, JMM.

71. Kahn, *Uncommon Threads*, 196; Cahn, *Man's Concern*, esp. 8; Paul I. Umansky, "The Story of Sinai Hospital," *Generations* (Fall 1998): 13–16.

72. Joseph Katz VF, JMM; *Sun*, Nov. 11, 1992, 11C; "Jack L. Levin, Champion of Causes," *Generations* (Apr. 1985): 3.

73. *ATFS*, 152, 126.

74. Ibid., 145–46.

75. *JT*, Dec. 19, 1919, 4; Sept. 24, 1919, 2. Although owned by a Pittsburgh family, the *Jewish Times* was locally run.

76. *ATFS*, 263–64, xvi.

77. Moore, *At Home*, 16.

78. Michael Miller, "The Organization and Early Years of Menorah Lodge in Baltimore City," JMM, 1990.108.7; Federation of Jewish Women's Organizations Records, MS 82, JMM; *Sun*, Nov. 23, 1919, 16.

79. "Associated Jewish Charities Officially Formed," *JT*, Jan. 21, 1921; Cahn, *Man's Concern*, 9–10; Alexandra Lee Levin, *Dare to Be Different: A Biography of Louis H. Levin* (New York: Bloch, 1972); Israel Goldman, "Louis Levin: Master Builder of the Baltimore Jewish Community," 1966, JMM, 2007.51.6; J. Vincenza Scarpaci, "Louis H. Levin of Baltimore: A Pioneer in

Cultural Pluralism," *MHM* (June 1992): 183–92; Levy quoted in "The Associated: Ninety Years of Promises Kept," Associated Annual Report, June 2010, 2, Associated VF, JMM.

80. Cahn, *Man's Concern*, 13–14.

81. Hymen Saye, "The Baltimore Talmud Torah," *Generations* (June 1981): 19; *JT*, Jan. 28, 1921, 8 (Levy); July 13, 1923, 24 (Efros).

82. Melissa Klapper, "The Debate over Jewish Education," *Generations* (Fall 1996): 17.

83. Cahn, *Man's Concern*, 14–15; "Levindale's Record Is Long and Noble," *Jewish Press*, Sept. 29, 1950.

84. Edith Lauer and Gertrude Glick, "Experiments in Flexibility: A Study of Inter-Agency Relationships," *Jewish Social Service Quarterly* (June 1936): 376–80; Edith Lauer, "How We Found Our Foster Homes," *Jewish Social Service Quarterly* (Sept. 1928): 57–58.

85. Umansky, "The Story of Sinai Hospital," 14.

86. Joseph F. Hecht, *History of the Jewish Big Brother League* (Baltimore: N.p., 1971); 1925 YMHA study, 124–25.

87. Rose Esterson, "History of the YM and YWHA of Baltimore," Dedication Book, 1930, Associated Collection, folder 301, JMM.

88. David Kaufman, *Shul with a Pool: The "Synagogue-Center" in American Jewish History* (Waltham, MA: Brandeis University Press, 1999), 86–88, 112; 1925 YMHA study, 125. On the importance of the YMHA to interwar Jewish social life, see Sandler, *Jewish Baltimore*, 125–27.

89. "Reasons Y" leaflet, 1926, Associated Collection, folder 293, JMM; 1925 YMHA study, 137.

90. Louis Cahn, "When Fundraising Was Fun," *Generations* (June 1980): 16; "Shall the 'Y' Close Its Doors?" *JT*, Sept. 16, 1932; Ruth Smith Coppage, "Sinai Hospital: Its Past and Present," *Alumni Magazine*, May 1985; *JT*, Oct. 28, 1932, 27.

91. Associated board minutes, 1931–1932, Associated Collection, JMM; Jewish Social Service Bureau report, *JT*, Feb. 17, 1933; Cahn, *Man's Concern*, 21–22.

92. Quoted in "Address of Walter Sondheim," Jan. 22, 1933, Associated Collection, box 21, JMM.

93. *Sun*, Jan. 23, 1933, 14.

94. Beth S. Wenger, *New York Jews and the Great Depression: Uncertain Promise* (New Haven, CT: Yale University Press, 1996), 137–38, 142, 155–59.

95. Deborah R. Weiner, "A Club of Their Own: Suburban and Woodholme through the Years," *Generations* (2004): 9.

96. Kahn, *Uncommon Threads*, 183–84; Weiner, "Club of Their Own."

97. Rubin Livov, untitled [History of the Workmen's Circle in Baltimore], n.d., Workmen's Circle VF, JMM.

98. Mlynover Verein Collection, MS 36; Lutzker Verein Collection, MS 39; Hebrew Young Men's Sick Relief Association Collection, MS 207, all JMM.

99. Brith Sholom, *Bulletin*, May 1932, MS 146, folder 38, JMM.

100. 1925 YMHA study, 81–82. Baltimore Jews followed the pattern described by Daniel Soyer in *Jewish Immigrant Associations and American Identity in New York, 1880–1939* (Detroit, MI: Wayne State University Press, 1997).

101. Rivkin scrapbook, 1905–1987, JMM, 2012.106; "Talk Presented by Lester Levy at the Jewish Historical Society, May 1965," Reuben Rivkin VF, JMM. See also *Sun*, Aug. 30, 1920, 7; Feb. 13, 1922, 14; Livov, untitled [History of the Workmen's Circle].

102. *Sun*, July 10, 1921, 18; Levin, *Vision*, 239–98. On divisions in the Zionist movement,

see Melvin Urofsky, *American Zionism from Herzl to the Holocaust* (Lincoln: University of Nebraska Press, 1995).

103. *JT*, Aug. 11, 1922, 11; *Sun*, Aug. 9, 1922, 22. The 1925 YMHA study lists Baltimore's many Zionist groups, 76–77.

104. On Sonneborn, see *MAJC*, 197; Herman Seidel, "Baltimore: Cornerstone of Labor Zionism," in *A Pictorial History of Maryland Jewry*, ed. Abraham Glushakow (Baltimore: Jewish Voice Publishing, 1955), 148–49; *JT*, Aug. 30, 1929, 10; *Baltimore Post*, Sept. 5, 1929. On Hadassah, see, for example, *JT*, June 29, 1933, 8.

105. *Sun*, July 18, 1933, 3; Friedenwald Family Papers, MS 161, folder 272, JMM; *JT*, Mar. 20, 1936, 26; Mar. 27, 1936, 14; Apr. 3, 1936, 20; Apr. 10, 1936, 22; Herman Seidel Papers, MS 13, folder 516, JMM.

106. On Reform anti-Zionism in Baltimore, see Abba Solomon, *The Speech and Its Context* (N.p.: Abba Solomon, 2011), 70; "Farband Labor Zionist Order," in Glushakow, *Pictorial History*, 119.

107. On the national conflict, see, for example, *ATFS*; Wise to Rosenau, Apr. 10, 1933, Friedenwald Family Papers, folder 272, JMM. See folders 237, 241, 272, and 276 for correspondence among Wise, Friedenwald, and Sobeloff.

108. Sobeloff to Wise, Apr. 24, 1933, Friedenwald Family Papers, folder 241, JMM.

109. *JT*, May 19, 1933, 12.

110. Friedenwald Family Papers, folders 23, 237, 242, 272, 276, JMM; *Sun*, Mar. 31, 1933, 20; Anita Kassof, Avi Y. Decter, and Deborah R. Weiner, eds., *Lives Lost, Lives Found: Baltimore's German Jewish Refugees, 1933-1945* (Baltimore: Jewish Museum of Maryland, 2004).

111. Sobeloff to Herman Seidel, Jan. 12, 1937, Herman Seidel Papers, JMM; Friedenwald Family Papers, folders 275–76, JMM. See Jeffrey S. Gurock, ed., *America, American Jews, and the Holocaust* (New York: Routledge, 1998), 216, on the Tydings resolution; and more generally, Henry L. Feingold, "Who Shall Bear the Guilt for the Holocaust? The Human Dilemma," in *The American Jewish Experience*, ed. Jonathan D. Sarna (New York: Holmes and Meier, 1997), 274–92.

112. Rachel Skutch, *Deeds to Live By* (Baltimore: Baltimore Branch of the National Council of Jewish Women, 1968), 76–78; Kassof et al., *Lives Lost*. For Levy's wrenching correspondence with people for whom she was unable to secure visas, see Karen Falk, *Of Hats and Harmonies: The Recollections of Baltimore's Lester S. Levy* (Baltimore: Jewish Museum of Maryland, 2005).

113. Kassof et al., *Lives Lost*; Falk, *Of Hats and Harmonies*.

114. Leo Kanner Papers, MS 205, JMM.

115. *Lives Lost* exhibition files, JMM.

116. Gertrude Hirschler, *To Love Mercy: The Story of the Chevra Ahavas Chesed of Baltimore* (Baltimore: N.p., 1972); Moses Schwab, "Memories of Shearith Israel," Shearith Israel VF, JMM.

117. Schwab, "Memories of Shearith Israel," 4.

118. Jeffrey S. Gurock, "American Judaism between the Two World Wars," in *The Columbia History of Jews and Judaism in America*, ed. Marc Lee Raphael (New York: Columbia University Press, 2008), 95; Moore, *At Home*; Kaufman, *Shul with a Pool*; Wenger, *New York Jews*, 166 (quote).

119. Jan Bernhardt Schein, *On Three Pillars: The History of Chizuk Amuno Congregation, 1871-1996* (Baltimore: Chizuk Amuno, 2000), 147–87.

120. 1925 YMHA study, 43–44.

121. Arthur Hertzberg, *A Jew in America: My Life and a People's Struggle for Identity* (San

Francisco: Harper, 2002), 13–15, 27–28; Abraham Glushakow, *Maryland Bicentennial Jewish Book* (Baltimore: Jewish Voice Publishing, 1975), 160. See also Melvin J. Sykes, "Orthodoxy in East Baltimore: A Retrospect," *Generations* (Fall 1999): 25–31.

122. Rabbi Shmuel Dovid Siegel, "Some Highlights of the First Forty Years of the Adas," Adas 75th Anniversary Program, 1993, Adath B'nei Israel VF, JMM.

123. 1925 YMHA study, 39–40; Adath B'nei Israel Records, 1920–1953, MS 114, JMM; US Census, 1910 and 1920, on Rae Mechanic. Adath B'nei Israel shared characteristics of the national Young Israel movement, but was not affiliated.

124. *JT*, Dec. 19, 1919, 2; June 27, 1924, 6; Glushakow, *Maryland Bicentennial*.

125. Arthur J. Magida, "Immersed in Torah," *JT*, Nov. 26, 1993, 46–51 (quote, 49); William B. Helmreich, *The World of the Yeshiva: An Intimate Portrait of Orthodox Jewry* (Hoboken, NJ: KTAV, 2000).

126. *STCM*.

127. London, "Shul Mentsch," 20–21.

128. US Census, 1920, 1930. The three congregations, founded between 1919 and 1921, built their synagogues in the mid-1920s. *STCM*.

129. Martha J. Vill, "Park Heights: A Study of a Jewish Neighborhood," unpublished paper, 1979, BNHP, 18 (first quote); Sandler, *Jewish Baltimore*, 177.

130. 1925 YMHA study, 42–43; *Beth Tfiloh Fifteenth Anniversary Memorial History* (Baltimore: Beth Tfiloh Congregation, 1936), 15.

131. *Beth Tfiloh Fifteenth Anniversary*, 20, 25; "From Strength to Strength: Beth Tfiloh Congregation 1921–1981," 9, Beth Tfiloh VF, JMM.

132. Samuel Rosenblatt, OH 143, June 15, 1981, JMM; "From Strength to Strength," 11.

133. *Beth Tfiloh Fifteenth Anniversary*, 9, 50; Rosenblatt, OH. On the national picture, see Jonathan D. Sarna, *American Judaism: A History* (New Haven, CT: Yale University Press, 2004).

134. "The Guardians of the City: The Rabbis Who Keep Baltimore's Jewish Tradition Alive," *Jewish Mail*, Oct. 1953, 4.

135. *JT*, Apr. 3, 1936, 50. Tabak and Drazin both graduated from the Rabbi Isaac Elchanan Theological Seminary, which became part of Yeshiva University.

136. Sarna, *American Judaism*, 213.

137. *JT*, June 27, 1924, 6 (quote); Aug. 10, 1934, 7.

138. Ibid., July 13, 1923, 24 (quote); 1925 YMHA study, 49–50; *JT*, Apr. 17, 1936, 12.

139. Schein, *On Three Pillars*, 187; Abraham Shusterman, *Legacy of a Liberal: The Miracle of Har Sinai Congregation* (Baltimore: Har Sinai Congregation, 1967), 55.

140. *Sun*, Nov. 30, 1919, 16.

141. Ibid., Apr. 22, 1936, 24; May 1, 1936, 13; Feb. 26, 1939, CS6; Sept. 29, 1996, J6.

142. Ibid., Sept. 29, 1996, J6; *JT*, Apr. 17, 24, and May 1, 1936; *Sun*, Apr. 20, 1936, 18; Shusterman, *Legacy*, 53.

143. Ford required his dealerships to carry the paper, guaranteeing a wide distribution.

144. On antisemitism during the interwar era, see, for example, *ATFS*.

145. *Sun*, Apr. 19, 1936, 18; Apr. 23, 1936, 26; Apr. 21, 1936, 24; Apr. 14, 1936, 28.

146. David "Dutch" Baer, OH 114, June 12, 1980, JMM; Minnie Schneider, OH 66, May 12, 1977, JMM; Paper quoted in Ellie Ginsburg, "American Jews and the Holocaust: History, Memory, and Identity," MA thesis, University of Maryland, Baltimore County. See also Perry Siegel, OH 248, May 1, 1988; Ida Marton, OH 177, Feb. 21, 1983; Martin Lev, OH 301, Apr. 4, 1994; Milton Schwartz, OH 676, Nov. 9, 2005, all JMM.

- - - - - - - - - - - - -

147. Isadore Livov, OH 687, June 7, 2006; Aaron Smelkinson, OH 620, July 9, 2004; Edward Attman, OH 678, Nov. 28, 2005; Blanche Green, OH 681, Mar. 10, 2006; Rosalie Abrams, OH 49, Jan. 23, 1977, all JMM; Catherine Mancuso, OH 175, Sept. 21, 1979; John Pente, OH 96, July 23, 1979; Joseph Sergi, OH 139, Aug.21, 1979, all BNHP.

148. Sandler, "Front-Row Seat," 27.

149. Norma Wolod, OH 687, June 7, 2006, JMM.

150. 1925 YMHA study, 102.

151. *The Green Bag* (City College yearbook), 1923, 186.

152. Gilbert Sandler, "City Forever!" *JT*, Dec. 30, 2005, 57–58.

153. *VOTE! The Life of Sadie Crockin*, 2010, JMM exhibition files; *Baltimore Post*, Oct. 23, 1929; Kahn, *Uncommon Threads*.

154. Sidney Needle to Isaac Potts, May 11, 1939, folder 121, BJC Records.

155. Decter and Martens, *Enterprising Emporiums*, 71; Dirk Bonker, "Matters of Public Knowledge: The Baltimore *Jewish Times* and Nazi Germany's War against the Jews, 1933–1942," in Kassof et al., *Lives Lost*, 68–69.

156. Friedenwald correspondence, Friedenwald Family Papers, folders 269, 271, 273, JMM; *JT*, Sept. 30, 1932; Clementine Kaufman, "A Rabbi's Daughter Remembers," *Generations* (Fall 1999): 1–5.

157. *ATFS*, 238–39.

158. Leon Sachs, OH 174, Oct. 11, 1979, BNHP; Sachs, "Review," 6 (quote).

159. *Sun*, June 13, 1939, 24; June 14, 1939, 24.

160. *JT*, June 16, 1939, 13; Maurice Shochatt columns, *JT*, June 23 and 30, 1939; *Sun*, July 7, 1939, 24.

161. See Harvey Wheeler, "Yesterday's Robin Hood: The Rise and Fall of Baltimore's Trenton Democratic Club," *American Quarterly* 7 (Winter 1955): 337, on the latent power of the city's Jewish population.

162. Sandler, *Jewish Baltimore*, 160–63; *Sun*, Aug. 2, 1921, 9; Sept. 25, 1926, 24; Dec. 31, 1933, 20.

163. *NIMN*, 112 (first quote); Baer, OH (second quote). See also Sandler, *Jewish Baltimore*, 164.

164. Wheeler, "Yesterday's Robin Hood."

165. Ibid.; *NIMN*, 113; Baer, OH; Louis Bluefeld, OH 159, May 24, 1978, BNHP.

166. Sandler, *Jewish Baltimore*, 163 (quote); Jacob Edelman VF, JMM; *Sun*, Nov. 30, 1965, A19.

167. Garrett Power, "Public Service and Private Interests: A Chronicle of the Professional Life of Philip B. Perlman," *Journal of Southern Legal History* (1995–1996): 61–70. Ironically, as the US solicitor general, Perlman went on to successfully argue *Shelley v. Kraemer*, the 1948 Supreme Court case that made restrictive covenants against blacks and other minorities unenforceable.

168. *Sun*, Feb. 20, 1931, 4; *AA*, Mar. 4, 1933, 21; Wheeler, "Yesterday's Robin Hood," 339.

169. Argersinger, *Toward a New Deal*, 184.

170. Arnold, "Last of the Good Old Days"; Avrum K. Rifman, "Jewish Public Officials," *Generations* 1 (Dec. 1978): 17–28; *Sun*, Jan. 5, 1966, A11; Anthony Lewis, "Our Extraordinary Solicitor General," *Reporter*, May 5, 1955, 27.

171. Moore, *At Home*, chap. 8, "The Rise of the Jewish Democrat."

172. *VOTE!* exhibition files; Samuel Neistadt Papers, MS 175, folder 1, JMM; Deborah R. Weiner, "Ten in the Twentieth: Baltimore Jews and Social Justice," *Generations* (2009–2010): 164 (on Moses); Argersinger, *Making the Amalgamated*, 75–78, 108; Argersinger, *Toward a New Deal*; Skotnes, *New Deal*.

173. Wenger, *New York Jews*, 149.

174. Argersinger, *Toward a New Deal*, chap. 2; "JSSB [Jewish Social Service Bureau] Resumes Service Program," *JT*, Oct. 27, 1933; Cahn, *Man's Concern*, 22–23.

175. Cahn, *Man's Concern*, 23; *Sun*, Jan. 19, 1938, 22.

176. Wolman was the world's foremost expert on water supplies. He invented the process for chlorinating drinking water, set bacterial standards, oversaw the development of modern municipal and national water systems, and advised other nations on water issues.

177. *Sun*, Sept. 12, 1937, M5; Oct. 31, 1937, 20; Hymen Saye, *Lee L. Dopkin, Humanitarian, Champion of Social Justice* (Baltimore: Jewish Historical Society of Maryland, 1981).

178. *Sun*, Jan. 6, 1936, 16.

179. Skotnes, *New Deal*; Leonard M. Helfgott, "Enduring Idealism: Baltimore Jews in the Communist Party," *Generations* (2009–2010): 74–87. Ades headed the Baltimore branch of International Labor Defense, the Communist-backed group that defended the Scottsboro Boys.

180. Lillian Howard Potter, "Political Cooperation, Economic Competition: Relationships between Jewish and Black Communities in Baltimore, Maryland, 1930–1940," 16, paper presented at "Making Diversity Work: 250 Years of Baltimore History" conference, Nov. 15–16, 1995.

181. Weiner, "Ten in the Twentieth"; "Late Rabbi Was Staunch Interracialist," *AA*, Oct. 25, 1941; *AA*, Feb. 25, 1933, 11; Oct. 31, 1942, 14.

182. Other articles described violent confrontations outside Jewish-owned stores: "Husband Sues Jewish Grocer," *AA*, Jan. 2, 1920; "Jewish Boy Kills Botts," *AA*, Apr. 3, 1920.

183. Thomas Edsall, "Pennsylvania Avenue Declining for Generation," *Evening Sun*, May 10, 1967.

184. Andor Skotnes, "'Buy Where You Can Work': Boycotting for Jobs in African-American Baltimore, 1933–1934," *Journal of Social History* 27 (Summer 1994): 754.

185. Mickey Steinberg, interview by Deborah R. Weiner, Aug. 20, 2008.

186. Ruth Stewart, OH, 2008, "Baltimore '68: Riots and Rebirth" project, Langsdale Library Special Collections, University of Baltimore. See also Juanita Crider and Harold Knight, both OH, 2008, in the same collection, archives.ubalt.edu/bsr/oral-histories/index.html.

187. *NIMN*, 183. On African American grievances against Jews, see Skotnes, *New Deal*, 160–61.

188. Kohn, "Hochschild, Kohn." For a full account, see Paul A. Kramer, "White Sales: The Racial Politics of Baltimore's Jewish-Owned Department Stores, 1935–1965," in Decter and Martens, *Enterprising Emporiums*, 37–59.

189. Skotnes, *New Deal*, 283.

190. Edward Israel, "Jew Hatred among Negroes," *Crisis* 43 (Feb. 1936): 39. Jackson's response is in the April issue, 122.

191. Kramer, "White Sales," 42; Michael J. Lisicky, *Hutzler's: Where Baltimore Shops* (Charleston, SC: History Press, 2009), 143; Sandler, "H-K Days."

192. Sandler, *Jewish Baltimore*, 133; Krimmel and Liebowitz, "Now Playing at the Hippodrome"; Maryland Historical Society Library Department, "The Velvet Kind: The Sweet Story of Hendlers Creamery," mdhs.org/underbelly/2017/07/06/the-velvet-kind-the-sweet-story -of-hendlers-creamery/; Brunn memoir. On Shecter, see *Sun*, Nov. 11, 1992, C11.

193. Weiner, "Ten in the Twentieth," 164–65.

194. Mary Gabriel, *The Art of Acquiring: A Portrait of Etta and Claribel Cone* (Baltimore: Bancroft Press, 2002); *Saidie A. May Collection: Catalogue of an Exhibition* (Baltimore: Baltimore Museum of Art, 1972); Weiner, "Always Have Kind Words."

195. Blanche Klasmer Cohen, "Benjamin Klasmer's Contribution to Baltimore's Musical History," *MHM* 72 (Summer 1977): 272–76.

196. "Milton Bates," *Sun,* Apr. 28, 2007; *Sun,* July 13, 2007, B6; Pietila, "Sid Weinberg."

197. Jerry Leiber and Mike Stoller, *Hound Dog: The Leiber and Stoller Autobiography* (New York, Simon and Schuster, 2010), 10.

198. *ATFS,* xvi, 36, 188.

199. Ibid., 90; *Sun,* Mar. 9, 1980, A16.

Chapter 5.
From Baltimore to Pikesville

1. Martin Kohn, "Hochschild, Kohn and Company: A Personal Account," 1979, Hochschild, Kohn VF, JMM. The branch actually opened in 1947. See K. Meghan Gross, ed., "Chronology: Baltimore's Downtown Department Stores," *Generations* (2001): 57.

2. Quoted in Martha J. Vill, "Park Heights: A Study of a Jewish Neighborhood," 31, unpublished paper, 1979, BNHP.

3. This includes Jews who still lived within the city limits. "The Jewish Community of Greater Baltimore: A Population Study," Associated Jewish Charities of Baltimore, 1968, JMM, 1994.95.4 (hereafter Associated 1968 community study), 14.

4. *American Jewish Year Book* 44 (1942–1943); 55 (1954); 60 (1959); Associated 1968 community study; US Census, 1940–1980. Although the city's population declined from the 1950s onward, the entire metro area's population kept growing. Jewish suburban life attracted many sociological studies in the 1950s and 1960s, such as Judith R. Kramer and Seymour Leventman, *Children of the Gilded Ghetto: Conflict Resolutions of Three Generations of American Jews* (New Haven, CT: Yale University Press, 1961).

5. Rona Hirsch, "The Comeback Kid," *JT,* Nov. 3, 1995.

6. "Soldier Says War Does Not Change Fighters," unidentified Baltimore newspaper article, c. 1943, World War II VF, JMM; Edna Jontiff, "World War II Story," 26, Memoir Collection, JMM.

7. Albert Goldstein's war diary, in the possession of Eric Goldstein.

8. On the Jewish GI experience, see Deborah Dash Moore, *GI Jews: How World War II Changed a Generation* (Cambridge, MA: Harvard University Press, 2006).

9. Colonel Bernard Feingold, "A Tribute in Memory of Staff Sergeant Isadore S. Jachman," *Generations* (June 1981): 34–39. Even years after the war ended, *Jewish Times* obituaries announced the funerals of service members whose remains had finally been returned for burial. For example, the May 14, 1948, issue announced three such burials (40).

10. Vill, "Park Heights," 26–27; Gilbert Sandler, *Home Front Baltimore: An Album of Stories from World War II* (Baltimore: Johns Hopkins University Press, 2011); *Har Sinai Yearbook 1942,* MS 54, box 1, folder 16, JMM; YMHA 1943 Annual Report, 10–17, JMM, 89.12.3.

11. Ibid., 10; Suzanne Ellery Greene, *Baltimore: An Illustrated History* (Woodland Hills, CA: Windsor Hill, 1980), 271; Sandler, *Home Front,* 59, 71.

12. Kohn, "Hochschild, Kohn," n.p.

13. Baltimore Jewish Council Records (hereafter BJC Records), MS 107, boxes 5 and 6, JMM.

14. "Bethlehem-Fairfield," BJC memo, BJC Records, folder 26 (first quote); *Fairfield Yardbird* (Local 43 newspaper), Nov. 21, 1942 (second quote); *AA,* Nov. 21, 1942, 21. See Kenneth D. Durr, *Behind the Backlash: White Working-Class Politics in Baltimore, 1940–1980* (Chapel Hill: University of North Carolina Press, 2003), on racial conflict, Communism, and the CIO at the shipyards.

15. Milt Seif, "Autobiography," Memoir Collection, JMM; "Memorandum of Complaint,"

Sept. 9, 1941, BJC Records, folder 31; "Report of Investigator on Fact-Finding," Dec. 10, 1944, BJC Records, folder 28. For more cases, see folders 22, 25, 26.

16. Clifton R. Jones, "Invasion and Racial Attitudes: A Study of Housing in a Border City," *Social Forces* 27 (Mar. 1949): 285–90; *NIMN*.

17. Untitled notes from meeting at St. Martin's Church, Feb. 16, 1945, BJC Records, folder 333 (it appears that Mrs. Norman Carey, who had just moved into the neighborhood, attended the meeting and reported the results to the BJC); see also *AA*, Mar. 10, 1945, 16.

18. Leon Sachs, "Review of Baltimore Jewish Council Program," c. 1958, 11, BJC VF, JMM; correspondence between Maurice Sturm and Leon Sachs, 1946–1947, BJC Records, folder 333. See Durr, *Behind the Backlash*, for another perspective on the Fulton Avenue episode.

19. Sachs, "Review," 10.

20. Paul A. Kramer, "White Sales: The Racial Politics of Baltimore's Jewish-Owned Department Stores, 1935–1965," in *Enterprising Emporiums: The Jewish Department Stores of Downtown Baltimore*, ed. Avi Y. Decter and Melissa Martens (Baltimore: Jewish Museum of Maryland, 2001), 48–49.

21. *Sun*, Jan. 31, 1945, 11; *AA*, Mar. 10, 1945, 16; Mar. 17, 1945, 20. Repeal of Jim Crow laws was finally achieved in 1951. *Washington Post*, Feb. 16, 1951, B2.

22. Moore, *GI Jews*, 10. See *ATFH*; Gary Gerstle, *American Crucible: Race and Nation in the Twentieth Century* (Princeton, NJ: Princeton University Press, 2001).

23. *ATFH*, 28. On returning veterans, see Moore, *GI Jews*.

24. Yiddish-English newspaper ad, Nov. 1943, JMM, 1987.143.2; *Sun*, Dec. 1, 1942; Patti Murphy Dohn, "Holocaust Remembrance Day," *Catholic Review*, Feb. 27, 2013 (on Goldstein). On the national picture, see Jonathan D. Sarna, *American Judaism: A History* (New Haven, CT: Yale University Press, 2004), 258–64.

25. Irene Siegel, "Starting Out," *Generations* (2005–2006): 71–81.

26. Ibid., 77.

27. See, for example, Kenneth T. Jackson, *Crabgrass Frontier: The Suburbanization of the United States* (New York: Oxford University Press, 1985); Thomas Sugrue, *The Origins of the Urban Crisis: Race and Inequality in Postwar Detroit* (Princeton, NJ: Princeton University Press, 1996).

28. *Jews on the Move: Baltimore and the Suburban Exodus, 1945-1968* (2013), JMM exhibition, research files.

29. Ibid.

30. *ATFH*, 143.

31. Rose Cohen, OH 630, Apr. 24, 2001, JMM.

32. W. Edward Orser, *Blockbusting in Baltimore: The Edmondson Village Story* (Lexington: University Press of Kentucky, 1997); *NIMN*. On similar Jewish suburbanization rates in other cities, see *ATFH*, 144–45 (Newark); Lila Corwin Berman, "Jewish Urban Politics in the City and Beyond," *Journal of American History* (Sept. 2012): 492–519 (Detroit).

33. Larry Singer, "The Quest," *Baltimore Magazine*, Dec. 1972, 38; Minnie Levy Conn, OH 69, June 20, 1979, BNHP. See Vill, "Park Heights," on the impact of the West Side Expressway.

34. Steve Liebowitz, "The End of a Jewish Neighborhood: The Life and Death of Lower Park Heights," *Generations* (Fall 1998): 4–7; *STCM*.

35. "Baltimore Survey of Jewish Attitudes," American Jewish Committee, 1963 (hereafter 1963 attitudes survey), 8, JMM, 2011.81.1; Associated 1968 community study, 31, 53–55. On Jewish geographic mobility in the postwar era, see Deborah Dash Moore, *To the Golden Cities: Pursuing the American Jewish Dream in Miami and L.A.* (New York: Free Press, 1994).

----

36. Associated 1968 community study, 6, 14, 17–25; Laura Scism, "Part II — The Suburban Migration," *Baltimore News-American*, Feb. 1979, 4, part of her five-part series, "Jewish Baltimore: From Lombard Street to Pikesville." Located in the far northwest corner of Baltimore City, Upper Park Heights was technically inside the city limits, but it remained relatively undeveloped until after World War II and took on many of the features of a postwar suburb. Its suburban character was reinforced in the early 1960s with the construction of Northern Parkway, a six-lane thoroughfare that cut it off from Lower Park Heights. Scism referred to Upper Park Heights and Mount Washington (also located above Northern Parkway) as "suburban-style neighborhoods."

37. Scism, "Part II — The Suburban Migration," 3.

38. *Jews on the Move* research files.

39. *Sun*, May 17, 1948, 11; May 22, 1948, 6.

40. *Evening Sun*, Dec. 19, 1972, C1.

41. See *STCM* for a chronology of synagogue openings and mergers.

42. "Study of Recreational and Informal Educational Activities, Baltimore, by the Jewish Welfare Board," Associated Jewish Charities, 1947, 1–8, 88, JMM, 1995.98.51; Louis F. Cahn, *Man's Concern for Man: The First Fifty Years of the Associated Jewish Charities and Welfare Fund of Baltimore* (Baltimore: Associated Jewish Charities and Welfare Fund, 1970), 32–36. On Northern Parkway, see *Sun*, Aug. 23, 1959, FE3.

43. Cahn, *Man's Concern*, 35; Vill, "Park Heights," 31.

44. *Jews on the Move* research files.

45. Associated 1968 community study; Vill, "Park Heights," 34; Scism, "Part V — Keeping the Faith," 10, in her "Jewish Baltimore" (quote).

46. *JT*, Feb. 23, 2007, 53–54.

47. Associated 1968 community study, 43–45, 49–51. The 1970 figure is from *Evening Sun*, Dec. 19, 1972, C1.

48. *JT*, Feb. 23, 2007, 53 (quote); Barry Kessler, "Bedlam with Corned Beef on the Side," *Generations* (Fall 1993): 5; *Sun*, Sept. 3, 2010, T8 (on Suburban House).

49. Evan Serpick, "Diner: An Oral History," *Baltimore Magazine*, Apr. 2012; Michael Olesker, *Journeys to the Heart of Baltimore* (Baltimore: Johns Hopkins University Press, 2001), chap. 11.

50. Sarna, *American Judaism*, 283; Riv-Ellen Prell, "Community and the Discourse of Elegy: The Postwar Suburban Debate," in *Imagining the American Jewish Community*, ed. Jack Wertheimer (Hanover, NH: Brandeis University Press, 2007), 67, 70, 73; *ATFH*, 147.

51. Paul Haspel, "Avalon Lost: Suburbanization and Its Discontents in Barry Levinson's *Avalon*," *Journal of American Culture* 31 (Dec. 2008): 383–92; Eric A. Goldman, "*Avalon* and *Liberty Heights*: Toward a Better Understanding of the American Jewish Experience through Cinema," *AJH* 91 (Mar. 2003): 109–27; Warren Rosenberg, "Coming Out of the Ethnic Closet: Jewishness in the Films of Barry Levinson," *Shofar* 22 (Fall 2003): 29–43. Levinson was criticized for not explicitly identifying his characters as Jewish (though they obviously were). The autobiographical nature of the film is revealed in the choice of the name Krichinsky, Levinson's mother's maiden name.

52. Siegel, "Starting Out," 78. On the rise of the nuclear family and the role of the housewife, see Elaine Tyler May, *Homeward Bound: American Families in the Cold War Era* (New York: Basic, 1990).

53. Rosalie Silber Abrams, OH 49, Jan. 23, 1977, 13, JMM; Abrams, OH 626, May 4, 2001, 27, JMM; *Sun*, Mar. 1, 2009, A22; "Rosalie Silber Abrams," biography, Maryland Women's Hall of Fame, msa.maryland.gov/msa/educ/exhibits/womenshall/html/abrams.html.

----

54. Special Committee on Youth Problems, minutes, Dec. 8, 1958, and June 10, 1959; Special Committee on Youth Problems, "Community Report," June 1959; "Associated Jewish Charities: Jewish Youth Committee," all JMM, 1984.34.1–3.

55. For the seamier side of postwar Baltimore Jewish youth culture, see Chip Silverman, *Diner Guys* (New York: Citadel, 1989).

56. Sarna, *American Judaism*, 274. On the role of religion versus ethnicity in shaping American Jewish identity in the postwar era, see Eric L. Goldstein, *The Price of Whiteness: Jews, Race, and American Identity* (Princeton, NJ: Princeton University Press, 2006), 206–8.

57. Jan Schein, *On Three Pillars: The History of Chizuk Amuno Congregation, 1871–1996* (Baltimore: Chizuk Amuno, 2000), 187; *JT*, Apr. 8, 1955, 3.

58. Schein, *On Three Pillars*, 198; Jewish Women's Archive, profile of Bess Fishman, jwa .org; Riv-Ellen Prell, ed., *Women Remaking American Judaism* (Detroit, MI: Wayne State University Press, 2007), 120.

59. *JT*, Sept. 16, 1955, 101 (Goldman); Abraham Glushakow, *Maryland Bicentennial Jewish Book* (Baltimore: Jewish Voice Publishing, 1975), 154. On the synagogue building boom, see Sarna, *American Judaism*, 279.

60. *JT*, Apr. 8, 1955, 3.

61. Scism, "Part V—Keeping the Faith"; Rabbi Samuel Rosenblatt, OH 143, June 15, 1981, JMM.

62. *Sun*, Nov. 15, 1971, B1; Rabbi Uri Miller Papers, MS 79, folders 2 and 4, JMM; *Sun*, Jan. 3, 2001, B1. On the new national focus on education, see Sarna, *American Judaism*, 279.

63. Glushakow, *Maryland Bicentennial*, 58 (first quote); "Modernistic New Synagogue to House Beth El Activities," *Sun*, May 11, 1948, 13.

64. Schein, *On Three Pillars*, has an excellent account of the controversy, 205–14. On the Orthodox reaction, see, for example, *JT*, Jan. 30, 1948, 29; Apr. 30, 1948, 45; May 7, 1948, 38.

65. Sarna, *American Judaism*, 284.

66. *ATFH*, 148; 1963 attitudes survey, 59–60.

67. *JT*, Jan. 30, 1948, 45; Eli Schlossberg, "Baltimore: Are We Better Off Today?" *Where What When*, Mar. 2010. Beth Israel and Beth El, though instantly popular, were the only Conservative synagogues founded in the mid-twentieth century, giving Baltimore a total of three (with Chizuk Amuno) until the 1970s. See *STCM*.

68. Council of Orthodox Congregations of Baltimore minutes, May 19, 1958; June 2, 1958; Aug. 18, 1958; Nov. 28, 1960, MS 144, box 1, folder 6, JMM.

69. *JT*, Apr. 30, 1946, 47; *Sun*, Dec. 2, 1946, 15; "Ner Israel Rabbinical College Authorized to Confer Doctor Degree," Ner Israel press release, 1952, Ner Israel VF, JMM; Arthur J. Magida, "Immersed in Torah," *JT*, Nov. 26, 1993, 46–51; *Sun*, Nov. 30, 1993, B2 (quote).

70. Eli W. Schlossberg, "A Nostalgic Glimpse at Baltimore: 1955 to 2007," *Where What When*, June 2007; Schein, *On Three Pillars*, 213; *Sun*, Jan. 8, 1968, C18.

71. *STCM*, 87; torahinstitute.org; *Sun*, June 8, 1978, D1.

72. *JT*, Oct. 11, 18, 25, Nov. 1, 1957; Schlossberg, "Baltimore: Are We Better Off Today? Part 3," *Where What When*, May 2010 (on Kaplan). On the growing national tendency of ultra-Orthodox leaders to disassociate from other forms of Judaism, see Jeffrey S. Gurock, *American Jewish Orthodoxy in Historical Perspective* (Hoboken, NJ: KTAV, 1996).

73. *Sun*, Dec. 3, 1973, B1.

74. The controversy lasted from late 1977 to early 1979, when the Associated finally acted. Council of Orthodox Jewish Congregations minutes, Oct. 24, 1977, and Feb. 26, 1979, MS 144, box 2, folder 10; *JT*, Feb. 2, 1979, 14; *Sun*, Jan. 26, 1979, C1; Scism, "Part V—Keeping the Faith."

---

75. Avi Y. Decter and Deborah R. Weiner, eds., "Chronology: Maryland and Israel," *Generations* (2007–2008): 112; *Sun*, Dec. 3, 1973, B1. On American Jewry's increasing attachment to Israel, see Gerald Sorin, *Tradition Transformed: The Jewish Experience in America* (Baltimore: Johns Hopkins University Press, 1997), 214; *ATFH*, 201–12.

76. "Rudolf Sonneborn Dies," *New York Times*, June 4, 1986; letter from Ben-Gurion to Rudolf Sonneborn, Jan. 2, 1967, JMM, 1999.104.4; Alexandra Lee Levin, *Vision: A Biography of Harry Friedenwald* (Philadelphia: Jewish Publication Society of America, 1964), 403.

77. *Sun*, Apr. 11, 1984, F1; Ruth Gruber, *Exodus 1947: The Ship That Launched a Nation* (New York: Random House, 1999).

78. Raphael Ben-Yosef, "Mahal Days," *Generations* (2007–2008): 54–59; *Sun*, May 20, 1948, 38.

79. Morris Lazaron, "Why I Was a Zionist and Why I Now Am Not," reprinted in *Generations* (2007–2008): 50 (first quote); Thomas A. Kolsky, *Jews against Zionism: The American Council for Judaism, 1942–1948* (Philadelphia: Temple University Press, 1992); Morris Lazaron, "Jewish Postwar Problems," *JT*, June 12, 1942, 16 (second quote); *Sun*, May 6, 1948, 40.

80. *Sun*, Sept. 15, 1947, 8; Sept. 22, 1947, 5; Leon Sachs, OH 257, 20–21, JMM; Rose Greenberg, *The Chronicle of Baltimore Hebrew Congregation, 1830–1975* (Baltimore: Baltimore Hebrew Congregation, 1976), 57.

81. Zvi Ganin, *An Uneasy Relationship: American Jewish Leadership and Israel, 1948–1957* (Syracuse, NY: Syracuse University Press, 2005).

82. Ganin, *An Uneasy Relationship*; Mark K. Bauman, "The Blaustein–Ben-Gurion Agreement: A Milestone in Israel-Diaspora Relations," *Generations* (2007–2008): 70–83 (quotes, 74–75).

83. Hirsch, "Comeback Kid."

84. Bradley Burston, "The Exodus Effect," *Haaretz*, Nov. 9, 2012; M. M. Silver, *Our Exodus: Leon Uris and the Americanization of Israel's Founding Story* (Detroit, MI: Wayne State University Press, 2010), 2.

85. Cahn, *Man's Concern*, 43–44; Lutzker Verein Collection, MS 39, JMM; *Jews on the Move* research files.

86. Federation of Jewish Women's Organizations Records, MS 82, JMM; *Sun*, Oct. 9, 1960, E1.

87. *Sun*, Sept. 28, 1964, 19; Apr. 7, 1963, FY1.

88. Sorin, *Tradition Transformed*, 218.

89. Sachs, "Review," 18–19.

90. 1963 attitudes survey, 26–28.

91. Elsbeth Levy Bothe, OH 628, Sept. 14, 2002, 67–68, JMM.

92. BJC Records, folders 88, 883, 932; Sachs, OH 257; *NIMN*, 133–34.

93. Neil Smith, *American Empire: Roosevelt's Geographer and the Prelude to Globalization* (Berkeley: University of California Press, 2004), 247.

94. Sachs, OH 257; Sachs to William Logan, Nov. 2, 1954, BJC Records, folder 883. See also Jason Kalman, "Dark Places around the University: The Johns Hopkins University Admissions Quota and the Jewish Community, 1945–1951," *Hebrew Union College Annual* (2013): 233–79.

95. Sachs, "Review," 8 (quote); BJC resolution and form letter to Jewish leaders, c. 1948, BJC Records, folder 344.

96. Meeting and conversation notes, BJC Records, folder 349 (quote); see also *NIMN*, 135–38, 142. David Sarnoff was the president of RCA and the founder of the nation's first television network, NBC.

----

97. *JT*, June 19, 1953, 14; *Sun*, June 16, 1953, 36; Sachs, "Review," 9–10. For more, see *NIMN*, 134.

98. Sachs, "Review," 10.

99. Ibid., 7 (quote); Sachs, OH 174, BNHP; *Sun*, Mar. 15, 1962, 54; Barbara Pash, "When Jews and Blacks Marched Together," *JT*, Nov. 10, 1978, 40–42.

100. For further analysis, see Rosenberg, "Coming Out of the Ethnic Closet"; Goldman, "*Avalon* and *Liberty Heights*."

101. Leonard J. Fein, *Where Are We? The Inner Life of America's Jews* (New York: Harper and Row, 1988), 186–87.

102. Silverman, *Diner Guys*; Eddi Fiegel, *Dream a Little Dream of Me: The Life of Cass Elliot* (Chicago: Chicago Review Press, 2005).

103. Hazel Dickens and Bill C. Malone, *Working Girl Blues: The Life and Music of Hazel Dickens* (Urbana: University of Illinois Press, 2008), 7.

104. Deborah Chessler obituary, *New York Daily News*, Oct. 12, 2012. See also Deborah Chessler biography, allmusic.com/artist/deborah-chessler-mn0000192894.

105. See, for example, Kurt Schmoke interview in "Separate Lives: Voices on Race and Segregation in Baltimore," *Urbanite*, Feb. 2010; and Rev. Harold L. Knight, OH, 2008, "Baltimore '68: Riots and Rebirth" project, Langsdale Library Special Collections, University of Baltimore, archives.ubalt.edu/bsr/oral-histories/index.html.

106. "Through their Eyes," *Baltimore Magazine*, Feb. 2014, 158 (Cole); "Separate Lives" (McCrimmon); Lee Sartain, *Borders of Equality: The NAACP and the Baltimore Civil Rights Struggle, 1914–1970* (Jackson: University Press of Mississippi, 2013), 145 (Western).

107. See Cheryl Lynn Greenberg, *Troubling the Waters: Black-Jewish Relations in the American Century* (Princeton, NJ: Princeton University Press, 2006), chapter 4.

108. Michael Olesker, *Journeys*, chaps. 11 and 12. Quote is from *Jews on the Move* research files.

109. Elizabeth M. Nix and Deborah R. Weiner, "Pivot in Perception: The Impact of the 1968 Riots on Three Baltimore Business Districts," in *Baltimore '68: Riots and Rebirth in an American City*, ed. Jessica I. Elfenbein, Thomas L. Hollowak, and Elizabeth M. Nix (Philadelphia: Temple University Press, 2011), 180–207 (Wickham quote, 191). On credit, see Harold Knight's and others' oral histories in "Baltimore '68: Riots and Rebirth," archives.ubalt.edu/bsr/oral-histories/index.html; "Separate Lives."

110. Nix and Weiner, "Pivot," 191.

111. *Sun*, Oct. 20, 1943, 6; Nov. 8, 1958, 7; Mark Reutter, "The Abandoners—Who, What, and Why," *Sun*, Oct. 6, 1972.

112. Jones, "Invasion," 288; *NIMN*, 96–104. On Goldseker, see especially Orser, *Blockbusting*, 96–97, 171–72.

113. Garrett Power, "Apartheid Baltimore Style: The Residential Segregation Ordinances of 1910–1913," *Maryland Law Review* (1983): 289–328 (quote, 321).

114. *NIMN*, 108–9, 184; *AA*, Feb. 20, 1962. For a balanced analysis of blockbusters, see Orser, *Blockbusting*.

115. Sartain, *Borders*, 5; Sachs, OH 174, 27. On the border city aspect of race relations in Baltimore, see Howell S. Baum, *Brown in Baltimore: School Desegregation and the Limits of Liberalism* (Ithaca, NY: Cornell University Press, 2010); C. Fraser Smith, *Here Lies Jim Crow: Civil Rights in Maryland* (Baltimore: Johns Hopkins University Press, 2008); Ron Cassie, "And Service for All," *Baltimore Magazine*, Jan. 2015, 84–89. *Sun* articles of the era provide ample evidence of the rabid opposition of whites to desegregation. See, for example, *Sun*, Jan. 14, 1966, C24.

- - - - - - - - - - - - -

116. *AA*, Jan. 22, 1955, 6; Read's Drug Store VF, JMM.

117. *AA*, June 4, 1960, 2; July 23, 1960, 1.

118. Kramer, "White Sales"; Kohn, "Hochschild, Kohn," n.p.

119. Kramer, "White Sales," 50–54 (quote, 51).

120. Gilbert Sandler, "Demonstrators: Reform Rabbis Confront Segregation," *Generations* (2009–2010): 104–11; *Sun*, Feb. 8, 1962, 52 (quote).

121. "Statement by Joseph Meyerhoff on Pending Open Housing Legislation," Mar. 1967, BJC Records, folder 124, JMM.

122. Pash, "When Jews and Blacks Marched"; *Sun*, June 4, 1961, B42. On southern Jews, see Clive Webb, *Fight against Fear: Southern Jews and Black Civil Rights* (Athens: University of Georgia Press, 2003).

123. *Sun*, July 12, 1948, 26; July 18, 1948; *AA*, Aug. 21, 2013; Barry Kessler and Anita Kassof, "Match Point: Fighting Racial Discrimination in Druid Hill Park," *Generations* (2004): 43–53; Pash, "When Jews and Blacks Marched."

124. Marshall Levin obituary, *Sun*, Feb. 3, 2004; Aaron M. Glazer, "Course Correction," *City Paper* (Baltimore), Sept. 5, 2001; *Sun*, Mar. 15, 1962, 54; June 5, 1962, 42; Feb. 25, 1964, 36; Michael L. Mark, *But Not Next Door: Baltimore Neighborhoods, Inc.* (Baltimore: BNI, 2002); Ellsworth E. Rosen, "When a Negro Moves Next Door," *Saturday Evening Post*, Apr. 4, 1959.

125. Pash, "When Jews and Blacks Marched" (quote, 41); Sandler, "Demonstrators"; Uri Miller VF, JMM.

126. *Sun*, Dec. 21, 1961.

127. Sartain, *Borders*; *NIMN*; Baum, *Brown in Baltimore*.

128. Greenberg, *Troubling the Waters*, 165–68; Sachs, OH 174, 22–23; Nix and Weiner, "Pivot."

129. *Sun*, Aug. 14, 1967; Jan. 27, 1968.

130. Nix and Weiner, "Pivot"; "Loans for Merchants Who Suffered Losses in 1968 Riots," Hebrew Free Loan Society Collection, MS 149, folder 1549, JMM.

131. Nix and Weiner, "Pivot"; Hilda Perl Goodwin, "Dad's Store, 1920–1968," *Generations* (2005–2006): 68.

132. Nix and Weiner, "Pivot," 199 (quote); Pash, "When Jews and Blacks Marched"; "A Struggle, a Hope for City Clergy: Bringing the Communities Together," *Evening Sun*, Jan. 30, 1969.

133. *Sun*, Sept. 10, 1970, C22; Samuel Friedel obituaries, *Sun*, Mar. 22 and 23, 1979.

134. *Sun*, Mar. 26, 1971, C26.

135. Abrams, OH 49, 5, JMM; *Sun*, Apr. 3, 1971. Baltimore County surrounds the city but does not include it; Baltimore City and Baltimore County are separate entities.

136. See, for example, Matthew Frye Jacobson, *Roots Too: White Ethnic Revival in Post–Civil Rights America* (Cambridge, MA: Harvard University Press, 2006).

137. Mark Bowden, "Bossin' Around: A History of How Things Got Done in Baltimore," *City Paper*, June 29, 1979. See also *Sun*, Sept. 5, 1971, TS20.

138. "Material in Baltimore Jewish Council Files Pertaining to Jack Pollack's Embarrassment of Jewish Community," BJC VF, JMM.

139. *AA*, Nov. 11, 1950, 1 (quote); Harvey Wheeler, "Yesterday's Robin Hood: The Rise and Fall of Baltimore's Trenton Democratic Club," *American Quarterly* 7 (Winter 1955): 343.

140. *Sun*, Feb. 26, 1959. See also Bowden, "Bossin' Around."

141. Bowden, "Bossin' Around."

142. *NIMN*, 124.

- - - - - - - - - - - - - -

143. On Kovens's relationship with Willie Adams, see *Sun*, Mar. 19, 1979, A8; C. Fraser Smith, "100 Years: Willie Don Meets 'Big Chief,' " *Baltimore Magazine*, June 2007, baltimoremagazine.com/2007/6/6/100-years-willie-don-meets-big-chief.

144. *Sun*, Aug. 31, 2015, 1, 11; Sept. 4, 2015, 1, 17, 19.

145. Ibid., Aug. 31, 2015, 1, 11; Sept. 4, 2015, 1, 17, 19.

146. Ibid., Sept. 5, 1971, TS20.

147. Abrams, OH 626, 41; Stephen Sachs, OH 742, Aug. 3, 2010, JMM; Hyman Pressman obituary, *Sun*, Mar. 16, 1996.

148. C. Fraser Smith, *William Donald Schaefer: A Political Biography* (Baltimore: Johns Hopkins University Press, 1999); *Washington Post*, Oct. 3, 1982, A1 (McKeldin).

149. Durr, *Behind the Backlash*; *Sun*, July 19, 1946, 48.

150. Leonard Helfgott, "Enduring Idealism: Baltimore Jews in the Communist Party," *Generations* (2009–2010): 74–87; Vernon L. Pedersen, *The Communist Party in Maryland, 1919–1957* (Urbana: University of Illinois Press, 2000). HUAC targeted the Baltimore area because of the city's role in the defense industry.

151. The Catonsville Nine were Catholic antiwar activists, including the priests Daniel and Philip Berrigan, who burned draft records they took from the Catonsville, Maryland, draft board office.

152. *Sun*, May 30, 2003, B5; Helfgott, "Enduring Idealism."

153. Weiner, "Ten in the Twentieth," 171 (Rehfeld); Mark, *But Not Next Door*.

154. *Sun*, Sept. 23, 1954, 42; Dec. 11, 1954, 6; Jan. 15, 1956, 38. See also *The Inner Harbor Book* (Baltimore: City of Baltimore Department of Planning, 1984); Jim Duffy, "Baltimore Gets a New Downtown," *Baltimore Magazine*, Nov. 2007.

155. Duffy, "Baltimore Gets a New Downtown"; Martin L. Millspaugh, "The Inner Harbor Story," *Urban Land* (Apr. 2003): 36–41.

156. Michael Yockel, "Walter Sondheim Is Born," *Baltimore Magazine*, Oct. 2007, baltimoremagazine.com/2007/10/10/100-years-walter-sondheim-is-born. See also Duffy, "Baltimore Gets a New Downtown"; *Sun*, Apr. 16, 1972, A24.

157. Scism, "Part IV—The Most Influential Jews in Town," 6, in her "Jewish Baltimore."

158. Joan Jacobson, *A Spirit of Change: Honoring 50 Years of the Center Club* (Baltimore: Center Club, 2012).

159. M. Hirsh Goldberg, *Joseph Meyerhoff: A Portrait* (Baltimore: N.p., 1987), 38; Scism, "Part IV—The Most Influential Jews" (Hackerman); *Sun*, July 3, 1977, B1 (Frenkil). On Panitz, Christianna McCausland, "Modernist Oasis," *Style*, Sept. 2007; Michael Yockel, "Requiem 2012: Our Loss," *Baltimore Magazine*, Jan. 2013, baltimoremagazine.net (quote).

160. On Weinberg, see *Sun*, Nov. 7, 1973, C26; Dec. 27, 1984, A1 (quote); Oct. 21, 2001, F2. On Kaufman, see Reutter, "The Abandoners."

161. *Sun*, Sept. 1, 1951, 1.

162. Deborah R. Weiner, "Always Have Kind Words for the Place That Feeds You: Jews on 'The Block,' " *Generations* (2003): 16.

163. Sugrue, *Origins of the Urban Crisis*; "Baltimore: Retailing's Wasteland," *Clothes*, Feb. 1, 1976, 23–28; US Census, 1950–2010.

164. *Sun*, July 5, 2008, B2 (Shaw); Feb. 8, 2004, B4 (Becker); Frances Berman profile, Jewish Women's Archive, jwa.org; *Sun*, Dec. 26, 2008, A8 (Jacobs); Dec. 29, 1999 (Myers).

165. "Baltimore: Retailing's Wasteland"; Kohn, "Hochschild, Kohn"; *Sun*, Nov. 7, 1973, C26; Mark Cohen, "Desperate Days for the Dowager," *Baltimore Magazine*, Dec. 1988, 86–90; Joel Hutzler, "Reasons for Failure of the Hutzler Store," memo, Hutzler Brothers Company VF,

JMM; K. Meghan Gross, "Chronology: Baltimore's Downtown Department Stores," *Generations* (2001): 58–59.

166. Diane L. Jacobsohn, "City of Champions: Major League Sports and Baltimore Jews," *Generations* (2004): 56.

167. Jacobsohn, "City of Champions."

168. Ibid.; Olesker, *Journeys*.

169. *Sun*, Oct. 8, 1951, MS9; Sept. 1, 1954, 36.

170. Ibid., May 4, 1969, 28; Robin Z. Waldman, "Equine Passion: The Cohen Family at Pimlico Race Course," *Generations* (2004): 30–41.

171. *Sun*, Mar. 24, 1978, C1; Sept. 16, 1982, C1; Sept. 17, 1982, B1.

172. Reuben Kramer VF, JMM; "Art Outside," brochure for Druid Hill Park Art Festival, 2014; *Sun*, Jan. 2, 1994, 1E (Gunts quote). See also Jacob Glushakow, "Brief Burst of Glory," *Generations* (Fall 1998): 2–3; *Sun*, May 25, 1953, 30; Avi Y. Decter, ed., "Chronology: Entertaining Maryland," *Generations* (2003): 79, 81.

173. Decter, "Chronology: Entertaining Maryland," 77–79.

174. Berman, "Jewish Urban Politics," 492.

Epilogue.

1. Phil Jacobs, "Is There a Jewish Future in Randallstown?" *JT*, Jan. 24, 1986, 51–54; "The Jewish Community of Greater Baltimore: A Population Study," Associated Jewish Charities of Baltimore, 1968, JMM, 1994.95.4 (hereafter Associated 1968 community study); "Baltimore Jewry 1975: A Demographic Study," Associated Jewish Charities and Welfare Fund, Baltimore Jewish Population Studies VF, JMM (hereafter Associated 1975 community study); "Jewish Population Study of Greater Baltimore," Associated Jewish Charities and Welfare Fund, 1986, Baltimore Jewish Population Studies VF, JMM (hereafter Associated 1986 community study); Steve Liebowitz, "Paradise Lost: A Retrospective of Liberty Road's Jewish Community," *Generations* (Fall 2000): 23–29.

2. *JT*, Jan. 24, Feb. 7, Mar. 7, 1986.

3. Jacobs, "Is There a Jewish Future?" 51, 54.

4. According to the "2010 Greater Baltimore Jewish Community Study," Associated: Jewish Community Federation of Baltimore (hereafter Associated 2010 community study), and "Jewish Community Study of New York, 2011," UJA Federation of New York, 32 percent of Jews in both Baltimore and New York were Orthodox. Both studies can be found at jewishdatabank.org.

5. Associated 2010 community study; Ira M. Sheskin, "Population Size and Geographic Distribution," in *Comparisons of Jewish Communities: A Compendium of Tables and Bar Charts*, 2012, North American Jewish Data Bank Report No. 5, jewishdatabank.org.

6. Associated community studies of 1968, 1975, 1986, 2010; "Jewish Community Study of Greater Baltimore, 1999," Associated: Jewish Community Federation of Baltimore, 2001, Baltimore Jewish Population Studies VF, JMM (hereafter Associated 1999 community study). The ratio of Jews living in Northwest Baltimore dropped from 90 percent in 1968 to 85 percent in 1975 to 80 in 1986 to 75 in 1999. Since much of the Jewish population growth after 1999 occurred in the Orthodox community in Upper Park Heights, it is no surprise that the percentage crept back up to 77 percent in 2010.

7. Associated community studies of 1968, 1986, 2010. The *American Jewish Year Book* for 2012 put Baltimore's Jewish population at 115,400, much higher than the 2010 community study. The discrepancy came from its use of the federally defined "standard metropolitan statistical area," which, unlike the community studies, includes Howard County. Using the

---

American Jewish Year Book's method, Baltimore in 2012 was the nation's twentieth-largest metropolitan area and had the tenth-largest Jewish community. See jewishdatabank.org.

8. In 1975, less than 2 percent of Baltimore Jews lived in Owings Mills, slightly more than Roland Park's 1.5 percent. Randallstown was home to almost 15 percent of the Jewish population.

9. Liebowitz, "Paradise Lost"; Jay Lechtman, "What's Wrong with Randallstown?" *JT*, July 31, 1992, 16.

10. *Sun*, Nov. 4, 1973, A22.

11. Ibid., Feb. 6, 1978, A1.

12. Barbara Pash, "A Cornerstone Called CHAI," *JT*, Sept. 19, 2008, 52.

13. *JT*, May 3, 1974, 6–9.

14. Pash, "A Cornerstone"; Simone Ellin, "CHAI: Making a Stand in Upper Park Heights," *Generations* (2009–2010): 129.

15. Deborah R. Weiner, "Ten in the Twentieth: Baltimore Jews and Social Justice," *Generations* (2009–2010): 171 (Rehfeld); Ellin, "CHAI." In 2010 controversy erupted when a member of the Shomrim citizens' patrol had an altercation with an African American teen. The Shomrim member was eventually convicted of assault and false imprisonment. Afterward, CHAI hosted discussions between black and Jewish residents that helped to diffuse the situation. Edward Erickson Jr., "Racial Tensions May Ease after Shomrim Conflict," *City Paper*, July 4, 2012.

16. Andrew A. Buerger, "Are We One?" and Alan Feiler and Phil Jacobs, "Now Open for Shabbat," both *JT*, May 29, 2009.

17. Associated 2010 community study, 101; Arthur J. Magida, "Flocking to the Promised Land," *JT*, Sept. 11, 1992, 64–68.

18. Nathan Gutman, "Baltimore Roiled by Abuse Charge against Late Rabbi," *Forward*, Apr. 27, 2007.

19. Jonathan Rosenblum, "Rabbi Naftoli Neuberger, zt"l, and Us," *Cross-Currents*, Nov. 9, 2005, cross-currents.com/archives/2005/11/09/rabbi-naftoli-neuberger-ztl-and-us/#ixzz32DJgCLti; Arthur J. Magida, "Immersed in Torah," *JT*, Nov. 26, 1993, 46–51; Neil Rubin, "Analysis: What's Different?" *JT*, May 22, 2009, 41.

20. Arthur J. Magida and Gary Rosenblatt, "Orthodox Judaism: A Surge to the Right," *JT*, June 9, 1989, 54. Heinemann's anger at the *Jewish Times* stemmed from its 2007 investigation of sexual abuse allegations against a long-deceased former principal of the Talmudical Academy. See Gutman, "Baltimore Roiled."

21. Rubin, "Analysis," 41.

22. Baltimore was the third city in the nation to have an eruv, after New York and Miami. Letter to community from Bert Miller, Jan. 1981, Rogers Avenue Synagogue Collection, MS 87, box 5, folder 186, JMM (first quote); *Sun*, June 8, 1978, D1 (second quote).

23. Margie Pencak, "Seven Mile Market: The Store That Jack Built," *Where What When*, May 2010; *Sun*, Nov. 30, 2012, A1, on Northwest Citizens' Patrol. In 1994 Miller resigned after charges of fiscal improprieties related to the eruv directory. Alan Feiler, "Eruv President Resigns," *JT*, Aug. 5, 1994.

24. Margie Pencak, "Baltimore's Frum Community: It's Not All Black and White," *Generations* (Fall 2000): 30–34; Magida, "Flocking"; Magida and Rosenblatt, "Orthodox Judaism."

25. Rubin, "Analysis," 41; Associated 2010 community study; "A Portrait of Jewish Americans," Pew Research Center, 2013, pewforum.org/2013/10/01/jewish-american-beliefs-attitudes-culture-survey.

- - - - - - - - - - - - - -

26. On the rise of day schools nationwide, see Jonathan Sarna, *American Judaism: A History* (New Haven, CT: Yale University Press, 2004), 328–29.

27. *Sun*, July 8, 1984, SM8; Simone Ellin, "Opening the Tent," *JT*, May 29, 2014, jewishtimes .com/23695/opening-the-tent/news; Nacha Cattan, "Baltimore Shul Tests Conservatives' Policy on Gay Vows," *Forward*, Sept. 26, 2003. On trends in the Reform and Conservative movements, see Sarna, *American Judaism*; and Jack Wertheimer, *A People Divided: Judaism in Contemporary America* (Hanover, NH: Brandeis University Press, 1993), 102.

28. Rubin, "Analysis"; Associated 1999 and 2010 community studies; Feiler and Jacobs, "Now Open," 24.

29. Feiler and Jacobs, "Now Open," 24.

30. Buerger, "Are We One?" 10.

31. Harvey Karch, interview by Deborah R. Weiner, Apr. 17, 2014; Magida, "Flocking," 65.

32. Associated 1968 community study, 32; Associated 1999 community study, 21, 26–27.

33. *JT*, July 28, 1989, 6.

34. Magida and Rosenblatt, "Orthodox Judaism," 56; *Sun*, May 9, 2011, A2; Joel Shurkin, "Baltimore Paper Goes on Auction Block," *Forward*, Apr. 6, 2012; Wertheimer, *A People Divided*; Samuel G. Freedman, *Jew vs. Jew: The Struggle for the Soul of American Jewry* (New York: Simon and Schuster, 2000). The new owners of the *Jewish Times*, unlike Buerger, remained convinced that the newspaper could appeal to all segments of the community. In 2013 they hired a Chabad rabbi and journalist as editor in chief.

35. Neil Rubin, "Changing Faces," *JT*, Jan. 14, 2011; "The Associated, Weinberg Foundation Announce Next Phase of the Day School Initiative," associated.org/page.aspx?id=217246; Magida, "Flocking."

36. Ira Rifkin, "Orthodoxy Struggles with 'Frum or Frummer'?" *JT*, Dec. 15, 2006; Maayan Jaffe, "Eyes Wide Open," *JT*, Jan. 18, 2013.

37. *JT*, Mar. 8, 1974, 7; *Sun*, Mar. 10, 1974, A28.

38. *Sun*, Nov. 5, 2003, A1; Rifkin, "Orthodoxy Struggles," (quote, 46). The decision was prompted by the Orthodox Union's new requirement that all of its member synagogues have a *mechitza*. Of the small number of Orthodox Union synagogues nationwide that lacked one, some, unlike Beth Tfiloh, disaffiliated and joined the Conservative movement. *Wall Street Journal*, Mar. 23, 2007, W13.

39. Beth Tfiloh website, bethtfiloh.com.

40. Jewish Women's Archive, jwa.org (Weinberg); Eli W. Schlossberg, "Baltimore: Are We Better Off Today?" *Where What When*, Mar. 2010.

41. Associated 2010 Annual Report, Associated VF, JMM; Nina Beth Cardin, "Keepers of the Earth: The Jewish Environmental Movement Comes of Age," *Generations* (2009-2010): 136-45.

42. *JT*, June 25, 1993, 55–57; Associated 2010 community study. On the recession, see Rubin, "Changing Faces"; and Heather Norris, "Turning Point," *JT*, Oct. 10, 2013. On other philanthropic priorities, see Associated 2010 Annual Report.

43. Maayan Jaffe, "Day School at Baltimore Hebrew Closing Its Doors," *JT*, May 16, 2013; *Sun*, June 20, 2009, A1.

44. Phyllis M. Hersh and Naomi Kellman, "History of the JCC of Greater Baltimore," Sept. 2003, Jewish Community Center VF, JMM; Tatyana Kolchinskaya, "Feeling the Warmth of the Baltimore Community," *JT*, Feb. 17, 1989; Gene Oishi, "Soviet Jews in Area Find Adjustment Difficult," *Sun*, June 4, 1978, A4. For a lively look at Russian immigrant culture, see Van Smith, "Moscow Nights: Getting Down with Baltimore's Burgeoning Eastern Bloc," *City Paper*, Mar. 13, 2002.

----

45. Alan Feiler, "The Culture Within," *JT*, Aug. 16, 1991, 53. See also Magida, "Immersed"; and Rosenblum, "Rabbi Naftoli Neuberger."

46. *JT* quoted in Fabian Kolker obituary, *Sun*, Oct. 8, 2000, B6.

47. "Shoshana Cardin Is Unanimous Pick to Chair Conference of Presidents," Jewish Telegraphic Agency, Dec. 19, 1990; Shoshana Cardin memoir, Memoir Collection, JMM.

48. *Sun*, Apr. 8, 2007, G1; Aug. 27, 2010, A1. See also "Jews Seek Higher Office in Local and State Politics," *JT*, July 20, 2012, 42.

49. Michael Anft and Molly Rath, "The End," *City Paper*, Dec. 1, 1999 (Schmoke). On Rikki Spector, see *Sun*, Jan. 3, 2016; Nov. 9, 2016.

50. *Sun*, Oct. 28, 2012, H1.

51. Ibid., Feb. 11, 2014, A12. A notable exception in today's Baltimore is Kevin Plank, the (non-Jewish) head of Under Armour.

52. Frank Kuznik, "We Need More Angels," *Baltimore Magazine*, Dec. 1990, 40–45, with sidebars by Mark Cohen, "Harry's Last Hurrah," 43; and Lisa Chalmers, "The Most Generous People," 45. In 2001, four of the city's top eight foundations came from Jewish family fortunes (Harry and Jeanette Weinberg, Jacob and Hilda Blaustein, Morris Goldseker, and Aaron and Lily Straus), with the Weinberg Foundation coming in second overall to the Annie E. Casey Foundation. "Largest Charitable Foundations in the Baltimore Area," *Baltimore Business Journal 2001 Book of Lists*, bizjournals.com/baltimore.

53. See, for example, Michael Dresser, "Sage Adviser, Key Figure in City's Growth," *Sun*, Feb. 16, 2007, 1A (quote); C. Fraser Smith, "Sondheim's Legacy of Courage," *Sun*, Feb. 25, 2007.

54. Associated 2010 community study, 31.

55. "Who Is Zanvyl Krieger?" krieger.jhu.edu/about/zanvyl_krieger. However, it must be noted that the largest Jewish donor to Baltimore universities is a New Yorker: Hopkins alumnus Michael Bloomberg, who has given his alma mater more than $1 billion. See *New York Times*, Jan. 27, 2013, A1.

56. *Sun*, May 2, 2013, A18; "The Next Generation," *Cincinnati Magazine*, Sept. 1990.

57. See bethambaltimore.org; B. Boyd, "Great 'Mysterian' Marc Steiner Celebrates 20 Years on Baltimore Air," Apr. 1, 2013, baltimorefishbowl.com/stories/great-mysterian-marc -steiner-celebrates-20-years-on-baltimore-air.

58. The quote is from Olesker, *Michael Olesker's Baltimore: If You Live Here, You're Home* (Baltimore: Johns Hopkins University Press, 1995), iv. See also Olesker, *Journeys to the Heart of Baltimore* (Baltimore: Johns Hopkins University Press, 2001); Gilbert Sandler, *Jewish Baltimore: A Family Album* (Baltimore: Johns Hopkins University Press, 2000); Sandler, *Small-Town Baltimore: An Album of Memories* (Baltimore: Johns Hopkins University Press, 2002).

59. On the effort to save the Lloyd Street Synagogue, see *The Synagogue Speaks* exhibition files, JMM; on the museum's history, see " 'I Think It Will Go': Robert Weinberg Creates the Jewish Heritage Center," *Generations* (Winter 2002): 56–73.

60. According to the 2014 Associated synagogue directory, there were nine synagogues on Park Heights Avenue, with dozens more in the surrounding streets of Upper Park Heights, Pikesville, and Owings Mills. See jlinkbalt.org.

Index

Aaronsohn, Reuben, 154
Abraham Lincoln Brigade, 238
Abrahams, Isaac, 24
Abrams, Rosalie Silber, 13, 264–65, 289–90,
  292, 293
acculturation, 2, 15, 30–33, 71–77, 147, 150,
  154, 157, 186–88, 220, 240, 242, 313; and
  Americanization, 163–74, 179, 180–82, 207,
  209–10, 213, 223–24. *See also* assimilation
Act Concerning Religion (Toleration Act,
  1649), 20
Adams, Willie, 291
Adath B'nei Israel (The Adas), 222, 243, 269
Ades, Bernard, 237–38
Ades, Harry and Simon, 134
African Americans, 180, 181, 191, 296, 347n14;
  discrimination against, 183–84, 233, 282;
  efforts to disenfranchise, 15, 166–67, 233,
  235; and immigrant labor, 111–12, 120; and
  Jewish-owned department stores, 238, 239,
  251, 279, 284; and Jews in politics, 15, 233,
  235, 238, 251, 285–86, 288–91, 293, 316; Jim
  Crow laws against, 4, 15, 235, 238, 239, 245,
  251; and neighborhood Jewish businesses,
  14, 195–98, 238–39, 282, 287–88, 349n44;
  and 1968 riots, 245, 287–88, 296; racism
  against, 184, 239, 249–51, 284; relations with
  Jews, 14–15, 122, 184, 212, 230, 235, 237–38,
  240, 245, 251, 280–84, 299, 301, 304–5. *See
  also* free blacks; slavery
Afro-American (newspaper), 122, 235, 237, 238,
  283

agricultural colonies, Jewish, 125–27
Agudas Achim Anshe Sphard Congregation,
  243
Agudas B'nai Zion, 155
Agudath Israel Congregation, 319
Ahrens, Jacob, 77
Aitz Chaim Congregation, 155, 176
Albin, Leon, 194
alcohol, 120, 142; Jews as producers and
  purveyors of, 18, 23, 25, 26, 60, 117. *See also*
  Prohibition
Alpha Zeta Omega, 206
Altfeld, E. Milton, 235, 251
Amalgamated Clothing Workers of America
  (ACWA), 138, 160, 167, 190–91, 206, 236
American Civil Liberties Union, 236
American Council for Judaism, 274
American Federation for Lithuanian Jews, 252
American Jewish Committee, 176, 217, 275
American Jewish Congress, 177, 207, 217
American Jewish Relief Committee (AJRC),
  176
American Legion, 228
American Party. *See* Know-Nothings
American Society for the Melioration of the
  Condition of the Jews (ASMCJ), 67–68. *See
  also* missionaries
Amity Club, 213
anarchism, 120, 151, 152, 157, 159
Annapolis, MD, 20, 21, 22, 23, 43, 44, 98
Anshe Chesed Bialystok (congregation), 103
Anshe Sphard Congregation, 222

Benjamin, Esther, 32
Benjamin, Hannah, 32
Benjamin, Levi, 51
Benjamin, Samuel, 32
Benjamin, Solomon, 32
Ben-Yosef, Raphael (Ralph Finkel), 273
Berg, Jimmy, 309
Berger, Frank, 176
Berlin, Germany, 68, 125
Berman, Barnett, 186
Berman, Frances, 297
Bernstein, Manny, 282–83
Beth Am Synagogue, 318
Beth El Congregation, 268, 269
Beth Israel Congregation, 260, 269
Beth Jacob Congregation, 220, 260, 287
Bethlehem Steel, 112, 195; shipyards of, 249–50
Beth Rachel Society, 138
Beth Tfiloh Congregation, 223–25, 226, 260,
    266, 268, 274, 311; day school, 267, 308, 309,
    310, 311
Bialystok, Poland, 103
Bikur Cholim (congregation), 95, 103, 143
Binswanger, David, 97
Bisgyer, Maurice, 179
Black-Jewish Forum of Baltimore (BLEWS), 304
Blaustein, Harry "Heinie," 196
Blaustein, Jacob, 195, 275, 315
Blaustein, Louis, 195
Blaustein–Ben-Gurion agreement, 275
Blaustein family, 296, 298, 316
Block, The, 11, 198–99, 241, 296, 299
blockade runners (Civil War), 86, 88, 91-92, 93
blockbusting, 250–51, 257, 282–83
Bloomfield, Maurice, 117
Bluefeld, Louis, 234–35
Blumberg, Albert, 237, 293
Blumberg, Dorothy, 293
Blumenberg, Leopold, 76, 88–89, 93–94
B'nai Abraham and Yehuda Laib Family Circle,
    252
B'nai B'rith, 64, 75, 76, 161; Jeschurun Lodge
    No. 3 of, 65; Menorah Lodge of, 208
B'nai Israel Congregation, 103, 142, 143, 145,
    311, 319
Board of Jewish Education, 210, 226–27,
    267–68
Bobroisker Beneficial Circle, 136
Bohemia: Jewish immigrants from, 29, 32, 40,

57, 84, 97; non-Jewish immigrants from,
    112, 131, 138, 232
Boston, MA, 17, 23; compared to Baltimore as
    Jewish center, 2, 108, 109, 111, 150, 151
Bothe, Elsbeth Levy, 278
Bouton, Edward, 182, 239
Bowman, Isaiah, 204, 279
boxers, Jewish, 196, 198, 233, 349n50
Brager-Gutman's, 297–98
Breidenbach, Hesse, 54, 55
Bremen, Germany, 1, 5, 57–58, 111
Bridge, Melvin, 233
B'rith Abraham, Independent Order, 136, 161, 215
Brith Sholom, Independent Order, 161–63, 215
Broening, William F., 176, 235
brokerage and exchange business, 17–19, 28, 29,
    34. See also banking
Brown v. Board of Education, 284, 287
Brunn, Bianca, 1
Brunn, Gustav, 1–2, 240
Buchman, Harold, 294
Buerger, Andy, 309
Bund (Jewish Worker's Bund), 107, 157, 160
Burgunder, Benjamin, 63
butchers, kosher, 145–47, 186. See also kashrut;
    shochtim

Cahn, Louis, 209, 212, 260
Camp Airy and Camp Louise, 210
Cardin, Benjamin, 293, 315
Cardin, Shoshana, 315
Carliner, Sam, 299
Carlin's Park, 187, 189, 215
Carroll of Carrollton, Charles, 118
Catholics, 20, 210, 237, 248, 250, 251, 258;
    Baltimore as a center for, 119, 125; prejudice
    against, 66, 70, 232; relations with Jews, 121,
    122, 250, 363n151
cemeteries: Jewish, 33, 78–79, 80, 137, 176, 271,
    312; Jews buried in Christian, 33
Center Club, 296, 316
Center Stage, 299
Central Conference of American Rabbis, 177,
    337n157
Central European ("German") Jews in Balti-
    more, 53–103, 114–18, 123–25, 126; relations
    with Eastern European Jews, 104–5, 117–18,
    122–23, 125, 127, 163–78, 207–8, 213, 215, 220,
    270, 278–79, 319

Central High School. *See* City College

Centre Market, 51, 60–63

CHAI (Comprehensive Housing Assistance, Inc.), 304, 305, 306, 312

CHANA (Counseling, Helpline and Aid Network for Abused Women), 311, 312

Chanukah House, 302

charities. *See* philanthropy

Charles Center, 295, 296, 297, 299

Charles Center<N>Inner Harbor Management Inc., 295

Charleston, SC, 19, 96

Chessler, Shirley "Deborah," 281

Chevra Ahavas Chesed, 219, 271

Chicago, IL, 73, 347n14; compared with Baltimore as Jewish center, 8, 54, 94, 108, 109, 111, 112, 150; as source of unauthorized kosher meat, 145, 147

Chideckel, Maurice, 153, 341n71

Children of Zion, 155

Chizuk Amuno Congregation, 156, 210, 222, 252, 270, 286–87, 318; acculturated Orthodoxy of, 102, 125, 164, 210; fluctuating membership of, 220–21, 227, 266; ritual innovation at, 224, 225, 268–69, 311; slow shift to Conservative movement, 225, 226, 268–69; synagogue buildings of, 145, 173, 266–67, 318

Cincinnati, OH, 5, 28, 82

circumcision, 28, 30, 33, 79, 82, 330n22

City College (formerly Central High School), 11, 97, 230, 231, 233, 246, 279, 281, 316

civic life of Baltimore Jews, 34–49, 64–71, 93–94, 114–15, 159, 160–63, 165–67, 169–70, 171, 229, 238, 240, 242, 281, 294–99, 316–18. *See also* Jew Bill; politics

civil rights movement, 15, 245, 251, 280, 284–87

Civil War, 2, 86–94; Jewish military service in, 76, 93–94

Cleosophic Dramatic and Literary Society, 75

Cleveland, OH, 59, 111, 347n14

Cleveland Conference (1855), 84–85

clothing industry. *See* clothing retailers; garment industry

clothing retailers, 51, 59–60, 63, 86–87, 114, 297

Clover Club, 123

Clover Theater, 199

Cohan, Levi, 21

Cohen, Ben and Herman, 202, 298, 299

Cohen, Benjamin I., 40, 48, 91

Cohen, Edward, 91

Cohen, Elizabeth, 33

Cohen, Jacob I. Jr., 28, 36, 40, 50, 65, 91, 98, 326n53; as advocate for Jew Bill, 10, 41–49, 328n99; lottery business of, 18, 29, 34, 38–39

Cohen, Judith, 28, 41

Cohen, Max, 198–99, 241

Cohen, Mendes, 117, 339n32

Cohen, Mendes I., 40, 98, 326n53

Cohen, Philip I., 40

Cohen, Rose, 257

Cohen, Sydney, 201

Cohen family, 28, 30, 32, 33, 36, 41, 49, 50, 326n53

Cohn, Michael, 152, 157

Collmus, Levi, 32, 40

Columbia, MD, 316

Committee for Downtown, 294–95

communal life, 8–10, 27, 30, 32–34, 49–52, 53–54, 72–76, 135–38, 143–45, 167–69, 176–77, 206–20, 271–76, 304–6, 311–15. *See also* philanthropy; and specific communal institutions

Communist Party, 237, 250, 293–94

Concordia Association, 53, 98, 100–101, 117, 123

Cone, Claribel and Etta, 240–41

Congress of Racial Equality (CORE), 284, 287

Conn, Minnie, 257

Conservative Judaism, 10, 224–25, 226, 252, 276, 307, 308, 311; post-World War II growth, 260, 268, 269. *See also* religious life, Jewish

conversion to Christianity, 32, 68, 119

convict servants, 21–23. *See also* indentured servants

Cooper, Isidor, 282

Council of Orthodox Congregations, 269

craftspeople, Jewish, 5, 22, 25, 28, 32, 60, 134, 140

crime, 8; committed by Jews, 21–23, 51, 65, 70–71, 142, 199–200, 233, 296–97. *See also* juvenile delinquency

Crockin, Emil, 208

Crockin, Sadie, 208, 231–32, 236

Cumberland, MD, 59

Curran, William, 233–34

D'Alesandro, Thomas Jr., 230, 234, 290, 298

Dalsheimer, Helen, 266
Daughters in Israel, 164, 173
Daughters of Zion, 155
Davidove, Emanuel, 196–97
Davison, Rosalee, 202
defense industry, World War II, 245, 248, 249;
    Jewish workers and union organizers in,
    250, 293–94
delicatessens, 1, 11–12, 139, 160, 193, 201, 284,
    287; as gathering places, 187, 220, 240, 242,
    262–63. *See also* restaurants
Democratic Party, 13, 66, 68, 70–71, 88, 91, 93,
    98, 115, 160, 161, 162, 166, 200, 233–36, 293,
    316; Breckinridge faction of, 88, 335n110;
    pro-Union faction of, 93
Democratic Republican Party ("Republicans"),
    37–39, 44, 46, 48, 66
Demokrat (newspaper), 68
Denaburg, Israel, 116
department stores, 15, 63, 114, 201–2, 244, 248,
    316; and downtown decline, 294–95, 297–
    98; importance in Baltimore commercial
    life, 114–15, 193, 239–40. *See also* African
    Americans; *and under specific stores*
Detroit, MI, 111, 300, 347n6, 347n14
Deutsch, Solomon, 101
Deutsche Correspondent, 68–69, 75, 121, 122
dietary laws, Jewish. *See* kashrut
Diner (movie), 263
discrimination against Jews: economic,
    189–90, 203–5, 232, 249–50; residential, 11,
    180, 182–184, 258, 278–80; social, 13 76, 115,
    117. *See also* antisemitism; nativism; quotas
Dopkin, Lee, 237
Drazin, Nathan, 216, 225
Druid Hill Park, 185, 187, 201, 216, 219, 220, 223,
    224, 254, 255, 258, 299; interracial tennis
    protest at, 285, 293, 294
dry goods business, 23, 32, 51, 58, 59–60, 63, 69,
    86, 87, 94, 95, 96, 97, 142. *See also* depart-
    ment stores
Dumbarton Heights, 185, 259
Dyer, John M., 51, 65–66, 80, 98, 331n38
Dyer, Leon, 65–66, 80, 331n38

East Baltimore, 319; acculturation in, 139, 142,
    143, 144, 147, 150; during interwar period,
    199, 210, 222, 229, 230, 237, 260, 311; as hub
    for Central European Jews, 80, 82, 173;

institutional and religious life in, 155, 157,
    160, 176, 214, 215, 226; as Jewish immigrant
    neighborhood, 6, 118, 122, 127, 128–31;
    moving away from, 11, 180, 184–86, 210,
    291; politics in, 161, 164, 165, 166, 167, 170;
    settlement work in, 143, 164, 172–73, 179.
    See also Old Town
East Baltimore Boys, 206
Eastern European Jews in Baltimore, 23, 29, 50,
    57, 95–96, 103, 104–14, 118–22, 127–63; rela-
    tions with Central European Jews, 104–5,
    117–18, 122–23, 125, 127, 163–178, 207–8, 213,
    215, 220, 270, 278–79, 319
Eastern High School, 230
Easterwood Park, 185, 187, 206, 242
Eckhaus, Carol, 186
economic life, Jewish, 17–18, 23–30, 50–51,
    58–64, 94–97, 111–12, 127–40, 189–206,
    261–63
Eddie Jacobs menswear, 297
Edelman, Jacob, 190–91, 206, 235, 286
Edmondson Village, 244; shopping center, 296
education, secular: in German-language
    schools, 76–77; in Jewish private day
    schools, 76, 136–37; in public schools, 97,
    101, 139, 147, 230–31, 233, 281. *See also* Jewish
    education
Efros, Israel, 209–10
Einhorn, David, 101; antislavery views of, 7, 13,
    89, 90, 91; issues prayer book *Olat Tamid*
    (1855), 84; as radical reformer, 7, 8, 13, 83–85
Eisenberg family, 221
Elliott, Cass (Ellen Naomi Cohen), 281
Ellison, Daniel, 235
Emden (ship), 227–28, 232
English language, adopted by Jewish im-
    migrants, 53, 75–76, 101–2, 123, 125, 143,
    146–47, 151, 159, 164, 169
entertainment industry, 196–99, 240
Epstein, Jacob, 3, 5, 135, 137, 168, 169, 176, 192,
    208, 212, 240
eruv, in Northwest Baltimore, 270, 307
Esterson, Rose, 211
Etting, Elizabeth (Betsy), 32
Etting, Frances (Fanny), 31, 32
Etting, Rachel Gratz, 28, 39
Etting, Reuben, 25, 28, 29, 32, 37–38
Etting, Samuel, 40, 42, 49
Etting, Shinah, 25

German language, used by Jews, 53, 57, 68–69, 75, 76
German Society of Maryland, 36
German states (pre-unification): Jewish immigrants from, 24, 28, 29, 50, 56, 57–58; Jewish life in, 54–56; non-Jewish immigrants from, 36, 51, 57–58, 66, 68, 70, 75. *See also* Germany; *and specific locations*
Germany, 1, 217–19, 227, 232, 270
Gibbons, James Cardinal, 121, 122
GI Bill of Rights, 254, 262, 270
Ginsberg, Solomon, 135, 168
Glaser, Ida and Mendel, 141
Glaser, Milton, 200
Glass, Ben and Philip, 196
Glick, Gertrude, 210
Glick, Rose Shanis, 202
Glushakow, Jacob, 299
Goldberg, George, 200, 296
Goldberg, Harry, 196–97
Golden, Ed, 299
Goldman, Israel, 266, 286–87
Goldschmidt, Jonas, 76
Goldseker, Morris, 282
Goldstein, Albert, 245
Goldstein, Rubin, 150
Goldstein, Sol, 252–53
Goldstone, Herbert, 203
Gomborov, Israel, 341n71
Goodman, Philip, 290–91
Goodwin, Hilda, 288
Gordonia Labor Zionist youth camp, 215
Gordon Sea Food, 242
Gorfine, Emanuel, 228
Grady, Harold, 290–91
Gratz, Barnard and Michael, 23–24
Gratz, Rachel. *See* Etting, Rachel Gratz
Gratz, Rebecca, 26
Great Britain, 17, 21–23, 24, 25, 26, 27, 37, 38, 40; Jewish immigrants from, 29, 50, 57; Palestine under rule of, 174, 272, 274. *See also* Revolutionary War; War of 1812
Great Depression, 199–204, 212–13, 220, 235, 236, 245, 299. *See also* New Deal
Greater Baltimore Committee, 294–95
Greenbaum, Daniel, 97
Greenstein, Harry, 212–13, 237
Greif, L. & Brother, 116, 127–28, 133
Greif, Levi, 59, 63, 94

grocers, 23, 51, 59, 64, 102, 132, 134, 194, 195, 242
Guinzberg, Aaron, 76, 84
Gutman, Arthur, 201–2
Gutman, Joel, 63
Gutman's Department Store, 114, 193, 201–2. *See also* Brager-Gutman's
Guttmacher, Adolph, 123, 125, 167
Guttmacher, Laura, 209, 210
Gwynns Falls Junior High School, 233

Hackerman, Willard, 204, 296, 316
Hadassah, 206, 215, 231
Hagerstown, MD, 28, 59
Hamburg, Germany, 58, 104; Hamburg Temple, 77
Hamburger, Isaac, 63
Hamburger family, 185
Hammerman, Robert, 316
Harkavy, Alexander, 152–53
Harlem Theatre, 196–98
Harmony Circle, 73, 100, 337n147
Harris, James M., 70
Harrison Street, 51, 62–63, 103, 180
Harrison, Albertina and Samuel, 132
Harry and Jeanette Weinberg Foundation, 316–17
Har Sinai Congregation, 101, 247–49; activism of rabbi Edward Israel, 190, 226, 237; advance of Reform at, 77–79, 80, 82–86, 102, 103, 123–24; led by anti-Zionist rabbi Charles A. Rubenstein, 167, 177–78; led by David Einhorn, 7, 8, 53, 83–85, 89–90, 91; suburbanization of, 227, 266
Hart, Jacob, 23, 24
Har Zion Congregation, 227
Hashomer Hadati, 216
Hashomer Hatzair, 216
Hasidic Jews, 142, 222, 270
Ha-Techia Zionist Society, 173
Hauer, Moshe, 309
havurot, 308
Hebrew Assistance Society, 64, 72, 331n30, 331n31. *See also* Hebrew Benevolent Society
Hebrew Benevolent Society, 53, 72, 73–74, 76, 87, 98–99, 100, 104, 163, 185, 210, 331n30. *See also* Hebrew Assistance Society
Hebrew Children's Sheltering and Protective Association, 137
Hebrew Education Society, 164

66, 68, 70, 94, 120, 122, 130, 138, 160, 229, 233, 290

Isaac Bar Levinsohn Hebrew Literary Society, 151, 152, 169, 208. *See also* Russian Night School

Israel, Baltimore Jews and, 272–76, 297, 313, 315

Israel, Edward, 190, 226, 228, 229, 236, 237, 238, 239

Israelis in Baltimore, 6, 305

Israelson family, 194

Italian immigrants and Italian Americans, 112, 130, 133, 138, 160, 183, 185, 191, 198, 229, 230, 280

Jachman, Isadore, 247

Jack Lewis Funeral Home, 176

Jackson, Howard, 227–28

Jackson, Lillie Mae, 239, 283, 287

Jacobs, Barnard, 28, 30

Jacobs, Joseph, 51

Jacobs, Moses, 30

Jacobs, Phil, 301

Jacobs, Samuel, 324n14

Jew Bill (1826), 10, 13, 19, 35, 36, 43–49, 51, 53, 65; universal version of, 44–46, 328n99

Jewish Big Brother League, 206, 210

Jewish Cemetery Association, 312

Jewish Children's Society, 210

Jewish Chronicle (newspaper), 101

Jewish Comment (newspaper), 142, 164, 167, 177–78, 207, 208

Jewish Community Center (Owings Mills), 16, 272, 301, 303, 306, 309

Jewish Community Center (Park Heights), 260, 261, 304, 305, 313

Jewish education, 209, 226, 227, 267–68, 307, 313. *See also* Board of Jewish Education; *and specific schools*

Jewish Educational Alliance (JEA), 173, 177, 179, 186, 188, 206, 210, 230, 241, 260; JEA Alumni, 206

Jewish Family Services, 313

Jewish Legion in Palestine, 174–75

Jewish Museum of Maryland, 319

Jewish Social Service Bureau (Jewish Family and Children's Bureau), 210

Jewish Theological Seminary (JTS), 224

Jewish Times, 201, 206–7, 212, 216, 228, 233, 242, 245, 246, 274, 301, 303, 314, 365n20; and

religious conflict, 269, 271–72, 306, 309–10; suburbanization and, 258–62

Jewish Welfare Board, 176

"Jews Burying Ground" (1786), 33. *See also* cemeteries

Johns Hopkins University, 114, 117, 164, 217, 237, 265, 317; quotas at, 203–4, 278–79

Johnson-Reed Act (1924), 346n2

Jontiff, Edna, 246

Joseph A. Bank menswear, 297

Joseph Meyerhoff Symphony Hall, 16, 299

juvenile delinquency, 142, 210, 229. *See also* crime

Kahn, Amelia, 62

Kahn, Dorothy, 210

Kahn, Phil, 199, 204

Kahn, Samuel, 62

Kaiser, Alois, 156

Kamenetz, Kevin, 316

Kanner, Leo, 218

Kaplan, Louis L., 267–68, 271

Kardinsky family, 110

kashrut (Jewish dietary laws), 30, 33, 82, 130, 143, 145, 146, 147, 150. *See also* shochtim

Katkow, Herman, 282

Katz, Joseph, 204

Katzenberg, Berney Jr., 186

Katzenstein, Alvin, 200–201

Katzenstein, Louis, 200

Kaufman, Herbert, 282, 296

Kayam Farm, 312

Keiser, Marcia Smith, 187

Kennedy, Thomas, 44, 46

Kishinev pogrom (1903), 121

Klasmer, Benjamin, 241–42

Knapp, Frederick, 76, 77

Know-Nothings (American Party), 13, 66–67, 68, 69, 70, 88, 89, 91, 93, 98, 120, 331n40

Kohn, Martin, 239, 244, 248, 284

Kolker, Dan, 230

Kolker, Fabian, 314–15

Kolker, Jonathan, 304

Kovens, Irvin, 290–91

Kovno (Kaunas), Lithuania, 107, 135, 143

Kramer, Reuben, 299

Kravetz, Abraham, 6

Kres, Isadore, 162

Krick, Perna, 299

Mandy, Sylvia, 223

Manning-Shaw Realty, 283

manufacturers, Jews as, 29, 30, 88, 96, 133, 161, 166, 192. *See also under* garment industry

Maril, Herman, 299

Market Street, 18, 23, 26, 35. *See also* Baltimore Street

marriage, 30, 33, 51, 141–42, 246, 255, 264; between Central and Eastern European Jews, 208; officiants, 30, 33, 51, 143. *See also* intermarriage

Marshall, Thurgood, 228, 285

Maryland Club, 117

Marylander Apartments, 280

Maryland General Assembly, 43–46, 48, 49, 51; Jewish members of, 98, 161, 166, 228, 235, 251, 265, 291, 292, 293

Maryland State Colonization Association, 36

Maryland state legislature. *See* Maryland General Assembly

Maskil El Dol Society, 138

Masliansky, Zvi Hirsh, 155, 166

Masonic lodges, 76, 77, 140, 333n75

May, Saidie Adler, 241

McCarthyism, 242, 293–94

McCormick Spice Company, 1, 190

McKeldin, Theodore Roosevelt, 291, 293

Meadowbrook Swimming Club, 279, 280

Meals on Wheels, 276

Mechanic, Morris, and Mechanic Theatre, 299

Mechanic, Rae, 222

Mechanical Company of Baltimore, 39, 328n83

Mendelssohn Literary Society, 75

Mervis, Moshe Falk, 155

Methodists, 33, 68, 93, 237

Meyerhoff, Joseph: as philanthropist and civic leader, 13, 260, 296, 298–99, 316; as real estate developer, 183, 195, 280, 285

Meyerhoff family, 195, 316

Mickle, Robert, 32

Mikveh Israel Congregation (Philadelphia), 33

Miles, Clarence, 294–95, 296, 298

military service, Jewish. *See* Jewish Legion in Palestine; militias; *and specific wars*

militias, Jewish service in, 25, 39–41, 46, 48–49, 69

Miller, Bert, 307

Miller, J. Jefferson, 294–95

Miller, Morris, 159

Miller, Uri, 287

Millum, Moses, 51

Mirmelstein, Abraham, 247

missionaries, Christian, 66–68, 69, 73, 99, 119, 222

Mitchell, Clarence III, 283

Mitchell, Parren, 288, 293

Mizrachi Party, 155, 215–16

Montgomery County, 4

Monumental Theatre (Orpheum Theatre), 147, 154

Monument Street Y. *See* Young Men's/Women's Hebrew Association

Mordecai, David, 96

Mordecai, Mordecai Moses, 23, 25, 28, 30, 32–33, 107

Mordecai, Moses, 23

Mordecai, Moses Cohen, 96

Morgan State College, 284

Morgn zhurnal (newspaper), 154

Morris, George, 280

Mortara Affair, 69–70

Moses, Bessie, 240

Moses, Hortense, 208

Moses, Jacob, 40

Moses, Jacob M., 156, 169–71, 208, 236, 240, 243

Moses Montefiore Hebrew Congregation, 128

Mount Washington, 185, 279, 280

mutual assistance societies, 63–64, 72, 79, 219, 312. *See also* landsmanshaften

Myer Atkin's Democratic Club, 236

Myers, Israel, 191–92, 297

Myers, John, 25–28

Myers, Moses, 25–26

Nates and Leons, 11–12, 187, 193, 240, 284, 287

Nathan, Lyon, 25

National Association for the Advancement of Colored People (NAACP), 228, 239, 280, 284, 285; *Crisis* magazine, 239, 287

National Brewing Company, 298

National Conference of Christians and Jews, 232

National Council of Jewish Women, Baltimore branch (NCJW), 212, 218, 276

National Refugee Service, 218

Native Americans, 23, 40, 65

nativism, 66–68, 70, 71, 118–119, 120, 174, 179, 228, 232, 346n2. *See also* antisemitism; Know-Nothings

Nattans, Arthur Sr., 284

naturalization, 56, 65, 68, 120, 159, 160, 167, 314

Nazism, 8, 216, 217–19, 227, 246, 251

Needle, Sidney, 238

Neistadt, Samuel, 206, 236, 242

Ner Israel Rabbinical College, 8, 9, 218, 222–23, 260, 270, 306, 307, 311, 314

Netherlands. *See* Holland

Netivot Shalom, 311

networks, 3, 5, 6, 27, 30, 215, 218; family and kinship, 1, 185; social, 204, 206, 207, 217, 276

Neuberger, Herman, 270, 271, 306, 314

New Deal, 191, 201, 203, 212–13, 215, 235–37

New Orleans, LA, 28

New York, NY, 23, 28, 33, 55, 90, 125, 127, 154, 155, 166, 217, 250, 272, 314, 347n14; Jewish life in Baltimore compared to, 8, 11, 22, 54, 108–9, 111, 130, 146, 149, 150, 151–52, 157, 159, 160, 222, 225, 270, 302; Jews moving to Baltimore from, 250, 306, 310; size of Baltimore compared to, 19, 26, 50, 94

New York Dairy Lunch Room, 186

Norfolk, VA, 25–26, 276

North Avenue, 185, 187, 212, 242, 258, 262, 284, 288

North Baltimore, 182

Northeast Baltimore, 183

North German Lloyd shipping line, 6, 95, 111

Northwest Baltimore, 11, 13, 16, 179, 208, 229, 240, 272, 277, 281, 317; as Jewish district, 180–89, 195, 206–7, 213, 242, 302–3, 319; Jewish institutions in, 210, 222–23, 227, 307, 312; Jews and blacks in, 212, 238, 304; and politics, 233, 288, 290, 291, 316; and suburbanization, 244–45, 257–61

Northwest Baltimore Corporation, 304

Northwest Citizens' Patrol, 307, 312

Northwood, 182, 294

Novick, Jacob, 131

Oasis nightclub, 199, 297

Ober Law, 293

Odd Fellows, 76, 77

Odessa, Ukraine, 107, 150

Offitt, Buck, 200

Oheb Shalom Congregation, 156, 226, 227, 266,

267, 319; advance of reform at, 102, 103, 123; early religious identity of, 79–80, 82–83, 86; led by Benjamin Szold, 8, 53, 83–84, 85, 90, 101, 156; led by William Rosenau, 123, 149, 167, 176, 199; synagogues of, 80, 123–34, 268

Ohr Hamizrach Congregation, 314, 319

Old Bay seasoning, 1–2, 240

Olden, David, 32

Old Town, 29, 49, 51. *See also* East Baltimore

Olesker, Michael, 263, 318–19

O'Neill's department store, 294

Orioles (vocal group), 281

Orpheum Theatre. *See* Monumental Theatre

Orthodox Judaism, 4, 10, 16, 164, 170–73, 176, 242, 243, 252, 276, 313, 319; Baltimore as hospitable place for, 8, 114, 125, 254; and Eastern European immigrants, 140, 142–50, 152, 157; institutional growth of, 222–224, 245, 270, 307; in interwar era, 207, 210, 213, 215, 216, 218–19, 221, 225–27; late twentieth century resurgence of, 301, 302, 304, 306–10; and nineteenth-century acculturation, 79, 80, 82, 85, 102–3, 125; "open Orthodoxy," 311; in post–World War II era, 260, 267, 268–69, 271, 272. *See also* religious life, Jewish

Osterman, Joseph, 51

overseas trade, Jews in, 18, 23, 26, 27, 29, 37

Owings Mills, 272, 301, 303, 305, 317

Palestine, 10, 154, 155, 174–75, 177, 215, 216, 246, 272, 274, 344n128

Palm Beach, FL, 302

Panic of 1819, 26, 30, 33–34, 50

Panitz, Stanley, 294, 296

Paper, Maurice, 229

Paper, Samuel, 199

Park Heights, 188, 223, 230, 254, 294, 310; Lower, 185–87, 222, 243, 257, 258, 304, 318; Upper, 15, 185, 227, 256, 258–61, 270, 289, 301, 303–6, 316, 317, 358n36

Park Heights Avenue, 123–24, 186, 187, 258, 260, 261, 302, 304, 314, 319

Parker (Pollokoff), Royal, 299

Park School, 232, 278, 279

Pats, Sharon, 288

Patterson Park, 150, 185

pawnbrokers, 19, 51, 60, 63, 70, 199, 202

Pearlstone Center, 312

peddlers, 25, 35, 28, 29, 30, 40, 55, 58–59, 60, 135, 137

Pennsylvania Avenue, 128, 194, 200, 238, 282–83

Perlman, Philip, 235

Petach Tikvah Congregation, 223

Peters, Madison, 121

Philadelphia, PA, 22, 23, 24, 25, 28, 29, 32, 33, 38, 40, 91, 94, 96, 97, 161, 276, 316, 347n14; compared to Baltimore as Jewish center, 8, 54, 108, 109, 111, 112, 150; as rival to Baltimore, 4, 19, 26, 50

philanthropy: directed at non-Jewish causes, 72–73, 98–99, 313, 316; within Jewish community, 53, 72–75, 98–100, 104, 107, 137–38, 160, 163–65, 167–69, 181, 201, 208–9, 210–12. *See also specific organizations*

Phoenix Club, 123, 208, 213

Pikesville, 185, 244, 245, 258, 260–64, 270, 289, 300–302, 304, 306, 317

Pikesville High School, 261

Pimlico, 11, 262; racetrack, 188, 198, 298, 299

Pimlico Junior High School, 281

Pioneers of Liberty (New York), 151–52

Pittsburgh, PA, 28, 347n6, 350n75

Pittsburgh Platform (1885), 337n157

Poale Zion. *See* Labor Zionists

pogroms, 107–8, 109, 121, 154, 338n11

Poland: Jewish immigrants from, 29, 50, 57, 95, 103, 107, 109, 120, 140, 191, 246; non-Jewish immigrants from, 122, 130. *See also specific locations*

Polan Katz, 192

Polish Americans, 229, 250

politics, 35, 36–38, 65–66, 68, 69, 70–71, 80, 88–91, 93, 97–98, 114–15, 118, 120, 160–63, 165–67, 181, 233–37, 288–94, 315–16; Jewish office holders, 15, 37–38, 41, 43, 46, 48, 49, 50, 65, 98, 161, 166, 228, 235, 251, 265, 288–94, 315–16; political clubs, 188, 206, 236

Pollack, James "Jack," 200, 233–35, 238, 290–91

Pollack, Morton Curran, 234

Polliakoff, Manuel, 247

Pollock, Elias (Joseph Smith), 25, 29–30

Polt, Gilbert and Leslie, 256

Pompeian Olive Oil, 192

population, Jewish. *See* Baltimore: Jewish population of

Porges, Ida, 130, 145

Portney, Jack, 198

Posen, 57, 68, 95, 170

Posvohler Friendly Society, 136

Potts, Isaac, 232

Pratt Street Riot (1861), 91–92

prayer books. *See* liturgy

Preakness Stakes, 298

President Warfield (ship). *See Exodus 1947*

Pressman, Hyman, 293

professions, Jews in: 97, 101, 114, 134, 202–6, 262

Progressive Labor Lyceum, 144, 159, 187, 344n136. *See also* Workmen's Circle

Prohibition, 199–200, 235

prostitution, 142, 296

Protestant Episcopal Church, 32, 68

Protestants, 20, 66–68, 73, 121. *See also specific churches and denominations*

Prussia, 51, 56, 57, 76, 95

Pryse, Harriet, 32

Purim Association, 100

quotas: in medical and law schools, 203, 278–79; in private schools, 232. *See also* antisemitism; discrimination against Jews

Rabbi Isaac Elchanan Theological Seminary, 224, 353n135

Rafalsky, Nizel, 174

Rainess, Izzy, 198

Ranchleigh, 254

Randallstown, 245, 258, 260, 269, 301–5

Raphall, Morris J., 90

Rappaport, Isadore, 196, 240

Rayner, Isidor, 15, 97–98, 101, 115, 117–18, 166–67, 339n32

Rayner, William S., 58–59, 85, 93, 97, 99–100, 117

Read's Drug Store, 284

real estate: discriminatory practices regarding, 180, 182–184, 279–80, 304; Jewish involvement in, 13, 183, 195, 250, 254, 258–59, 262, 279–80, 282–83, 296

Reconstructionist Judaism, 10, 308

Reform Judaism, 8, 164, 210, 215, 224, 227, 252, 260, 266, 267, 269, 276, 287, 308; advance of, after Civil War, 101–2, 103, 123–35 337n157; early ideological incoherency of, 77–86; opposition to among traditionalists, 78,

Reform Judaism (*cont.*)

102, 216, 225, 271, 306; rabbis as ideologists
of, 7, 79, 83–85; and Zionism, 167, 177–78,
216, 226, 242–43, 274. *See also* religious life,
Jewish

Rehfeld, Ruth, 294, 304

Rehiné, Zalma, 33

Reisterstown Road Plaza, 261–62

Religious Good Will League, 232

religious life, Jewish, 7–9, 10, 30–34, 49–50,
51–52, 77–86, 101–3, 123–25, 126, 140–50,
220–27, 265–71, 306–11; conflict over, 78,
102, 207, 268–69, 271–72, 306, 309–10. *See
also different denominations*

Republican Party, 88–89, 93, 98, 115, 161, 162,
166, 234, 235, 242, 291, 293, 316. *See also*
Democratic Republican Party

Republican Society of Baltimore, 38, 39

residential patterns, Jewish, 10, 11, 13, 29,
60–61, 117, 128–30, 182, 184–86, 244–46,
257–58, 261, 301, 302–4

restaurants, 186, 199, 263, 307, 309; racial integration of, 284–85. *See also* delicatessens

Revolutionary War, 19–20, 23, 24–25, 29, 39;
Jewish service in, 17, 25

Rice, Abraham, 8, 77–78, 79, 82, 85

Richmond, VA, 19, 28, 32, 33, 38, 91

Rifman, Avrum, 150

Rifman, Chaim-Shemon and Zeesla-Baile, 150

Rivkin, Reuben, 215, 231, 242

Rodeph Shalom Congregation (Philadelphia),
33

Roland Park, 182, 239, 303

Roland Park Company, 182, 183, 185, 280

Rosen, Morton, 233

Rosenau, William, 123, 125, 149, 167, 177–78,
199, 210, 216, 217

Rosenblatt, Josef, 224

Rosenblatt, Samuel, 224, 260

Rosenbloom, Carroll, 298

Rosenbluth, Ronnie, 309

Rosenbush, Lou, 291

Rosenfeld, Edward, 299

Rosenfeld, Goody, 100

Rosenfeld, Merrill, 176

Rosenthal, Ada, 204, 210

Rothman, Donald, 299

Rothschild, Amalie, 13, 299

rowhouses, 13, 135, 180

Rubenstein, Charles A., 167, 177–78, 207

Rubin, Neil, 306–7

Rubinstein, Rubin, 250

Ruderman, Faiga, 222

Ruderman, Jacob, 222, 270

Russell, Esther Mordecai, 25

Russell, Philip Moses, 25

Russian Empire: Jewish life in, 106–8, 109;
pre-1880 arrivals from, 95, 103. *See also*
pogroms; *and specific regions*

Russian Night School, 169, 208

Russian, Sheila, 308

Rutter, Thomas, 29

Sachs, Barbara, 255

Sachs, Leon, 182, 184, 204, 232, 251, 274,
278–80, 284, 287, 293. *See also* Baltimore
Jewish Council

Sachs, Stephen, 293, 294

Sachs Drug Store, 187

Sachs family, 133

Sachs-Kohen, Elissa, 308

Saffron, Israel, 183

Sale, Samuel, 53

Salsbury, Julius, 297

Sandler, Gilbert, 181, 230, 318–19

San Francisco, CA, 54, 66

Sapolsky, Buddy, 309

Sapperstein, Ike, 200, 242, 296

Sauber, Adolph, 155, 161, 162

Saye, Hymen, 209, 226

Schaefer, William Donald, 293, 295, 296, 298

Schanfarber, Tobias, 123, 125

Schapiro, John, 298

Schapiro, Morris, 192, 298

Scheib, Heinrich, 76, 77

Schlossberg, Eli, 269, 311

Schlossberg, Lena, 127–28

Schloss Brothers, 133

Schmoke, Kurt, 316

Schnaper, David, 243

Schneeberger, Henry, 102, 125, 156, 164, 343n15

Schneider, Minnie, 229

Schochet, Abraham S., 154, 161

Schoeneman's, J., clothing manufacturer,
190–91

Schwab, Simon, 218–19, 220, 223, 270, 271

Schwartz, Abraham N., 143, 146, 149, 222, 270

Schwartz, Carmi, 304

Weiner, Esther and Morty, 255
Weissager, William, 161, 341n71
Wertheim, Alexander, 33
West Baltimore, 181, 238, 240
West Baltimore General Hospital, 240
Western High School, 281
West Point (United States Military Academy), 40
Where, What, When (magazine), 309, 311
Whig Party, 65–66
white flight, 15, 245, 250, 257, 282, 286, 301, 304, 305
Whiting-Turner Company, 204, 296
wholesale industry, 192, 297
Wickham, DeWayne, 282
Wide-Awakes (paramilitary unit), 88–89
Wiener, Charles J., 97, 101
Wiener, Moritz, 68–69, 97
Wiesenfeld, Betsy Friedenwald, 64, 73–74
Wiesenfeld, Moses, 62–63, 64, 80, 86–87, 88, 90, 91, 92, 93, 94, 100, 335n121, 337n147
Willen, Martin, 247
Williams, Frances, 32
Windsor Hills, 15, 185, 286
Wire, The (TV show), 318
Wise, Isaac Mayer, 82–83
Wise, Stephen, 217
Wohlberg, Mitchell, 311
Wolf, Moses, 97
Wolman, Abel, 237
Wolod, Norma Livov, 230
women, Jewish, 264, 281; boycott kosher meat outlets, 147; in business, 193, 199, 202, 262, 296, 297; in garment industry, 127–28, 131, 190–91; organizations of, 73–75, 137–38, 156, 164, 170, 206, 208, 211, 212, 218, 221, 236, 265, 276, 308, 311, 315; in politics, 236, 265, 293, 316; in professions, 203, 204, 210, 262; in religious life, 220, 224–25, 266, 268. *See also* gender
Woodberry, 230
Woodholme Country Club, 213
Workingmen's Educational Society, 151–52
Workmen's Circle (Arbeter Ring), 144, 150, 157–59, 206, 214, 216, 285. *See also* Progressive Labor Lyceum
World War I, 174–78, 180, 189–90, 192; Jewish service in, 174–76

World War II, 245, 246–54; homefront, 247–48; Jewish service in, 246–47

Yeshiva Torah Ve-Emunah (Hebrew Parochial School), 222. *See also* Talmudical Academy
Yeshivat Rambam, 308, 310, 313
Yiddish, 119, 131, 138, 166, 171, 176, 207, 215, 223, 246, 252, 262, 270; among Central European Jews, 54, 75; libraries, 157–58, 159; newspapers, 151, 152–54, 161, 214; radio, 187; in religious education, 143, 146–47, 164; schools, 159, 214; theater, 140, 154, 186
Yidisher progress (newspaper), 153
Yidishes tageblat (newspaper), 154
York, PA, 25
Youngelson, Nat, 187
Young Ladies Benevolent Society, 138
Young Men's Progressive Labor Society, 157–58
Young Men's/Women's Hebrew Association (Y), 206, 211, 212, 248, 260
Young Progressives of Maryland, 285
Yousem, Jonas, 194
youth culture, 140, 147, 162, 187–89, 207, 265, 281

Zager Protective Association, 136
Zamoiski, Calman and Joseph, 196
Zetzer, Rose, 203, 206
Zion Association. *See* Hevrat Tsiyon
Zionism, 8–9, 10, 107, 154–57, 159, 163, 167, 169, 170, 171, 173, 174, 176, 177–78, 181, 206, 207, 213, 225, 226, 243; activities during interwar era, 215–17; and anti-Zionists, 274; and founding of Israel, 272–74; varieties of. *See also* Israel; Palestine
Zionist Congress, First (1897), 8–9, 10 155
Zionist Organization of America, 215. *See also* Federation of American Zionists
Zion Lutheran Church, 76